Völkerrecht und Außenpolitik

Edited by
Prof. Dr. Oliver Dörr
Prof. Dr. Jörn Axel Kämmerer
Prof. Dr. Markus Krajewski

Vol. 95

Sören Sommer

# Franco-German Armaments Collaboration

Legal Aspects and Options in the context
of the European Defence Policy

**Nomos**

This dissertation has been funded by the Konrad-Adenauer-Stiftung.

**The Deutsche Nationalbibliothek** lists this publication in the
Deutsche Nationalbibliografie; detailed bibliographic data
are available on the Internet at http://dnb.d-nb.de

a.t.: Glasgow, Univ., Diss., 2023

ISBN     978-3-7560-1825-3 (Print)
         978-3-7489-4488-1 (ePDF)


**British Library Cataloguing-in-Publication Data**
A catalogue record for this book is available from the British Library.

ISBN     978-3-7560-1825-3 (Print)
         978-3-7489-4488-1 (ePDF)


**Library of Congress Cataloging-in-Publication Data**
Sommer, Sören
Franco-German Armaments Collaboration
Legal Aspects and Options
Sören Sommer
324 pp.
Includes bibliographic references.

ISBN     978-3-7560-1825-3 (Print)
         978-3-7489-4488-1 (ePDF)

Onlineversion
Nomos eLibrary

1st Edition 2024
© Nomos Verlagsgesellschaft, Baden-Baden, Germany 2024. Overall responsibility
for manufacturing (printing and production) lies with Nomos Verlagsgesellschaft mbH
& Co. KG.

# Abstract

Russia's 2022 invasion of Ukraine marks the preliminary low point in Europe's increasingly challenging geopolitical environment. Against this backdrop, Europe now realises its immense defence capability gaps. To close these gaps, efficient and reliable armaments cooperation in Europe is urgently required. However, this objective need is contrasted by opposing national sovereignty concerns.

Franco-German armaments collaboration is situated in this field of tension. This thesis evaluates the legal framework for Franco-German armaments collaboration in the context of the European Defence Policy, analysing whether reliable rules are established which ensure that collaborative armaments projects are consistently realised. Furthermore, possible options to overcome existing legal deficits are pointed out.

This thesis shows that the bilateral Franco-German legal framework for armaments collaboration is not sufficiently reliable to ensure the consistent realisation of joint armaments projects. This is due to lacking convergence of armaments export regimes in particular, which is rooted in national sovereignty concerns. Subsequently, EU law as an alternative, potentially more reliable legal framework for armaments cooperation is analysed. However, this thesis also shows that EU law is likewise not sufficiently reliable to ensure the consistent realisation of armaments projects. This is due to the European Capabilities and Armaments Policy's fragmented and primarily intergovernmental arrangement, which allows the EU Member States to avoid armaments-related commitments and prevents the EU from establishing a comprehensive regime for armaments procurement and armaments exports. Overcoming these shortcomings would require a change of the EU framework for armaments cooperation. Due to national sovereignty concerns vis-à-vis surrendering national security and defence competences to the EU, enhancing the corresponding framework is currently unfeasible. Therefore, the European frameworks for defence capability development do not meet Europe's needs in the face of its increasingly challenging geopolitical environment and remain to be urgently enhanced.

# Acknowledgments

I would like to express my sincere gratitude to everyone who has supported me throughout my PhD journey. First and foremost, I gratefully acknowledge the funding received towards my PhD from the Konrad Adenauer Foundation. This financial support has been instrumental in enabling me to pursue my research and complete my thesis.

Furthermore, I am immensely grateful to my academic supervisors, Prof. Dr. Jörg Philipp Terhechte, Prof. Dr. Christian Tams, and Prof. Dr. Robin Geiß. Their guidance, encouragement, and intellectual rigor have been invaluable in shaping my ideas and helping me to navigate the complexities of the research process, especially during the challenging times of the Covid pandemic.

I would also like to thank my PhD colleagues who provided helpful feedback during the course of my research. Their input and perspectives have been more than helpful in the advancement of my research and improved the clarity, coherence, and readability of my work.

Finally, I would like to express my appreciation to my family and friends for their unwavering support and encouragement. Their patience and belief in me have been a constant source of motivation and inspiration, and I could not have completed this journey without them.

# Table of Contents

# List of Abbreviations

| | |
|---|---|
| ATT | Arms Trade Treaty |
| AWG | Foreign Trade Law (*Außenwirtschaftsgesetz*) |
| AWV | Foreign Trade Regulation (*Außenwirtschaftsverordnung*) |
| BAFA | German Federal Agency for Economic Affairs and Export Control (*Bundesamt für Wirtschaft und Ausfuhrkontrolle*) |
| BPFA | Bureau de Programme Franco-Allemand |
| BVerfG | German Federal Constitutional Court (*Bundesverfassungsgericht*) |
| CARD | Coordinated Annual Review on Defence |
| CCP | Common Commercial Policy |
| CDP | Capability Development Plan |
| CFSP | Common Foreign and Security Policy |
| CIEEMG | Inter-Ministerial Commission for the Study of the Export of War Materials (*Commission interministérielle pour l'étude des exportations de matériels de guerre*) |
| CJEU | Court of Justice of the European Union |
| COARM | Working Group on Conventional Arms Exports |
| CoC | Code of Conduct |
| CoCs | Codes of Conduct |
| CP | Common Position |
| CSDP | Common Security and Defence Policy |
| EC | European Communities |
| ECAP | European Capabilities and Armaments Policy |
| ECSC | European Coal and Steel Community |
| EDA | European Defence Agency |

| | |
|---|---|
| EDC | European Defence Community |
| EDEM | European Defence Equipment Market |
| EDF | European Defence Fund |
| EDP | European Defence Policy |
| EDTIB | Defence Technological and Industrial Base |
| EDU | European Defence Union |
| ESDP | European Security and Defence Policy |
| EU | European Union |
| EUMC | EU Military Committee |
| EUMS | EU Military Staff |
| FCAS | Future Combat Air System |
| FFA | Farnborough Framework Agreement |
| GG | German Basic Law (*Grundgesetz*) |
| KrWaffKontrG | War Weapons Control Act (*Kriegswaffenkontrollgesetz*) |
| LoI | Letter of Intent |
| MENA | Middle East and Northern Africa |
| MGCS | Main Ground Combat System |
| NATO | North Atlantic Treaty Organization |
| NFGAAE | New Franco-German Agreement on Armaments Exports |
| OCCAR | Organisation Conjointe de Coopération en matière d'Armement |
| PESCO | Permanent Structured Cooperation |
| PSC | Political and Security Committee |
| RDC | Rapid Deployment Capacity |
| R&D | Research and Development |
| SDA | Schmidt Debré Agreement |
| TEU | Treaty on European Union |
| TFEU | Treaty on the Functioning of the European Union |
| UK | United Kingdom |

| | |
|---|---|
| UN | United Nations |
| US | United States of America |
| VCLT | Vienna Convention on the Law of Treaties |
| WEAG | Western European Armaments Group |
| WEAO | Western European Armaments Organisation |
| WEU | Western European Union |

Der 24. Februar 2022 markiert eine Zeitenwende
in der Geschichte unseres Kontinents.
Olaf Scholz[1]

---

1 Olaf Scholz, 'Regierungserklärung von Bundeskanzler Olaf Scholz am 27. Februar 2022' (*Bundesregierung*, 27 February 2022) <https://www.bundesregierung.de/b reg-de/suche/regierungserklaerung-von-bundeskanzler-olaf-scholz-am-27-februar-202 2-2008356> accessed 30 March 2023.

# 1. Introduction

'The 24th of February 2022 marks a historical turning point in the history of our continent.'[2] These are the words of German *Bundeskanzler* Scholz three days after Russia launched its barbaric attack on Ukraine. It finally recognises the (potentially only preliminary) low point in Europe's increasingly challenging geopolitical environment. Faced with an all-out war on its continent, an unstable neighbourhood in the MENA region, a return to global power politics, the disintegration of the rules-based international order, and an extreme dependency on the United States to guarantee its security, Europe now realises its immense defence capability gaps.

However, the historical turning point ('*Zeitenwende*') had already been foreshadowed in 2014, following the Russian annexation of Crimea, and later during the Trump presidency which questioned the American security guarantee. This launched a rethinking and re-evaluation of defence policy and defence capabilities in Europe. It subsequently triggered several developments which will be central to this thesis. Their relevance was ultimately cemented following Russia's all-out invasion in 2022.

The first major development in this context, which will later also be the starting point of analysis in this thesis, is the 2019 Franco-German Aachen Treaty. In this treaty, Germany and France agreed to strengthen their bilateral armaments cooperation[3] and subsequently initiated large-scale armaments projects. Besides financial and defence-strategic motives, as large-scale armaments projects are increasingly unfeasible to be realised in Europe by one State alone, the enhanced Franco-German armaments cooperation is intended to boost the EU's Common Security and Defence Policy (CSDP) and strengthen European defence capabilities.

---

2  ibid.
3  In broader as well as subject-specific language usage, the terms "armaments cooperation" and "armaments collaboration" are generally used synonymously. They are not meant as categorical distinctions in this thesis. In case of distinctions between both terms, this is meant to emphasize different intensity levels of cooperation. However, this does not affect analysis and findings of this thesis. For further remarks see Baudouin Heuninckx, 'A Primer to Collaborative Defence Procurement in Europe: Troubles, Achievements and Prospects' [2008] Public Procurement Law Review 17(3) 123, 123–145.

As the economically most powerful and politically most influential Member States in the EU, the Franco-German "couple" has always been the main driver of European integration. The strengthened Franco-German armaments cooperation can be viewed as an example of that "avant-garde" mentality. It can also be regarded as a continuation of Member States clinging to national sovereignty[4] and conducting armaments cooperation within exclusive intergovernmental formats on an ad hoc basis.

The Franco-German bilateral defence integration principally contrasts a common European approach to defence and armaments integration. In this regard, it is noteworthy that the CSDP has significantly accelerated over the last years, especially since the Russian annexation of Crimea. The most relevant outcomes of this process are Permanent Structured Cooperation (PESCO) and the European Defence Fund (EDF), which play a central role for European capability development to achieve strategic autonomy and are based on a Franco-German initiative. These are the second major developments which this thesis will focus on.

Europe's increasingly challenging geopolitical environment requires robust defence capabilities. In Europe, efficient defence capability development today requires armaments cooperation to compensate their spiralling development costs and to ensure interoperability between the Member States' armed forces to facilitate defence cooperation and integration.

However, as in other areas of integration, since the early beginnings of European integration after World War II until today, there have been inherent contradictions in these cooperation and integration steps, particularly on two levels, which become particularly evident in the area of defence and armaments integration: the intention of a genuine common defence and armaments policy is contrasted by continuously nationally oriented and formulated defence policies. In the following parts, the underlying dialectic will be further elaborated: how can the geopolitical necessity for cooperation in the armaments sector be met in view of continuing national sovereignty reservations that would have to be overcome? The contradictions between Nation State thinking and progressive defence integration for more than seventy years have resulted in today's highly fragmented and

---

4 Referring to the power of a country to govern itself, see Collins Dictionary, 'sovereignty' <https://www.collinsdictionary.com/de/worterbuch/englisch/sovereignty> (*Collins Dictionary*, 2023) accessed 11 April 2023; Duden, 'Souveränität' <https://www.duden.de/rechtschreibung/Souveraenitaet> (*Duden*, 2023) accessed 11 April 2023.

sometimes even contradictory legal frameworks for European defence and armaments cooperation and their dysfunctional governance systems.

These challenges have in the past and continue to significantly affect armaments cooperation in Europe to this day – in particular if Germany participates. The central contentious issue revolves around diverging armaments export policies. Germany pursues an export policy that is viewed as highly restrictive and often unpredictable by its partners. For France in particular, which pursues a less restrictive export policy, it constitutes a significant problem if Germany blocks French exports of jointly produced armaments. In the past, this has repeatedly led to failures of Franco-German armaments cooperation.

In the author's view, this situation constitutes a severe problem for Europe's long-term ability to defend itself. Faced with its decreasing economic, demographic, and political weight on a global scale, it will have to significantly rely on an efficient and autonomous defence industry to safeguard its ability to act in foreign and security affairs.

By now, it is clear that European armaments cooperation is indispensable to face the increasingly challenging geopolitical environment. Franco-German armaments cooperation plays a significant role in this context. However, are the underlying legal frameworks designed to ensure the realisation of armaments projects even sufficiently reliable in this regard considering the contradictions mentioned above? If not, these are bad omens for the *Zeitenwende.*

## 1.1. Research Questions and Objectives

Why does this thesis focus on Franco-German armaments collaboration? In the previous part, reference has already been made to the central role these two States play in the European integration process. Both their available economic and political resources as well as their "motor of integration" function in the process of European integration explain and justify this focus.

Since the 1950s, after the end of World War II and shortly after the end of Franco-German "hereditary enmity", the Franco-German relationship overall, but more specifically their armaments cooperation, has been ambivalent and sometimes contradictory. On the one hand, the necessity and desire for reconciliation and cooperation were coupled in the face of the Cold War. On the other hand, national egoisms, historical sensitivities, and strategic divergences have lived on, and they have significantly influenced and often adversely affected the realisation of joint armaments projects. The most relevant manifestation of that divergence can be observed with regard to lacking convergence of armaments export policies. This has repeatedly led to failures of Franco-German armaments cooperation.

Against the backdrop of these challenges, there is an obvious need for a reliable legal framework to ensure that large-scale collaborative armaments projects can be consistently realised.

The central research objective of this dissertation is thus to evaluate the legal framework for Franco-German armaments collaboration in the context of the European Defence Policy, analysing whether reliable rules are established which ensure that collaborative projects are consistently realised and to point out possible options to overcome existing deficits.

To evaluate the reliability of the legal framework for Franco-German armaments collaboration in the context of the European Defence Policy, this thesis seeks to answer the following research questions:

1. What are the main challenges of Franco-German armaments collaboration?
2. Is the bilateral Franco-German legal framework for armaments collaboration sufficiently reliable to ensure that large-scale armaments projects will be consistently realised against the backdrop of these challenges?
3. Does EU law offer a more reliable alternative framework for armaments cooperation instead?
4. What are the deficits in terms of legal reliability and how can they be addressed to achieve more reliability in European armaments cooperation?
5. What consequences follow for future Franco-German armaments collaboration in the context of the European Defence Policy?

This thesis will reach the following conclusions:

1. The main challenges of Franco-German armaments collaboration stem from their diverging national interests and strategic cultures. They manifest themselves in lacking convergence of armaments exports regimes. Sufficient convergence of exports of armaments stemming from joint projects is a prerequisite for reliable armaments collaboration, meaning that joint armaments projects are realised. Lacking convergence therefore endangers the success of Franco-German armaments cooperation as a whole.

2. The bilateral Franco-German legal framework for armaments collaboration is not sufficiently reliable to ensure that large-scale armaments projects will be consistently realised because it fails to establish sufficiently reliable rules to deal with armaments exports stemming from joint projects.

3. Therefore, this thesis will turn to EU law as a potentially more reliable alternative framework for armaments cooperation than the bilateral Franco-German legal framework. This thesis will show that EU law in its current form is likewise not sufficiently reliable to ensure the consistent realisation of European defence capability development.

4. This is because of the European Capabilities and Armaments Policy's fragmented and primarily intergovernmental arrangement, which allows the Member States to avoid armaments-related commitments and prevents the EU from establishing a comprehensive regime for armaments procurement and armaments exports. Overcoming these shortcomings would require a change of the European framework for armaments cooperation as it is established by the Lisbon Treaty. Due to continuing national sovereignty concerns vis-à-vis surrendering national security and defence competences, enhancing the European framework for armaments cooperation is currently unfeasible.

5. This entails three major consequences. Firstly, this means that intergovernmental forms of European (including Franco-German) armaments cooperation within and outside the European framework will persist for the time being. Secondly, the frameworks for armaments cooperation will thus remain fragmented and unreliable, both within and outside the framework of the EU. Thirdly, this in turn entails continuing significant deficits in terms of reliable and efficient European defence capability development which is required to ensure Europe's strategic autonomy in the context of Europe's increasingly challenging geopolitical environment.

## 1.2. "Reliability" as an Analytical Tool

The key terms "reliability" and "unreliability" (including their adjective and plural variations) are thereby central to this analysis and will now be explained.

Generally, law can serve various purposes.[5] In theory, law can bring social order by providing legal certainty and predictability and thus prevent legal conflicts. In case of legal conflicts, law can offer solutions to solve such conflicts. Law can also serve as a means for integration, by harmonising rules and establishing a common interpretation of these rules.

Reliability can depend on several factors. Factors determining the benchmark for reliability on the legal level are the following in this thesis:

- The legal commitments which underlie the collaborative projects and make up the legal frameworks are distinct and unambiguous.
- They are uniformly interpreted by all State parties to the projects.
- They are binding for all State parties.
- They are uniformly observed and applied by all State parties.
- There are sanctions for non-compliance.
- There is a mechanism to enforce compliance, to sanction non-compliance, and to settle disputes in cases of conflicts between the State parties.
- The commitments are established long-term with a view to the long R&D phases of the collaborative armaments projects.

These factors, which constitute legal "reliability", are used in this thesis to evaluate the legal frameworks for Franco-German and European armaments cooperation in terms of their ability to effectively ensure the conduct of States regarding consistently realising their large-scale armaments projects. They are principally separate from the States' own objectives and agreements under public international law.

It is submitted that reliable European armaments cooperation (i.e. the effective and consistent realisation of joint armaments projects), including Franco-German armaments collaboration, requires legal reliability (legal level) which enables and ensures that reliable cooperation can be realised against the backdrop of several distinct challenges (political level) which frequently cause armaments cooperation in Europe to fail.

In addition to the legal level, "reliability" issues in armaments cooperation in Europe (in this thesis especially with regard to Franco-German armaments collaboration) could also be observed on a political and a project level. All three levels are interlinked. However, since the focus of this thesis is on legal unreliability (i.e. deficits in the legal frameworks

---

5 Reinhold Zippelius, *Grundbegriffe der Rechts- und Staatssoziologie* (Mohr Siebeck 2012) 51–88; Frank Dietrich, 'Recht als Sonderfall einer Normordnung' in Eric Hilgendorf and Jan Joerden (eds), *Handbuch Rechtsphilosophie* (J.B. Metzler Verlag 2017) 2–6.

for armaments cooperation in Europe preventing effective realisation of armaments projects), project level reliability will not be part of any deeper analysis in this thesis.

When it comes to the legal level, this thesis will show that the legal frameworks for armaments cooperation in Europe (including Franco-German armaments collaboration) fall short of the benchmark for reliability stated above in a number of ways and thus are overall deficient.

The legal frameworks for Franco-German and European armaments cooperation do not (adequately) provide for legal certainty and predictability and thus do not prevent legal (and related political) conflicts.

Many of the rules established to enable armaments cooperation are ambiguous and leave a margin of discretion, as this thesis will show. Instead of preventing conflicts by providing legal certainty and predictability, the frameworks for armaments cooperation in Europe thus entail the potential for conflict if one side perceives a certain rule interpretation and application (or also non-application) by the other side as a violation.

The lack of legal certainty and predictability when it comes to interpreting and applying legal commitments is furthered by (potential) conflicts of norms which arise from unclarified constitutionality questions, unclear norm relationships, or lacking harmonisation. As this thesis will show, in some cases, this could mean that commitments made to enable armaments cooperation must be withdrawn if they are ultimately judged as unconstitutional or violating other domestic, international or European norms.

In case of conflicts arising out of (at least perceived) non-application of commitments, lacking mechanisms for dispute settlement and enforcement further the risk that ultimately joint armaments projects are not realised because conflicts are not solved and partner States will then simply refrain from armaments cooperation if they do not see their legitimate expectations fulfilled or even see their interests threatened.

Also, commitments made in Franco-German and European armaments cooperation can usually be easily withdrawn. Since large-scale armaments projects are usually realised over decades and thus require legal and political certainty, predictability and therefore reliable long-term commitments, the lack thereof means short-term political shifts are therefore a constant risk that these projects are cancelled at any point.

On a side note and in the context of European capability development, this thesis will furthermore show how lacking legal harmonisation and resulting legal fragmentation is directly linked to fiscal and defence-strategic efficiency losses. European armaments projects could often be more efficiently realised and employed if there was further legal defence-related harmonisation.

States therefore do not fully make use of law as a means for armaments cooperation. Considering the number of legal unreliability factors (preventing effective and consistent realisation of joint armaments projects) in the therefore deficient legal frameworks which were intended to enable the realisation of armaments projects, the question is: why does this legal unreliability exist?

To answer this question, we have to leave the legal level and turn to the political level. Legal unreliability exists because law reflects existing political interests and realities. Armaments cooperation in Europe in that regard is a prime example of diverging and even contrasting national interests and this field of tension can be illustrated extraordinarily well on the basis of the (therefore fragmented, partially contradictory, and unreliable) legal frameworks.

Existing legal unreliability is the direct result of political contradictions and divergences. On the one hand, there is a political will and interest for armaments cooperation (arising out of geopolitical and economic necessities) and for realising joint armaments projects. On the other hand, States are not willing to give up (substantial) national sovereignty[6] in defence-related matters, meaning the pursuit of their own national defence-related interests without interference. Since they fear the loss of national sovereignty in armaments cooperation, they avoid those legal commitments that would be necessary to increase reliability of armaments cooperation in terms of efficient and consistent realisation of armaments projects.

This peculiar dialectic leads to the paradox outcome that those legal commitments ultimately made (as concessions and preconditions[7]) to enable armaments cooperation are politically intended to enable "reliable" armaments cooperation (i.e. ensure the efficient and consistent realisation of joint projects) but at the same time are meant to safeguard national defence-related interests as much as possible, which is how they become legally unreliable when it comes to ensuring the efficient and consistent realisation of joint armaments projects.

---

6  As already cited in part *1. Introduction*, sovereignty refers to the power of a country to govern itself, see (n 4).

7  In the case of armaments cooperation for example non-veto principles in armament export policies or juste retour principles in production shares, see part *2. The Context: Franco-German Armaments Collaboration and European Armaments Cooperation.*

Furthermore, since these interests are divergent between States, those legal commitments ultimately made to enable armaments cooperation require political compromises and entail sovereignty losses after all.

Well, you can't have your cake and eat it too. The result are these flexible, fragmented, partially contradictory, and overall unreliable legal frameworks for armaments cooperation in Europe, which this thesis will show.

The failure of the European States to establish reliable legal rules and frameworks for armaments cooperation, which are not characterised by the legal deficits mentioned above, due to their national sovereignty concerns is thus one factor of "political unreliability". Reliable armaments cooperation requires far-reaching legal commitments to enable the consistent realisation of large-scale armaments projects due to the long development periods of these projects and because of partially diverging and contrasting national interests. These commitments come at the loss of national sovereignty. While the European States want reliable armaments cooperation due to the increasing geopolitical and fiscal pressures, the fact that they also want to retain their respective sovereignty over defence-related matters makes armaments cooperation in Europe politically unreliable.

It is important to note at this point that this thesis' assessment of lacking legal reliability (in the legal frameworks for armaments cooperation) remains principally unaffected from the valid objection that there certainly are pragmatic and politically understandable reasons (i.e. national sovereignty concerns) to establish these legal frameworks in their present design. Otherwise, the participating States would not agree to them in the first place. However, this does not make the frameworks less deficient, it only explains existing deficits from a political perspective.

Another political unreliability factor refers to how States then deal with the lack of legal reliability in the legal frameworks and potentially try to exploit it. The less of the legal reliability factors stated above are reflected in the legal frameworks, the easier it is for States to not comply with their commitments. This in turn could mean that joint armaments projects are then ultimately not realised.

Since armaments cooperation has this aspect that – while having fiscal and defence-strategic advantages – it comes at the loss of national sovereignty, this always entails a lack of certainty and predictability regarding the political long-term commitment of participating States to joint armaments projects, including the fulfilment of legal commitments given as a precondition.

Potential political shifts and thus potential revaluations of national interests and the perceived advantages (defence capability development) or disadvantages (loss of sovereignty) of armaments cooperation in combination with the lack of reliable legal commitments made in intergovernmental armaments formats always entail the risk that joint armaments projects are ultimately not realised because commitments made (as preconditions) are not fulfilled (or perceived as not fulfilled) at some point. This risk is negatively reinforced by the long development periods which are required especially for large-scale armaments projects.

It has been stated above that commitments made in armaments cooperation frameworks usually serve this dual-purpose of enabling (allegedly "reliable") armaments cooperation against the backdrop of diverging national defence-related interests, which these frameworks also safeguard and need to reconcile. This is a precondition for armaments cooperation.

Despite the creation of unreliable legal frameworks for armaments cooperation, States participating in armaments cooperation expect that these commitments made in these frameworks are fulfilled, since their national interests are affected. However, if these commitments are then not fulfilled or at least perceived as not fulfilled, which is likely considering the various reliability gaps in the legal frameworks and the diverging and often volatile national interests, those participating States who regard them as not fulfilled are likely to refrain from cooperating to protect their national interests. Joint armaments projects are then also not realised.

Ultimately, this means that the efficient and consistent realisation of large-scale armaments projects in Europe is primarily dependent on a corresponding political will by the participating States. Firstly, this means creating reliable rules and frameworks to enable the consistent realisation these projects. Secondly, it means complying with their commitments. This in turn presupposes that States politically commit to armaments cooperation by finding convergence of national interests and strategic cultures to reduce sovereignty concerns and other perceived disadvantages.

How these challenges and constraints need be addressed and how political convergence can be found is left to other academic disciplines. Again, this thesis primarily focuses on the legal frameworks and presents options for enhancements provided political convergence is found. However, it is important to keep these contexts in mind, as they help to understand the continuing challenges of armaments cooperation in Europe, the flawed configuration and limits of the underlying frameworks, and the background constraints that exist when making proposals for enhancements.

## 1.3. Research Methods and Approach

This thesis applies a doctrinal legal research methodology to assess the legal frameworks of (bilateral) Franco-German and European armaments cooperation. Doctrinal legal research has been defined as '[r]esearch which provides a systematic exposition of the rules governing a particular legal category, analyses the relationship between rules, explains areas of difficulty and, perhaps, predicts future developments.'[8] "Doctrine" refers to '[a] synthesis of various rules, principles, norms, interpretive guidelines and values. It explains, makes coherent or justifies a segment of the law as part of a larger system of law.'[9]

Doctrinal legal research is the standard methodology in legal scholarship[10] and presents itself as the most adequate methodology to analyse the research questions stated in part *1.1. Research Questions and Objectives*. Although in the research interests of this thesis, this type of methodology is expanded to overcome its known shortcomings (see below). In retrospect, it can be confirmed that this approach was the most adequate methodology for this thesis.

Firstly, this thesis provides a systematic and detailed exposition of the legal frameworks of Franco-German and European armaments cooperation. In that process, it clarifies the relationship between both frameworks and their norms. Furthermore, this thesis also explains areas of difficulty by identifying deficits in the legal frameworks. And lastly, this thesis might not make predictions, but it lays out proposals and scenarios for potential future legal enhancements and political developments.

The systematic and detailed exposition of the legal frameworks of Franco-German and European armaments cooperation is divided between a historical and political contextual analysis and a legal dogmatic analysis.

---

8   Defined by the Pearce Committee and cited in Terry Hutchinson and Nigel Duncan, 'Defining and Describing What We Do: Doctrinal Legal Research' (2012) 17 Deakin Law Review 83, 101.

9   Trischa Mann, *Australian Law Dictionary* (OUP 2010) 197.

10   Hutchinson and Duncan (n 8) 99; Terry Hutchinson, 'Doctrinal Research' in Dawn Watkins and Mandy Burton (eds), *Research Methods in Law* (2nd edn, Routledge 2018) 9–10.

This is because the current state of these frameworks, their (intended) purposes and their deficits can only be really understood in their historical and political contexts.

One of these deficits is the fragmentation of these frameworks. A doctrinal legal research methodology also allows for systematically gathering, organising and then analysing the different frameworks and their relationship, which is later needed to analyse the frameworks as a whole and is an academic contribution in itself. This further underlines the adequacy of applying a doctrinal legal research methodology.

Within these frameworks, this thesis further aims at identifying legal norm-specific and structural deficits. Legal hermeneutics allows for interpretation of legal norms.[11] Legal interpretation in this context is to be understood as clarifying the substance and purpose of legal norms.[12] Legal interpretation is usually divided into semantic, systematic/contextual, teleological, and historical modes of interpretation.[13] This thesis applies all these modes of interpretation based on epistemological considerations.

Semantic interpretation refers to the interpretation of a law based on its literal meaning.[14] As the most basic mode of interpretation it will not be further elaborated here. More relevant are systematic (also known as contextual), teleological, and historical modes of interpretation.

Systematic interpretation argues with the consistency and coherency of a legal system.[15] This approach allows to analyse different norms in their relationship and status to other norms and to identify structural legal gaps and inconsistencies. This in turn is useful to explain convergencies and divergencies in legal systems and is of particular relevance for this thesis as fragmentation and divergence is a central issue throughout. Partially, systematic interpretation will also be useful to analyse certain norms, their status and relationship to others, particularly within small, more coherent and consistent sections[16] of the legal frameworks that are analysed in this thesis. Generally, however, since the process of armaments integration in

---

11  Matthias Klatt, 'Juristische Hermeneutik' in Eric Hilgendorf and Jan Joerden (eds), *Handbuch Rechtsphilosophie* (J.B. Metzler Verlag 2017) 224.

12  ibid. 225.

13  ibid. 226–227.

14  ibid. 226.

15  ibid. 227.

16  An example would be the evolutive clause in Art. 42(2) TEU in the context of the CSDP, see part *3.2.1.1. Towards a European Defence Union and potential consequences for European Armaments Cooperation.*

Europe is far from being consolidated, the usefulness of systematic interpretation as a means to analyse the research questions of this thesis is
limited.

Teleological interpretation is meant to determine the purpose of a
norm.[17] In this regard, a further distinction can be made between subjective-teleological interpretation (see below) and objective-teleological interpretation. Objective-teleological interpretation analyses norms in light
of a reasonable or necessary purpose. Teleological interpretations usually
include follow-up arguments, which evaluate the effects of different interpretation results. This often is done with regard to ethical discussions,[18]
however this thesis views them in light of practical political considerations,
i.e. enabling reliable armaments cooperation.

Historical interpretation analyses the genesis of legal systems and their
norms.[19] In this regard, a further distinction is made between subjective-semantic and subjective-teleological interpretation. Subjective-semantic interpretation refers to the word usage by the historical lawmaker. Subjective-
teleological interpretation by contrast analyses the intended purposes of
a historical lawmaker when drafting the norm. These purposes can be de-
duced from various materials surrounding the drafting process of a norm.[20]
For this thesis, subjective-teleological interpretation is essential to analyse
its research questions, as many of the current deficits can be explained
in their historical contexts. Furthermore, it is also revealing to compare
the original purposes of a norm with its applications and effects today.
To support its historical norm interpretation, this thesis will rely on an
extensive contextual section (see below for further details).

The legal frameworks and their norms for Franco-German and European armaments cooperation are interpreted in this thesis with a view to
their usefulness in terms of enabling reliable armaments cooperation. The
extensive contextual section (see below for further details) also serves the
purpose in this regard to determine the factors for reliable armaments
cooperation. The substances and purposes of the legal frameworks and
their norms following their interpretation in this thesis can then be assessed
against the backdrop of these factors. In this regard it will be noteworthy
whether and why the frameworks and norms are designed to facilitate

---

17  Klatt (n 11) 227.
18  ibid.
19  Ignacio Czeguhn, 'Rechtsgeschichte' in Eric Hilgendorf and Jan Joerden (eds), *Hand-
    buch Rechtsphilosophie* (J.B. Metzler Verlag 2017) 67.
20  Klatt (n 11) 226–227.

armaments cooperation and succeed in that objective, whether and why they are designed to facilitate armaments cooperation but fail to achieve that objective, or whether and why they are specifically designed to prevent reliable armaments cooperation. If they undermine reliable armaments cooperation, they are regarded as deficient. Such assessments are not typical in conventional teleological interpretation, but they are necessary to answer the research questions of this thesis.

In a final step, based on the identified deficits in the legal frameworks, this thesis makes proposals for legal enhancements and assesses them against the backdrop of social realities. This also allows the author to outline some possible scenarios for future legal and political developments.

A recurring criticism of (at least conventional) doctrinal legal research is its narrow view, focusing only on the "letter of the law" and neglecting social contexts. Law does not and is not developed in a legal vacuum. Today, law is therefore increasingly observed through a variety of disciplinary lenses, for example history, political theory, sociology, or hermeneutics.[21] Without a systematic understanding and study of the social background of legal norms, their genesis, intended purposes, and impact, doctrinal legal research only provides an incomplete picture.[22]

To better understand the contexts of the current legal frameworks for Franco-German and European armaments cooperation, this thesis therefore partially breaks through disciplinary barriers and specifically takes social, historical, and political contexts into account to explain the current state of the legal frameworks and considers them as background constraints when developing proposals for further legal development. This is why the first main section focuses so extensively on the contexts of Franco-German and European armaments cooperation.

European law specifically has been described as positivised treaty law which is subject to changing interests.[23] It is situated in the particular field of tension between pre-positivist normative demands and the interests of the Member States and the European institutions.[24] The centre of attention

---

21 Shane Kilcommins, 'Doctrinal Legal Method (Black-Letterism): assumptions, commitments and shortcomings' (*University of Limerick*, 2015) <https://core.ac.uk/downl oad/pdf/84112166.pdf> accessed 6 April 2023.

22 Ishwara Bhat, *Idea and Methods of Legal Research* (OUP 2020) 161.

23 Benno Zabel, 'Europarecht' in Eric Hilgendorf and Jan Joerden (eds), *Handbuch Rechtsphilosophie* (J.B. Metzler Verlag 2017) 57.

24 Benno Zabel, 'Europa denken. Das Recht der Moderne zwischen staatlicher und entstaatlichter Freiheitsverwirklichung' in Wilfried Griesser (ed), *Die Philosophie und*

revolves around the different forms of institutionalisation, constitutionalisation, and rule of law in Europe.[25] This thesis will contribute to this discussion by analysing the specific issue of armaments cooperation in Europe. For it to be a meaningful contribution, it is essential to also consider the different social interests and constraints that continue to determine European integration.

To better understand the approach of this thesis when it comes to analysing its research questions, the approach will now be presented in detail.

This thesis is structured in the following way: It consists of two main sections. The first main section (part *2. The Context: Franco-German Armaments Collaboration and European Armaments Cooperation*) presents and analyses the context of Franco-German armaments collaboration and European armaments cooperation. This context-setting section serves a quadruple purpose. Firstly, it introduces the complex subject of Franco-German and European armaments cooperation. Secondly, the existing challenges of Franco-German and European armaments cooperation are carved out. Thirdly, it explains the fragmentation of the current legal frameworks for armaments cooperation in Europe (this will be relied on in the second main section's parts *3.1. Unreliabilities of Franco-German Armaments Collaboration in the Bilateral Framework*, *3.2. European Union Law – a more reliable legal framework for Armaments Collaboration?*, and *3.3. Multilateral European Armaments Cooperation – unreliable but effective?*). Lastly, it establishes the historical, political, social, and cultural background constraints which limit any proposals for legal change and development that are made in this thesis (part *3.2.2. Making European Armaments Cooperation reliable?*). European defence and armaments cooperation is a highly political subject and does not occur in a legal vacuum. Without an understanding of the context as a determining factor, the current state of the legal framework as well as constraints for its potential further development are incomprehensible.

The second main section (part *3. Franco-German Armaments Collaboration -unreliable legal frameworks*) analyses the legal framework for Franco-German armaments collaboration against the backdrop of the first main section's findings (in part *2. The Context: Franco-German Armaments Col-*

---

*Europa. Zur Kategoriengeschichte der "europäischen Einigung"* (Königshausen&Neumann 2015) 19–41.

25  Zabel (n 23) 56.

*laboration and European Armaments Cooperation*). The legal framework for Franco-German armaments collaboration consists of bilateral agreements (part *3.1. Unreliabilities of Franco-German Armaments Collaboration in the Bilateral Framework*) and EU law (part *3.2. European Union Law – a more reliable legal framework for Armaments Collaboration?*).

Subsequently, the subparts of this thesis will be presented in detail.

Part *2. The Context: Franco-German Armaments Collaboration and European Armaments Cooperation* is concerned with Franco-German armaments cooperation in particular and European armaments cooperation in general. The process of increasing armaments cooperation will be referred to as armaments integration in this thesis.

This dissertation's point of reference is the current Franco-German armaments collaboration on the basis of the 2019 Aachen Treaty. This research projects analyses this cooperation in the broader context of the European Defence Policy. In this regard, Franco-German armaments integration represents only a partial aspect of European defence integration. Therefore, the subsequent analysis begins with the European context.

The first part of the contextual analysis (part *2.1.1. Historical Evolution of European Defence and Armaments Integration*) starts with an exposition of the historical evolution of European defence and armaments integration[26], in particular on the basis of EU primary law evolution. Noteworthy steps in this process include the failure of the European Defence Community (EDC), the belated launch of European defence integration as a consequence of the Yugoslav wars after the St Malo summit, ultimately concluding in the Lisbon Treaty. The purpose of this part is to demonstrate the difficulties of launching European defence and armaments integration against national sovereignty concerns in the EU. These national sovereignty concerns pose the central obstacle to European armaments integration and explain the legal fragmentation of the European frameworks for armaments cooperation. This intermediate conclusion will appear throughout the legal analysis of the European framework (part *3.2. European Union Law – a more reliable legal framework for Armaments Collaboration?*) to explain existing unreliabilities and will also serve as the main background constraint limiting proposals for legal change and development (made in part *3.2.2. Making European Armaments Cooperation reliable?*).

---

26  As will be shown, European armaments integration is a central element of European defence integration.

The subsequent part (part *2.1.2. Historical Evolution of the Franco-German Armaments Collaboration*) presents and analyses the historical evolution of Franco-German armaments collaboration. This process develops in parallel to developments on the European level. The purpose of this part is to demonstrate the difficulties of Franco-German armaments collaboration which are rooted in their diverging national interests and strategic cultures. The consequentially arising conflicts manifest themselves in particular in the different armaments exports regimes of both States. These challenges continue to significantly influence Franco-German armaments collaboration to this day and require a reliable legal framework to address these issues. This aspect will become relevant especially when analysing the Franco-German bilateral framework for armaments collaboration (part *3.1 Unreliabilities of Franco German Armaments Collaboration in the Bilateral Framework*).

The following part (part *2.2. Current Context: State of European Defence Integration and Franco-German Armaments Cooperation*) is subdivided to present and analyse the current state of European defence and armaments integration (part *2.2.1. European Defence and Armaments Integration today*) and the current state of Franco-German armaments collaboration (part *2.2.2. Franco-German Armaments Cooperation today*).

In a first step (part *2.2.1. European Defence and Armaments Integration today*), the current state of European defence and armaments integration will be presented and analysed as it presents itself in 2023. It will be shown that Europe continues to have immense defence capability gaps and how important armaments cooperation is in that context to close these gaps. Several developments following the annexation of Crimea will be presented and it will be shown that the current state of cooperation is inadequate to effectively close Europe's capability gaps. Again, this is the consequence of continuing national sovereignty reservations, which prevent European defence and armaments integration to develop further. This intermediate conclusion will be revisited in part *3.2. European Union Law – a more reliable legal framework for Armaments Collaboration?* and analysed in detail from a legal perspective.

In a second step (part *2.2.2. Franco-German Armaments Cooperation today*), we will return to the Franco-German context. In the beginning, this part will discuss the relaunch of Franco-German armaments collaboration as a consequence of Europe's increasingly challenging geopolitical environment. Recurring issues which were discussed in part *2.1.2. Historical Evolution of the Franco-German Armaments Collaboration* will be revisited.

The purpose of this part is to demonstrate the continuing diverging national interests and strategic cultures of both States, in particular with regard to armaments exports. These issues continue to endanger Franco-German armaments collaboration. The existing legal framework, which is intended to overcome these issues, will be analysed in part 3.*1. Unreliabilities of Franco-German Armaments Collaboration in the Bilateral Framework* with a view to whether it is sufficiently reliable to ensure the consistent realisation of large-scale armaments projects of the two partners.

This concludes the first main section (part 2. The Context: Franco-German Armaments Collaboration and European Armaments Cooperation) of this thesis. We will now turn to the second main section (part 3. Franco-German Armaments Collaboration – unreliable legal frameworks) and the current framework for Franco-German armaments collaboration. This framework is composed of bilateral agreements (part 3.1. Unreliabilities of Franco-German Armaments Collaboration in the Bilateral Framework) and EU law (part 3.2. European Union Law – a more reliable legal framework for Armaments Collaboration?). In this context, EU law is both part of the framework for Franco-German armaments collaboration as well as a potential alternative framework for European armaments projects, which will be shown later.

Part 3.1. begins with an analysis of the bilateral legal framework for Franco-German armaments collaboration. Franco-German armaments cooperation started out long before European armaments integration and it is therefore the starting point of this section. This bilateral framework is analysed with a view to existing deficits that endanger the success of Franco-German armaments collaboration. Starting point of this analysis is the 1963 Elysée Treaty (part 3.*1.1. Foundations of Franco-German Armaments Collaboration – the Elysée Treaty*) as well as the supplementary 1972 Schmidt Debré Agreement (part 3.*1.2. Mistakes were made in Franco-German Armaments Collaboration – the Schmidt Debré Agreement*) to regulate the contentious issue of armaments exports. This part will conclude that the legal framework at the time was not sufficient to ensure a lasting and constructive bilateral armaments cooperation. The following decade-long period without noteworthy armaments cooperation concluded with the 2019 Aachen Treaty (part 3.*1.4. Let's try again – the Aachen Treaty*), relaunching Franco-German armaments collaboration. Relevant in this context is again a supplementary agreement (part 3.*1.5. Mistakes were remade? – the New Franco-German Agreement on Armaments Exports*), which regulates the continuing contentious issue of diverging armaments exports regimes. This part will reach the conclusion that the further developed legal framework for Franco-German armaments collaboration continues to not provide a sufficiently reliable legal basis for lasting and constructive bilateral armaments cooperation (part *3.1.6. Intermediate Conclusions – need for a different approach*).

Here follows an analysis of the European framework for armaments cooperation as a potentially alternative and more reliable legal framework for Franco-German armaments projects (part *3.2. European Union Law – a more reliable legal framework for Armaments Collaboration?*). Armaments cooperation in Europe is increasingly conducted within EU structures. The European framework will likewise be analysed with a view to its reliability to ensure the consistent realisation of large-scale armaments projects In this context, the following part (part *3.2.1. European Armaments Cooperation – torn between intergovernmentalism and supranationalism*) will introduce the field of tension of intergovernmental and supranational EU law governing European armaments cooperation. In the following parts, the resulting fragmented legal framework will be further analysed in its sub-elements. These encompass the (potential) development towards a European Defence Union (part *3.2.1.1. Towards a European Defence Union and potential consequences for European Armaments Cooperation*), the existing structures for European armaments cooperation (part *3.2.1.2. The Future of European Armaments Cooperation and PESCO*), the European armaments policy (part *3.2.1.3. The European Armaments Policy and its future*), and a potential regulatory framework for European armaments exports (part *3.2.1.4. Towards a Comprehensive European Armaments Export Regime?*). Identified deficits will be discussed and part *3.2.2. Making European Armaments Cooperation reliable?* will then discuss proposals how European armaments cooperation could be made reliable long term on that basis. When discussing these proposals, this thesis will take the background constraints identified in part *2. The Context: Franco-German Armaments Collaboration and European Armaments Cooperation* into account.

Following the conclusion that the European framework for armaments cooperation in its current form likewise does not provide sufficient reliability to consistently ensure the realisation of large-scale armaments projects and that a necessary adjustment of the European legal framework remains out of sight for the foreseeable future, part *3.3. Multilateral European Armaments Cooperation – unreliable but effective?* will return to multilateral European armaments cooperation more broadly and will discuss its formats as a more practical way forward. This will include a discussion of the compatibility of multilateral armaments cooperation with EU law.

The final part of this thesis (part *4. Conclusion and Outlook – The Future of Franco-German Armaments Collaboration in the context of the European Defence Policy*) will summarise the intermediate conclusions of each part and on that basis will then reflect on the future of Franco-German armaments cooperation in the context of the European Defence Policy.

Two primary limitations to this research should be noted. Firstly, it is important to note that although this thesis takes political, cultural, social, and historically rooted conditions as explanatory factors and background constraints into account, this work is ultimately a systematic legal evaluation of Franco-German armaments collaboration. Proposals to enhance the frameworks for armaments cooperation in Europe are thus made from a legal perspective and assessed against the backdrop of the identified background constraints. These proposals may someday serve as options for political action provided these background constraints change and necessary legal change thus becomes possible, for example if immense geopolitical pressure forces Europe to further rethink its defence policies. How these background constraints need be addressed and overcome in detail however is left to other academic disciplines. Secondly, this research focuses exclusively on armaments cooperation in Europe, Franco-German collaboration in particular. Transatlantic cooperation formats (within NATO structures or on a bilateral basis) are excluded from this research to not distract from the central objectives of this thesis.

## 1.4. State of the Art and Relevance

Despite its topicality and increasing relevance, the subject of Franco-German armaments collaboration in the context of the (rapidly developing) European Defence Policy has so far received little scholarly attention, especially from legal scholars. This thesis aims to fill this existing gap in legal scholarship.

Existing research of this subject is almost exclusively historical and political. A systematic legal analysis does not exist. Franco-German and multilateral armaments collaboration have generally received little legal scholarly attention. European armaments cooperation has received more attention by comparison, but far less than other areas of EU law. Noteworthy contributions by Kielmansegg and Trybus are referenced in this thesis.

Furthermore, in the context of the rapidly developing European Defence Policy, large parts of the existing legal scholarship are at least partially outdated. Moreover, there are only isolated proposals how to enhance the legal frameworks for European armaments cooperation and so far, they have not been merged, enhanced, and evaluated, especially in the context of Franco-German armaments collaboration. This is also because the frameworks for armaments cooperation in Europe are highly fragmented and partially contradictory. These academic gaps underline the need for clarification by this thesis.

Against this backdrop, this thesis therefore fills academic gaps by providing a systematic legal analysis and assessment of the subject of Franco-German armaments collaboration in the context of the European Defence Policy, by combining existing legal, political and historical research in this area, by identifying conditions for successful Franco-German armaments collaboration, by methodologically organising the existing legal frameworks and identifying existing deficits, and on that basis by formulating proposals for possible enhancements to ensure a more consistent realisation of large-scale armaments projects.

In addition to its academic contributions, this research is also politically highly relevant. As stated above, Russia's attack on Ukraine has underlined Europe's increasingly challenging and less rules-based geopolitical environment. Faced with this environment and its decreasing global influence, Europe needs to pool its resources to retain its ability to act. In the area of defence, this means efficient defence and armaments cooperation. However, this objective need is contrasted by continuing subjective national sovereignty concerns. Whether Europe succeeds in enhancing its defence capability development thus becomes a fateful question.

The results of this research might be useful someday to serve as course for political action. The identified deficits contribute to Europe's self-analysis of its defence-political shortcomings. It offers perspectives how these shortcomings could be overcome someday, provided there is a corresponding political will. Presuming that geopolitical pressure will most likely increase, this day could come fast.

# 2. The Context: Franco-German Armaments Collaboration and European Armaments Cooperation

This first section of this thesis is meant to provide some contextual historical and political background information necessary to better understand the current legal and political challenges that continue to characterise Franco-German armaments cooperation in the context of the European Defence Policy (EDP) today. They also serve as significant background constraints for any proposals regarding legal change and development discussed in the later parts of this thesis.

The following parts are subdivided according to thematic and historical aspects. Thematically, a brief overview over both European defence and armaments integration and Franco-German armaments cooperation will be provided respectively. While Franco-German armaments cooperation can partially be located within the EDP framework, many joint projects have traditionally been bilaterally realised and are only recently increasingly Europeanised.

This is why this part is also subdivided according to historical aspects. As will be shown, European defence integration and armaments cooperation was almost non-existent after World War II until the 1990s and has only around the year 2017 started to develop noticeably. Likewise, European armaments cooperation and more specifically Franco-German armaments collaboration during the first period has exclusively taken place on a bi- and multilateral basis outside the European Union (EU) framework (thus referred to as "trans-European") but has been more and more integrated into EU structures since the 1990s and especially since 2017. This is why the parts on European defence and armaments integration and Franco-German armaments cooperation are divided with regards to developments between the periods 1951 and 2017 and then with regard to current developments after 2017.

## 2.1. Historical Context: Evolution of European Defence Integration and Franco-German Armaments Cooperation

This section will begin with the historical evolution of European defence integration and Franco-German armaments cooperation.

European defence (and armaments) integration is the story of a latecomer. The following part will review the long road to European defence and armament integration. Starting more than thirty years after broader European (mostly economic) integration, the process of defence and armaments integration remains overall incomplete to this day. This is because defence integration deeply touches upon national sovereignty interests and the EU Member States remain reluctant regarding any cessation of their sovereign powers to the supranational level till date.

The second part of the historical overview will briefly discuss the ups and downs of Franco-German armament collaboration in the past. Over the years, Franco-German armament collaboration was often unsuccessful due to their diverging positions on armaments exports.

### 2.1.1. Historical Evolution of European Defence and Armaments Integration

Thoughts on how to develop a European Security and Defence Policy have existed for a long time.[27] The current legal framework for European defence and armaments integration cannot be analysed without an understanding of the historical and social conditions preceding its evolution, which continue to influence legal developments in this area of law today. The European treaties, EU legislation and the case law by the Court of Justice of the European Union (CJEU) are strongly characterised by their historical contexts. These consist of various political, social, economic, cultural, and military factors, which have been in a constant state of flux over the last 70 years of European defence integration.

Political integration is considered to be a process where political competences are conferred from the national to the international (in the EU's

---

27 Sebastian Graf von Kielmansegg, 'The Historical Development of EU Defence Policy: Lessons for the Future?' (*Verfassungsblog*, 25 March 2019) <https://verfassungsb log.de/historical-development-lessons-for-the-future%ef%bb%bf> accessed 8 October 2019; Jörg Terhechte, 'EUV Art. 42 [Aufgaben und Tätigkeiten; Europäische Verteidigungsagentur]' in Ulrich Becker et al. (eds), *EU-Kommentar* (4th edn, Nomos 2019) 373.

case to the so-called supranational) level and are thus withdrawn from the exclusive sovereignty of the State.[28] European integration has been defined as the voluntary surrender of national competences and sovereignty rights to the European supranational level and thus the formation of a coherent political and legal system autonomous from the individual Member States of the EU.[29] Integration is thus different from international cooperation, which is usually restricted to certain policy areas and does not include (comprehensive) cessation of national sovereignty to a supranational level.[30]

As will be discussed below and which is incremental for any politico-legal reflections on European defence and armaments integration, the matter of national sovereignty over security and defence matters (which includes armaments questions) and its surrender to the supranational level has been one of the most contentious issues of the European integration process for more than 70 years now. National power over security and defence matters lie at the heart of sovereign statehood and the European Member States' long-time unwillingness for any cessation of national competences in this policy area has immensely hampered European defence and armaments integration in the past and continues to be a nearly insurmountable obstacle to this day, making further integration steps very difficult and preventing reliable and successful European armaments collaboration.

The realisation of a consistent and comprehensive European Capabilities and Armaments Policy (ECAP) remains one of the central challenges of European defence integration. As will be discussed in more detail below, armaments matters were historically excluded from the European integration process due to the Member States' concerns to give up national sovereignty over security and defence policy issues and their diverging economic and defence-industrial interests.[31] Legally, this state is still apparent in what is

---

28  Frank Schimmelfennig, *Internationale Politik* (4th edn, utb 2015) 290.

29  Christian Welz and Christian Engel, 'Traditionsbestände politikwissenschaftlicher Integrationstheorien: Die Europäische Gemeinschaft im Spannungsfeld von Integration und Kooperation' in Armin von Bogdandy (ed), *Die europäische Option. Eine interdisziplinäre Analyse über Herkunft, Stand und Perspektiven der europäischen Integration* (Nomos 1993).

30  Marcel Kotthoff, *Die Entwicklung der deutsch-französischen Sicherheitskooperation seit dem Ende des Ost-West-Konflikts* (Springer 2011) 21.

31  Thorsten Kingreen and Bernhard Wegener, 'Art. 346' in Christian Calliess and Matthias Ruffert (eds), *EUV/AEUV* (6th edn, C.H.Beck 2022) 2619; Daniel Dittert, 'Artikel 346' in Hans von der Groeben et al., *Europäisches Unionsrecht* (7th edn, Nomos 2015) 1995.

today Art. 346(1)(b) TFEU[32], the infamous armaments exception provision that has been part of EU law since the Treaty of Rome (Art. 223[33]) and for a long time has been extensively used by the Member States to prevent any supranational harmonisation in the area of armaments and limit the potential role of the EU. Moreover, the armaments exception allowed the Member States to favour their respective armaments industries and resulted in the fragmented and deficient armaments structures that continue to characterise the EU's Defence Technological and Industrial Base (EDTIB) to this day.[34]

This non-Europe in defence matters is seemingly contrary to the fact that originally, European integration in general was strongly motivated by peace, security and armaments considerations.[35] A central lesson from the devastating experiences of World War II was the need to overcome national competitions and antagonisms and instead to cooperate and integrate in multiple policy fields to ensure lasting peace in Europe. The foundation of the European Coal and Steel Community (ECSC) in 1951 aimed at regulating the European coal and steel industries (the key war-enabling industries) by a centralised authority at a supranational level[36], thus making war 'not merely unthinkable, but materially impossible'[37]. It was the starting point of the European integration project that ultimately led to the EU of today.

However, after the failure of the supranational EDC in 1954 due to the opposition of the French *Assemblée Nationale* over sovereignty concerns, the European integration process subsequently became exclusively about economic integration, with deeper security and defence integration becoming more relevant only more than thirty years later in the aftermath of

---

32  Consolidated version of the Treaty on the Functioning of the European Union (TFEU) [2016] OJ C202/1.

33  EC Treaty (Treaty of Rome) [1957].

34  Florian Seiler, *Rüstungsintegration: Frankreich, die Bundesrepublik Deutschland und die Europäische Verteidigungsgemeinschaft 1950 bis 1954* (De Gruyter 2015) 1; Martin Trybus, *European Union Law and Defence Integration* (Hart Publishing 2005) 395; Kingreen and Wegener (n 31) 2619; Dittert (n 31) 1995.

35  Trybus (n 34) 9–50.

36  ibid. 20.

37  Robert Schuman, 'The Schuman Declaration' (*EU*, 9 May 1950) <https://europa.eu/european-union/about-eu/symbols/europe-day/schuman-declaration_en> accessed 16 February 2022.

the Yugoslav Wars[38] and then again in the face of the current geopolitical challenges which the EU and its Member States face today (see part *2.2.1. European Defence and Armaments Integration today*).

Instead, with the Treaties of Rome in 1957, European integration became a (very successful) economic project establishing a Single Market while security and defence cooperation matters were dealt with in intergovernmental formats like the Western European Union (WEU) and the North Atlantic Treaty Organisation (NATO) outside the framework of the European Communities (EC).[39] Since the European Member States considered foreign, security, defence and armaments policies as their exclusively national prerogative, armaments matters were explicitly excluded from the Rome Treaty and a national security exceptions for situations where armaments overlapped with the common market (for example in cases of armaments exports, intra-Community transfers of defence products, defence procurement, State aids and defence-industrial competition) was introduced in the form of the aforementioned Art. 223 EC Treaty.[40] The regulation of armaments thus remained an exclusive Member State competence. Considering the generally comprehensive creation of a European common market by the EC Treaty, the introduction of the armaments exception in the EC Treaty meant that a significant part of that market deliberately remained outside the scope of application of EU (at the time Community) law and largely remains that way today.

From today's perspective, the EDC is remarkable both in regard to how far-reaching it would have been in terms of supranational integration and loss of national sovereignty as well as the reason for its ultimate failure being French (and other European States') sovereignty concerns, which will reappear throughout this thesis as a background constraint regarding potential legal change and development of European armaments regulation.

The EDC would have been a supranational defence organisation with integrated European armed forces, mutual assistance, a common administration, and a comprehensive armaments and procurement system. This would have encompassed a designated commission responsible for common programmes for armaments, equipment, supply, infrastructure, research, and regulating armaments exports. Joint armaments projects were

---

38 Sebastian Graf von Kielmansegg, 'Die verteidigungspolitischen Kompetenzen der Europäischen Union' [2006] 2 Europarecht 182.

39 Trybus (n 34) 22–43.

40 ibid. 396.

meant to be financed from a common budget. As will be become clearer below, the EDC concept for European defence integration at the time was much more profound than what is even theoretically available under EU law today.

The main reason for the EDC's failure was its supranational structure. Since the national competence over security and defence issues is considered to lie at the heart of sovereign statehood, its transfer to a supranational organisation ultimately proved to be too controversial. This is relevant because this controversy over ceding national security and defence competences to the supranational level lasts until today and continues to deeply impact European armaments integration. It is the reason why the EU's Common Foreign and Security Policy (CFSP) and the Common Security and Defence Policy (CSDP) have remained intergovernmental since their earliest beginnings and are today the only area of EU Treaty law that is not supranational.[41]

After the failure of the EDC and until the 1990s, the Western European countries then organised their military security through NATO and armaments cooperation via ad hoc bi- and multilateral intergovernmental cooperative armaments programmes. This meant only insignificant losses of sovereignty for the Member States and a pragmatic way to realise armaments projects due to the flexible intergovernmental arrangements and usually with few participating States, but at the cost of political, industrial and legal fragmentation of the European defence and armaments framework.

Consequently, during the period ranging from the 1950s to the 1990s, joint trans-European armaments projects were intentionally left outside the Community/EU framework and took place within ad hoc bi- or multilateral cooperative armaments programmes, such as the WEU's Western European Armaments Group (WEAG) and Western European Armaments Organisation (WEAO).

During the Cold War period, defence and armaments matters were of strong relevance which translated to (overall) high defence budgets[42] (com-

---

41 ibid. 22–43; Seiler (n 34) 3–4.
42 The European Member States' defence spending since 1949 can be tracked via the Stockholm International Peace Research Institute (SIPRI) Military Expenditure Database: https://milex.sipri.org/sipri; see also Diego Lopes da Silva et al., 'Trends in World Military Expenditure, 2021' (*SIPRI*, April 2022) <https://www.sipri.org/sites/d efault/files/2022-04/fs_2204_milex_2021_0.pdf> accessed 1 September 2022.

pared to European defence budgets today[43]) and a strong political will for armaments cooperation.

(Trans-)European armaments cooperation back then and to this day remains mainly motivated by defence-strategic and economic considerations. Trans-European collaborative armaments projects usually cover the most expensive and technologically advanced projects, which the individual European State is not able to finance and develop on its own. To reduce costs, participating States rely on increased joint production (under the economic concept of economies of scale). Such projects usually also feature high costs and therefore public investment into the R&D and production phases. Historically, the investing States therefore expected a "fair return" for its investment in the form of industrial participation of its national defence industry for defence-industrial capability, fiscal, and employment reasons. This is called the "juste retour principle"[44] and has historically been a significant obstacle to efficient armaments cooperation in Europe, as it led to costly and inefficient duplications of the Member States' defence industries and a fragmented, unregulated armaments market within Europe. This was further reinforced by the fact that Member States participating in the collaborative projects thus directly fulfilled their defence procurement needs instead of by defence awards following a competitive procurement procedure.[45]

---

43  European Commission, Joint Communication to the European Parliament, the European Council, the Council, the European Economic and Social Committee and the Committee of the Regions on the Defence Investment Gaps Analysis and Way Forward, JOIN/2022/24 final, 18 May 2022.

44  The problem of the juste retour principle arises out of the fact that the place (or rather places) of production of the joint armaments system is not determined according to criteria of technical and industrial competence but is rather proportionally based on each participating State's financial contribution to the joint project. As a consequence, most defence projects undertaken under the juste retour principle are plagued by exploding costs and project delay. Nevertheless, most cooperative armaments projects have conventionally been undertaken under the juste retour principle, which is rooted in national sovereignty consideration and national security interests, mainly funding its own defence industry instead of other's, see Christian Mölling, *Der europäische Rüstungssektor Zwischen nationaler Politik und industrieller Globalisierung* (SWP 2015) 12; Ronja Kempin, 'Die deutsch-französische Zusammenarbeit in der Sicherheits- und Verteidigungspolitik – Vernunftehe vor dem Aus?' [2012] 5 Zeitschrift für Außen- und Sicherheitspolitik 203, 210.

45  Martin Trybus, *Buying Defence and Security in Europe* (CUP 2014) 53–54; Jean-Paul Hébert, 'D'une Production Commune à Une Production Unique? La Coopération Européenne En Matière d'armement Comme Moyen de Renforcement de l'autonomie Stratégique Européenne' in Jean-Paul Hébert and Jean Hamiot (eds),

Moreover, since its early beginnings, (trans-)European armaments cooperation has been plagued by several distinct political challenges that prevented reliable and consistent armaments collaboration between European States and is both the root for and expressed by today's legal fragmentation. Despite the need and will for armaments cooperation, especially until the 1990s, (Western) European States heavily favoured national defence industry champions and protected their indigenous defence industries against foreign competition. As a political and legal consequence, the defence industry was exempted from Internal Market integration (again, see the aforementioned Art. 223 EC Treaty), because the Member States wanted to prevent any transfer of authority over armaments to the European Commission,[46] which in turn led to deeply fragmented and individual defence markets within the European Communities (EC), and armaments cooperation took place in loose and often unreliable[47] ad hoc formats and under the juste retour principle.[48] Furthermore, due to the importance of the United States (US) for European defence considerations during the Cold War, trans-European armaments cooperation often also involved the US and only became almost exclusively European during the 1990s, due to concerns over the US's defence-political reliability after the Cold War and due to a lack of market and technological access in the US to the disadvantage of the European defence manufacturers. In other words, until the 1990s, European armaments cooperation was distinctly not an integrated European policy matter.[49]

---

*Histoire de La Coopération Européenne dans l'armement* (CNRS Editions 2004) 201–217.

46  Catherine Hoeffler, 'Differentiated Integration in CSDP Through Defence Market Integration' [2019] 6(2) European Review of International Studies 43, 52.

47  Meaning participating States avoided significant long-term commitments in armaments projects and reserved the right to withdraw from armaments projects at any point. Very prominent is the French withdrawal from the Eurofighter development in 1984 due to disagreements with regard to equipment, system leadership, knowledge transfer and production shares. As will be discussed in parts *2.1.2. Historical Evolution of the Franco-German Armaments Collaboration* and *2.2.2. Franco-German Armaments Cooperation today,* disagreements over armaments exports were also a frequent cause for States to not collaborate in armaments.

48  Luke Butler, Transatlantic Defence Procurement (CUP 2017).

49  Trybus (n 45) 53.

2.1.1.1. The Belated Launch of the CSDP

It was at that time that defence and security matters really came back onto the European integration agenda. The dialectic development of the CSDP to this day is distinctively event-driven and follows dialectic principles. The lacking ability to act against and react to the atrocities of the Yugoslav Wars as a result of Europe's capability gap (the difference between defence aspirations in terms of strategic autonomy and military reality in terms of dependency on the US in key defence capabilities), the dissolution of the Warsaw Pact, European fears regarding the reliability of the American security guarantee, disagreements over burden sharing, and a renewed will for deeper European integration gave European defence integration a new impetus.[50] This also concerned armaments integration in particular. Following the end of the Cold War, decreasing defence budgets (especially for defence investments) coupled with spiralling costs for R&D of complex defence projects became increasingly difficult to finance even for the larger European Member States and furthered the European capability gaps. However, maintaining key defence (industrial) capabilities remained a political objective. Since the national defence industries were not able to survive through national procurement alone, especially in times of decreasing defence investments, struggled to compete with the US defence industry that benefitted from an enormous, well-protected domestic market and the largest defence budget in the world, and thus pushed for enhanced European armaments cooperation,[51] such cooperation was regarded as indispensable and increasingly took place in a multitude of multinational initiatives at different levels and with varying State participation, leading to a highly fragmented institutional landscape.[52]

In this regard, it is also important to note that especially in the beginning of European defence integration, defence integration meant a fundamental shift away from the conventional self-perception and self-conception of the EC (and later the EU) as a purely civilian power.[53] This partially also explains the underdeveloped state of the CSDP to this day. Over the next two decades, the treaties of Maastricht, Amsterdam, Nice, the failed EU Constitutional Treaty, and finally the Lisbon Treaty increasingly aimed at

---

50  Kielmansegg (n 27).
51  Hoeffler (n 46) 55–56.
52  ibid. 52.
53  Kielmansegg (n 27).

overcoming the separation between European defence integration outside the EU's structures and mainstream European (economic) integration.[54] In this process, armaments integration in particular to close Europe's capability gaps has played a central part.[55]

In 1992, the Maastricht Treaty first introduced the European CFSP in Title V of the Treaty on European Union (TEU-Maastricht)[56], which formed the intergovernmental "Second Pillar" of the then EU, but still struggled with the integration of defence matters and thus relied on the WEU as the military arm of the EU in terms of providing the EU with defence operational capabilities.[57] While the WEU was tasked to implement decisions and actions of the EU that had defence implications, the EU nevertheless finally became a defence policy actor after more than thirty years of European integration. Art. J.1(1) TEU-Maastricht set out a broad obligation for the EU and its Member States to define and implement a CFSP 'covering all areas of foreign and security policy.'

During the preparation of the Maastricht Treaty and as a consequence of frequent armaments exports by European arms manufacturers to conflict zones, repressive regimes and even embargoed countries during the 1980s and 1990s, which became particularly apparent during the 1991 Gulf war, in which Western coalition troops were confronted with Iraqi military equipment that was exported by Western countries to Iraq briefly before, the need for a common European approach to armaments exports, non-proliferation and stricter and more transparent rules for armaments export control became relevant for the development of the new CFSP. As a result, convergence, coordination and harmonisation of the export control policies of the Member States became a priority.[58] However, out of respect for

---

54  Trybus (n 34) 108.
55  Sebastian Graf von Kielmansegg, 'Auf dem Weg zur Europäischen Armee? Ambitionen und Grenzen des Unionsrechts bei der Schaffung integrierter Streitkräfte' in Sebastian Graf von Kielmansegg et al. (eds), *Multinationalität und Integration im militärischen Bereich. Eine rechtliche Perspektive* (Nomos 2018) 80–81.
56  Consolidated Version of the Treaty on European Union (TEU-Maastricht) [1992] OJ C325/5.
57  Art. J.4(2) TEU-Maastricht; Trybus (n 34) 100.
58  Simone Wisotzki and Max Mutschler, 'No common position! European arms export control in crisis' [2021] 10 Zeitschrift für Friedens- und Konfliktforschung 273, 273–275; Mark Bromley, 'The Review of the EU Common Position on Arms Exports: Prospects for Strenghtened Controls' [2012] 7 Non-Proliferation Papers 1, 3; Susanne Hansen, 'Taking ambiguity seriously: Explaining the indeterminacy of the European Union conventional arms export control regime' [2016] 22(1) European Journal of

Member State sovereignty, CFSP and armaments export matters continued to remain outside the scope of supranational law and where instead dealt with intergovernmentally.[59] Therefore, convergence and harmonisation of Member State export control policies began to take form via implementation of common assessment criteria which included human rights and conflict prevention considerations.[60] In 1991, the Council of the EU established the Working Group on Conventional Arms Exports (COARM) as a forum to facilitate Member State armaments export convergence. By 1998, the European Council formalised these common assessment criteria in the EU Code of Conduct (CoC) on arms exports, a non-binding soft law agreement, which in 2008 developed into legally binding EU law as a Council Common Position (CP) defining common rules for armaments exports[61], making the EU the only regional organisation to have established a legally binding arrangement on conventional armaments exports. This today provides the legal limitations stemming from EU law regarding Member States' margins of discretion when licencing armaments exports and will be further discussed in part *3.2.1.4. Towards a Comprehensive European Arms Export Regime?*. It is however noteworthy in this context to point out that already at that time, any attempt to increase political and legal convergence of Member States' armaments export policies (especially if binding at the EU level) was highly controversial due to established sovereignty concerns.[62] The Member States' resistance in this area of law remains virtually unchanged to this day and significantly limits current attempts to overcome the legal fragmentation of European armaments export regimes

---

International Relations 192, 198; Jan Grebe, 'For a Europeanisation of Arms Export Controls. More power for Brussels will lead to a stronger Common Foreign and Security Policy of the EU' (*Bundesakademie für Sicherheitspolitik*, 2018) <https://www.baks.bund.de/en/working-papers/2018/for-a-europeanisation-of-arms-export-controls-more-power-for-brussels-will-lead> accessed 23 June 2020.

59  Matthias Pechstein, 'Die Intergouvernementalität der GASP nach Lissabon: Kompetenz-, Wirkungs-, Haftungs- und Grundrechtsfragen' [2010] 65(9) JZ 425, 425–432; Hansen (n 58) 202.

60  See Annex VII, European Council, European Council Presidency Conclusions 28 and 29 June 1991, SN 151/3/91, 29 June 1991; Diederik Cops et al., *Towards Europeanized arms export controls? Comparing control systems in EU Member States* (Flemish Peace Institute 2017) 35.

61  Council Common Position 2008/944/CFSP of 8 December 2008 defining common rules governing control of exports of military technology and equipment [2008] OJ L335/99.

62  Hansen (n 58) 198; Grebe (n 58).

and resulting unreliabilities of European armaments collaboration (see part *3.2.2. Making European Armaments Cooperation reliable?*).

Further relevant for the subsequent discussions of this thesis (see *part 3.2.1.1 Towards a European Defence Union and potential consequences for European Armaments Cooperation in particular*) is the common defence policy development process that started with the Maastricht Treaty. According to Art. J.4(1) TEU-Maastricht, the CFSP shall include 'the eventual framing of a common defence policy, which might in time lead to a common defence.' This provision represents the central provision for European defence integration to this day, although it has successively been changed in the following treaties and became more defence integration committed (see below).

### 2.1.1.2. The Introduction of European Armaments Cooperation to CSDP

At the same time, armaments cooperation continued to take place outside of common European structures. In 1998, the intergovernmental armaments management agency *Organisation Conjointe de Coopération en matière d'Armement* (OCCAR) was created by France, Germany, Italy, and the United Kingdom (UK). Belgium joined in 2003, Spain in 2005. OCCAR was based on a Franco-German initiative[63] and continues to be a central multilateral organisation for trans-European armaments collaboration to this day. The role of OCCAR within European armaments cooperation and defence integration will be discussed in part *3.3.1. Multilateral European Armaments Cooperation*).

Finally in 1997, the Amsterdam Treaty[64] added a common defence policy to the CFSP[65], which is today (post-Lisbon)[66] known as the CSDP. After the Yugoslav Wars had shown that the EU had little capacity for action, a security and defence policy dimension was added to the "Second Pillar" of the EU at the time. Furthermore, the 1992 Petersberg tasks formulated

---

63  Seiler (n 34) 3.
64  Treaty of Amsterdam amending the Treaty on European Union, the Treaties establishing the European Communities and certain related acts (TEU-Amsterdam) [1997] OJ C340/1.
65  TEU-Amsterdam, Title V: Provisions on a Common Foreign and Security Policy, Art. J.7(1).
66  Treaty of Lisbon amending the Treaty on European Union and the Treaty establishing the European Community (Lisbon Treaty) [2007] OJ C306/1.

by the WEU were integrated into the TEU[67] and the EU began building its own politico-military institutions and operational capabilities over the following years.[68] The wording of Art. J.4(1) TEU-Maastricht's 'eventual framing of a common defence policy' was changed to a now 'progressive framing of a common defence policy [...] which might lead to a common defence.'[69] This wording, which was then later changed again to a 'progressive framing of a common Union defence policy' which 'will lead to a common defence (Art. 42(2) subpara. 1 TEU) in the Lisbon Treaty, lays the basis for a potential, but far-reaching evolutionary process of European defence integration. This will be relevant for the legal discussions in part *3.2.1.1. Towards a European Defence Union and potential consequences for European Armaments Cooperation.*

The Amsterdam Treaty further introduced a provision of armaments cooperation to Community law. According to Art. J.7(1) TEU-Amsterdam, Member States would cooperate, where appropriate, in the field of armaments in order to support the progressive framing of the common defence policy. The Amsterdam Treaty recognised the importance of armaments cooperation (which at the time took place exclusively outside the common European framework) for a common EDP for the first time, but did not yet develop it within said common European framework due to continuing Member State sovereignty concerns over security and defence matters.[70]

This Member State resistance to armaments integration started to increasingly erode in the following year during the 1998 Franco-British summit at St Malo. Due to a growing realisation among the EU Member States regarding their ineffectiveness in security and defence matters during the Yugoslav wars, a widening defence capability gap following the end of the Cold War and a resulting and continuing dependence on the US for European defence coupled with the realisation that purely national efforts were politically and economically unfeasible, the need for increased European cooperation in defence and security matters (including armaments in order to ensure their effectiveness) had become obvious.[71] This applied particularly to the UK, which traditionally had been highly opposed to

---

67 Art. J.7(2) TEU-Amsterdam; Kielmansegg (n 38) 182.
68 Kielmansegg (n 27).
69 Art. J.7(1) TEU-Amsterdam.
70 Trybus (n 34) 61–66.
71 Trybus (n 34) 94–95; Maartje Rutten, 'From St-Malo to Nice European Defence: core documents' [2001] 47 Chaillot Paper 1.

deeper defence integration within EU structures and providing the EU with autonomous defence structures (which today form the CSDP) due to national sovereignty concerns regarding security and defence matters and in order to avoid any (potentially costly) duplication of NATO defence structures.[72] Nevertheless, following a UK initiative, the French and British governments held a summit in St Malo and in their Joint Declaration on European Defence[73], both governments referred directly to the CFSP and its more intergovernmental basis and demanded that the Union had a 'capacity for autonomous action, backed up by credible military forces, the means to decide to use them and a readiness to do so, in order to respond to international crises.' For the first time since the failure of the EDC, the establishment of a European military force was back on the agenda and subsequently (in the 2001 Nice Treaty[74]) little by little found its way into EU primary law. Post-Lisbon, they have taken the form of the so-called EU Battlegroups[75].

To have the capacity for autonomous action carried out by credible military forces, the Franco-British couple in St Malo also recognised the need for a strong and competitive EDTIB. The Franco-British Joint Declaration therefore also stressed the need for a 'strong and competitive European defence industry and technology' and subsequently, defence and armaments cooperation has become central to the CSDP.

The goals of the St Malo Declaration were made an EU objective six months later at the Cologne European Council[76] and then further developed at the 1999 Helsinki summit, where the EU was provided with new political bodies and structures, namely the Political and Security Com-

---

72  Kielmansegg (n 27); Hoeffler (n 46) 54.
73  Governments of France and the United Kingdom, 'Joint Declaration on European Defence' (*cvce*, 4 December 1998) <https://www.cvce.eu/obj/franco_british_st_ma lo_declaration_4_december_1998-en-f3cd16fb-fc37-4d52-936f-c8e9bc80f24f.html> accessed 1 March 2022.
74  Treaty of Nice amending the Treaty on European Union, the Treaties establishing the European Communities and certain related acts (TEU-Nice) [2001] OJ C80/1.
75  Military units made up of different Member States' troop contributions. As of 2022, the Battlegroup concept is currently being reworked to become the EU's Rapid Deployment Capacity (RDC), see EEAS, 'A Strategic Compass for Security and Defence' (*EEAS*, 2022) <https://www.eeas.europa.eu/sites/default/files/documents/strategic_c ompass_en3_web.pdf> accessed 24 April 2022.
76  Declaration of the European Council on Strengthening the Common European Policy on Security and Defence, European Council Meeting in Cologne 1999, see Rutten (n 71) Paper 42–43.

mittee (PSC), the Military Committee (EUMC) and the Military Staff (EUMS), within the Council to enable the EU to carry out military operations. The so-called Helsinki Headline Goal (also build on the St Malo Declaration) set a military capability target for 2003 of mobilising 50.000 – 60.000 joint European troops within 60 days as a European Rapid Reaction Force deployable in crises situations within the terms of the Petersberg Tasks. After this goal had not been met in 2003 and again in 2010, the Member States subsequently created the aforementioned smaller EU Battlegroups (consisting of 1.500 troops, deployable after 10 days). Despite these politically far-reaching objectives, legal change did not occur in a corresponding manner, as the intergovernmental structure of the CFSP framework remained unchanged.[77] The European Rapid Reaction Force did not mark the beginning of a European army (which does not exist till today) and did not even establish its autonomy for action. Rather, the Member States remained in control of their respective armed forces and the CFSP remained committed to the principle of unanimity, out of respect for Member State sovereignty.[78]

Despite the intergovernmental approach for armaments cooperation within the EU framework, which started after the St Malo summit, intergovernmental armaments cooperation continued to take place and be shaped outside EU structures. Also in 1998, France, Germany, Italy, Spain, Sweden and the UK signed the Letter of Intent (LoI), which by 2000 became the Farnborough Framework Agreement[79] (FFA), a political and legal framework for cross-border defence-industrial restructuring[80]. The objective to maintain defence-industrial capacities in Europe also had to deal with the globalizing dynamics of defence industries after the end of the Cold War. Confronted with shrinking domestic and foreign defence markets, US defence firms engaged in a series of mergers and acquisitions. This was seen as a threat to the survival of the European defence manufactures,

---

77  Pechstein (n 59) 425–432.
78  Trybus (n 34) 99; Pechstein (n 59) 426.
79  Framework Agreement Between the French Republic, the Federal Republic of Germany, the Italian Republic, the Kingdom of Spain, the Kingdom of Sweden, and the United Kingdom of Great Britain and Northern Ireland Concerning Measures to Facilitate the Restructuring and Operation of the European Defence Industry (FFA) (France, Germany, Italy, Spain, Sweden, United Kingdom) (27 July 2000).
80  A noteworthy example is Airbus which is a result of a cross-border merger.

which were thus encouraged by their governments to do likewise.[81] The FFA will also be further discussed in part *3.3.1. Multilateral European Armaments Cooperation*. However, for the context of this thesis, it is relevant to note that the agreement also covers the area of export procedures (Arts. 1(d), 12 – 18), a result of diverging stances on armaments exports between the six States (particularly due to Germany's more restrictive armaments export policy, see parts *2.1.2. Historical Evolution of the Franco-German Armaments Collaboration* and *2.2.2. Franco-German Armaments Cooperation today*). This was in particular with regard to Germany's non-application of the 1972 Franco-German Schmidt Debré Agreement's (SDA[82]) non-veto principle[83], which led to significant disagreements over armaments exports between Germany and France and became a significant obstacle to their bilateral armaments collaboration. The SDA and the non-veto principle will be discussed in detail in parts *2.1.2. Historical Evolution of the Franco-German Armaments Collaboration* and especially *3.1.2. Schmidt Debré Agreement*. Instead, the FFA introduced consensus-based rules for exports, (intended) to reliably regulate exports of jointly produced armaments and therefore to strengthen the European defence industry (although the non-veto principle was not formally dropped). The consensus principle made consensus among the participating States over exports of jointly produced armaments the guiding principle for collaborative armaments production. The collaborating States jointly drew up lists of permissible destinations for exports. The removal of destination States from those lists required to be based on objective criteria, namely political changes in the situation of the destination States. At the time, this meant a significant deviation from previous export policies in Europe, where the ultimate responsibility for armaments exports lied with the State responsible for the final part

---

81  Burkard Schmitt, 'From Cooperation to Integration: Defence and Aerospace Industries in Europe' [2000] 40 Chaillot Papers 1, 5–14.

82  Agreement on the Export of Jointly Developed and/or Produced Armaments (SDA) (*Vereinbarung über die Ausfuhr von gemeinsam entwickelten und/oder gefertigten Kriegswaffen und sonstigem Rüstungsmaterial / Accord sur les exportations vers les pays tiers des matériels d'armement développés et/ou produits en cooperation*) (Germany-France) (1972).

83  A non-veto principle in intergovernmental armaments export agreements stipulates that neither State party will prevent the other from exporting or authorising exports of jointly developed or produced armaments to third countries, see also parts *2.1.2. Historical Evolution of the Franco-German Armaments Collaboration* and *3.1.2. Mistakes were made in Franco-German Armaments Collaboration – the Schmidt Debré Agreement*.

of production and where suppliers of sub-components authorized or denied their exports accordingly. Under the FFA, such decisions were taken jointly. By introducing the consensus principle, the States participating in joint defence projects intended to avoid unilateral (restrictive) decisions on armaments exports based on political preferences or changes in national administration. For many subsequent collaborative armaments projects, the FFA provided a reliable framework for armaments collaboration, as all State parties adhered to their commitments. The new 2019 Franco-German agreement on armaments exports features a return to the non-veto principle. Potential legal and political consequences will be discussed in parts *2.2.2. Franco-German Armaments Cooperation today* and especially *3.1.5. New Franco-German Agreement on Armaments Exports*.

Due to the aforementioned changing geopolitical environment post-Cold War and due to a lack of reciprocity regarding market and technological access to the disadvantage of the European armaments industry, during the 1990s trans-European collaborative armaments projects became almost exclusively European (meaning without US participation) and occurred more and more in the context of more permanent structures, such as OCCAR (outside the common European framework) and after 2004 the European Defence Agency (EDA) (within the common European framework).

After the UK had given up its traditional and fundamental opposition against deeper defence integration and providing the EU with autonomous defence structures during the 1998 St Malo summit, in 2001, the Maastricht and then the Amsterdam Treaties' security and defence policy provisions were transformed into the European Security and Defence Policy (ESDP) of the Nice Treaty, which is today known under the term CSDP. However, despite the political momentum towards autonomous European defence capabilities, they were featured only in a limited fashion in the Nice Treaty. While the sections on the WEU providing the EU with operational capabilities, which were prominently featured in the Treaties of Maastricht and Amsterdam, were then deleted in the Nice Treaty (Art. 17 TEU-Nice), meaning the EU now assumed direct responsibility for its own operational capabilities,[84] the ESDP remained limited to the Petersberg Tasks stipulated in Art. 17(2) TEU-Nice. The Nice Treaty failed to introduce further provisions promoting European armaments cooperation, to establish a European armaments agency and to integrate the various European armaments initia-

---

84  Trybus (n 34) 100; Terhechte (n 27) 373.

tives and relevant WEAG and WEAO structures into the EU framework.[85] Only after the creation of EDA in 2004, which today coordinates European armaments cooperation, and the Lisbon Treaty's introduction of a mutual defence clause (Art. 42(7) TEU-Lisbon), the WEU finally became redundant and dissolved in 2011. The only existing provision on armaments cooperation in Art. 17(1) subpara. 3 TEU-Nice (remaining the same as Art. J.7(1) TEU-Amsterdam) only stipulated that Member States would cooperate, where they would consider it appropriate, in the field of armaments to support the progressive framing of the common defence policy. This very limited provision which only reflected the already existing reality of intergovernmental trans-European armaments cooperation was also a reflection of the continuing existence of the armaments exception, at the time expressed in Art. 296(1)(b) TEU-Nice, which Member States were not willing to abolish and which prevented harmonisation of armaments matters within EU structures. This legal reality of lacking armaments integration was strongly contrasted by the political, strategic and economic realities of needing to strengthen the EDTIB, which had become apparent in the 1990s. The flawed attempt to overcome the armaments exception in EU primary law via intergovernmental and defence-industrial cooperation continued to reinforce the existing fragmentation of the European armaments market.[86] As a consequence, armaments cooperation within EU structures remained dormant until the creation of EDA in 2004.

In 2003, the European Commission's Communication *European Defence–Industrial and Market Issues: Towards an EU Defence Equipment Policy*[87] identified standardisation, monitoring of defence-related industries, intra-Community transfers, competition rules, export of dual-use goods and research as fields in which, in addition to procurement rules, action was proposed. This was followed up in 2004 by the Commission's Green Paper on 'Defence Procurement'[88] which set out the objective of moving towards the creation of a genuine European Defence Equipment Market (EDEM) and establishing EDA, in order to overcome the costly fragmenta-

---

85  Trybus (n 34) 105.
86  Sascha Dietrich, 'Die rechtlichen Grundlagen der Verteidigungspolitik der Europäischen Union' [2006] 66 Zeitschrift für ausländisches öffentliches Recht und Völkerrecht 663, 682.
87  European Commission, European Defence–Industrial and Market Issues: Towards an EU Defence Equipment Policy, COM/2003/0113 final, 12 March 2003.
88  European Commission, Green Paper Defence procurement, COM/2004/608 final, 23 September 2004.

tion of the European defence market and strengthen the EDTIB. This is important as it provides the starting point for the Commission to become regulatorily active in the field of armaments, extending its famous role as the "motor of integration" from Internal Market integration to defence matters and thus adding significant momentum to the ongoing erosion of the traditional intergovernmental-supranational divide between Internal Market regulation and defence matters (see also part *3.2.1. European Armaments Cooperation – torn between intergovernmentalism and supranationalism*).

In 2004, EDA was created by the Council.[89] Although formally termed "European Defence Agency", EDA is rather the EU's armaments agency. It is intergovernmental[90] and promotes intra-EU armaments cooperation. In principle, EDA thus continues the work of the aforementioned WEAG and WEAO by facilitating the development of European defence capabilities, setting up common European standards for armaments equipment, and strengthen the EDTIB and the EDEM.[91] The roles of the European Commission, the European Parliament and the CJEU relating to EDA were intentionally marginalised. However, under Lisbon, the TEU establishes a link for cooperation between EDA and the Commission (Art. 45(2) TEU). Via EDA's statute[92] (Preamble para. 7), EDA is today also linked to other actors, including LoI Group and OCCAR. It is relevant to note that EDA only plays a supporting role in armaments cooperation, without policy-making power. EDA's Codes of Conduct[93] (CoCs) are soft law. This arises

---

89 Council Joint Action 2004/551/CFSP of 12 July 2004 on the establishment of the European Defence Agency [2004] OJ L245/17.

90 According to Art. 45(1) TEU, it is subject to the authority of the Council and according to Art. 8(1) Council Decision 2015/1835 of 12 October 2015 defining the statute, seat and operational rules of the European Defence Agency [2015] OJ L266/55, each Member State is equally represented in EDA's steering board (EDA's decision-making body).

91 Tom Dyson and Theodore Konstadinides, *European Defence Cooperation in EU Law and IR Theory* (Palgrave Macmillan 2013) 97.

92 Council Decision 2015/1835 (n 90).

93 See for example EDA's CoCs on Defence Procurement (2005), on Offsets (2008), on Pooling & Sharing (2012), on Security & Supply (2014) or on REACH Defence Exemptions (2015); EDA, The Code of Conduct on Defence Procurement of the EU Member States participating in the European Defence Agency [2005] available via <https://eda.europa.eu/docs/documents/code-of-conduct-on-defence-procurement.pdf?sfvrs> accessed 7 October 2022; EDA, 'Bringing Transparency into the European Defence Equipment Market: Code of Conduct on Offsets comes into force' (*EDA*, 1 July 2009) <https://eda.europa.eu/docs/news/EDA_-_Code_of_Conduct_on_Offsets_Comes_into_Force.pdf?Status=Master> accessed 18 December 2022; EDA, 'Code

again from the intergovernmental CSDP structure and the aforementioned armaments exception in Art. 346(1)(b) TFEU (under the Lisbon Treaty).[94] Together with the principle of voluntariness regarding participation in EDA (Art. 45(2) TEU), the institutional design of EDA again reflects the larger Member State sovereignty concerns over ceding national defence competences to the supranational level.[95] The role of EDA in European armaments cooperation will be discussed in detail in part *3.2.1.2. The Future of European Armaments Cooperation and PESCO.*

2.1.1.3. European Defence and Armaments Integration after Lisbon

The 2007 Lisbon Treaty significantly consolidated the CFSP and the ESDP, which under the Lisbon Treaty was finally termed CSDP (Arts. 42–46 TEU, Protocols 1, 10 and 11 and Declarations 13 and 14). The Lisbon Treaty's CSDP provides the legal basis for EU defence integration today, with the option to further develop into a common defence (Art. 42(2) TEU). The CSDP as the operative part of the CFSP[96] encompasses several civilian and military assets to cover the EU's crises management (expanded Petersberg tasks, specified in Art. 43(1) TEU), it features a mutual assistance clause (Art. 42(7) TEU) and features provisions for enhanced armaments cooperation: PESCO (Arts. 42(6), 46 and Protocol No. 10 TEU). This results from the aforementioned European capability gap. Besides PESCO (which was only initiated in 2017), the CSDP places a strong emphasis on strengthening the EU's operative capabilities for civilian and military missions (Art. 42(1) TEU). Under Art. 42(3) TEU, the EU Member States are obligated to improve their military capabilities, including via armaments cooperation and

---

of Conduct on Pooling & Sharing' (*EDA*, 2012) <https://eda.europa.eu/docs/news/c ode-of-conduct.pdf> accessed 17 December 2022; EDA, The Code of Best Practice in the Supply Chain [2014] available via <https://eda.europa.eu/docs/documents/EDA _Code_of_Best_Practice_in_the_Supply_Chain> accessed 17 December 2022; EDA, 'REACH' (*EDA*, 2015) <https://eda.europa.eu/what-we-do/all-activities/activities-sea rch/reach> accessed 17 December 2022.

94  Susanna Fortunato, 'Article 40 The Relationship Between Powers and Competences Under the TEU and Under the TFEU' in Hermann-Josef Blanke and Stelio Mangiameli (eds), *The Treaty on European Union (TEU) A Commentary* (Springer 2013) 1220.

95  Hoeffler (n 46) 52.

96  Dietrich (n 86) 664.

facilitated by EDA (Art. 45 TEU), which thus plays a central role in the Lisbon Treaty's CSDP.[97]

It is again noteworthy that EU law is today almost entirely supranational and that only the CFSP/CSDP have remained exclusively intergovernmental[98], which usually[99] means that unanimity is required in the decision-making process by the European Council and the Council (Arts. 24 (1), 31 (1), 42 TEU), that the operational capability of the EU depends on the voluntary contributions by the Member States (Arts. 42(1), 31(4), 44 TEU) and that the jurisdiction of the CJEU is excluded (Art. 24(1) TEU).[100] At the same time, the roles of the European Commission, the European Parliament and the CJEU are intentionally marginalised. The CFSP is not an exclusive competence of the EU and the Member States therefore remain in control over their respective national foreign and security policies.[101] Again, this is because security and defence matters lie at the heart of State sovereignty. This perspective has been further underlined by the German Federal Constitutional Court (*Bundesverfassungsgericht*, abbreviated BVerfG), which ruled in its 2009 "Lisbon judgement" that the CSDP does not involve a transfer of power to the EU level that violates Germany's sovereignty and constitutional identity ('*zur Wahrung des unantastbaren Kerngehalts der Verfassungsidentität des Grundgesetzes*'[102]).

Nevertheless, CSDP matters have since Lisbon become frequently linked to supranational policy fields, in particular with regard to armaments, due to the European Commission's activism in this field since the 1990s and due to the Member States' need for a strong, competitive and innovative EDTIB as part of an effective CSDP.[103] This step-by-step process since the St Malo summit led to the Commission increasingly engaging in arma-

---

97 Terhechte (n 27) 373–374.

98 Pechstein (n 59) 425–432.

99 With some notable exceptions relating to EDA (Art. 45(2) TEU) and PESCO (Art. 46(2)-(4)), to which majority voting applies.

100 Pechstein (n 59) 425–432; Dyson and Konstadinides (n 91) 76–80.

101 Walter Frenz, 'Die neue GASP' [2010] 70 Zeitschrift für ausländisches öffentliches Recht und Völkerrecht 487, 492; Pechstein (n 59) 426.

102 BVerfG, Beschluss des Zweiten Senats vom 30. Juni 2009 – 2 BvE 2/08, at 240.

103 Dyson and Konstadinides (n 91) 88; Kielmansegg (n 27); Hoeffler (n 46) 55; Daniel Fiott, 'Strategic autonomy: towards 'European sovereignty' in defence?' [2018] 12 European Union Institute for Security Studies 1.

ments policy and integrating armaments matters into EU competences[104], despite the Member States' concerns.[105] Besides intergovernmental armaments cooperation, this concerns in particular supranational regulation via the Commission's Internal Market competence, to improve the EU's regulatory framework for armaments.[106]

Likewise, the Lisbon Treaty has also expressly linked its supranational policies to the European armaments policy, which is introduced under Art. 42(3) TEU. Art. 45(2) TEU requires that the (intergovernmental) EDA and the (supranational) Commission work in liaison when necessary. This concerns in particular the ECAP today, thus further bridging the traditional intergovernmental-supranational divide in European armaments matters (see also parts *3.2.1.2. The Future of European Armaments Cooperation and PESCO* and *3.2.1.3. The European Armaments Policy and its future*).

However, every supranational action in the field of armaments continues to be impeded by the traditional national armaments exception in (since Lisbon) Art. 346(1)(b) TFEU that has existed since the Treaties of Rome and exempts the area of armaments from the application of the EU's Internal Market rules (see above). As will be discussed at length in part *3.2.1.3. The European Armaments Policy and its future*, this provision has for the longest time exempted armaments from supranational harmonisation (again, on purpose, due to the sovereignty concerns of the Member States[107]). This provision thus has been traditionally interpreted widely by the Member States, meaning as a general, categorical, and automatic exception of hard defence equipment from the application of EU primary law. It was widely accepted that the Member States retained unlimited jurisdiction over armaments matters and that their national security concerns automatically overruled the objectives of the Internal Market. It has been pointed out that due to the lack of judicial interpretation, the armaments exception was thus open to abuse and successfully invoked accordingly for the longest time, which significantly hampered the creation of an EDEM

---

104 Chantal Lavallée, 'The European Commission's Position in the Field of Security and Defence: An Unconventional Actor at a Meeting Point' [2011] 12(4) Perspectives on European Politics and Society 371, 371–389.

105 Hoeffler (n 46) 52.

106 Ulrika Mörth, 'Competing Frames in the European Commission – the case of the defence industry and equipment issue' [2000] 7(2) Journal of European Public Policy 173, 173–189.

107 Hoeffler (n 46) 52; Kingreen and Wegener (n 31) 2619; Dittert (n 31) 1995.

and European defence integration.[108] This situation has likewise changed since the 1990s, in particular due to the Commission's actions before the CJEU to defend a restrictive reading of the scope of Art. 346(1)(b) TFEU. Consequently, the broadly interpreted armaments exception has since then been significantly limited by the CJEU in several judgements (see part *3.2.1.3. The European Armaments Policy and its future*), ruling that the exception needs to be narrowly construed and balance Internal Market and national security interests.[109] Nevertheless, it continues to restrict the Commission's regulative competences. The Member States thus continue to procure primarily domestically[110] by relying on Art. 346(1)(b) TFEU or by using the exceptions provided for in the Defence Package legislation.

This "Defence Package" was adopted in 2009 by the Council (and the Parliament), following proposals by the Commission. The legislative part consists of two directives designed to improve the functioning of the Single Market for defence and security products. The first deals with transfers of defence-related products[111] and the second with defence procurement[112]. They will be discussed in detail in part *3.2.1.3. The European Armaments Policy and its future*.

While the Commission has become regulatory active in the field of armaments, in particular to establish an EDEM and to support the EDTIB, armaments cooperation as such has remained intergovernmental and based on the principle of voluntariness.[113] However, since the creation of EDA (and the initiation of PESCO in 2017), this intergovernmental cooperation now takes largely place within EU structures (as opposed to non-EU structures).

---

108 Trybus (n 34) 150.

109 ibid. 396.

110 EDA, 'EDA finds record European defence spending in 2020 with slump in collaborative expenditure' (*EDA*, 6 December 2021) <https://eda.europa.eu/news-and-even ts/news/2021/12/06/eda-finds-record-european-defence-spending-in-2020-with-slu mp-in-collaborative-expenditure> accessed 16 April 2022.

111 Directive 2009/43/EC of the European Parliament and of the Council of 6 May 2009 simplifying terms and conditions of transfers of defence-related products within the Community [2009] OJ L146/1.

112 Directive 2009/81/EC of the European Parliament and of the Council of 13 July 2009 on the coordination of procedures for the award of certain works contracts, supply contracts and service contracts by contracting authorities or entities in the fields of defence and security, and amending Directives 2004/17/EC and 2004/18/EC [2009] OJ L216/76.

113 Samuel Faure, 'Varieties of international co-operation: France's "flexilateral" policy in the Context of Brexit' [2019] 17 French Politics 1, 1–25.

Also in 2009, the EU's dual-use regulation[114] was passed by the Council to further harmonise European armaments export policies, in conjunction with the aforementioned EU CP on armaments exports[115]. The fact that this legislation was passed by the Council and not the Commission underlines the continuing intergovernmental dimension of European armaments integration and the restrictions posed by Art. 346(1)(b) TFEU when it comes to supranational armaments regulation.

With regard to the integration of armaments-related issues into the CSDP and its supranational links, two hybrid dynamics thus have played a central role. Firstly, armaments integration has been promoted by the Commission and partially arranged within its supranational Internal Market framework to establish a genuine EDEM and apply the EU's Single Market rules to the European defence industry to enhance economic and defence-strategic efficiency. Secondly, since Europe's inability to act during the Yugoslav Wars, armaments integration has also been promoted by the Member States in order to close their aforementioned capability gaps. This has been arranged within intergovernmental defence policy frameworks, such as PESCO.[116] The debates on European defence capability development and the subsequent creation of EDA, the Defence Package legislation, and PESCO demonstrate the close interdependencies between the defence-industrial and military-operational elements of the CSDP.[117] Armaments matters are central in the CSDP. It also shows the ongoing divide between supranational and intergovernmental governments in the area of ECAP (see will be further discussed in part *3.2.1. European Armaments Cooperation – torn between intergovernmentalism and supranationalism*).

### 2.1.1.4. Intermediate Conclusions – European defence integration as an ongoing process

It took a long time for the EU and its Member States to recognize the fact that in order to be able to act in foreign policy affairs, it had to change from being a purely civilian and economic actor to being also a military

---

114 Council Regulation (EC) No 428/2009 of 5 May 2009 setting up a Community regime for the control of exports, transfer, brokering and transit of dual-use items [2009] OJ L134/1.
115 (n 61).
116 Hoeffler (n 46) 53.
117 ibid. 56.

actor and thus develop a CSDP.[118] The fact that the European defence (and armaments) policy had been dealt with outside the European integration framework for more than thirty years has consequences until today. Despite the geopolitical relevance of the CSDP, other policy areas within the EU are much more dominant and consolidated, especially with regard to the Internal Market, both in terms of further progression and level of competences.[119] This concerns specifically the intergovernmental arrangement of the CSDP that leaves security and defence competences primarily with the Member States and not the EU, reflecting Member State sovereignty concerns over ceding national security and defence competences to the supranational level.

Furthermore, the Member States' motivations and visions of deeper defence integration have always been very different. While some Member States like Germany and France have also regarded European defence integration and the EU becoming a defence actor as serving the wider European integration process, others like the UK in particular were even after St Malo much more reluctant.[120] In the past, this has hindered European defence and armaments integration significantly in terms of the EU's role in this policy field and it continues to be a great obstacle for further integration and legal development to this day. It is also interesting to note in this context that much defence-political development, especially with regard to armaments, is legally linked to the Internal Market and not to the CSDP under the TEU, simply due to the fact that this is where the EU is primarily able to act despite Member States' sovereignty concerns, even if Art. 346(1)(b) TFEU continues to impede supranational action.

The different political, social, economic, cultural and military factors that influenced, enabled and often prevented European defence integration (both within and outside the common European framework) since its early beginnings after World War II shaped the legal development and configuration of what today is known as the CSDP and ECAP.[121] They continue to explain current regulatory complexities, the legal fragmentation in the European security, defence and armaments cooperation frameworks, the contradictions between visions and realities, and set the background constraints for any proposals for legal change and development.

---

118   Dietrich (n 86) 665.
119   Kielmansegg (n 55) 67.
120   Kielmansegg (n 55) 67–68.
121   Kielmansegg (n 55) 68.

European defence integration has been described as an ongoing process towards the uncertain goal of a common defence.[122] This process now takes place increasingly within the legal frameworks based on the European treaties, which inter alia create political, military and financial commitments and establish defence- and armaments-specific institutions. These frameworks are characterised by significant legal fragmentation in terms of competent institutions both inside and outside (meaning within various international intergovernmental organisations and frameworks, such as OCCAR and FFA, which continue to exist despite the EU's CSDP) the EU framework and the tense relationship between intergovernmental and supranational configurations in EU law regarding the defence and armaments policy fields.[123]

Despite the overall significant development of the CSDP and the ECAP since the end of the 1990s, they have remained overall incomplete. After the 2009 Defence Package, CSDP matters (including armaments) lost political priority due to the EU's various political crises (in particular the financial crisis and the migration crisis) and little progress was made in the area of defence integration. Since the CSDP is particularly event-driven, this situation only changed in 2017 due to the EU's increasingly challenging geopolitical environment, which will be discussed in part *2.2.1. European Defence and Armament Integration today*. Before PESCO, the EDF, and CARD were initiated, the Member States did not fully make use of the possibilities offered by the Lisbon Treaty. Significant deficits persisted over time with regard to the EU's institutional configuration and the different national strategic cultures, which especially in the past prevented a systematic coordination of national armaments policies due to lacking Member State convergence in the matter. Despite the significant development of European armaments integration until 2017, it remained overall incomplete and failed to establish an effective and comprehensive ECAP, including creating a Single Market for defence equipment and an integrated procurement system, and finding convergence on armaments exports.

---

122  Trybus (n 34) 395.
123  ibid. 395.

## 2.1.2. Historical Evolution of the Franco-German Armaments Collaboration

In this part, the historical evolution of Franco-German[124] armaments collaboration will be briefly discussed. This period ranges from the year of 1963, in which the Elysée Treaty[125] was signed, initiating Franco-German armaments cooperation after World War II, to the year of 2017, where Germany and France reinitiated their armaments cooperation (this will be discussed in *part 2.2.2. Franco-German Armaments Cooperation today*) after two decades without significant cooperation.

The causes for this long period without significant cooperation will be the centre of discussion in this part. Adequately analysing current issues of Franco-German armaments collaboration is not possible without putting them into their historical context. It will therefore be shown which factors originally led to the failure of Franco-German armaments collaboration in the past and then in part *2.2.2. Franco-German Armaments Cooperation today* how these causes for failure problematically still apply today. To prevent another failure of the current Franco-German armaments collaboration, it is necessary to politically and legally mitigate these causes of failure.

As discussed in the previous part (*2.1.1. Historical Evolution of European Defence and Armaments Integration*), European armaments integration only began in the 1990s and is still not completed. Until the 1990s, armaments cooperation in Europe therefore took place exclusively outside EU structures on ad hoc, multilateral and intergovernmental bases.[126] Franco-German armaments cooperation is an example of that modus operandi.

As will be shown in this part, Franco-German armaments cooperation became less and less steady over the years. There are several examples of successful joint projects, but many also failed due to diverging political and economic interests and were consequently either not realised, or on a costly exclusive national basis or on an alternative multilateral

---

124 In those parts of this thesis discussing the historical context of Franco-German armaments collaboration, "Germany" refers to the Federal Republic of Germany (before 1990 also "Western Germany").

125 Treaty between the Federal Republic of Germany and the French Republic on Franco-German cooperation (Elysée Treaty) (*Vertrag zwischen der Bundesrepublik Deutschland und der Französischen Republik über die deutsch-französische Zusammenarbeit / Traité d'amitié franco-allemand*) (Germany-France) (22 January 1963).

126 Butler (n 48).

basis without German participation (so-called "German-free" armaments production, meaning in cooperation with other partners but purposefully without German participation or components to avoid Germany's expressly restrictive and unpredictable[127] export policy[128]). The intergovernmental legal frameworks governing Franco-German armaments collaboration were by nature arranged in a flexible, but also unreliable manner, meaning both States avoided significant commitments due to sovereignty concerns, which in turn meant they could easily terminate their cooperation over political disagreements, such as unresolved disputes over armaments exports or juste retour arrangements (for legal analysis see part *3.1. Unreliabilities of Franco-German Armaments Collaboration in the Bilateral Framework*).

### 2.1.2.1. Launching Franco-German Armaments Collaboration

The central agreement that paved the way for Franco-German reconciliation after World War II and for subsequent bilateral cooperation in many policy fields is the 1963 Elysée Treaty (see also part *3.1.1. Elysée Treaty* for legal analysis), signed by the French President de Gaulle and the German Chancellor Adenauer. This bilateral treaty is generally considered as one of the driving factors of European integration,[129] but it also initiated the intergovernmental Franco-German defence and armaments cooperation.[130] Although small-scale bilateral political and defence-industrial cooperation existed before the Elysée Treaty, the level of bilateral defence integration unleashed by the Elysée Treaty was unprecedented on a global and historical

---

127 Katja Keul and Reinhard Bütikofer, 'Gegenseitiges Vertrauen durch gemeinsame Exportkontrolle. Eine Erwiderung auf Anne-Marie Descôtes' (*Bundesakademie für Sicherheitspolitik*, 2019) <https://www.baks.bund.de/en/node/2024> accessed 21 June 2020.

128 Hans Atzpodien, 'Deutscher Rüstungsexport. Restriktionen, Regelungsbedarfe und der europäische Kontext' (*Bundesakademie für Sicherheitspolitik*, 2019) <https://www.baks.bund.de/de/arbeitspapiere/2019/deutscher-ruestungsexport-restriktionen-regelungsbedarfe-und-der-europaeische> accessed 21 June 2020; Lucie Béraud-Sudreau, 'Building Franco-German Consensus on Arms Exports' [2019] 61(4) Survival 79, 80.

129 Eckart Klein, 'Der Elysée-Vertrag vom 22. Januar 1963' in Tilman Bezzenberger et al. (eds), *Die deutsch-französischen Rechtsbeziehungen, Europa und die Welt. Les relations juridiques franco-allemandes, l'Europe et le monde* (Nomos 2014) 258–259.

130 Jörg Ukrow, 'Élysée 2.0 im Lichte des Europarechts – Der Vertrag von Aachen und die „immer engere Union"' [2019] 22(1) Zeitschrift für Europarechtliche Studien 3.

scale.[131] The Elysée Treaty's foreign and security policy aspect is central and features close cooperation and coordination between the governments of Germany and France in this area. This includes a common defence policy conception and also comprehensive armaments collaboration.

### 2.1.2.2. Diverging National Interests and Strategic Cultures

The reasons for Franco-German armaments cooperation at the time were diverse but have generally remained the same to this day (see part *2.2.2. Franco-German Armaments Cooperation today*). They are first and foremost motivated by fiscal considerations, but geopolitical and European integrational factors[132] also played an important role.

After World War II, France had a strong interest to prevent another war with Germany and thus closer policy cooperation with Germany (on a bilateral basis, but also within broader European integration) was regarded as a means to achieve this objective. Furthermore, France as a global power with geopolitical interests but economically weakened by the war also needed the post-war economically revitalized Germany to realise its ambitious large-scale armaments programmes.[133]

Another French lesson from World War II was to formulate a security policy ensuring a French autonomous defence industry safeguarding France's national strategic autonomy so that France would not depend on foreign allies again in case of another war. For France, (national) strategic autonomy entails to this day sovereignty over security and defence matters and an autonomous defence industry which serves to provide the French military with the necessary capabilities to act autonomously and conduct global military operations. Armaments cooperation with Germany was in this context also seen as a means to maintain Franco-German armaments

---

131 Wissenschaftliche Dienste Deutscher Bundestag, 'Die deutsch-französische Rüstungskooperation. Bilaterale deutsch-französische sowie multilaterale Entwicklungs- und Beschaffungsprojekte mit deutscher und französischer Beteiligung (WD 2 – 3000 – 070/18)' (*WD*, 2018) <https://www.bundestag.de/resource/blob/57 6770/c5359790a0d6d943e4ccb2900cc6d3a1/wd-2-070-18-pdf-data.pdf> accessed 21 October 2021.

132 Klein (n 129) 248–250.

133 Kotthoff (n 30) 51–50.

industrial capacities in Europe and protect the French defence industry against US competition.[134]

This means that Franco-German armaments cooperation was strongly motivated by economic and geostrategic necessities from its outset, much rather than political conviction for deeper integration. This has been a cause for frictions. Defence integration and armaments cooperation directly touch upon national sovereignty and are at the very core of statehood and national autonomy. This has made Franco-German armaments cooperation traditionally a "marriage of convenience". Such cooperation usually took place if both States were unable to procure armaments on a solely national basis and if the perceived advantages to cooperate (i.e. cost sharing and economies of scale) outweighed the perceived disadvantages (i.e. loss of defence autonomy and sharing sensitive knowledge). Otherwise, such co-operation was avoided and armaments projects were either not realised or on a purely national basis or in cooperation with different partners. Specifically France faces the dilemma since the end of World War II between pursuing its global geopolitical aspirations and its fiscal constraints which compel it to defence and armaments integration.[135] But also generally, it has increasingly become difficult for the European States after World War II to procure large-scale armaments projects on a purely national basis, even for the larger States.[136] This is why Germany and France are committed since the Elysée Treaty to European armaments integration (until the 1990s this happened outside EU structures, see part *2.1.1. Historical Evolution of European Defence and Armaments Integration*, and since then increasingly within EU structures, see part *2.2.1. European Defence and Armaments Integration today*) for defence-political and industrial reasons.[137]

No Franco-German armaments collaboration also occurred frequently between 1963 and 2017 due to failures to find convergence of the politically and historically rooted different national security and defence interests of both States and their very different respective strategic cultures. These obstacles have also been discussed in the context of European defence

---

134    Lucie Béraud-Sudreau, 'The policy model for French arms exports' [2016] 58(475–476) Adelphi Series 19, 19–29; Seiler (n 34) 45–59.

135    Barbara Kunz, 'Defending Europe? A Stocktaking of French and German Visions for European Defense' [2015] 41 Institut de Recherche Stratégique de l'Ecole Militaire; Hoeffler (n 46) 53–55.

136    Heuninckx (n 3) 123.

137    Hoeffler (n 46) 53–55.

integration (see part *2.1.1. Historical Evolution of European Defence and Armaments Integration*), where they also apply.

France traditionally views itself as a global power and as mentioned above, is particularly concerned about its sovereignty. As a permanent member of the United Nations (UN) Security Council and being frequently involved in military operations around the globe, it had and has distinctly other geopolitical and military requisitions than the peaceful trading power Germany, which after World War II was primarily concerned with Western integration and adhered to a minimalist foreign policy.[138]

### 2.1.2.3. Diverging Positions on Armaments Exports impeding Franco-German Armaments Collaboration in the past

The differences in Germany's and France's respective strategic cultures further extended to both States' different stances on armaments exports. In the past, Germany and France pursued very different armaments export policies and to this day both States have a difficult time converging in this matter (see part *2.2.2. Franco-German Armaments Cooperation today*). While Germany traditionally (since World War II) pursues a rather restrictive armaments policy, often explicitly under humanitarian and human rights considerations, France's export policy has been less strict and is to this day primarily guided by economic and national security interests.[139]

Historically, armaments exports play a marginal part in France's political debate. Public discourse across all political parties is dominated mainly by the concept of (national) strategic autonomy, which is central in France's foreign and defence policy. This objective is pursued by retaining and strengthening the French defence industry, which is also regarded as having significant economic benefits in terms of employment.[140] However, since the French national defence market is too small to serve as the only market for the French defence industry in an economically viable manner, armaments exports are regarded as a suitable means to lower costs for R&D through economies of scale by sharing costs with foreign armaments

---

138  Kunz (n 135) 29; Kotthoff (n 30) 49; Kempin (n 44) 204.
139  Kunz (n 135) 28.
140  Béraud-Sudreau (n 134) 19–29; Cops et al. (n 60) 59.

buyers.[141] This is why France pursues a pragmatic and more indiscriminate armaments export policy than Germany.[142]

Armaments production restarted in Germany in the mid-1950s, however exporting armaments only became legal during the 1960s (around the same time Franco-German armaments cooperation was first initiated). Since Germany adhered to a minimalist foreign policy and prioritized international peace and stability after World War II, strict limits on arms exports were imposed.[143]

Despite the very different security and defence policies of both States, there has been a very close bilateral relationship since the signing of the Elysée Treaty that led to bilateral and European integration, not only in security and defence matters.[144] Problematically, the different stances on armaments exports became a central point of contention between Germany and France in the context of their bilateral armaments cooperation and led to many joint projects not being realised.

A restrictive stance on armaments exports becomes a challenge for the cooperation partner who is potentially unable to export armaments stemming from joint production[145] when the export restrictive partner has the power to veto such exports (export control). To overcome this issue, Germany and France signed the so-called Schmidt Debré Agreement (abbreviated SDA, for legal analysis see part *3.1.2. Schmidt Debré Agreement*) in 1972, which deals explicitly with export rules concerning jointly produced armaments to enable the bilateral armaments cooperation. This was main-

---

141 Atzpodien (n 128); Lucie Béraud-Sudreau, 'Towards convergence in European arms export policies: How to overcome the Franco-German stalemate?' (Atlantic Community, 29 August 2019) <https://atlantic-community.org/towards-convergence-in-european-arms-export-policies-how-to-overcome-the-franco-german-stalemate/> accessed 22 June 2020; Ministère des Armées, 'Revue Stratégique de Défense et de Sécurité Nationale' (*gouv.fr*, 2017) <https://www.diplomatie.gouv.fr/IMG/pdf/2017-rs-def1018_cle0b6ef5-1.pdf> accessed 26 October 2020; Anne-Marie Descôtes, 'Vom „German-free" zum gegenseitigen Vertrauen' (*Bundesakademie für Sicherheitspolitik*, 2019) <https://www.google.com/url?sa=t&rct=j&q=&esrc=s&source=web&cd=1&cad=rja&uact=8&ved=2ahUKEwjPi5SCrOLiAhWLUhUIHUIGAzsQFjAAegQIAhAB&url=https%3A%2F%2Fwww.baks.bund.de%2Fde%2Farbeitspapiere%2F2019%2Fvom-german-free-zum-gegenseitigen-vertrauen&usg=AOvVaw3w30k-lzufGnct9yxMHABx> accessed 11 June 2020; Béraud-Sudreau (n 134) 23–24.
142 Descôtes (n 141); Béraud-Sudreau (n 141).
143 Cops et al. (n 60) 56.
144 Kempin (n 44) 205.
145 Or where components produced by a partner State are used and integrated into the export-destined armaments system by the other.

ly intended by stipulating a non-veto principle, which basically provided that neither government would prevent the other from exporting or from authorising exports of jointly produced or developed armaments to third countries.

In the first two decades following the conclusion of the SDA, both States largely refrained from applying their respective export control laws in the interest of successful cooperative armaments production and subsequently several joint armaments projects, like the development of the *Hot* and *Milan* anti-tank rockets, were successfully jointly realised.

Until 1999, the German government mostly adhered to the SDA, denied export licences only in isolated cases, and in such cases consulted the French government in accordance with the SDA's consultation mechanism. Such a case was for example the planned French export of *Hot* and *Milan* anti-tank rockets to China in 1977 (which then did not take place for other reasons). In 1999 however, the German Government vetoed the export of a *Tiger* helicopter to Turkey and in the following years, it tightened its armaments export control regime and began to repeatedly hinder the export of armaments that were jointly produced or only slowly delivered export licences when it came to supplying French armaments producers with German sub-components (at least it was perceived that way by France).[146] These repeated refusals to authorize the export of armaments was considered by observers and by France as repeated breaches of the SDA and reinforced public opinion in France that collaborating with Germany in armaments matters was disadvantageous for France.[147]

The divergence of armaments export policies between Germany and France then became even more apparent following the 2015 Saudi-led intervention in Yemen and the 2018 assassination of Washington post journalist

---

146 Ulrich Krotz, *Flying Tiger International Relations Theory and the Politics of Advanced Weapons* (OUP 2011) 149–151; Diedrik Cops and Aurelie Buytart, 'Sustainable EU funding of European defence cooperation' [2019] Policy Brief Flemish Peace Institute 1, 9.

147 Béraud-Sudreau (n 136); Lorenz Hemicker, 'Rechtliche Zweifel an deutsch-französischem Rüstungsabkommen' (*FAZ*, 26 February 2020) <https://www.faz.net/aktuel l/politik/inland/bundeswehr-uni-kritisiert-deutsch-franzoesisches-ruestungsabkom men-16649444.html?premium=0x79c76a4a56672c7a0fd0c63c954fe016&GEPC=Sha re_SMS> accessed 22 June 2020.

Jamal Khashoggi,[148] causing Germany to render its export policy even stricter.[149]

There are several examples for significant discord between France (or other European partners) and Germany over vetoed armaments exports. In particular noteworthy German export denials in this context were the planned exports of French *Aravis* transport vehicles to Saudi Arabia in 2012[150] and of British *Eurofighter Typhoon Meteor* missiles to Saudi Arabia in 2019[151]. Several other exports of armaments stemming from joint projects were likely also vetoed by Germany without public knowledge.[152] These cases are significant because firstly this led to increasingly "German-free" trans-European armaments projects.[153] This divergence of armaments exports did not only prevent successful Franco-German armaments cooperation but was also a significant obstacle to trans-European armaments cooperation in general. It meant that Germany, being the economically most powerful and politically arguably most influential European State, was increasingly excluded from joint armaments projects, which heavily impeded the goal of building-up a strong EDTIB.[154] Secondly, the French experiences with Germany's restrictive and unpredictable armaments export policy played a significant role during the negotiations of the 2019 Aachen Treaty[155] and the reinitiation of Franco-German armaments collaboration. Consequently, they led to the signing of a new bilateral agreement

---

148  Béraud-Sudreau (n 141).

149  Christian Schubert, 'Zweifel an der Harmonie' (*FAZ*, 16 October 2019) <https://ww w.faz.net/aktuell/wirtschaft/deutschland-und-frankreich-zweifel-an-der-harmonie-1 6436447.html> accessed 18 August 2020.

150  SPON, 'Frankreich beklagt Blockade von Rüstungsdeal durch Berlin' (*SPON*, 24 December 2012) <https://www.spiegel.de/politik/ausland/bundesregierung-soll-ru estungsgeschaefte-mit-saudi-arabien-blockieren-a-874593.html> accessed 25 May 2022.

151  Michel Cabirol, 'Eurofighter, A330 MRTT, Casa C295, H145 ... bloqués à l'export: Berlin fragilise Airbus' (*La Tribune*, 25 February 2019) <https://www.latribune.fr/en treprises-finance/industrie/aeronautique-defense/eurofighter-a330-mrtt-casa-c295 -h145-bloques-a-l-export-berlin-fragilise-airbus-808239.html> accessed 30 October 2021.

152  Béraud-Sudreau (n 128) 79–81; Descôtes (n 141).

153  Atzpodien (n 128); Béraud-Sudreau (n 128) 80.

154  Béraud-Sudreau (n 128) 80.

155  Treaty between the Federal Republic of Germany and the French Republic on Franco-German cooperation and integration (Aachen Treaty) (*Vertrag zwischen der Bundesrepublik Deutschland und der Französischen Republik über die deutsch-fran-zösische Zusammenarbeit und Integration / Traité sur la coopération et l'intégration franco-allemandes*) (Germany-France) (22 January 2019).

on armaments exports (see part *3.1.5. New Franco-German Agreement on Armaments Export*s), which is like the SDA earlier intended to prevent Germany from blocking French armaments exports[156] and which's reliability will likely determine whether the current Franco-German armaments collaboration succeeds or fails (see part *2.2.2. Franco-German Armaments Cooperation today*).

It is important to stress that at first, the Elysée Treaty was followed by a long period of fruitful bilateral defence and armaments cooperation which demonstrates that it is feasible if both sides are willing to adhere to their commitments. The best-known example for the enhanced Franco-German defence cooperation is certainly the Franco-German Brigade, yet there are also several successful (but also unsuccessful) armaments projects that relate to Franco-German defence cooperation. They will be mentioned further below.

Armaments cooperation was the dominant aspect of Franco-German defence cooperation for the longest time.[157] This was also because harmonising the diverging national positions on security and defence in the area of armaments was easier than in other defence policy areas.[158] In the years following the signing of the Elysée Treaty, Franco-German armaments cooperation was thus subsequently enhanced. In 1970, both States created the *Bureau de Programme Franco-Allemand* (BPFA) to better coordinate their existing armaments cooperation, although no large-scale joint projects were initiated after France left the integrated military structures of NATO in 1966 and Germany subsequently concentrated on defence and armaments cooperation with the US.[159]

The mid-1980s then witnessed a revitalization of Franco-German armaments cooperation. The SDA had already been signed in 1972 and then in 1987, the Franco-German Defence and Security Council was established (which in 2017 reinitiated the Franco-German armaments cooperation, see part *2.2.2. Franco-German Armaments Cooperation today*) and the following years were characterized by ever-closer armaments cooperation, as the need for closer cooperation grew stronger due to strategic, political and industrial needs. Since the signing of the Elysée Treaty, the cooperation and interdependence between Germany's and France's armaments industries

---

156  Descôtes (n 141).
157  Kotthoff (n 30) 53.
158  Heuninckx (n 3) 123–145.
159  Seiler (n 34) 54–59.

had become closer and there was a strong and shared will to maintain key defence-industrial capacities in Europe. Furthermore, there was an increasing fiscal need for France to cooperate with Germany during the 1980s. Consequently, both States initiated several[160] new large-scale projects.[161]

Noteworthy examples for successful Franco-German armaments cooperation in the past and facilitated by the SDA are the development of the anti-tank weapons *HOT* and *MILAN*, the *Roland* missile, the transport aircraft *Transall* or the attack helicopter *Tiger*.[162] However, there are also many examples where Franco-German armaments cooperation failed and joint projects were not realised, because France withdrew from joint projects, chose to develop projects on its own or in a "German-free" manner.[163] Very prominent is the French withdrawal from the Eurofighter development in 1984 due to disagreements with regard to equipment, system leadership, knowledge transfer and production shares (a scenario which is still present among Germany and Spain with regard to the development of FCAS, see *2.2.2. Franco-German Armaments Cooperation today*) and consequently France's unilateral development of the Rafale fighter jet instead.

The end of the Cold War finally made Franco-German armaments cooperation even more difficult. The end of the Warsaw Pact significantly reduced the perceived need for high defence budgets and also for armaments cooperation. France subsequently further arranged its armaments policy to specifically support its own national prestigious armaments industry.[164] Germany successively implemented a stricter policy on armaments exports towards the end of the 1990s (as mentioned above and in part *3.1.2. Schmidt Debré Agreement*), which France perceived as a violation of the 1972 SDA and thus saw no basis for further armaments collaboration with Germany. Consequently, France (if at all) cooperated increasingly with other European partners (like Italy or the UK) and avoided cooperating with Germany in armaments matters until 2017.[165]

---

160 Wissenschaftliche Dienste Deutscher Bundestag (n 131) 3–4.
161 Wissenschaftliche Dienste Deutscher Bundestag (n 131) 5–6.
162 Hébert (n 45) 201–217.
163 Thorsten Jungholt, 'Geschäft mit dem Tod oder Beitrag für Deutschlands Sicherheit?' (*Welt*, 13 March 2019) <https://www.welt.de/politik/deutschland/article19027 6603/Ruestungsexporte-Geschaeft-mit-dem-Tod-oder-Beitrag-zur-Sicherheit.html> accessed 15 November 2021.
164 Wissenschaftliche Dienste Deutscher Bundestag (n 131) 5–6; Kempin (n 44) 210.
165 Kempin (n 44) 210.

2.1.2.4. Intermediate Conclusions – no collaboration without exports

This part has briefly shown how Franco-German armaments cooperation has historically been primarily dependent on economic and geopolitical factors requiring such cooperation. France is traditionally particularly concerned about its sovereignty and strategic autonomy in armaments matters since World War II. This is why it has a large interest in its autonomous defence industry and only cooperates out of economic and geopolitical necessity. In this context, armaments exports play a central role. To lower costs for developing and producing large-scale armaments projects, armaments exports are regarded as necessary since the French national defence market is too small to be exclusively served by the French armaments industry only and cost-effectivness is generated through economies of scale and armaments exports. This also means that when France is unable to export armaments stemming from joint projects because its cooperation partner blocks French armaments exports, it refrains from armaments cooperation.

In the case of Franco-German armaments collaboration, both States' divergence of armaments exports policies is a significant challenge. Germany's particular restrictive armaments export policy, which is more concerned about human rights than strategic interests and extends to armaments exports stemming from collaborative projects, is difficult to reconcile with France's rather indiscriminate armaments export policy. A bilateral agreement intended to achieve bilateral armaments export policy convergence, thereby cater to France's defence-industrial and armaments exports needs and thus enable Franco-German armaments cooperation ultimately proved unreliable for France in the past in that regard (see also part *3.1.2. Mistakes were made in Franco-German Armaments Collaboration – the Schmidt Debré Agreement*). Consequently, Franco-German armaments cooperation failed for decades.

## 2.2. Current Context: State of European Defence Integration and Franco-German Armaments Cooperation

This part is meant to provide an overview of the current legal and political developments and challenges of European defence integration and Franco-German armaments collaboration. This contextual part is relevant to better understand the current deficits of both frameworks, which will be further discussed in the later analytical parts of this thesis. At the same time, this contextual part further carves out the need for enhancements of these frameworks and the background constraints which limit any proposals for potential further legal change and development. They will also be further discussed in the later parts of this thesis.

### 2.2.1. European Defence and Armaments Integration today

Considering that the EU started out as a purely civilian integration project and that the CSDP effectively began its gradual development only in the 1990s, the CSDP has come quite a long way. As part of the CFSP, it is potentially comprehensive.[166] According to Art. 24(1) TEU, the EU's competence in CFSP matters shall cover all areas of foreign policy and all questions relating to the EU's security, including the progressive framing of a common defence policy that might lead to a common defence.

The CSDP of the Lisbon Treaty features a variety of tasks and initiatives, ranging from the 1992 Petersberg tasks which are today included in the CSDP (Art. 43 TEU), mutual defence in cases of armed aggression (Art. 42(7) TEU), EU-led military operations[167], and especially PESCO, which was activated in 2017[168] and functions as a framework for 25 of the 27 EU Member States to converge and cooperated more closely in defence capability development. The CSDP today may eventually lead to a common defence of the EU, when the European Council unanimously so decides (Art. 42(2) TEU). There is currently much discussion as to how this might develop.

In defence matters, more than in any other policy field, the Member States continue to guard their sovereignty. The EU's role in defence policy is still a controversial matter and the Member States suspiciously guard their sovereignty rights and prevent any development of the CSDP beyond their control. From a broader perspective, the intergovernmental[169] CSDP

---

166 Frenz (n 101) 488–491.

167 For example the European Training Mission Mali (EUTM), based on Arts. 42, 43 TEU.

168 Council Decision (CFSP) 2017/2315 of 11 December 2017 establishing permanent structured cooperation (PESCO) and determining the list of participating Member States [2017] OJ L331/57.

169 The intergovernmental structure of the CSDP is in particular based on the principle of unanimity in decision-makings (Arts. 31(1) subpara. 1, 42(4) TEU), the exclusion of legislative acts (Art. 24(1) subpara. 2), and the exclusion of the CJEU's jurisdiction (Art. 275 TFEU).

due to Member States' concerns regarding the cessation of security and defence competences to the EU is a continuing obstacle to the CSDP's effectiveness as it hampers the decision-making process and therefore the EU's ability to act as a defence policy actor. An effective and operative security and defence policy demands a fast ability to act and react, since international crises are not manageable by long and complicated decision-making processes (usually based on unanimity).[170] The CSDP's lacking effectiveness is also the reason why many European security and defence initiatives continue to take place outside the CSDP and instead are based on ad hoc arrangements, for example the European Intervention Initiative (EI2) or the Franco-British Lancaster House Treaties. This in turn further undermines the CSDP's effectiveness and leads to defence fragmentation and continuing policy divergence, instead of a common approach. Franco-German defence cooperation, for instance in the form of the Franco-German Brigade but also the current exclusive Franco-German armaments cooperation, is also a notable example in this regard.

Besides intergovernmental defence cooperation outside the CSDP framework, the CSDP itself is likewise characterised by legal and political fragmentation and multi-track development. This is because to enable defence integration, the CSDP must be flexible due to the Member States' divergence of strategic cultures and security interests. When it comes to defence cooperation within the CSDP, the Member States are picking and choosing which forms of defence cooperation they wish to pursue. European defence cooperation is thus yet another example of different speeds of integration in Europe. The Danish opt-out of the CSDP for the last thirty years, the so-called Irish-clause which safeguards certain Member States' neutrality, or the varying levels of participation in the Pooling[171] & Sharing[172] initiative

---

170  Sebastian Graf von Kielmansegg, 'Gemeinsame Verteidigung und Verteidigungspolitik' in Stefan Kadelbach (ed), *Die Welt und Wir. Die Außenbeziehungen der Europäischen Union* (Nomos 2017) 283.

171  Certain capabilities or logistical components are pooled by several Member States for common usage.

172  Certain capabilities or logistical components are provided by certain Member States and made available to the others.

and now in PESCO[173] are noteworthy examples for the different levels of European defence integration.[174]

Generally, lacking Member State convergence in security and defence matters due to the differing national strategic cultures and security interests continues to impede the enhancement of the CSDP. There are large differences with regard to military action, defence spending, or the role of the defence industry between neutral Member States like Malta or Ireland and Member States like France, which is constantly involved in military operations around the globe. This lack of convergence in security and defence matters is also a reason why the Member States continue to adhere to the intergovernmental structure of the CSDP, including the principle of unanimity, where the Member States can maintain their sovereignty over these matters.[175] Further developing the CSDP (including armaments integration) thus requires Member State convergence in national strategic cultures and common defence policy interests.[176] Fundamental changes to the CFSP/CSDP (i.e. supranationalisation by Treaty amendment) in order to facilitate the decision-making processes and render these policy-areas more effective are however bound to fail against the Member States sovereignty reservations in the foreseeable future (see also part *3.2.1.2. The Future of European Armaments Cooperation and PESCO*).[177]

The intergovernmental structure of the CFSP/CSDP further results from the central role of the European Council and the Council as the main

---

173 Today only Malta does not participate. Following a recent referendum on 1 June 2022, Denmark has now decided to participate in all aspects of CSDP, see EEAS, 'Denmark: Statement by the High Representative on the outcome of the referendum on the opt-out in defence matters' (*EEAS*, 1 June 2022) <https://www.eeas.europa. eu/eeas/denmark-statement-high-representative-outcome-referendum-opt-out-de fence-matters_en> accessed 17 December 2022; this includes PESCO, see Council of the EU, 'EU defence cooperation: Council welcomes Denmark into PESCO and launches the 5th wave of new PESCO projects' (*EU*, 23 May 2023) <https://www.co nsilium.europa.eu/en/press/press-releases/2023/05/23/eu-defence-cooperation-cou ncil-welcomes-denmark-into-pesco-and-launches-the-5th-wave-of-new-pesco-proje cts/> accessed 10 December 2023.

174 Sebastian Graf von Kielmanssegg, 'The Common Foreign and Security Policy – A Pool of Flexibility Models' in Thomas Giegerich et al. (eds), *Flexibility in the EU and Beyond. How Much Differentiation can European Integration Bear?* (Nomos 2017) 145.

175 Kielmansegg (n 170) 284.

176 Steven Blockmans and Giovanni Faleg, 'More Union in European Defence' [2015] Centre for European Policy Studies 14; Kielmansegg (n 170) 284.

177 Kielmansegg (n 170) 283.

decision-making bodies (Arts. 22, 26 TEU). By contrast, the European Commission and the European Parliament play virtually no role in the decision-making process.[178] Furthermore, CFSP/CSDP actions and decisions are not subject to judicial review by the CJEU (Arts. 24(1) subpara. 1 TEU, 275 TFEU), except where they borderline with Internal Market issues (to some degree), which is of particular relevance for the ECAP (for legal analysis see part 3.2.1.3. *The European Armaments Policy and its future*). Otherwise, no other enforcement mechanism exists. As discussed throughout this thesis, this is due to the Member States' sovereignty concerns (see also part 2.1.1. *Historical Evolution of European Defence and Armaments Integration*). The limited role of the CJEU in CFSP matters is the result of the Member States' concerns regarding a body of EU law being created by judicial activism comparable to developments regarding to supranational law in the area of Single Market integration, which they wanted to avoid in foreign and security matters.[179]

## 2.2.1.1. A New Impetus for CSDP

As discussed in the previous part, in the first years following the Lisbon Treaty's entry into force, the CSDP did not change substantially. Through the Lisbon Treaty, an ECAP (conducted by EDA) had come within the scope of primary EU law and the CSDP (via Art. 45 TEU), however armaments cooperation continued to take place outside common European structures. European regulation for armaments exports in the form of the EU's CP on armaments exports[180] and the EU's dual-use regulation[181] as well as legislation to regulate (and promote) the European defence market in the form of the aforementioned Defence Package had been introduced around the same time as the Lisbon Treaty's entry into force.

However, since 2017, the historically event-driven CSDP has witnessed a historical push due to the EU's increasingly challenging geopolitical environment, which recently found its current and dramatic low point in

---

178  Florika Fink-Hooijer, 'The Common Foreign and Security Policy of the European Union' [1994] 5 European Journal of International Law 173, 184.

179  Trybus (n 34) 79; Nanette Neuwahl, 'A Partner with a Troubled Personality: EU Treaty-Making in Matters of CFSP and JHA after Amsterdam' [1998] 3(2) European Foreign Affairs Review 177, 177–195.

180  (n 61).

181  (n 114).

Russia's 2022 war against Ukraine. But even before that, the other various conflicts and crises and resulting geopolitical instability, for example the Russian annexation of Crimea in 2014, the civil wars in Syria and Libya since 2011 and the consequential migration crisis, the EU's 'system rivalry'[182] with China, the UK's withdrawal from the EU, and uncertainties to the US's security guarantee and NATO commitment[183] revived the CSDP, which has consequently become one of the most dynamic fields of European integration.

These geopolitical challenges provided a window of opportunity for European defence integration and since 2017, several significant initiatives have thus been initiated to enhance European military capabilities and achieve European strategic autonomy, in particular in the field of European armaments cooperation.[184] These efforts are however limited by the Member States continuing divergence of security and defence policy interests.

Following the "Brexit", France and Germany took the initiative to give European security and defence integration new momentum. On 28 June 2016 (five days after the Brexit referendum), the then foreign ministers of France and Germany published a paper titled *Ein starkes Europa in einer unsicheren Welt*[185] ("A strong Europe in an uncertain world"), where they reiterated the need for a CSDP of the EU and thus deeper European security and defence integration by further developing the CSDP. They stated that France and Germany should work towards making the EU step-by-step an independent and global actor internationally, which is in line with France's larger visions for European strategic autonomy. The most relevant outcome of this initiative subsequently became the activation of PESCO and the EDF in 2017 following the Franco-German Ministerial Council summit

---

182 European Commission, Joint Communication to the European Parliament, the European Council and the Council: EU-China – A strategic outlook, JOIN/2019/5 final, 12 March 2019.

183 Benjamin Schreer, 'Trump, NATO and the future of Europe's defence' [2019] 164(1) The RUSI Journal 10.

184 Jan Anderson, 'European defence collaboration. Back to the future' [2015] 19 European Union Institute for Security Studies 1.

185 Jean-Marc Ayrault and Frank-Walter Steinmeier, 'Ein starkes Europa in einer unsicheren Welt' (*Ministère de l'Europe et des Affaires Étrangères*, 28 June 2016) <https://www.diplomatie.gouv.fr/de/neuigkeiten/article/ein-starkes-europa-in-einer-unsicheren-welt-28-06-16> accessed 14 June 2022.

(see part *2.2.2. Franco-German Armaments Cooperation today*) and the subsequent establishment by the Council[186].

PESCO is legally based on Arts. 42(6), 46 and Protocol No. 10 TEU. It is a common platform for European cooperation on enhancing joint military capabilities within the CSDP framework, in particular with regard to increasing and coordinating defence spending, cooperating in armaments projects, and pooling and sharing of military capabilities and making them available to the EU. PESCO represents a step forward from the previous loose Pooling & Sharing initiatives and now consolidates European capability development within a common framework. Participation within PESCO and with regard to PESCO projects occurs on a voluntary basis. PESCO is thus a special type of enhanced cooperation, granting wide margins of flexibility.[187] Furthermore, PESCO is linked to the EDF (see below), which provides additional funding for capability projects developed within PESCO.[188] It is also linked to EDA. According to Art. 1(a) Protocol No. 10 TEU, the Member States participating in PESCO develop their defence capacities more intensely via EDA and according to Art. 2(e) take part, where appropriate, in the development of major joint or European equipment programmes in EDA framework. According to Art. 3 Protocol No. 10 TEU, EDA shall contribute to the regular assessment of the participating Member States PESCO contributions. Within PESCO, the PSC, the EUMC, the EUMS, and EDA are involved in developing and implementing joint policies and projects. Furthermore, PESCO encompasses regulatory instruments that normatively address the Member States' legislative and administrative defence policies. PESCO obligations are not enforceable by the CJEU, however they are enforced by a centralized oversight regime. The implementation of PESCO decisions is structured by a schedule and

---

186 (n 168); Regulation (EU) 2021/697 of the European Parliament and of the Council of 29 April 2021 establishing the European Defence Fund and repealing Regulation (EU) 2018/1092 [2021] OJ L170/149; formerly Regulation (EU) 2018/1092 of the European Parliament and of the Council of 18 July 2018 establishing the European Defence Industrial Development Programme aiming at supporting the competitiveness and innovation capacity of the Union's defence industry [2018] OJ L200/30.

187 Daniel Fiott et al., 'Permanent structured cooperation: What's in a name?' [2017] 142 Chaillot Paper 18; François-Xavier Priollaud and David Siritzky, *Le Traité de Lisbonne Texte et Commentaire Article par Article des nouveaux Traités Européens (TUE-TFUE)* (La Documentation française 2008) 107.

188 European Commission, 'The European Defence Fund' (*European Commission*, 28 April 2021) <https://ec.europa.eu/defence-industry-space/document/downl oad/69aa3194-4361-48a5-807b-1a2635b91fe8_en> accessed 25 November 2021.

sequenced phases. Member States are obligated to report their progress, efforts and plans regarding implementation. PESCO uses CARD (see below) as a monitoring system to evaluate progress against the benchmarks of the capability development priorities and the annual national implementation plans. Ultimately, PESCO obligations are sanctionable by the Council's right to exclude non-complying Member States from PESCO by qualified majority vote. While PESCO continues to be arranged in an exclusively intergovernmental manner (which is traditionally typical for CSDP matters), together with the supranationally administered EDF, it forms a new intergovernmental-supranational hybrid for European armaments cooperation. PESCO will be further discussed in part *3.2.1.2. The Future of European Armaments Cooperation and PESCO.*

Besides PESCO, the EDF[189] is the second major development in European armaments cooperation and has also been created in 2017. It is legally based on the European Commission's Single Market competences (Arts. 173, 182(4), 183, 188(2) TFEU for 'Industry' and 'Research and technological development and space'). The EDF co-finances collaborative capability projects between three (sometimes two) or more Member States or associated countries. PESCO projects are eligible to receive additional funding. The overall objective of the EDF is to generate cost-efficiencies, reduce duplications and overcome the EDEM fragmentation. It thus addresses the industrial dimension of strategic autonomy by strengthening the EDTIB. The EDF focuses mainly on collaborative R&D and acquisition of defence capabilities. The EDF is administered by the Commission, opening the path for supranational defence capability development (see below). However, since the EDF's legal basis lies in the Commission's Single Market competences, the Commission has no mandate to determine specific capabilities. This competence remains with the Member States. Furthermore, the EDF Regulation makes it clear that its funding shall not have any influence over the Member States' export decisions over those armaments that were developed with EDF funding (see Arts. 20(9), 23(3) EDF Regulation). This was the result of rigid opposition by the Member States (France in particular) against any EU authority over armaments exports.[190] The opportunity

---

189 Regulation (EU) 2021/697 (n 186); formerly Regulation (EU) 2018/1092 (n 186).
190 Sophia Besch, 'No escaping an arms export policy' (*Centre for European Reform*, 10 October 2019) <https://www.cer.eu/in-the-press/no-escaping-arms-export-policy> accessed 22 June 2020.

for potential further export harmonisation on the EU level has thus been missed.

Arisen out of the EU's increasingly challenging geopolitical environment and besides being a framework for defence cooperation, PESCO and the EDF have the potential to promote convergence among the Member States towards a common defence approach. This is why their initiation are regarded as the starting points towards a European Defence Union (EDU) (for legal analysis see part *3.2.1.1. Towards a European Defence Union and potential consequences for European Armaments Cooperation*) and are considered incremental in the process of closing Europe's capability gap and working towards strategic autonomy.[191]

A third significant development since 2017 is the Coordinated Annual Review on Defence (CARD). The EU's 2016 Global Strategy[192] called for the 'gradual synchronisation and mutual adaptation of national defence planning cycles and capability development practices.' CARD is the outcome of this goal. This intergovernmental initiative is conducted by EDA and assesses the Member States' defence capabilities on the basis of voluntary information provided by the Member States to better coordinate defence spending and identify possible collaborative armaments projects.[193] It also monitors PESCO.

---

191 Bundesministerium der Verteidigung, 'PESCO Permanent Structured Cooperation: Ein Meilenstein auf dem Weg zur Verteidigungsunion' (*BMVG*, 13 November 2017) <https://www.bmvg.de/de/aktuelles/pesco-ein-meilenstein-auf-dem-weg-zur-verte idigungsunion-19806> accessed 22 April 2022; EDA, 'Germany – From PESCO to a European Defence Union' (*EDA*, 2017) <https://eda.europa.eu/webzine/issue15/co ver-story/pesco-drivers-the-floor-is-yours#exampleAccordion2> accessed 22 April 2022; European Commission, 'A European Defence Fund: €5.5 billion per year to boost Europe's defence capabilities' (*European Commission*, 7 June 2017) <https://ec .europa.eu/commission/presscorner/detail/en/IP_17_1508> accessed 22 April 2022.

192 EEAS, 'EU Global Strategy' (*EEAS*, 28 June 2016) <https://www.eeas.europa.e u/eu-global-strategy_en> accessed 13 June 2020, endorsed by the Council, see Council of the European Union, Council conclusions on the Global Strategy on the European Union's Foreign and Security Policy – Council conclusions (17 October 2016), CFSP/PESC 814 CSDP/PSDC 572, 17 October 2016.

193 Council of the European Union, Council conclusions on implementing the EU Global Strategy in the area of Security and Defence – Council conclusions (14 November 2016), CFSP/PESC 906 CSDP/PSDC 637 COPS 327 POLMIL 127 CIVCOM 219, 14 November 2016.

### 2.2.1.2. Europe's Capability Gap

European "strategic autonomy" is currently one of the central catchwords in European defence integration discussions. Usually insinuating the capacity for autonomous action in security and defence matters, including reducing dependencies on the US in Europe's case,[194] the idea is particularly promoted by the French president Macron[195], but also appears in several EU documents[196], in particular in the EU's 2016 Global Strategy[197], which is the EU's doctrine to improve the effectiveness of the EU's and its Member States main security and defence priorities. In this context, strategic autonomy plays a central role in connection with strengthening and reforming the CSDP. This in turn requires enhancing the European defence capabilities, specifically through armaments cooperation to improve interoperability, effectiveness, and efficiency.

Closing Europe's capability gap is the key concern of the CSDP since the St Malo summit.[198] Europe's capacity to defend itself and manage international crises is severely restricted, despite the CSDP ambitions and the geopolitical challenges in reality, due to underfinancing of defence budgets[199] and low spending for R&D.[200] A recent example for Europe's inability to act in crisis management has been the troop withdrawal from Afghanistan, which the participating European States were unable to car-

---

194  Barbara Lippert et al. (eds), 'European Strategic Autonomy' [2019] 4 SWP Research Paper 1.

195  Emmanuel Macron, 'Initiative for Europe' (*ouest-france*, 26 September 2017) <http://international.blogs.ouest-france.fr/archive/2017/09/29/macron-sorbon ne-verbatim-europe-18583.html> accessed 13 April 2022; Florence Parly, 'Minister sets out defence priorities for French EU presidency in 2022' (*French Embassy in London*, 14 December 2021) <https://uk.ambafrance.org/Minister-sets-out-defence -priorities-for-French-EU-presidency-in-2022> accessed 10 January 2022.

196  See for example European Council, European Council 19/20 December 2013 Conclusions, EUCO 217/13, 20 December 2013.

197  EEAS, 'EU Global Strategy' (*EEAS*, 28 June 2016) <https://www.eeas.europa.eu/ eu-global-strategy_en> accessed 13 June 2020, endorsed by the Council, 'Council conclusions on the Global Strategy on the European Union's Foreign and Security Policy – Council conclusions (17 October 2016)' (*Council of the European Union*, 17 October 2016) <https://data.consilium.europa.eu/doc/document/ST-13202-2016-IN IT/en/pdf> accessed 13 June 2020.

198  Kielmansegg (n 27).

199  The Commission estimates the European defence investment gap at around 160 billion euro, see European Commission (n 43).

200  ibid.

ry out without the US's assistance.[201] Generally, the European States rely massively on the US for key defence capabilities. The current war in Ukraine has dramatically underlined this dependency once more.[202] To realise CSDP tasks (Art. 43(1) TEU), the EU has to rely on the military capabilities of the Member States (Art. 42(1) TEU), which are qualitatively and quantitatively deficient. Especially the smaller Member States have very limited capabilities, but generally, all Member States have to concentrate on certain capabilities due to budgetary constraints.[203] These capability gaps translate to the inefficiency of the CSDP.[204] The solution to overcome these gaps lies in armaments cooperation and the Europeanization of the fragmented armaments markets.[205] Despite several initiatives since 2017 (in particular PESCO, EDF, and CARD) to improve European armaments co-operation and promote the European armaments market and thus achieve European strategic autonomy and make the Member States' enhanced military capabilities available to the EU,[206] the ECAP continues to be in need of enhancement. The impact of these new initiatives in terms of scope, ambition and legally binding force remains limited and inadequate to close Europe's capability gap.[207]

### 2.2.1.3. The Necessity and Challenges of European Armaments Cooperation

In the context of achieving European strategic autonomy, armaments cooperation plays a central role. The EU's (and its Member States') ability to act in foreign and security policy affairs will – amongst other determinators

---

201  Charles Michel, 'The chaotic withdrawal in Afghanistan forces us to accelerate honest thinking about European defence' (*europa*, 2 September 2021) <https://www .consilium.europa.eu/en/european-council/president/news/2021/09/02/20210902-p ec-newsletter-afghanistan/> accessed 16 June 2022.

202  Christian Weisflog, 'Der Krieg in der Ukraine offenbart. Ohne den Beistand der USA gibt es kein freies und sicheres Europa' (*NZZ*, 24 June 2022) <https://www.nzz. ch/meinung/ukraine-krieg-die-usa-sind-europas-geringgeschaetzter-schutzengel-ld. 1686754?reduced=true> accessed 13 April 2023.

203  Kielmansegg (n 170) 285.

204  ibid. 286.

205  James Rogers and Andrea Gilli, 'Enabling the future European military capabilities 2013–2025: challenges and avenues' [2013] European Union Institute for Security 1, 16–57.

206  Kielmansegg (n 55) 80–81.

207  Kielmansegg (n 27).

– also be decided in regards to whether Europe manages to establish a genuine and autonomous European Defence Technological and Industrial Base (EDTIB) that is able to close Europe's capability gap, reduces dependencies on the US[208] and enables autonomous action in crises situations based on shared and interoperable military systems.[209] The current Franco-German armaments projects (although outside the CSDP framework) are examples for creating such autonomous defence capabilities.[210]

Problematically, lacking Member State convergence in security and defence matters also obstructs the integration process in the area of armaments. To this day, there is no systematic and effective coordination of the Member States' armaments and armaments export policies on the European level due to national sovereignty concerns. Besides the geopolitical necessity, armaments cooperation is also particularly driven by economic interests.[211] States cooperate in armaments projects if they perceive economic benefits, but refrain from cooperating if they see economic disadvantages or risks to their national defence industries (see also part *2.1.2. Historical Evolution of the Franco-German Armaments Collaboration*). For the same reasons, the process of opening up the national armaments markets to enable more efficient defence procurement is still incomplete. These are known challenges for the European armaments industries.[212]

---

208 Gerhard Hegmann, 'Europas Rüstungskonzerne wollen auf US-Technik verzichten' (*Welt*, 02 August 2020) <https://www.welt.de/wirtschaft/article212684375/Europas -Ruestungskonzerne-wollen-auf-US-Technik-verzichten.html> accessed 29 October 2021.

209 Kielmansegg (n 170) 286; Jacques Favin Levêque, 'L'Europe de la Défense après Lisbonne: enjeux, réalités et perspectives' in Aurélien Raccah (ed), *Le traité de Lisbonne De nouvelles compétences pour l'Union européene?* (L'Harmattan 2012) 187.

210 Gerhard Hegmann, 'Der neue Superfighter ist der Schlüssel für Europas Verteidigungsstrategie' (*Welt*, 29 July 2020) <https://www.welt.de/wirtschaft/plus21241227 9/Der-Superfighter-ist-der-Schluessel-fuer-Europas-Verteidigungsstrategie.html> accessed 30 October 2021.

211 Felix Biermann and Moritz Weiss, 'Power without a cause? Germany's conflict avoidance and the integration of European defence procurement' [2021] 43(2) Journal of European Integration 227, 230.

212 See for example the German 2020 Strategy Paper on Strengthening the Security and Defence Industry that acknowledges the need for an effective and competitive German and European EDTIB and thus clear rules for European armaments cooperation, see Bundesregierung, 'Strategy Paper of the Federal Government on Strengthening the Security and Defence Industry' (*BMWK*, 14 February 2020) <https://www.bmwk.de/Redaktion/DE/Downloads/S-T/strategiepapier-staerk ung-sicherits-und-verteidigungsindustrie-en.pdf?__blob=publicationFile&v=4> accessed 19 June 2022.

European armaments cooperation continues to be fragmented. While PESCO now provides a common framework for European armaments cooperation within the CSDP framework, trans-European armaments cooperation on an ad-hoc bilateral (for example the current Franco-German cooperation, see part *3.1. Unreliabilities of Franco-German Armaments Collaboration in the Bilateral Framework*) or multilateral (within OCCAR or the FFA, see part *3.3.1. Multilateral European Armaments Cooperation*) basis continues to exist alongside.

Trans-European armaments cooperation (outside the EU framework) inherits several challenges to the CSDP. Firstly, they principally contrast common approaches on the European level. For reasons of feasibility, it is accepted that too many participating States in armaments projects can lead to higher costs for R&D due to the juste retour principle or differing national system requirements. For these reasons, the development of the *A400M* transport aircraft for example became significantly more challenging to execute.[213] Because of the difficulties of inclusive European armaments projects, the Franco-German armaments cooperation is arranged in an exclusive manner.[214] Poland's request to join the MGCS project was rejected by France, for reasons of feasibility and protectionism.[215] France in particular has a strong interest to support its national defence industry and does not want to share sensitive knowledge and production shares if not necessary for financial reasons.[216] This has the potential to undermine enhanced European armaments integration. Secondly, it leads to political and

---

213  Jocelyn Mawdsley, 'The A400M Project: From Flagship Project to Warning for European Defence Cooperation' [2013] Defence Studies 13(1) 14–32; Hébert (n 45) 201–217.

214  By now, Spain has been allowed to join the FCAS project, however the "onboarding" process took four years after the project was initiated by Germany and France during the 2017 Franco-German Ministerial Council summit.

215  Björn Müller, 'Die Hürden für Europas gemeinsamen Kampfpanzer' (*FAZ*, 31 October 2019) <https://www.faz.net/aktuell/politik/ausland/ruesten-fuer-europa-huerden-fuer-den-gemeinsamen-kampfpanzer-16439321-p2.html> accessed 2 December 2021; see also part *2.2.2. Franco-German Armaments Cooperation today*.

216  Thomas Hanke, 'Europas grösstes Rüstungsprojekt steckt in der Krise' (*NZZ*, 3 March 2021) <https://www.nzz.ch/international/ruestung-deutsch-franzoesisches-projekt-steckt-in-der-krise-ld.1604493> accessed 26 October 2022; Meta-Défense, 'SCAF, MGCS: Die Politik übernimmt wieder die Kontrolle über die deutsch-französische Rüstungsindustriekooperation' (*Meta-Défense*, 23 September 2022) <https://meta-defense.fr/de/2022/09/23/scaf-mgcs-Politiker-gewinnen-die-Kontrolle-%C3%BCber-die-deutsch-franz%C3%B6sische-Verteidigungsindustrie-Kooperation-zur%C3%BCck/> accessed 26 October 2022.

industrial fragmentation and costly duplication. This contrasts initiatives like PESCO which are designed to improve cost-effectiveness and avoid redundancies. The FCAS project for example is mirrored by a competing British-Italian-Swedish project.[217] The success of the CSDP and of PESCO will therefore also be measured in regards to how large-scale armaments projects like FCAS will be integrated into these formats.

Armaments cooperation primarily occurs to improve cost effectiveness and achieve system interoperability. Yet, cooperative capability programmes in the past (conducted on a multilateral basis outside of the CSDP framework) have not always reduced costs for R&D or improved interoperability. For example, trans-European collaboration on the development of the *Boxer* armoured vehicle or the *FREMM* frigates within the OCCAR framework have nevertheless entailed interoperability issues, due to different technical specifications downstream. Furthermore, collaborative projects often suffer from escalating costs due to frequent unreliability by the participating States in terms of system requirements, changing purchase orders, or outright withdrawal from the project (noteworthy is the French withdrawal from the Eurofighter development for example). The initiation of PESCO and the EDF as binding frameworks is also based on the hope to eliminate these unreliabilities.[218] It is agreed that only systematic common European approaches can address the major capability gaps.[219]

Furthermore, the national differences in defence procurement, technical system compatibility, inefficiencies when it comes to developing defence products, and the aforementioned national security exception provision for armaments (Art. 346(1)(b) TFEU) are ongoing obstacles to European armaments cooperation. The consolidation of the European defence industries and industrial collaboration are regarded as key elements to enhance the competitiveness of the EU defence industry and thus European defence capabilities, however they are limited by European defence market fragmentation and different armaments export policies and cultures among the Member States.[220]

---

217  Helen Warrel and Sylvia Pfeifer, 'Italy joins forces with UK in European fighter jet race' (*FT*, 11 September 2019) <https://www.ft.com/content/d8bcb02e-d49e-11e9-8367-807ebd53ab77> accessed 3 April 2022.

218  Fiott (n 187) 47–48.

219  Anderson (n 184) 4.

220  Béraud-Sudreau (n 128) 79.

Furthermore, Member States like Italy, Poland, Sweden (and formerly the UK) maintain close transatlantic links, meaning that any commitment to a European defence-industrial policy should not come at the expense of collaboration with the US.[221]

Despite the Commission's efforts to harmonize the European market for defence equipment, it remains fragmented and thus inefficient. As a bloc, the European armaments industry is responsible for approximately 25–30 % of the global arms trade.[222] Yet, defence procurement in Europe continues to take place primarily on a national basis, thus leading to costly and unnecessary duplications of defence-industrial capacities and R&D of different defence systems.[223] The strategic shifts in European defence policy (or rather policies) due to the increasingly challenging geopolitical environment has admittedly led to higher total defence spending in Europe, however collaborative expenditure has remained low. Despite the more challenging geopolitical environment, EDA data shows a significant reduction in European collaborative defence equipment procurement since 2016. In 2020, the Member States spent a total of 4.1 billion euro on the procurement of new equipment in cooperation with others, a fall of 13 % compared to 2019. Furthermore, the Member States conducted just 11 % of their total equipment procurement in cooperation with other Member States, falling well short of the 35 % collective benchmark, which is also a commitment under PESCO.[224] Up to 30 % of annual defence expenditures could be saved through pooling of procurement.[225]

Moreover, when it comes to the integration of Europe's defence industries, national protectionism of the Member States' defence industries continues to prevent the efficient development of European armaments

---

221 Jean-Pierre Maulny, 'No time like the present – Towards a genuine defence industrial base for the CSDP?' in Daniel Fiott (ed), *The CSDP in 2020* The EU's legacy and ambition in security and defence (EUISS 2020) 125–126.

222 The European Member States' arms transfers can be tracked via the Stockholm International Peace Research Institute (SIPRI) Arms Transfers Database: https://www.sipri.org/databases/armstransfers; see also Pieter Wezeman et al., 'Trends in International Arms Transfers, 2021' (*SIPRI*, March 2022) <https://www.sipri.org/sites/default/files/2022-03/fs_2203_at_2021.pdf> accessed 1 September 2022.

223 European Commission (n 43).

224 EDA (n 110).

225 David Bachmann et al. 'More European, More Connected and More Capable Building the European Armed Forces of the Future' (*Munich Security Conference*, 2017) <https://securityconference.org/assets/02_Dokumente/01_Publikationen/MSCEuropeanDefenceReport2017.pdf> accessed 26 October 2022.

programmes.[226] Again, this leads to costly and unnecessary duplications of defence-industrial capacities and R&D of different defence systems. As discussed throughout this thesis (see also part *2.1. Historical Context: Evolution of European Defence Integration and Franco-German Armaments Cooperation*), the Member States' protectionism is rooted in their respective national defence interests[227], specifically the objective of retaining (at least to a certain degree) national defence-industrial autonomy and to not limit their defence industries in capacity, capability and competitiveness due to economic and defence strategic interests. Furthermore, differing defence-industrial structures, concerns regarding technology transfer and divergence of armaments exports also significantly impede defence-industrial integration and the building-up of an EDTIB.[228]

The continuing defence-industrial and defence market fragmentation have significant adverse economic and defence-strategic consequences. While the US used 30 major weapons systems in 2017, the EU Member States used 178.[229] As a bloc, the EU is after the US the second biggest spender globally on defence.[230] Studies have shown that especially at a time of budgetary constraints, a more efficient use of public money could be achieved by reducing inefficient redundancies, achieving economies of scale, targeting projects that surpass individual Member States' capacities, and improving the competitiveness and functioning of the Single Market for defence. The lack of cooperation between Member States in the field of defence and security is estimated to cost annually between 25 billion and 100 billion euro.[231] From a defence-strategic perspective, improving defence-industrial collaboration will lead to a more effective CSDP because the Member States will use shared and interoperable defence systems and

---

226 Mawdsley (n 213) 14–32; Marc DeVore and Moritz Weiss, 'Who's in the cockpit? The political economy of collaborative aircraft decisions' [2014] 21(2) Review of International Political Economy 479, 497–533; Hébert (n 45) 201–217.

227 Trybus (n 34) 49.

228 Christian Mölling and Torben Schütz, 'European Armament Collaboration: What We Can Learn from History and Concepts' in Nikolaos Karampekios et al. (eds), *The Emergence of EU Defense Research Policy* (Springer 2018) 131; Seiler (n 34) 2.

229 Bachmann (n 225).

230 Global defence spending since 1949 can be tracked and compared via the Stockholm International Peace Research Institute (SIPRI) Military Expenditure Database: https://milex.sipri.org/sipri; see also Silva et al (n 42).

231 European Parliamentary Research Service, 'The Cost of Non-Europe in Common Security and Defence Policy' (*europa*, 2013) <https://www.europarl.europa.eu/RegData/etudes/etudes/join/2013/494466/IPOL-JOIN_ET%282013%29494466_EN.pdf> accessed 17 April 2022.

can rely on a strong and autonomous EDTIB, providing the Member States with necessary defence capabilities.

Especially the issue of armaments exports is discussed in detail throughout this thesis, due to its significance[232] as an obstacle to European armaments cooperation. In 2019, (at the time) German chancellor Merkel stressed the need for a common European culture of armaments exports during the Munich Security Conference and specifically noted the risks that otherwise joint weapon systems could potentially not be realised in Europe.[233] According to Merkel, deeper European defence integration, a common armaments policy and joint armaments development is not possible without having a common armaments export policy on the European level. It has been shown that the Europeanisation of defence policy and procurement and European defence-industrial consolidation (including bilateral initiatives, such as the Franco-German collaboration), which aims at increasing efficiency and innovation in these areas will only be successful if there is a reliable framework regarding common standards and exports of armaments.[234]

How further convergence on the European level with regard to armaments exports will develop remains to be seen and depends on the political will for compromise. It was also in 2019 that the former German defence minister von der Leyen (who is today the President of the European Commission) noted that Germany's highly restrictive position on armaments exports is not supported by the majority of the other EU Member States.[235] This is why the Franco-German convergence of armaments exports as expressed in their new bilateral agreement is potentially an important step in the direction of making armaments cooperation in Europe more reliable by finding convergence in export matters. Although questions to its reliability

---

232 Dominic Vogel, 'Future Combat Air System: Too Big to Fail' (*SWP*, 8 January 2021) <https://www.swp-berlin.org/publikation/armament-project-future-combat-air-sys tem-too-big-to-fail> accessed 12 April 2022.

233 Angela Merkel, 'Rede von Bundeskanzlerin Merkel zur 55. Münchner Sicherheitskonferenz am 16. Februar 2019 in München' (*bundeskanzlerin*, 16 February 2019) <https://www.bundeskanzlerin.de/bkin-de/aktuelles/rede-von-bundeskanzlerin-me rkel-zur-55-muenchner-sicherheitskonferenz-am-16-februar-2019-in-muenchen-158 0936> accessed 21 October 2021.

234 Ernst&Young, *Rüstung und Beschaffung in Deutschland Stand und Herausforderungen, Dilemmata konstruktiv managen* (Ernst&Young 2017) 30.

235 Jungholt (n 163).

remain, the New Franco-German Agreement on Armaments Exports[236] (abbreviated NFGAAE) might be a model for similar agreements in the future ensuring reliable armaments cooperation.

Besides such bilateral agreements, there are also tendencies to further harmonise armaments export policies within the EU framework. The EU's CP on armaments exports[237] and the EU's Dual-Use Regulation[238] are the beginnings of such convergence, however their scope is limited. Germany for example favours further armaments export harmonisation on the European level.[239] France on the other hand remains deeply opposed to cede national competences over armaments exports to the supranational level.[240]

The success of European armaments cooperation within the frameworks of PESCO and the EDF will also depend on the level of European convergence of the different national defence-industrial and strategic interests. PESCO and the EDF initiatives show the revived interest of the Member States for (intergovernmental) defence-industrial cooperation after the period of defence integration stagnation after Lisbon.[241] This offers the potential that some of the shortcomings of European armaments cooperation can be addressed. Nevertheless, convergence on armaments exports has not yet been addressed by PESCO.

PESCO has been designed in an 'inclusive and ambitious'[242] fashion. According to Arts. 46 (1) TEU, Art. 1 Protocol 10, PESCO is open to all Member States. This is in line with German ideas for voluntary, open, integrative and inclusive European defence integration to enable conver-

---

236 Agreement between the Government of the Federal Republic of Germany and Government of the French Republic on Export Controls in the field of Armaments (NFGAAE) (*Abkommen zwischen der Regierung der Bundesrepublik Deutschland und der Regierung der Französischen Republik über Ausfuhrkontrollen im Rüstungsbereich / Accord sous forme d'échange de lettres entre le Gouvernement de la République française et le Gouvernement de la République fédérale d'Allemagne relatif au contrôle des exportations en matière de défense*) (Germany-France) (14 November 2019).

237 (n 61).

238 (n 114).

239 Bundesregierung, 'Koalitionsvertrag zwischen SPD, Bündnis 90/Die Grünen und FDP' (*Bundesregierung*, 2021) <https://www.bundesregierung.de/breg-de/service/gesetzesvorhaben/koalitionsvertrag-2021-1990800> accessed 24 March 2022.

240 Descôtes (n 141).

241 Antonio Calcara, 'Cooperation and non cooperation in European defence procurement' [2019] 42(6) Journal of European Integration 799.

242 Deutsch-Französischer Ministerrat, 'Gemeinsame Erklärung' (*France-Allemagne*, 13 July 2017) <https://www.france-allemagne.fr/Deutsch-Franzosischer-Ministerrat-am-in-Paris.html> accessed 16 December 2021.

gence in and emergence of a common defence culture (instead of further fragmentation) and takes into account the other Member States' concerns vis-à-vis Franco-German dominance within the EU after Brexit.

France originally had other plans for PESCO, favouring selective but ambitious defence integration with a focus on strategic autonomy and ability to act as priorities in European defence cooperation. This idea is reflected in EI2.[243] The Franco-German armaments collaboration is rather in line with France's ideas for European defence cooperation, entailing the risk of further defence fragmentation. This dialectic reflects again the continuing field of tension where European armaments cooperation is situated, between common integration aspirations and contrasting national sovereignty interests.

## 2.2.1.4. Armaments and the Single Market

For the longest time, defence and armaments matters were regarded as separate from other EU policy areas. Either outside (NATO, WEU) or since St Malo increasingly within the European framework (CSDP), they remained intentionally removed from supranational action. However, as discussed in the previous part, the Commission has increasingly become active in the field of armaments since then, alongside EDA.[244] At first with regard to establishing a Single Market for defence (via its Defence Package), recently also with regard to facilitating armaments cooperation (via the EDF). These efforts towards further adjusting the regulatory environment of defence and armaments (with the overall goal remaining a future EDU, whatever its final arrangement, see part *3.2.1.1. Towards a European Defence Union and potential consequences for European Armaments Cooperation*) are ongoing and will potentially also include further convergence regarding armaments exports.

This is because defence and armaments matters cannot be viewed separately from the Single Market. The need for a common regulatory framework for armaments arises out of the fact that European defence companies operate within the common market and their cross-border linkups and mergers have increased since the 1990s. Furthermore, defence matters

---

243  Hoeffler (n 46) 63; Steven Blockmans, 'The EU's modular approach to defence integration: an inclusive, ambitious and legally binding PESCO?' [2018] 55(6) Common Market Law Review 1785, 1812.

244  Hoeffler (n 46) 45.

have economic and social implications and thus an Internal Market dimension.[245] Finding a balance between the interests of the Internal Market and Member States' sovereignty concerns (in the case of armaments expressed in Art. 346 TFEU) is an ongoing struggle between the Member States and the EU, which has also led to several CJEU rulings in the matter (see part *3.2.1.3. The European Armaments Policy and its future*).

The European Commission, which today regards itself as 'geopolitical'[246], meaning as an international security policy actor, is by now active in the field of armaments and has implemented secondary law on several issues relating to defence-industrial policy (SMEs-targeted programmes, competitiveness-oriented measures)[247], procurement[248] and intra-European transfers of armaments[249] based on its Internal Market competence to create a genuine EDEM.[250]

Furthermore, not only does the Commission promote the Single Market for defence equipment, it actively supports the European defence industry, by complementing (on the basis of Art. 6(b) TFEU) the Member States' efforts in this field.[251] The supranationally administered EDF has further contributed to the supranationalisation of the European armaments cooperation and thus broadened EU defence integration beyond the strict (intergovernmental) limits of the CSDP.[252] The EDF represents for the first time in European defence integration supranational budget in CSDP matters, thus bridging the traditional supranational-intergovernmental divide in European armaments matters since the failure of the EDC, which would have included supranational defence procurement (see part *2.1.1. Historical Evolution of European Defence and Armaments Integration*).

---

245  Trybus (n 34) 123–125, 134–135.
246  European Commission, 'The von der Leyen Commission: One year on' (*European Commission*, 2020) <https://ec.europa.eu/info/sites/default/files/von-der-leyen-co mmission-one-year-on_en.pdf> accessed 11 September 2022.
247  Regulation (EU) 2018/1092 (n 186).
248  (n 112).
249  (n 111).
250  Hoeffler (n 46) 50; Nicolas Jabko, *Playing the Market: A Political Strategy for Uniting Europe, 1985 – 2005* (1st edn, Cornell University Press 2012) 26–41.
251  European Commission, Communication from the Commission to the European Parliament, the European Council, the Council, the European Economic and Social Committee and the Committee of the Regions, "European defence action plan", COM/2016/950 final, 30 November 2016.
252  Hoeffler (n 46) 64.

Notably, the Commission has principally no mandate for CSDP matters under EU primary law. According to Art 41(2) TEU, CFSP operating expenditure shall also be charged to the Union's budget, except for such expenditure arising from operations having military or defence implications. Instead of CSDP provisions, the legal basis for the Commission's activities related to the EDF is therefore construed from Arts. 173, 182(4), 183, 188(2) TFEU (for 'Industry' and 'Research and technological development and space'), being Internal Market competences. This is why the EDF addresses the industrial dimension of defence integration, promoting the EDTIB and the Single Market for defence. On the other hand, this means that the Commission has no managing powers when it comes to capability development, which remains intergovernmental. This in turn leaves European armaments cooperation fragmented and comprehensive common armaments policy coordination continues to be non-existent. Likewise, the Commission continues to not have a mandate to coordinate or regulate armaments exports (including EDF-financed armaments, except for dual-use goods, based on the Dual-Use Regulation[253] and the Commission's Internal Market competence (Art. 207 TFEU 'Common Commercial Policy'[254])). This will be further discussed in part *3.2.1.3. The European Armaments Policy and its future.*

Through the EDF, the Commission has become part of the (technically still) intergovernmental CSDP structure,[255] although within the narrow (contested) limits of the Treaties. The Commission has gone as far as the Treaties allow it to go, specifically with regard to the highly restricting armaments exception provision of Art. 346(1)(b) TFEU, due to which European armaments cooperation and the establishment of a Single Market for defence remains incomplete.

Despite the Commission's activities in the field of armaments, the (intergovernmental) EDA remains primarily responsible under EU primary law (Arts. 42(3), 45 TEU) to facilitate European armaments cooperation and close Europe's capability gap. According to Art. 42(3) subpara. 2 TEU, the Member States are tasked[256] to progressively improve their military

---

253 Regulation (EU) 2021/821 of the European Parliament and of the Council of 20 May 2021 setting up a Union regime for the control of exports, brokering, technical assistance, transit and transfer of dual-use items (recast) [2021] OJ L206/1.

254 Thomas Cottier and Lorena Trinberg, 'Artikel 207' in Hans von der Groeben et al. (eds), *Europäisches Unionsrecht* (7th edn, Nomos 2015) 310–351.

255 Hoeffler (n 46) 45.

256 Fortunato (n 94) 1220.

capabilities. EDA is tasked to support the Member States in this matter when it comes to R&D, procurement, stimulating cooperative projects, and strengthening the EDTIB (Art. 45(1)(a)–(e) TEU), for example via CARD or the EDF. Hence, EDA operates in an area concerned with the economic aspects of defence close to and potentially overlapping with Single Market matters.[257] EDA has played a significant part in facilitating European capability development[258] and contributing to the creation of an EDEM.[259] In this area, it cooperates with the Commission (Art. 45(2) TEU), also linking intergovernmental (i.e. CSDP) and supranational (i.e. Internal Market) policy areas.

Due to the principle of voluntariness regarding participation in EDA and in EDA programmes and projects, EDA is another of the CSDP's flexibility tools, in this case specifically for capability development and armaments cooperation. As in the other cases of flexibility in CSDP matters, this raises questions regarding coherence. EDA represents an umbrella for individual collaborative armaments projects. The Member States participating in EDA (until 2023 all Member States except Denmark[260]) are then free to choose in which projects they want to participate.[261] This will be further discussed in part *3.2.1.2. The Future of European Armaments Cooperation and PESCO.*

### 2.2.1.5. Intermediate Conclusions – European defence and armaments integration in 2023

The CSDP's "integration dividend" since the Russian annexation of Crimea in 2014 is ongoing and currently dramatically reinforced by Russia's 2022 invasion of Ukraine, which has underlined the need for effective and autonomous European defence capacities. The EU's recent Strategic Compass[262] particularly stresses the need for capability development by the

---

257  Trybus (n 45) 186–187.
258  Dyson and Konstadinides (n 91) 100.
259  Jörg Terhechte, 'EUV Art. 45 [Aufgaben der Europäischen Verteidigungsagentur]' in Ulrich Becker et al. (eds), *EU-Kommentar* (4th edn, Nomos 2019) 388.
260  As a consequence of Russia's attack of Ukraine, Denmark has joined EDA in 2023, see EDA, 'Denmark joins the European Defence Agency' (*EDA*, 25 March 2023) <https://defence-industry.eu/denmark-joins-the-european-defence-agency> accessed 27 March 2023.
261  Council Decision 2015/1835 (n 90) Arts. 19 (1), 20 (2); Terpan (n 261) 1269.
262  EEAS (n 75); the Strategic Compass was endorsed by the European Council on 25 March 2022, see European Council, 'European Council meeting (24 and 25

Member States and armaments cooperation to meet the current threats and challenges. The EU Member States agree with this assessment. The Strategic Compass was endorsed by the European Council on 25 March 2022 and most Member States (France[263] and Germany[264] in particular) have stressed the importance of further European defence integration and capability development, in particular through armaments collaboration.[265] Denmark, which had opted-out of the CSDP for thirty years, has now decided to participate in the CSDP.[266]

Nevertheless, despite the increasingly unstable geopolitical environment of the EU, which has significantly increased the relevance of European defence integration and the CSDP, their underlying conditions have not been fundamentally changed. NATO remains the cornerstone for collective defence and the EU Member States continue to reject any attempts for deeper defence integration that affects their ultimate sovereignty in defence matters. This is also the reason why the recent initiatives (PESCO, EDF, CARD, RDC) only build upon the established features of the CSDP.[267] They are less ambitious then often insinuated and are primarily concerned with closing Europe's capability gap,[268] today in particular with regard to achieving strategic autonomy and therefore enhance the Member States' military capabilities and make them available for the EU.

Despite the EU's increasingly unstable geopolitical environment, the Member States' reservation vis-à-vis ceding defence competences to the EU is not likely to change soon. The Member States have opted for the in-tergovernmental (and fragmented) solution, meaning selective cooperation and integration by their national armed forces and in armaments matters, and this trend will most likely continue in the future. This in turn signifi-

---

March 2022) – Conclusions' (*European Council*, 25 March 2022) <https://data.consi lium.europa.eu/doc/document/ST-1-2022-INIT/en/pdf> accessed 27 April 2022.

263  Emmanuel Macron, 'Speech by Emmanuel Macron at the closing ceremony of the Conference on the Future of Europe' (*europa.eu*, 10 May 2022) < https://presidence francaise.consilium.europa.eu/en/news/speech-by-emmanuel-macron-at-the-clos ing-ceremony-of-the-conference-on-the-future-of-europe/> accessed 13 June 2022; Parly (n 195).

264  Scholz (n 1).

265  European Council, 'The Versailles declaration' (*European Council*, 10 and 11 March 2022) <https://www.consilium.europa.eu/media/54773/20220311-versailles-declarat ion-en.pdf> accessed 2 September 2022.

266  Following a recent referendum on 1 June 2022, Denmark has now decided to participate in all aspects of CSDP, see EEAS (n 173).

267  Kielmansegg (n 27).

268  Kielmansegg (n 55) 80–81.

cantly restricts any proposals for further legal development in the area of defence and armaments integration. The lack of a common approach and significant commitments to European capability development continues to entail the risk of unreliability when it comes to realising large-scale defence projects.

Overall, European armaments integration remains incomplete in terms of closing Europe's capability gap and achieving efficiency gains. Especially Art. 346(1)(b) TFEU continues to impede further integration attempts. The Commission has gone as far as the Treaties permit to consolidate the EDTIB and stimulate armaments cooperation.

With PESCO, there are now common structures for European armaments cooperation. However, PESCO resembles traditional intergovernmental framework for trans-European armaments cooperation. Participation in PESCO and in PESCO projects is also voluntary. The participating Member States have made commitments to further their joint capability development, however concrete large-scale armaments projects are yet to be realised. Disputes over armaments exports continue to be a significant challenge for European armaments cooperation and are yet to be adequately addressed by PESCO or the EDF.

### 2.2.2. Franco-German Armaments Cooperation today

#### 2.2.2.1. Relaunching Franco-German Armaments Collaboration

The current Franco-German armaments collaboration, which is the starting point of this thesis, is politically based on the 2017 Franco-German Defence and Security Council conclusions that were published after the 2017 Franco-German Ministerial Council summit and is legally based on the 2019 Aachen Treaty (which will be further discussed in part *3.1.4. Aachen Treaty*).

During the 2017 Franco-German Ministerial Council summit (three years after the Russian annexation of Crimea), Germany and France renewed their will to collaborate in armaments production (after a period of two decades without significant cooperation, see part *2.1.2. Historical Evolution of the Franco-German Armaments Collaboration*) to further enhance their military capabilities. Several large-scale projects were thus initiated, in particular FCAS[269], MGCS[270], and the 'Eurodrone'[271] projects. Further-more, and this is both relevant for the context of the current Franco-German armaments collaboration as well as the legal discussions in parts *3.2.1.1. The Common Security and Defence Policy and its future* and *3.2.1.2. The European Armaments Policy and its future*, both States declared their will to enhance European security and defence and to strengthen the CSDP. As this requires that the EU is provided with the necessary capabilities to take military and civilian action, the EU Member States need to enhance their defence capabilities, since the EU relies on them to fulfil the CSDP tasks (see part *2.2.1. European Defence and Armaments Integration today*). Therefore, both States demanded the initiation of an 'inclusive and ambi-tious' Permanent Structured Cooperation (PESCO) and set the conditions for the creation of the EDF so that the EU becomes a fully-fledged global security actor possessing serious defence capabilities (for PESCO and EDF see also parts *3.2.1.2. The Future of European Armaments Cooperation and PESCO* and *3.2.1.3. The European Armaments Policy and its future*).[272]

The political decisions of the 2017 Franco-German Ministerial Council were then (in a broader manner) legally expressed in the 2019 Aachen Treaty, a follow-up agreement to the aforementioned 1963 Elysée Treaty. Among other issues relating to Franco-German bilateral cooperation, the Aachen Treaty sets out provisions on enhanced Franco-German security cooperation, including armaments collaboration, and on furthering Euro-pean defence integration and bolstering the EU's and its Member States' ability to act in matters relating to foreign affairs and security issues (for further discussions see part *3.1.4. Aachen Treaty*).

Considering the long period of stagnation and divergence of European security and defence cooperation and Franco-German defence and arma-ments cooperation, the Franco-German Defence and Security Council con-clusions and the Aachen Treaty are intended as both a clear pro-European signal and that the Franco-German "couple" plans to undertake more

---

269 A joint trans-European armaments project between Germany, France and since 2021 also Spain, which is meant to develop and produce a new fighter jet combined with drones, satellites and other aircrafts. FCAS is considered to be Europe's most import defence project, see Vogel (n 232).

270 A joint Franco-German armaments project, which is meant to develop a new battle tank.

271 The European MALE RPAS (medium-altitude, long-endurance remotely piloted air system) is a PESCO project between Germany, France, Italy, and Spain to develop a joint drone.

272 Deutsch-Französischer Ministerrat (n 241).

responsibility in European security and defence matters again. This was also necessary because of the UK's withdrawal from the EU. The 2017 Franco-German ministerial Council was held a year after the UK's 2016 withdrawal referendum. "Brexit" also meant that the EU lost a Member State with significant defence capabilities which despite its reservations against European defence integration has historically been instrumental in driving European defence (and armaments) integration together with France (see discussions regarding the Franco-British "couple" and the 1998 St Malo summit in part *2.1.1. Historical Evolution of European Defence and Armaments Integration*). This gap in European defence and armaments integration caused by the UK's withdrawal from the EU is now being filled by the Franco-German tandem. Together, both States have since then pushed the development of the traditionally event-driven CSDP and European armaments integration significantly forward, most importantly with regard to the creation of PESCO and the EDF, which represent new milestones in the area of European armaments cooperation.

Nevertheless, despite the Franco-German ambitions to strengthen European defence integration and armaments cooperation, the large-scale projects FCAS and MGCS are (at least for now) developed on a purely intergovernmental and multilateral basis outside PESCO.[273] Some observers argue that the newly increased Franco-German cooperation in the field of security and defence (including armaments production) 'is almost exclusively a result of the overall importance both States ascribe to their bilateral relationship.'[274] This has both national sovereignty reasons as well as practical reasons. Both France and Germany intent to retain national defence-industrial capacities for defence-strategic reasons. Furthermore, past collaborative projects (for example the development of the *A400M* transport aircraft[275]) have been significantly more challenging to execute

---

273 Kai Küstner, 'Lücken in der EU-Verteidigungsunion' (*tagesschau.de*, 14 December 2019), <https://www.tagesschau.de/ausland/pesco-105.html> accessed 13 April 2022; Sidney Dean, 'Main Ground Combat System (MGCS): A Status Report' (*European Security&Defence*, 23 January 2023) <https://euro-sd.com/2023/01/artic les/29122/main-ground-combat-system-mgcs-a-status-report/> accessed 7 March 2023.

274 Barbara Kunz and Ronja Kempin, 'The Treaty of Aachen. New Impetus for Franco-German Defense Cooperation?' (*IFRI*, 22 January 2019) <https://www.ifri.org/en/p ublications/editoriaux-de-lifri/treaty-aachen-new-impetus-franco-german-defense -cooperation> accessed 22 June 2020.

275 Mawdsley (n 213) 14–32.

with higher numbers of participating States which each had different defence requirements and disagreed over cost and productions shares which in turn led to higher development costs.[276] The development of FCAS and MGCS is therefore (for now) conducted on a trilateral (FCAS) and bilateral (MGCS) basis outside EU structures, while other projects (such as the Eurodrone) are developed as PESCO projects.

The fact that Franco-German armaments cooperation takes place both within and outside EU structures is contrary to a comprehensive and common European approach and leads to political, legal and industrial fragmentation in the area of European defence and armaments. Although partially, intergovernmental and ad hoc approaches (like the current Franco-German collaboration) facilitate trans-European armaments cooperation since these more flexible (but less reliable frameworks) mean States have to give up fewer sovereign powers in the area of defence and armaments and avoid far-reaching commitments. On the other hand, this also renders European armaments cooperation incomprehensive and defence cooperation less effective as these lose formats entail a variety of different programmes and frameworks (see also discussions in parts *2.2.1. European Defence and Armaments Integration today*, *3.2.1.2. The European Armaments Policy and its future*, and *3.3. Multilateral European Armaments Cooperation*).

However, even on the bilateral, intergovernmental level and despite a shared political interest to collaborate in armaments production, Franco-German collaboration is also not without frictions and characterised by several distinct political, economic, and legal challenges.

### 2.2.2.2. Necessities for Armaments Cooperation

In general, since the fall of the Iron Curtain (until the 2017 shift in EDP), defence budgets in Europe (including in France and Germany) have drastically decreased[277], while armaments development costs have risen. Coupled with the expected efficiency gains and lower and shared costs of armaments

---

276  Nana Brink, 'Die Wunderwaffe' (*Internationale Politik*, 1 May 2021) <https://internationalepolitik.de/de/die-wunderwaffe> accessed 13 April 2022.

277  The European Member States' defence spending since 1949 can be tracked via the Stockholm International Peace Research Institute (SIPRI) Military Expenditure Database: https://milex.sipri.org/sipri; see also Silva et al (n 42); see also European Commission (n 43).

production through economies of scale and sharing of technological know-how, European States are fiscally forced to cooperate in armaments production. Despite public declarations of the increased armaments cooperation being a pro-European signal, this financial necessity has also been a key reason for the initiation of the current Franco-German armaments collaboration.[278]

Furthermore, European (including Franco-German) armaments cooperation is driven by geopolitical necessity. The EU's increasingly challenging geopolitical environment and the derived need for European strategic autonomy requires that the Member States enhance their military capabilities, which is not possible without enhanced armaments cooperation and a strong EDTIB (see also part *2.2.1. European Defence and Armaments Integration today*).[279] Notably, it was also in 2019 (the year in which the Aachen Treaty was signed) when the French president Macron famously used the term 'brain death' (*'mort cérébrale'*[280]) to describe his perception of NATO's condition and the need for European strategic autonomy. Moreover, already back in 2017 (a few weeks before the Franco-German Ministerial Council summit which reinitiated the Franco-German armaments collaboration), the (at the time) German Chancellor Merkel said that Europe needed to take its destiny into its own hands and insinuated that it could no longer necessarily rely on the US' military protection.[281] This is why the preamble of the Aachen Treaty expressly states the need for a united, capable, sovereign and powerful EU (para. 3 of the Aachen Treaty's preamble), which is also in line with Macron's calls for European strategic autonomy[282].

---

278 Die Bundesregierung, 'Weissbuch 2016 Zur Sicherheitspolitik und der Zukunft der Bundeswehr' (*BMVG*, July 2016) <https://www.bmvg.de/resource/blob/13708/015 be272f8c0098f1537a491676bfc31/weissbuch2016-barrierefrei-data.pdf> accessed 26 October 2020; Ministère des Armées (n 141); Kunz (n 135) 92–93.

279 Die Bundesregierung (n 278); Ministère des Armées (n 141); Kunz (n 135) 92–93; Levêque (209) 187.

280 The Economist, 'Emmanuel Macron in his own words (French)' (*The Economist*, 7 November 2019) <https://www.economist.com/europe/2019/11/07/emmanuel-macr on-in-his-own-words-french> accessed 16 June 2021.

281 Handelsblatt, '"Wir Europäer müssen unser Schicksal in unsere eigene Hand nehmen"' (*Handelsblatt*, 28 May 2017) <https://www.handelsblatt.com/politik/d eutschland/angela-merkel-wir-europaeer-muessen-unser-schicksal-in-unsere-eige ne-hand-nehmen/19861340.html?ticket=ST-14653270-UNvsjicXuGBjWHnqEVPT -ap6> accessed 16 June 2021.

282 Macron (n 195).

Furthermore, there is also a strong defence-strategic necessity for Euro-pean armaments cooperation (both inside and outside EU structures). Since European armed forces (or rather, the armed forces of the EU Member States) increasingly operate within multinational battle groups of NATO, EU or other structures (for example EI2), this requires that they can operate on shared equipment. This in turn requires increased interop-erability and standardisation of European armaments which is facilitated through cooperation. Furthermore, the European States are able through armaments cooperation to procure military equipment that they would otherwise not be able to develop on their own due to lack of funds and technical or industrial capabilities. Armaments cooperation is therefore also regarded as strengthening European defence-industrial capacities which are the basis for European defence.[283]

### 2.2.2.3. Continuing Divergence and Challenges

Since trans-European armaments cooperation, including Franco-German collaboration, is primarily born out of necessity rather than pro-European conviction, such cooperation takes place on a flexible, intergovernmental and ad hoc basis, which safeguards States' sovereign interests in security and defence matters, and is also an important reason why such coopera-tion is usually avoided when States have the option to realise armaments projects on their own. This makes such trans-European armaments coop-eration (including Franco-German collaboration) inconsistent, since the European States only cooperate on a case-by-case basis and (despite for-mats like PESCO and the EDF today) avoid significant commitments when it comes to armaments integration. This in turn continues to entail industrial, political and legal fragmentation in the area of armaments coop-eration in Europe. Despite the need for a stronger EDTIB, there are still only few examples for increased European defence industrial consolidation, such as Airbus and KNDS, and European armaments cooperation (both inside and outside EU structures) continues to be low, with more than 80 % of defence procurement and more than 90 % of R&D being nationally conducted in 2017.[284]

---

283   Die Bundesregierung (n 278); Ministère des Armées (n 141); Kunz (n 135) 92–93.
284   European Commission, Launching the European Defence Fund, COM/2017/0295 final, 7 June 2017.

In the 2019 Aachen Treaty, France and Germany publicly declared that their bilateral defence and armaments cooperation is motivated by European integration considerations. However, as mentioned above, European armaments cooperation is generally primarily guided by economic, defence-strategic and political necessities and only to a lesser extent by European defence integration conviction. This also applies to the Franco-German collaboration. Much rather than common interests or similar positions, a key reason for both States to cooperate in this contentious policy area is the fact that both States are dependent on each other when it comes to realising these current large-scale projects due to financial and technical constraints. Especially France needs Germany as its partner to fund the ambitious armaments projects FCAS and MGCS which from the French point of interest serve to ensure France's global military ability to act.[285] It is important to note that if France could finance its large-scale armaments projects on its own, it would most likely not collaborate with Germany due to its diverging defence-industrial interests and concerns over armaments exports restrictions. The Franco-German armaments collaboration primarily arises out of the fact that France is forced to collaborate due to the large gap between its global military ambitions and its defence-industrial and financial capacities in reality.[286] This Franco-German "marriage of convenience" makes their armaments collaboration reliant on the basis that this condition continues to apply and that the perceived advantages of the collaboration prevail over France's and Germany's respective concerns regarding their collaboration due to their different defence strategic cultures and divergence of armaments export policy.

To this day, the diverse historical legacies and strategic cultures (see also of part *2.1.2. Historical Evolution of the Franco-German Armaments Collaboration*) both States and their different security and defence priorities continue to impede closer bilateral cooperation in the area of European defence integration in general and especially in the field of their armaments cooperation.[287]

France and Germany have very different defence-industrial structures and different defence policy requisitions. France is frequently involved in military operations around the globe and features a pyramid-structured defence industry where the French government sets guidelines in line

---

285  Kunz (n 135) 69–76.
286  Kempin (n 44) 210.
287  Béraud-Sudreau (n 128) 79.

with France's national security policy. The French State is closely linked to the nationally prestigious defence industry and protects it against European and global competition.[288] Since the de Gaulle era, part of that security policy is to ensure a French autonomous defence industry safeguarding France's national strategic autonomy.[289] Today, this also links to Macron's ideas for European strategic autonomy (partially an extension French national strategic autonomy considerations).[290] For France, strategic autonomy entails sovereignty over security and defence matters and an autonomous defence industry which serves to provide the French military with the necessary capabilities to act autonomously and conduct global military operations.[291] Albeit, France's defence-industrial autonomy has become increasingly difficult to maintain. Like the other EU Member States, France cannot sufficiently finance its (ambitious) defence capabilities on its own which forces France to cooperate in armaments matters with partner States (like Germany) even though this is incompatible with France's idea of defence-industrial autonomy.[292] This causes a problematic contradiction between French national defence aspirations and financial constraints in reality which makes armaments cooperation unstable and reliable on continuing necessity, not political conviction.

The German defence industry on the other hand is decentralised, more independent from the German government, features smaller armaments companies, and does not enjoy a prestigious status like the French defence industry in France.[293] Military operations are not the norm.[294] Therefore, Germany is less focussed on autonomy concerns, which also means that large-scale armaments projects are conventionally (at least until the 2022 Russian invasion of Ukraine, see below) not a political priority.[295] Since the defence industry and national strategic autonomy are not (compared to France) political priorities, there is a higher political acceptance to organize armaments matters within EU structures.[296]

---

288   Kunz (n 135) 91–92.
289   Béraud-Sudreau (n 134) 19–29.
290   Vogel (n 232).
291   Kempin (n 44) 210.
292   Kempin (n 44) 210.
293   Atzpodien (n 128).
294   Kempin (n 44) 210.
295   Kunz (n 135) 91–92.
296   Hoeffler (n 46) 53–55.

The structural differences of the French and German defence industries and national defence-strategic cultures complicate their bilateral armaments collaboration and have caused recurring disagreements.[297] Points
of contention have arisen out of the extensive approval procedures by
the German *Bundestag* with regard to the collaboration projects' funding
which from the French perspective prevent long-term planning. Furthermore, there are disagreements regarding cost distribution and production
shares (a juste retour debate[298]) and with regard to industrial competition,
technology transfer and system leadership. Especially challenging in this
context appears to be the competition between Airbus and Dassault, which
are now expected to collaborate on the FCAS project.[299]

Nevertheless, these challenges are not new for Franco-German armaments collaboration (see also part *2.1.2. Historical Evolution of the Franco-
German Armaments Collaboration*) and appear to be manageable. A continuing challenge, which has the potential to cause the ultimate failure of the
current Franco-German armaments collaboration, is however the ongoing
divergence of armaments exports policies. Despite a bilateral agreement
specifically regulating this issue (the NFGAAE, see part *3.1.5. New Franco-
German Agreement on Armaments Exports*), there is no sufficiently reliable
solution on how to handle exports of armaments stemming from their bilateral collaboration and thus ensure long-term Franco-German armaments
collaboration.

### 2.2.2.4. The Continuous Contentious Issue of Armaments Exports

Generally, the European armaments industries are highly dependent on exports because the European defence equipment market (or rather markets)
is too small and fragmented for national armaments industries which are
intended to be competitive, efficient and autonomous for defence-strategic
and economic reasons, especially in times of lower defence budgets after

---

297 Vogel (n 232).
298 (n 44).
299 Thomas Hanke, 'Rüstungskonzerne Airbus und Dassault bemühen sich um Rettung
von Mega-Projekt' (*Handelsblatt*, 8 March 2021) <https://www.handelsblatt.com/p
olitik/international/kampfflugzeugsystem-ruestungskonzerne-airbus-und-dassault
-bemuehen-sich-um-rettung-von-mega-projekt/26984414.html> accessed 25 March
2022; Michaela Wiegel, 'Ärger in Paris über Deutschlands Tempo' (*FAZ*, 24 March
2021) <https://www.faz.net/aktuell/politik/ausland/deutsch-franzoesische-ruestung
sprojekte-kommen-nicht-voran-17261344.html> accessed 25 March 2022.

the fall of the Iron Curtain.[300] German and France feature the largest defence industries in the EU and heavily rely on foreign defence markets to sustain their defence industries' economic viability through economies of scale[301] and in order to balance development costs.[302] Especially for France, armaments exports are considered part of the French armaments industry's business model and serve to safeguard France's national strategic defence autonomy.[303] France and Germany are the biggest armaments exporting countries in the EU.[304] Nevertheless, the positions on armaments exports are very different in both countries (see also part *2.1.2. Historical Evolution of the Franco-German Armaments Collaboration*).

France pursues a pragmatic and more indiscriminate armaments export policy which also serves as a foreign policy instrument.[305] Especially when compared to Germany, armaments exports are a lot less controversial.[306] This is also why in France's centralist presidential system the *Assemblée Nationale* has no substantial involvement in the armaments export control process.[307] The government's political criteria for licencing decisions are classified information and the parliament receives relevant substantive information only after the government has granted the licences, in an annual report on arms exports. This report is the only available tool for legislators to influence the French government's armaments export policy decisions and in the past, the parliament has made little use of it.[308] Although, the political climate has slightly changed over the past decade and human

---

300  Mölling (n 44) 27; Descôtes (n 141).

301  Atzpodien (n 128).

302  Béraud-Sudreau (n 141); Ministère des Armées (n 141); Descôtes (n 141).

303  Véronique Guillermard, 'Dassault appelle à une harmonisation des règles à l'export' (*Le Figaro*, 28 Feburary 2019) <https://www.lefigaro.fr/societes/2019/02/28/20005-2 0190228ARTFIG00295-dassault-appelle-a-une-harmonisation-des-regles-a-l-export. php> accessed 3 December 2021.

304  Pieter Wezeman et al., 'Trends in International Arms Transfers, 2020' (*SIPRI*, March 2021) <https://www.sipri.org/sites/default/files/2021-03/fs_2103_at_2020_v2.pdf> accessed 31 October 2021; Wezeman et al. (n 222).

305  Descôtes (n 141); Béraud-Sudreau (n 141).

306  Béraud-Sudreau (n 128) 85–86; Lucie Béraud-Sudreau et al. 'Réguler le commerce des armes par le Parlement et l'opinion publique: Comparaison du contrôle des exportations d'armement en Allemagne, France, Royaume-Uni et Suède' [2015] 48 Politique européenne 82, 99–103.

307  Béraud-Sudreau (n 134) 44–46.

308  Béraud-Sudreau (n 128) 87.

rights, foreign-policy choices and transparency vis-à-vis armaments exports are playing a more important role in the French debate.[309]

In Germany, armaments exports are much more controversial[310] than in France and the *Bundestag* is much more involved in the political debate. Like in France, armaments export decisions are made by the government, but the German members of parliament are vastly more active in this policy area and better informed. They have the right to information[311] from the German government (*"Kleine und Große Anfragen"*), the German government publishes all its licencing decisions[312], and there are annual and biannual governmental armaments export reports[313]. Although the German defence industry faces similar challenges as France's in terms of a national defence market which is too small to only serve the German armed forces in an economically viable manner (especially in times of decreasing defence

---

309 Commission de la défense nationale et des forces armées, 'Audition de Mme Florence Parly, ministre des Armées, sur le rapport au Parlement sur les exportations d'armement de la France' (*Assemblée nationale*, 4 July 2018) <https://www.assemblee-nationale.fr/dyn/15/comptes-rendus/cion_def/l15cion_def1718070_compte-rendu#> accessed 26 October 2022; Commission de la défense nationale et des forces armées, 'Audition de Mme Florence Parly, ministre des Armées, sur les opérations en cours et les exportations d'armement' (*Assemblée nationale*, 7 May 2019) <https://www.assemblee-nationale.fr/dyn/15/comptes-rendus/cion_def/l15cion_def1819032_compte-rendu#> accessed 26 October 2022; AFP, 'La gauche réclame la "transparence" sur la vente d'armes au Yémen' (*L'OBS*, 15 April 2019) <https://www.nouvelobs.com/politique/20190415.OBS11593/la-gauche-reclame-la-transparence-sur-la-vente-d-armes-au-yemen.html> accessed 26 October 2022; Manon Rescan, 'À l'Assemblée, des élus s'invitent dans le débat miné sur les ventes d'armes à l'Arabie saoudite' (*Le Monde*, 8 June 2019) <https://www.lemonde.fr/politique/article/2019/06/08/l-assemblee-s-invite-dans-le-debat-mine-sur-les-ventes-d-armes_5473357_823448.html> accessed 26 October 2022.
310 Atzpodien (n 128).
311 BVerfG, Urteil vom 21. Oktober 2014 – 2 BvE 5/11 at 1.
312 Bundesministerium für Wirtschaft und Klimaschutz, 'A Restrictive, Responsible Policy on the Export of Military Equipment' (*BMWK*, 2019) <https://www.bmwk.de/Redaktion/EN/Dossier/export-controls-for-military-equipment.html> accessed 26 October 2022.
313 See for example Bundesministerium für Wirtschaft und Klimaschutz, 'Bericht der Bundesregierung über ihre Exportpolitik für konventionelle Rüstungsgüter im Jahre 2020' (*BMWK*, 2020) <https://www.bmwk.de/Redaktion/DE/Downloads/B/bericht-der-bundesregierung-ueber-ihre-exportpolitik-fuer-konventionelle-ruestungsgueter-im-jahre-2020.pdf?__blob=publicationFile&v=6> accessed 26 October 2022.

budgets[314] after the fall of the Iron Curtain), since armaments exports are highly controversial in Germany, Germany pursues are very restrictive armaments export policy.[315] Whereas France primarily considers armaments exports under strategic aspects, Germany debates armaments exports mainly on moral grounds.[316]

The different positions on armaments exports have been a serious obstacle for Franco-German armaments collaboration in the past (see part *2.1.2. Historical Evolution of the Franco-German Armaments Collaboration*) and continue to threaten the success of the current collaboration (despite a current bilateral agreement on the issue which will be discussed in part *3.1.5. New Franco-German Agreement on Armaments Exports*). Until the renewed collaboration in 2017, collaborative large-scale armaments projects were not realised since France was unable to rely on Germany that it would not block French armaments exports stemming from joint projects. Germany's expressly 'restrictive'[317] stance threatens Franco-German armaments collaboration (as well as other trans-European armaments cooperation with German participation) and has isolated Germany in the past among its European partners, especially France. As mentioned earlier, armaments projects are much harder to finance without export options. Furthermore, the armaments industries of the European partner States face recurring problems when their legitimate expectations are not protected due to unreliable and non-transparent German export decisions. There are several examples where exports were outright denied despite prior production licences or where armaments producers were pressured by the German government not to export to certain third countries retroactively. This happened for example in the case of planned armaments exports to Saudi Arabia which were denied after the *Kashoggi* murder due to human rights concerns. For the European armaments producers this means having to

---

314  EDA, *Defence Data 2019–2020* (EDA 2021); SIPRI, 'SIPRI Military Expenditure Database' <https://milex.sipri.org/sipri> accessed 26 April 2022; European Commission (n 43).

315  Mölling (n 44) 27.

316  Kunz (n 135) 96.

317  See preamble of the German federal government's 2019 Political Principles for armaments exports, Bundesregierung, 'Politische Grundsätze der Bundesregierung für den Export von Kriegswaffen und sonstigen Rüstungsgütern' (*Bundesregierung*, 26 June 2019) <https://www.bmwi.de/Redaktion/DE/Pressemitteilungen/2019/2019 0626-bundesregierung-beschliesst-politische-grundsaetze-fuer-ruestungsexporte.h tml> accessed 5 April 2022.

pay contractual penalties. This unpredictability and lack of reliable rules for armaments exports makes producing armaments with Germany participation financially risky and in turn weakens the German and European armaments industries.[318] Consequently, trans-European armaments production frequently happens "German-free", meaning partner States avoid cooperating with Germany in armaments production as much as possible since they cannot be sure that they will be able to export armaments produced with German components. This in turn further weakens the German and European armaments industries as it leads to industrial fragmentation and non-participation of Germany, being the economically most powerful EU Member State.[319]

Germany's unpredictability and unreliability when it comes to licencing armaments exports is also one of the reasons why the FCAS project is mirrored by a competing British-Italian-Swedish project[320], which further underlines the lack of a comprehensive European approach to armaments cooperation. For the foregoing reasons, the French defence industry was very critical from the onset of the current Franco-German armaments collaboration due to concerns over Germany's restrictive armaments export control.[321] This is why finding convergence of armaments exports played an important role in the negotiation process of the 2019 Aachen Treaty[322] and subsequently led to a bilateral follow-up agreement regulating this contentious issue.

### 2.2.2.5. Need for Convergence of Armaments Export Policies

To avoid another failure of Franco-German armaments production collaboration, there was and is a definite need for Franco-German convergence of armaments export matters. This means a coordinated approach to armaments exports in order to facilitate the development of future large-scale armaments programmes and thus strengthen European defence.[323] If France

---

318  Atzpodien (n 128); Descôtes (n 141).
319  Atzpodien (n 128).
320  Warrel and Pfeifer (n 217).
321  Commission de la défense nationale et des forces armées, 'Audition de Monsieur Stéphane Mayer, président-directeur général de Nexter' (*Assemblé nationale*, 15 May 2019) <https://www.assemblee-nationale.fr/dyn/15/comptes-rendus/cion_def/l15cio n_def1819034_compte-rendu#.> accessed 26 October 2022.
322  Merkel (n 233).
323  Béraud-Sudreau (n 128).

cannot not rely on Germany to not block French armaments exports, France will not collaborate with Germany in armaments production[324] which in turn will have serious disadvantages for the EDTIB and European defence capabilities.[325] In other words, Franco-German armaments collaboration can only be guaranteed if there are reliable rules on how to deal with exports of armaments stemming from joint production that are compatible with both countries' armaments export cultures. However, converging in armaments export policy has been difficult due to legal and political factors.

Due to the need for European (including Franco-German in particular) armaments cooperation, there is partial political and legal convergence on the European level and significant convergence on the Franco-German bilateral level expressed by their new bilateral agreement on armaments exports. The NFGAAE is intended to resolve the most contentious issues between France and Germany by establishing a non-veto principle for armaments stemming from joint projects to enable the joint realisation of the current large-scale armaments projects.[326]

For now, the NFGAAE has sufficed so that Franco-German armaments collaboration could be reinitiated. Whether it will make Franco-German armaments collaboration more reliable in the long-term as French armaments exports cannot principally be blocked by Germany remains to be seen, as the new agreement resembles the failed SDA in many ways (see parts *2.1.2. Historical Evolution of the Franco-German Armaments Collaboration*, *3.1.2. Schmidt Debré Agreement*, and *3.1.5. New Franco-German Agreement on Armaments Exports*).

Furthermore, Germany and France share common European[327] and international[328] commitments which has also led to growing convergence of their respective armaments export control regimes (for more see part *3.2.1.4. Towards a Comprehensive European Arms Export Regime?*). Moreover, this provides a basis for further legal harmonisation and common

---

324 Descôtes (n 141).
325 Vogel (n 232).
326 Atzpodien (n 128).
327 In particular (n 61).
328 Such as the FFA, the Wassenaar Arrangement, the Missile Technology Control Regime, the Nuclear Non-Proliferation Treaty, the Chemical Weapons Convention, the Biological Weapons Convention, the Arms Trade Treaty, the Hague Code of Conduct against missile proliferation, the Anti-Personnel Mine Ban Convention, or UN Arms Embargos. Also, both countries participate in the UN Programme of Action on Small Arms, Proliferation Security Initiative, and the Global Initiative to Combat Nuclear Terrorism; Cops et al. (n 60) 38–39.

standards and procedures for armaments exports. For that to happen, further political convergence of armaments exports is required.

Further complicating European armaments cooperation with German participation is the fact that Germany's position on armaments exports in the context of European armaments cooperation is not only restrictive but also ambiguous. This also furthers the Franco-German armaments collaboration's unreliability.

In 2019 (when the Aachen Treaty and the NFGAAE were also signed), the German federal government updated its Political Principles on Armaments Exports, which also clarify the German government's stance on bilateral and European armaments cooperation (Preamble and section II(2) of the 2019 Political Principles).[329] On the one hand, the 2019 Political Principles stress the intent to further European armaments cooperation and to further convergence of armaments export policies by developing common approaches on the European level. This is expressly considered with regard to the CFSP, strengthening the EDTIB and to enhance defence cooperation in the context of the EDU (Preamble 2019 Political Principles). PESCO is also mentioned particular. In cases of armaments exports to EU Member States, NATO-allies and NATO-equivalent countries, such exports are principally unrestricted in order to enable trans-European armaments cooperation (section II(1) of the 2019 Political Principles). On the other hand, according to the Preamble of the 2019 Political Principles, Germany intends to continue to pursue a restrictive armaments export policy, where the armaments export decisions are made by the federal government on the basis of the *Kriegswaffenkontrollgesetz*[330], the *Außenwirtschaftsgesetz*[331], the EU's CP[332] on armaments exports and the 2013 Arms Trade Treaty[333] (section I(1) 2019 Political Principles).[334] While the export of armaments to EU Member States, NATO-allies and NATO-equivalent countries is principally

---

329  Bundesregierung (n 317).

330  1961 War Weapons Control Act (*Gesetz über die Kontrolle von Kriegswaffen (Ausführungsgesetz zu Artikel 26 Abs. 2 des Grundgesetzes)*) (KrWaffKontrG) (current version 19 December 2022).

331  2013 Foreign Trade Law (*Außenwirtschaftsgesetz*) (AWG) (current version 17 July 2020).

332  (n 61).

333  Arms Trade Treaty (ATT) (signed 2 April 2013, entered into force 24 December 2014) 3031 UNTS.

334  On a related note, this also further underlines that – contrary to Boysen's claims (see below) – the German federal government does not delegate its export competence to France.

unrestricted, armaments exports to third countries continue to be heavily restricted (section III 2019 Political Principles). This is the central point of contention between Germany and France regarding exports of armaments stemming from joint projects and potentially provides a risk for the future of their armaments collaboration.

Furthermore, the 2019 Political Principles state that the German federal government will not waive the possibility to intervene in export plans of cooperation partners and to enforce its Political Principles reserves the right in any case to oppose certain export plans of the cooperation partner in a consultation procedure. This makes convergence on the trans-European level more challenging as it always entails the possibility that Germany may veto armaments exports of its cooperation partners in the future which in turn might further enforce "German-free" armaments cooperation formats.

Even more challenging to find further European convergence of armaments exports is the fact that Germany's restrictive armaments export policy is well-established by the German constitution (Art. 26 GG) which heavily restricts attempts to make the German armaments export control regime less restrictive or to confer national licencing competences to the supranational level or a armaments project partner.[335] It is however relevant to point out that Art. 26 GG is not immune to change by the German legislator[336] provided sufficient political will. Concerns regarding the constitutionality of the 2019 follow-up agreement (NFGAAE) to the Aachen Treaty which addresses and regulates the contentious issue of armaments exports regarding jointly produced armaments have already been raised (this will be further discussed in *part 3.1.5. New Franco-German Agreement on Armaments Exports*) which in turn raises questions of the NFGAAE's long-term reliability.

Politically, there is also a lack of certainty and predictability regarding the long-term commitment of both States to their armaments cooperation and the governing agreements arising out of their aforementioned fundamentally different strategic cultures. The new Franco-German armaments cooperation is currently being designed to be viable for the next decades, but potential governmental shifts that lead to more restrictive armaments export policies in Germany or the revival of purely national defence ap-

---

335  Kunz (n 135) 96.
336  According to Art. 79(3) GG, only Arts. 1 and 20 GG are unalterable.

proaches in France[337] might seriously disrupt Franco-German armaments cooperation in the future, despite bilateral agreements which are meant to ensure its success.

The current German "traffic light" government coalition has agreed on passing a new national armaments export act which is intended to serve the purpose of furthering a restrictive armaments export policy. It is set to implement the EU's CP[338] on armaments exports, the German federal government's aforementioned (export restrictive) Political Principles, and to extent post-shipment controls for armaments exports. Furthermore, export licences for armaments exports to countries directly involved in the Yemen conflict will be principally denied.[339] It is to be expected that the anticipated new German armaments export act would in practice generally entail more restrictions for armaments exports to third countries (non-EU, non-NATO and non-NATO-equivalent countries). This in turn would likely weaken the EDTIB[340] and might potentially have adverse effects on the current Franco-German armaments collaboration as it might lead to situations again where Germany blocks French armaments exports despite the new bilateral agreement on armaments exports, which is not acceptable for France.

On the other hand, the 2022 Russian invasion in Ukraine has led to a historic turning point ('*Zeitenwende*') in Germany's strategic culture. German chancellor Scholz has declared the Franco-German armaments collaboration and European defence integration (including armaments cooperation) political priorities.[341] As mentioned earlier, this will not be feasible without more convergence of armaments exports.

However, this is currently speculation and as a result, like in the past (see part 2.1.2. *Historical Evolution of the Franco-German Armaments Collaboration*) when Franco-German armaments collaboration did not function properly in terms of realising joint projects, legal and political unreliability factors remain and continue to endanger the collaboration's long-term success.

---

337 Die Zeit, 'Marine Le Pen will Verteidigungsprojekte mit Deutschland stoppen' (*ZEIT*, 13 April 2022) <https://www.zeit.de/politik/ausland/2022-04/frankreich-marine-le-pen-verteidigung-deutschland-nato> accessed 13 April 2022.

338 (n 61).

339 Bundesregierung (239).

340 FAZ, 'Rüstungsindustrie warnt vor zu starken Exportbeschränkungen' (*FAZ*, 3 January 2022) <https://www.faz.net/aktuell/wirtschaft/mehr-wirtschaft/ruestungsindustrie-warnt-vor-starken-exportbeschraenkungen-17713099.html> accessed 4 January 2022.

341 Scholz (n 1).

The Franco-German controversy over armaments export convergence also reflects the EU's and its Member States' larger divide in the area of defence and armaments cooperation and export convergence.[342] In 2019, former German chancellor Merkel stressed the need for a common European culture of armaments exports during the Munich Security Conference and specifically noted the risks that otherwise joint weapon systems could potentially not be realised in Europe.[343] According to Merkel, deeper European defence integration, a common armaments policy and joint armaments development is not possible without having a common armaments export policy on the European level. It has been shown that the Europeanisation of defence policy and procurement and European defence-industrial consolidation (including bilateral initiatives, such as the Franco-German collaboration), which aims at increasing efficiency and innovation in these areas will only be successful if there is a reliable framework regarding common standards and exports of armaments.[344] How further convergence on the European level will develop remains to be seen and depends on the political will for compromise. It was also in 2019 that the former German defence minister von der Leyen (who is today the President of the Commission) noted that Germany's highly restrictive position on armaments exports is not supported by the majority of the other EU Member States.[345] This is why the Franco-German convergence of armaments exports as expressed in their new bilateral agreement is an important step in the direction of making European armaments cooperation more successful by finding convergence of export matters. Although questions to its reliability remain, the NFGAAE exports might be a model for similar agreements in the future ensuring successful European armaments cooperation (see also part *3.3.3. A Future for Multilateral European Armaments Cooperation?*).

### 2.2.2.6. Intermediate Conclusions – need for legal reliability to ensure successful collaboration

This part has provided the politico-legal backdrop against which the current Franco-German armaments collaboration was reinitiated and now takes place. Just as in the past, Franco-German armaments cooperation

---

342  Vogel (n 232).
343  Merkel (n 233).
344  Ernst&Young (n 234) 30.
345  Jungholt (n 163).

is born out of economic and geopolitical necessities and must withstand several distinct challenges. These challenges arise out of both States' diverging strategic cultures and national interests which manifest themselves in particular in the contentious issue of diverging armaments export policies.

France is still particularly concerned about its sovereignty and strategic autonomy in armaments matters. This is why it has a large interest in its autonomous defence industry and only cooperates out of economic and geopolitical necessity. In this context, armaments exports play a central role. To lower costs for developing and producing large-scale armaments projects, armaments exports are regarded as necessary since the French national defence market is too small to be exclusively served by the French armaments industry only and cost-effectivness is generated through economies of scale and armaments exports. Armaments exports are also an important foreign policy instrument for France. What follows is a rather indiscriminate armaments export policy and a refusal to collaborate on armaments projects if the perceived defence-industrial disadvantages of such collaboration outweigh the advantages. This is the case when France is unable to export armaments stemming from joint projects because its cooperation partner blocks French armaments exports.

This position is difficult to reconcile with Germany's particular restrictive armaments export policy, which is more concerned about human rights than strategic interests and extends to armaments exports stemming from collaborative projects.

The continuing divergence of armaments export policies has the potential to lead to another failure of Franco-German armaments collaboration which in turn will have significant adverse consequences for European defence capability development. To avoid such failure, political convergence of armaments exports and entailing reliable rules ensuring that commitments are upheld are therefore required.

For now, sufficient political convergence on armaments exports to reinitiate Franco-German armaments collaboration appears to have been found and is expressed by the NFGAAE. Whether its provisions are legally and politically sufficiently reliable however in the long run to ensure that the current large-scale armaments projects will ultimately be realised will be analysed in part *3.1.5. New Franco-German Agreement on Armaments Exports.*

# 3. Franco-German Armaments Collaboration – unreliable legal frameworks

Against the backdrop of the challenges of Franco-German armaments collaboration and European capability development discussed in the previous section, the current legal frameworks for Franco-German armaments collaboration will now be analysed with a view to whether they are sufficiently reliable from a legal perspective to ensure the efficient and consistent realisation of large-scale joint armaments projects.

The current legal frameworks for Franco German relations in the field of armaments cooperation comprise primarily of bilateral intergovernmental agreements, but EU law also plays a role. Both areas of law will therefore be analysed in this section. Furthermore, EU will also be discussed as an alternative legally more reliable framework for armaments cooperation in Europe and will be analysed especially in this regard.

## 3.1. Unreliabilities of Franco-German Armaments Collaboration in the Bilateral Framework

The first important building block of the legal puzzle characterising Franco-German armaments cooperation are the bilateral agreements between both States concerning the matter. They are the 1963 Elysée Treaty, the 1972 SDA, the 2019 Aachen Treaty, and the 2019 NFGAAE. From a legal perspective, in particular viewed from international law and from German and French administrative law, there is a need to clarify their legal status, substance and especially their reliability, since this has been a recurring challenge in the past for Franco-German armaments collaboration and will most likely also be a challenge in the future.

As described in parts *2.1.2. Historical Evolution of the Franco-German Armaments Collaboration* and *2.2.2. Franco-German Armaments Cooperation today*, Franco-German armaments cooperation has historically frequently been challenging and often unsuccessful, as many projects failed to be realised or even be initiated over the last decades. A (if not the) central point of contention has regularly been the question of diverging armaments export policies. Here lies therefore the focus of the following parts. In practice, Germany's armaments export policy has been (and still is) – for political reasons – more restrictive than France's. Consequently, the export of armaments stemming from Franco-German collaboration has been blocked several times by Germany. This has posed (and still poses) a severe issue for France, which – for political and economic reasons – traditionally has sought to export armaments stemming from joint projects and intends to likewise export armaments stemming from the current collaborative projects (in particular FCAS and MGCS). France will not collaborate with Germany in armaments production if it cannot rely on Germany to not block the export of armaments stemming from their collaboration.[346]

To enable their bilateral armaments cooperation, Germany and France have set up a bilateral framework, which is meant to find convergence of their differing armaments export regimes regarding the treatment of armaments exports stemming from joint projects. However, this framework has been highly unreliable in the past in this regard, which in turn prevented that large-scale joint armaments projects could be consistently realised. Problematically, the Franco-German framework for armaments collaboration in its current form continues to be characterised by many unreliabilities in this regard, which makes it questionable whether the current large-scale joint projects will ultimately be realised.

This lack of reliability is concerning. Another failure of Franco-German armaments collaboration would have significant adverse consequences for European defence capability development.[347] Firstly, these large-scale armaments projects, which are urgently required for European strategic autonomy and Europe's ability to defend itself, would then not be realised.

Furthermore, it is to be expected[348] that France would refrain from a third attempt to collaborate with Germany in armaments production for decades to come if the current Franco-German armaments collaboration failed again due to lack of sufficient convergence of armaments exports policies. This would likewise significantly undermine any current and future efforts to make Europe more resilient against geopolitical threats.

---

346  Descôtes (n 141).
347  Vogel (n 232).
348  Descôtes (n 141).

### 3.1.1. Foundations of Franco-German Armaments Collaboration – the Elysée Treaty

The first major agreement in the area of Franco-German armaments coop-eration (in fact bilateral Franco-German cooperation overall) is the 1963 Elysée Treaty, signed by the French President de Gaulle and the German Chancellor Adenauer and which initiated the subsequent bilateral arma-ments cooperation. The Elysée Treaty is still in force today. This bilateral treaty is also regarded as one of the driving factors[349] of general European integration as it symbolically ended centuries of wars between Germany and France and their so-called "hereditary enmity".[350]

Most notably, the Elysée Treaty stipulates a consultation mechanism, which requires regular meetings on all government levels[351], and that both governments coordinate their efforts in the areas of foreign policy, European policy, education and youth, and also regarding defence policy (section A, Art. 1(3) of the Elysée Treaty). This includes their armaments cooperation. According to section B, Art. 3 of the Elysée Treaty, in the area of armaments, both governments seek to organise a cooperation starting from the stage of drafting appropriate armaments projects and preparing the financial budgets. ('*Auf dem Gebiet der Rüstung bemühen sich die bei-den Regierungen, eine Gemeinschaftsarbeit vom Stadium der Ausarbeitung geeigneter Rüstungsvorhaben und der Vorbereitung der Finanzierungspläne an zu organisieren.*') This provision lays out the basis for Franco-German armaments cooperation to this day (although it is today extended by the provisions of the 2019 Aachen Treaty, see part *3.1.4. Let's try again – the Aachen Treaty*), and in the following years, several joint armaments projects were initiated.[352]

On a side note, the Franco-German Ministerial Council, which is based on the Elysée Treaty's consultation mechanism, announced in 2017[353] the reinitiation of Franco-German armaments collaboration (specifically, the

---

349  Ukrow (n 130).

350  Klein (n 129) 258–259.

351  The Franco-German Ministerial Council, which is based on the Elysée Treaty, announced the FCAS and MGCS projects and the initiation of PESCO in 2018 (Meseberg Declaration), see Bundesregierung, 'Erklärung von Meseberg' (*Bundesregierung*, 19 June 2018) <https://www.bundesregierung.de/breg-de/suche/er klaerung-von-meseberg-1140536> accessed 26 October 2022.

352  Kotthoff (n 30) 53.

353  Deutsch-Französischer Ministerrat (n 241).

FCAS and MGCS projects and the initiation of PESCO (see part *2.2.2. Franco-German Armaments Cooperation today*).

The Elysée Treaty's provision on armaments cooperation is (similar to the Aachen Treaty's provision on armaments cooperation later on) simply an expression of the political will (or rather intent, which is why the Treaty uses the term *'bemühen'*) of both States to collaborate in armaments production. There are no further provisions obligating the State parties to realise specific projects or implement certain legislation to deal with any further issues (like the issue of diverging armaments export policies and the treatment of exports of armaments stemming from joint projects) that might arise and thus ensure the consistent realisation of joint armaments projects. The issue of diverging armaments export policies was only addressed a few years later in the SDA, which will be analysed in the subsequent part.

The Elysée Treaty therefore only initiated Franco-German armaments cooperation originally. By failing to address the underlying challenges of that cooperation, it failed to make that cooperation sufficiently legally reliable in terms of ensuring that bilateral armaments projects could be consistently realised, which is underlined by the frequent failures of Franco-German armaments cooperation in the later years following the Elysée Treaty's entry into force (see part *2.1.2. Historical Evolution of the Franco-German Armaments Collaboration*).

Due to the Elysée Treaty's lack of further provisions on armaments cooperation and its failure to address any of the underlying challenges of Franco-German armaments cooperation, it will not be further discussed in this thesis. Instead, this thesis will now turn to the Elysée Treaty's follow-up agreement, the SDA, where the issue of diverging armaments export policies and the treatment of exports of armaments stemming from joint projects was then addressed and which is of central importance to understand how unreliabilities in the framework for Franco-German armaments cooperation have led to its ultimate failure in the past.


### 3.1.2. Mistakes were made in Franco-German Armaments Collaboration – the Schmidt Debré Agreement

The Schmidt Debré Agreement (abbreviated SDA) was signed in 1971 by the German defence minister Schmidt and in 1972 by the French defence minister Debré, after which it entered into force. It is the first Franco-German agreement which deals explicitly with converging export rules concerning jointly produced armaments to enable the bilateral armaments cooperation. The German version of the SDA has never been published (in fact it remains classified to this date) or ratified by the German Parliament). However, its contents are today known due to various letters by the German Federal Ministry for Defence to German armaments manufacturers.[354] Furthermore, the French version was published in 2000, in the annex to a parliamentary report[355].

### 3.1.2.1. Enabling Collaboration – non-veto of armaments exports

The SDA stipulates that neither government will prevent the other government from exporting or from authorising exports of jointly produced or developed armaments to third countries (the so-called "non-veto principle").[356] It further dictates that both governments shall (therefore) grant the necessary export licences for the delivery of (sub-)components to the exporting State without delay and in accordance with the national export control laws and procedures. The option to refuse an export licence of such components in a joint project may only be invoked in exceptional cases (Art. 2), in the case of Germany for example when there is a compelling reason to deny the export licence in accordance with § 7 KrWaffKontrG.[357]

---

354 Michael Brzoska and Hartmut Küchle, 'Folgen, Auswirkungen und Gestaltungsmöglichkeiten internationaler Abkommen für eine restriktive deutsche Rüstungsexportpolitik', 19 [2002] BICC 1, 11.

355 Jean-Claude Sandrier et al., 'Rapport d'information sur le contrôle des exportations d'armament' (*Assemblée nationale*, 25 April 2000) <http://www.assemblee-nation ale.fr/rap-info/i2334.asp> accessed 26 October 2022. This version is the primary reference point for this dissertation.

356 Sophia Besch and Beth Oppenheim, 'Up in arms: Warring over Europe's arms export regime' (*Center for European Reform*, 10 September 2019) <https://www.cer.e u/publications/archive/policy-brief/2019/arms-warring-over-europes-arms-export-r egime> accessed 30 January 2022.

357 However, in a 2019 response to a parliamentary inquiry, the German government stated that the SDA functions under the premise that both countries may sovereignly decide over armaments exports and that the respective national laws should be interpreted in the spirit of Franco-German collaboration, see Bundesregierung, 'Antwort der Bundesregierung auf die Kleine Anfrage der Abgeordneten Sevim Dağdelen, Heike Hänsel, Christine Buchholz, weiterer Abgeordneter und der Fraktion DIE LINKE – Drucksache 19/9317' (*Deutscher Bundestag*, 6 May 2019) <https:/ /dserver.bundestag.de/btd/19/099/1909902.pdf> accessed 26 October 2022.

Prior to denying an export licence, both governments shall consult each other (Art. 2). The SDA mentions several joint armaments projects of the past (see the annex of the SDA) and provides that future bilateral projects shall also be governed by it, except in cases of further special agreements (Art. 2).

### 3.1.2.2. Non-Veto Principle – from application to non-application

In the first two decades following the conclusion of the SDA, both States largely refrained from applying their respective export control laws to jointly produced armaments in line with the SDA and in the interest of enabling their bilateral armaments collaboration. In the following years, several joint armaments projects were thus successfully jointly realised, for example the development of the *HOT* and *Milan* anti-tank rockets (see part *2.1.2. Historical Evolution of the Franco-German armaments cooperation*). Germany's compliance with the provisions of the SDA was especially important for France to protect its legitimate expectations ("*Vertrauensschutz*") when it came to armaments exports as it could trust that Germany would also grant export licences for German (sub-)components (except in exceptional cases) which were later used in French armaments that were than exported to third countries.[358]

Until 1999, the German government mostly adhered to the agreement, considered only in isolated cases not granting export licences, and in such cases consulted the French government in accordance with the SDA's consultation mechanism. Such a case was for example the planned French export of *HOT* and *Milan* anti-tank rockets to China in 1977 (which then did not take place for other reasons).

In 1999 however, the German government vetoed the export of a *Tiger* helicopter to Turkey and in the following years it began to repeatedly deny the export of armaments that were jointly produced or only slowly delivered export licences when it came to supplying French armaments producers with German sub-components (at least it was perceived that way by France, see *2.1.2. Historical Evolution of the Franco-German Armaments Collaboration*).[359] Germany's repeated refusals to authorize the export of armaments until 2019 was rightfully seen by observers and by France as

---

358 Brzoska and Küchle (n 354) 12.
359 Krotz (n 146) 149–151; Cops and Buytart (n 146) 9.

repeated breaches of the SDA,[360] as Germany's frequent refusals to grant the necessary export licences for German armaments components either outright or in a timely manner clearly breached the SDA's Art. 2 provision that such export licences be only denied in exceptional cases.

The divergence of armaments export policies between Germany and France became even more apparent following the Saudi-led intervention in Yemen and the assassination of *Washington Post* journalist Jamal Khashoggi,[361] causing Germany to repeatedly refuse to grant export licences for jointly produced armaments (see also part *2.1.2. Historical Evolution of the Franco-German Armaments Collaboration* for examples).[362] As a consequence, the SDA's validity and reliability were until 2019 increasingly called into question and Germany's restrictive armaments export policy reinforced public opinion in France that collaborating with Germany in armaments matters was disadvantageous.[363]

Due to Germany's overall restrictive and partially unpredictable position on armaments exports and its either outright denial of granting or at least slow delivery of export licences for German components to French armaments productions, thereby violating the provisions of the SDA, French defence companies started to increasingly replace or avoid German components in their productions altogether (see parts *2.1.2. Historical Evolution of the Franco-German armaments cooperation* and *2.2.2. Franco-German armaments cooperation today* for "German-free" armaments projects) to circumvent Germany's restrictive export control rules.[364]

Against this backdrop, it was impossible to initiate new large-scale Franco-German collaborative armaments projects until 2019 (when a new bilateral agreement on armaments exports was signed, see part *3.1.5. Mistakes were remade? – the New Franco-German Agreement on Armaments Exports*), despite the 2017 Franco-German Ministerial Conference decision to reinitiate Franco-German armaments collaboration. This was simply because France saw no reliable basis for Franco-German armaments collaboration without the necessary reliable and for both sides satisfactory rules on exports of armaments stemming from joint productions.[365]

---

360 Hemicker (n 147).
361 Béraud-Sudreau (n 141).
362 Schubert (n 149).
363 Béraud-Sudreau (n 128); Hemicker (n 147).
364 Commission de la défense nationale et des forces armées (n 321).
365 Atzpodien (n 128); Descôtes (n 141).

### 3.1.2.3. Shortcomings and Germany's Non-Compliance

In 2019, Germany and France signed a new agreement on armaments exports (the NFGAAE, see part *3.1.4. New Franco-German Agreement on Armaments Exports*). Like the SDA, the NFGAAE is meant to reliably ensure that (principally) neither party blocks the other from exporting armaments stemming from joint production. This is a precondition for Franco-German armaments collaboration.

Because of this precondition, it is necessary to analyse the insufficiencies of the SDA and how the German government did de-facto stop applying the SDA in its licencing decisions for armaments exports stemming from Franco-German joint productions. If the NFGAAE closely resembles the SDA, especially in terms of its shortcomings, then also the NFGAAE might be legally unreliable which in turn endangers the ultimate success of the current Franco-German armaments collaboration, leading to a situation similar to the one of the last 20 years, where large-scale bilateral armaments projects could not be realised.

After the immediate conclusion of the SDA, Germany granted licences for its own armaments exports to third countries very restrictively (in accordance with the 1971 *"Politische Grundsätze der Bundesregierung für den Export von Kriegswaffen und sonstigen Rüstungsgütern"*, which translates to "Political Principles of the Federal Government for the Export of War Weapons and other Military Equipment"), while generally not applying its armaments export laws to exports of armaments stemming from Franco-German joint productions, in line with the SDA. This both enabled several collaborative armaments projects as well as let exports of armaments stemming from Franco-German joint projects rise significantly after 1972 and contributed to Germany's rise to one of the five most important armaments exporting countries globally.[366] Based on this new reality of armaments exports and due to domestic political pressure to further restrict German armaments exports (see also part *2.1.2. Historical Evolution of the Franco-German Armaments Collaboration*), by 1982, the German government saw a need to update its Political Principles, which had significant consequences for the application of the SDA.

---

366 Brzoska and Küchle (n 354) 12.

In its 1982 Political Principles[367] the German government set out to arrange consultation procedures in <u>all</u> newly concluded cooperation agreements from then on. These consultation procedures allow for objections of exports of armaments stemming from cooperative projects (section I.5. of the 1982 Political Principles). Corresponding provisions can also be found in a 1983 Anglo-German cooperation agreement that is similar to the SDA.[368]

This objective of the 1982 Political Principles was further reasserted in the German governments 2000 Political Principles (see section II.3.), where the German government reserved the right to oppose in any case certain export plans of the cooperation partner (here France) by consultation procedure to enforce its Political Principles on armaments exports. Committing to such a consultation procedure in any case to enforce its Political Principles (not only in exceptional cases relating to the KrWaffKontrG) strongly contrasts the SDA's Art. 2 protection of the legitimate expectation of the partner State (mainly France's) that export licences will be reliably granted. Section II.3 of the 2000 Political Principles is therefore irreconcilable with the SDA. Furthermore, in section II.2. of its 2000 Political Principles, the German government announced its intent to apply its (strict) export rules for third countries also to armaments exports stemming from cooperative projects, which further contradicted the SDA and hindered French armaments exports. The current 2019 Political Principles[369] reiterate these principles (see sections II.2. and II.3. of the 2019 Political Principles) again.

The incompatibilities of Germany's Political Principles with the SDA led until 2019 to the situation where Germany needed to either disregard its own Political Principles[370], modify or disregard the SDA, or conclude a new bilateral agreement that was compatible with its Political Principles.[371]

---

367 Bundesregierung, 'Politische Grundsätze der Bundesregierung für den Export von Kriegswaffen und sonstigen Rüstungsgütern vom 28.4.1982' (*Rüstungsexport-info*, 28 April 1982) <http://ruestungsexport-info.de/fileadmin/media/Dokumente/R%C3% BCstungsexporte___Recht/Politische_Grunds%C3%A4tze/Politische-Grundsaetze -1982.pdf> accessed 26 October 2022.

368 Brzoska and Küchle (n 354) 11–12.

369 Bundesregierung (n 317).

370 However, in the 2019 response to a parliamentary inquiry, the German government did not confirm that the application of the SDA lead to a lower level of German export control, see Bundesregierung (n 357).

371 Brzoska and Küchle (n 354) 12–13.

France and Germany ultimately opted for the last option by the end of 2019 (discussed in part *3.1.5. Mistakes were remade? – the New Franco-German Agreement on Armaments Exports*), although the German government still claimed that to implement its 2000 Political Principles there was no need to modify, renew or ignore the SDA.[372]

However, before the end of 2019, due to Germany's overall restrictive and partially unpredictable position on armaments exports and its either outright denial of granting or at least due to its perceived slow delivery of export licences for German components to French armaments productions, the SDA's validity and reliability was increasingly called into question[373] and considered to be outdated in the French perspective (something that has not been recognized by the German government[374]). In a 2000 French parliamentary report, it was (correctly from the French perspective[375]) stated that because Germany never published the SDA it was not legally binding under French constitutional law and that it only qualified as an intergovernmental agreement having the status of a political declaration (i.e. soft law). The report alleges that the agreement is not part of positive law in neither Germany nor France, and since Germany adjusted its export control policy in a way that is not compatible with the SDA, it appeared to be obsolete. Furthermore, because of the exception clause in Art. 2 of the SDA, there was no guarantee for France that Germany would ever reli-

---

372 'Nach Auffassung der Bundesregierung war, um die Politischen Grundsätze der Bundesregierung für den Export von Kriegswaffen und sonstigen Rüstungsgütern aus dem Jahr 2000 wirkungsvoll umzusetzen, das Schmidt-Debré-Abkommen nicht zu modifizieren, durch eine neue Vereinbarung abzulösen oder zu ignorieren.', see Bundesregierung (n 357).

373 Béraud-Sudreau (n 128); Hemicker (n 147).

374 'Die Bundesregierung hat keine Kenntnis, dass das Schmidt-Debré-Abkommen von französischer Seite in Frage gestellt wurde.', see Bundesregierung (n 357).

375 Under Art. 55 1958 French Constitution (*Constitution française*) (current version 4 October 1958), agreements are subject to the application by the other party (principle of *réciprocité*), see Nguyen Quoc Dinh, 'La Constitution de 1958 et le droit international' [1959] RDP 515, 557, '*une sorte de sanction – la privation des garanties du monisme – que la France appliquerait contre un État cosignataire avec elle d'un traité ou d'un accord, et qui lui porterait préjudice en n'exécutant pas les engagements pris envers elle.*', this allows France to suspend treaty obligations in the event that the other party fails to comply with its own obligations in order to ensure that no disadvantage arises for France due to the monist system (making a treaty directly applicable) while the other party likely has a different system); see also Thierry Renoux and Michel de Villiers, *Code constitutional* (10th edn, LexisNexis 2019) 1222–1223.

ably grant export licences for component parts. The report also mentions the above-mentioned case of the *Tiger* helicopter as an example, where Germany refused to authorize its export to Turkey. The report concludes that due to the SDA's unreliability, it could not serve as a basis for further integration in the area of European armaments integration.[376]

Moreover, it had been pointed out over the years that the SDA had become difficult to reconcile with Germany's own export control laws and Political Principles[377] and with Germany's overall restrictive and partially unpredictable conduct when it came to granting export licences for German (sub-)components for French armaments productions in a timely manner.[378] Still, despite contrary licencing practice, in a 2019 response to a parliamentary inquiry the German government stated that the SDA was in force since 1972 and did not confirm that it was not effective anymore.[379] To this date, there is no available confirmation on whether the SDA is not in force anymore. As mentioned earlier, Art. 2 of the SDA provides the possibility for further special agreements. It may be the case that the 2019 NFGAAE is regarded as such a special agreement. Alternatively, both States may potentially regard the NFGAAE as replacing the SDA following the international law principle of lex posterior derogat legi priori (in accordance with Art. 30(3) VCLT[380]).

From a German law perspective, it is difficult to classify the SDA because it was never published. It is most likely that (like the 2019 NF-GAAE) it qualifies as an administrative (intergovernmental) agreement (*"Verwaltungsabkommen"*) in accordance with Art. 59(2) sentence 2 GG, meant to regulate the modalities under which the German Federal Agency for Economic Affairs and Export Control (*Bundesamt für Wirtschaft und Ausfuhrkontrolle*, abbreviated BAFA) grants licences for exports of components for jointly produced armaments. Germany's administrative

---

376  Jean-Claude Sandrier et al. (n 355).

377  Brzoska and Küchle (n 354).

378  Béraud-Sudreau (n 128).

379  'Das Schmidt-Debré-Abkommen gilt seit dem 7. Februar 1972 und explizit unter der Prämisse, dass über den Export von Kriegswaffen und sonstigem Rüstungsmaterial die Regierungen beider Länder jeweils souverän entscheiden. Die einschlägigen nationalen Gesetze sollen im Geiste der deutsch-französischen Zusammenarbeit ausgelegt und angewandt werden.', see Bundesregierung (n 363).

380  Vienna Convention on the Law of Treaties (VCLT) (signed 23 May 1969, entered into force 27 January 1980) 1155 UNTS 331.

intergovernmental agreements are nevertheless binding agreements under international law.[381]

Whether Germany failed to deliver export licences without delay and therefore violated the SDA is a matter of interpretation (see also below). This is difficult to assess, however it was perceived that way by France, which in turn regarded the SDA as unreliable.

However, Germany's outright denials of export licences for components used in Franco-German joint productions on a frequent rather than an exceptional basis beginning in the 1990s clearly breached the SDA. Some licences were even denied for exports to countries to which other German armaments exports were authorized.

Consequently, German export control was considered as highly unpredictable by France and other European partners[382], despite an international agreement in the form of the SDA that was meant to ensure reliability in joint armaments export matters. Since France could not rely on the SDA, it consequently refrained from collaborating with Germany in armaments production.

However, when looking at the SDA and its provisions (the non-veto principle in particular) at a first glance, it appears that they are legally well-designed to find convergence and reliably regulate the difficult issue of armaments exports – especially considering both States' diverging stances on this issue – and thus enable their bilateral armaments cooperation. This is underlined by the fruitful Franco-German armaments cooperation in the first years after the SDA entered into force. The SDA's insufficiencies only become apparent later.

First and foremost, the shortcomings of the agreement can be traced to lacking enforceability and to Germany's failure to comply with its commitments due to domestic political reasons (see also parts *2.1.2. Historical Evolution of the Franco-German Armaments Collaboration* and *2.2.2. Franco-German Armaments Cooperation today*). The SDA features no enforcement mechanism.[383] The SDA's enforcement deficit is a legal unreliability, which in turn facilitates the possibility of non-compliance. Non-compliance however is politically motivated and depends on the level of necessity that

---

381 Michael Schweitzer and Hans-Georg Dederer, *Staatsrecht III* (12th edn, C.F. Müller 2020) 98–100, 112–114.

382 Keul and Bütikofer (n 127); Descôtes (n 141).

383 Although it could be argued that the consultation mechanism has some normative effect. However, it could ultimately also not ensure Germany's compliance with its SDA commitments.

is politically attributed to reliable armaments cooperation at the cost of national sovereignty.

After the fall of the Iron Curtain, joint defence capability development was not a political priority in Germany (but also in France) anymore (see part *2.1.2. Historical Evolution of the Franco-German Armaments Collaboration*). Moreover, from 1998 to 2005, the German federal government was for the first time ever led by a coalition of Social Democrats and Greens. This coalition pursued a more restrictive armaments export policy than the previous government and extended its restrictive policy to exports of armaments stemming from joint projects, thereby violating the SDA, even if that meant that Franco-German armaments cooperation was negatively affected. A year after this coalition came into power, Germany denied the export licence in the aforementioned case of the *Tiger* helicopter. Another year later, the coalition's updated Political Principles introduced that the German government reserved the right to oppose armaments exports in any case.

From a practical standpoint, it was certainly also more difficult to enforce an international agreement like the SDA when its existence and especially its contents remain basically unknown to the German public to this day and when it is unclear whether the agreement was/is in force or not. This likely also contributed to the SDA's perceived unreliability by France and armaments producers.

Furthermore, the SDA's provision that export licences shall be granted 'without delay' is not without ambiguity, which in turn entails legal unreliability. Licencing processes being administrative processes always require a certain amount of time. Not determining specific time periods for these processes in the SDA inhibits the risk that these processes could at least be perceived as being delayed, and that the bilateral cooperation is thus perceived as unreliable. France has perceived it that way.

Lastly and also problematically, the SDA's consultation mechanism can only be relied upon in case of an export licence denial, not if the licencing process was (at least perceived as being) delayed. This lack of a more effective mechanism for dispute settlement in the SDA is thus also a legal unreliability, because arising conflicts are not solved and the armaments cooperation is thus more likely to be terminated. The lack of a more effective dispute settlement mechanism likely reflects the (originally) legitimate expectations of both States in 1972 that the SDA commitments would be fulfilled in good faith to enable consistent bilateral armaments cooperation. They were not.

### 3.1.2.4. Intermediate Conclusions – no successful armaments collaboration without reliable rules for armaments exports

The fact that Germany was able to and complied less and less with the SDA's non-veto principle for domestic political reasons had significant adverse consequences for Franco-German armaments cooperation, as no large-scale joint armaments projects (in particular in the dimension of FCAS or MGCS) were thus realised because France consequently began to favour "German-free" forms of armaments collaboration instead.

As stated previously, this non-veto principle is a precondition for Franco-German armaments collaboration. In this regard, it was problematic that the SDA could not reliably ensure that Germany would reliably grant export licences for jointly produced armaments, causing France to refrain from collaborating with Germany in armaments production for two decades.

For the recently revived Franco-German armaments cooperation to be reliable, meaning the projects FCAS and MGCS will be ultimately realised, it is therefore necessary that the unreliabilities of the past bilateral agreements (the SDA in particular) are not repeated in the new bilateral agreements meant to enable the current Franco-German armaments collaboration. These new agreements must therefore be more reliable, meaning they find sufficient convergence of the issue of exports of armaments stemming from joint projects and then ensure that both States (Germany in particular, because of its failure to comply with the SDA in the past and its continuing ambivalent stance on armaments exports) consistently fulfil their commitments in the interest of realising their joint projects. Otherwise, there will be no future for Franco-German armaments cooperation.

### 3.1.4. Let's try again – the Aachen Treaty

The legal basis for the current (reinitiated) Franco-German armaments cooperation is provided by the Aachen Treaty. This "Treaty on Franco-German Cooperation and Integration" was signed on 22 January 2019 by the French President Macron and the German Chancellor Merkel. It is a bilateral agreement which is expressly referring to the above-mentioned Elysée

Treaty[384] and is regarded as an extension[385] and being complementary to it, intended to prepare both countries and the EU for 21st century challenges.[386] This includes the geopolitical challenges mentioned in parts *2.2.1. European Defence and Armaments Integration today* and *2.2.2. Franco-German Armaments Cooperation today,* for which France, Germany, and in fact Europe as a whole require an autonomous EDTIB and autonomous defence capabilities to maintain their ability to act in foreign and security matters.

Besides policy fields like European affairs, bilateral relations or sustainability, the Aachen Treaty therefore also contains provisions relating to peace, security and development, including armaments cooperation and defining a common approach to armaments exports (Chapter 2 of the Aachen Treaty). This stems from the shared critical view of both States regarding their own military capabilities.

According to Art. 4(3) Aachen Treaty, both States therefore intend to foster the competitiveness and consolidation of the EDTIB. They support the closest possible cooperation between their defence industries on the basis of mutual trust. To enable joint projects, both States agreed to develop a common approach for armaments exports. This goes beyond the Elysée Treaty's section B Art. 3 (see part *3.1.1. Foundations of Franco-German Armaments Collaboration – the Elysée Treaty*) which only stipulated that both States start a bilateral armaments cooperation. By contrast, the Aachen Treaty stipulates a closest possible armaments cooperation and explicitly refers to the EDTIB, which also places it in the broader context of the EU's CFSP (see part *3.2.1.3. The European Armaments Policy and its future*). The objective of developing a common approach for armaments exports reflects the long-standing central point of contention between the two States regarding the treatment of exports of armaments stemming from joint projects, which has hampered Franco-German armaments cooperation for at least two decades. France had made its participation in the current bilateral armaments cooperation conditional on such a legal clarification

---

384  Art. 27 Aachen Treaty.
385  While the Elysée Treaty was a Treaty on Franco-German cooperation, the Aachen Treaty is a Treaty on Franco-German Cooperation <u>and Integration</u>. With regard to bilateral integration, this is a novelty for both Germany and France. So far, both countries were only familiar with the EU integration perspective, now there is the possibility of a Franco-German integration dynamic (which is also interesting with regard to enhanced cooperation in accordance with Arts. 20 TEU, 326 ff. TFEU), see Ukrow (n 130) 8–9.
386  Ukrow (n 130); Besch (n 190); Kunz and Kempin (n 274).

and commitment by Germany. Without finding convergence of the issue of exports of armaments stemming from joint projects, the current bilateral armaments cooperation would not have been carried further.[387]

However, while the Aachen Treaty is meant to reinitiate bilateral Franco-German armaments cooperation, at the time of the Treaty's conclusion, this significant point of contention regarding the treatment of exports of armaments stemming from collaborative projects remained to be ultimately clarified. The Aachen Treaty only states that 'both States will develop a common approach regarding armaments exports' (Art. 4(3)), without making further specifications. This legal gap in the Aachen Treaty is noteworthy. The issue was only addressed by the end of 2019, when another (at first secret[388]) follow-up agreement to the Aachen Treaty on armaments exports (the NFGAAE) was concluded, which will now be discussed.

### 3.1.5. Mistakes were remade? – the New Franco-German Agreement on Armaments Exports

Due to Germany's restrictive und partially unpredictable conduct when it came to licensing armaments exports stemming from joint projects (thus violating the aforementioned SDA, see part *3.1.2. Mistakes were made in Franco-German Armaments Collaboration – the Schmidt Debré Agreement*), Germany and France did not collaborate in the field of armaments production for a two decades (see part *2.1.2. Historical Evolution of the Franco-German Armaments Collaboration*).[389]

This changed with the 2019 Aachen Treaty in which Germany and France committed to further integration[390] in the areas of defence and armaments. Specifically, this includes very close cooperation in the field of armaments production to realise the large-scale joint projects FCAS and MGCS (see part *2.2.2. Franco-German Armaments Collaboration today*). However, because of Germany's restrictive and partially unpredictable ar-

---

387 Descôtes (n 141).

388 SPON, 'Deutsch-französisches Geheimpapier regelt Waffenexporte neu' (*SPON*, 15 February 2019) <https://www.spiegel.de/politik/deutschland/ruestungsexporte-deu tsch-franzoesisches-geheimpapier-a-1253393.html> accessed 24 April 2023.

389 Marco Seliger, 'Die schwierige Geschichte der deutsch-französischen Rüstungsko-operation' (*NZZ*, 2 April 2019) <https://www.nzz.ch/international/deutsch-franzoes ische-ruestungskooperation-ist-muehselig-ld.1470274> accessed 15 June 2020.

390 The Aachen Treaty's title explicitly refers to Franco-German integration.

maments export policy as well as due to its (at least perceived) failure to comply with the SDA, France demanded political and legal assurances and greater predictability from Germany that it would not block France's exports of armaments stemming from joint projects (again).[391] Such convergence was then found in a follow-up agreement to the Aachen Treaty, which was signed on 23 October 2019 and entered into force on 14 November 2019, when it was published in the Official Journal of the French Republic.[392]

This new bilateral agreement (the NFGAAE) is in many ways similar to the 1972 SDA,[393] as will be shown below, however both States expect that this new agreement is generally better suited to enable joint defence programmes and enhance Franco-German armaments cooperation by addressing the difficult issue of diverging armaments export policies in a much more suitable way (a 'consensual, legally binding, stable and long-term solution'[394]). Paras. 5 and 6 of the NFGAAE's preamble reflect the past conflicts over licence denials or their (at least perceived) slow delivery for armaments exports stemming from joint projects and thus state that both States recognize the importance of a reliable transfer and export perspective for the economic and political success of the Franco-German industrial and governmental cooperation. The NFGAAE is meant to reduce the administrative burden on export controls to ensure the success of the

---

391  Atzpodien (n 128); Béraud-Sudreau (n 128); see also Preamble of the NFGAAE paras. 5 and 6 and also take into account the 2019 Aachen Treaty, where Germany and France committed to the closest possible cooperation between their defence industries on the basis of mutual trust and in the case of joint projects to develop a common approach for armaments exports (Preamble of the NFGAAE para. 7).

392  2019 Official Journal (*Décret n° 2019–1168 du 13 novembre 2019 portant publication de l'accord sous forme d'échange de lettres entre le Gouvernement de la République française et le Gouvernement de la République fédérale d'Allemagne relatif au contrôle des exportations en matière de défense (ensemble une annexe), signées à Paris le 23 octobre 2019 (1)*) (current version 13 November 2019); the agreement was also published by Germany after it entered into force, see 2019 Official Journal (*Bundesgesetzblatt Jahrgang 2019 Teil II Nr. 18*) (current version 14 November 2019) at 849.

393  Atzpodien (n 128).

394  Ministère de l'Europe et des Affaires Étrangères, 'Press release – Franco-German Agreement on Defence export controls (14 November 2019)' (*gouv.fr*, 14 November 2019) <https://www.diplomatie.gouv.fr/en/country-files/germany/events/articl e/franco-german-agreement-on-defence-export-controls-14-nov-19> accessed 27 October 2022.

joint programmes by facilitating the Franco-German (armaments) industrial partnerships.

### 3.1.5.1. Enabling Collaboration once more and another Non-Veto Principle

The NFGAAE is set to implement the aforementioned Aachen Treaty's provisions on armaments cooperation (see part *3.1.4. Let's try again – the Aachen Treaty*). It sets out rules and procedures for armaments exports in three cases: intergovernmental programmes (Art. 1), industrial cooperation (Art. 2), and components integrated in armaments outside such cooperation (Art. 3).

Art. 1(1) stipulates that both parties will mutually inform one another, well in advance of formal negotiations, of the opportunity of sales to third countries, and transfer the information needed for the other party's analysis. This mutual transfer of information includes discussions on the conditions permitting, from the exporting State's point of view, to conduct the export in compliance with common European and international commitments. According to Arts. 1(2) and 2(1), exports of armaments stemming from joint projects by one State party to a third country will not be blocked by the other State party, except on an exceptional basis which is when it compromises the first State Party's immediate interests or national security (non-veto principle). In such cases (Arts. 1(3) and 2(2)), there must be high-level consultations as soon as possible (within two months at most) to share analysis and identify appropriate solutions. Furthermore, the opposing party is under an obligation to make every effort to propose alternative solutions.

On top of the non-veto principle stipulated in Arts. 1(2) and 2(1), the NFGAAE stipulates a so-called "de-minimis" rule in Art. 3. Such a rule was not featured previously in the SDA. It applies to all armaments (components) which are covered by the EU Common Military List[395], but which are not covered by Arts. 1 and 2 and annex 2 of the NFGAAE, which were manufactured in one of the two involved States and are then exported and integrated into an armaments system which is manufactured by a manufac-

---

395 Common Military List of the European Union adopted by the Council on 17 February 2020
(equipment covered by Council Common Position 2008/944/CFSP defining common rules
governing the control of exports of military technology and equipment) [2020] OJ C85/1.

turer of the respective other State (Art. 3(1) in accordance with annex 1 part (1)).

According to the "de-minimis" rule, the export of such armaments (components) will be authorized and the necessary licences shall be granted without delay, except in exceptional cases where the licencing party's immediate interests or national security are compromised – provided they fall below the threshold of 20 percent of the final armaments system's value (Art. 3(2) in accordance with annex 1 part (2) NFGAAE), making them "minimal" ("de-minimis").

What makes the "de-minimis" rule special and go beyond the non-veto principle stipulated in Arts. 1(2) and 2(1) NFGAAE is that according to annex 1 part (5), if the "de minimis" rule is applied two further stipulations come into effect. Firstly, in such cases, the State party from which's territory the final armaments system is exported is solely responsible to check adherence with the State parties' common international and European obligations. Secondly, no end-use certificate or non-re-exportation certificate linked to the Franco-German export licence is required.

Furthermore, Art. 4 stipulates a permanent committee between both State parties to deal with further (potentially confidential) matters and to provide a forum for consultations.

In its preamble (paras. 1–4) the agreement also makes several important references to other relevant armaments rules. It refers to the shared European and international commitments in the field of arms export control and licencing of exports, in particular the Council CP on armaments exports[396] and the ATT[397]. It explicitly recognises the respective national arms export control regimes and competences to authorise armaments exports (including those stemming from joint projects).

As stated before, the different armaments export policies and rule applications of Germany and France have hindered their bilateral armaments cooperation in the past. The failure of the SDA due its unreliability, as Germany increasingly started to disregard it (see part *3.1.2. Mistakes were made in Franco-German Armaments Collaboration – the Schmidt Debré Agreement*), hampered Franco-German armaments cooperation for many years. For the current Franco-German armaments cooperation approach to be reliable, meaning the large-scale bilateral collaborative armaments

---

396  (n 61).
397  Arms Trade Treaty (signed 2 April 2013, entered into force 24 December 2014) 3031 UNTS (ATT).

projects (FCAS and MGCS specifically) will be realised, it is necessary that the NFGAAE is more reliable and cannot simply be disregarded by one party, in particular with regard to the aforementioned non-veto principle, which was incorporated into Art. 2 of the SDA and is now reiterated in Arts. 1 and 2 of the NFGAAE.

The main purpose of the NFGAAE is to more reliably ensure this time that both States generally do not block the other from exporting armaments, which (as argued previously) is a precondition for Franco-German armaments cooperation.[398] Nevertheless, since the NFGAAE is again (like the SDA) not ratified by the German *Bundestag*, concerns regarding the agreement's constitutionality (under German constitutional law) and therefore its reliability have already been raised (see below).

Furthermore, the NFGAAE remains potentially unreliable due to potential future non-compliance or withdrawal in case of governmental changes. Considering that the development of FCAS for example will not be completed before 2040 and potential exports will only be an issue after, political shifts during that period are likely and thus also put the bilateral armaments cooperation as a whole at risk of failure.

Again, if the current Franco-German armaments cooperation fails again due to unreliability issues, there will be no future for Franco-German armaments cooperation, which in turn will have serious adverse consequences for the development of Europe's CSDP and defence capabilities.[399]

To assess these risks, the NFGAAE's legal status, validity, and reliability will therefore be assessed in the subsequent parts.

### 3.1.5.2. Legal Status, Validity, and Reliability

The following parts assess the legal status and validity of the NFGAAE under international law and under both French but especially[400] German constitutional law. This is because concerns regarding the NFGAAE's constitutionality and legal validity have only been raised with regard to Ger-

---

398  Preamble New Agreement paras. 5 and 6; Descôtes (n 141).
399  Vogel (n 232).
400  This is because so far, Germany has been and remains to be the more unpredictable partner when it comes to armaments exports and the application of the NFGAAE. This is further underlined by the fact that a legal debate regarding the NFGAAE's constitutionality as well as a political debate with regard to the pros and cons of Franco-German armaments collaboration in general is only being held in Germany.

man law. This includes an analysis of the different views on the NFGAAE's constitutionality and compatibility with the respective domestic rules on armaments exports. From an international law perspective, the domestic constitutionality has no bearing on its bindingness of course,[401] however Germany might potentially be forced to withdraw from the agreement (which is possible under its Art. 5) if its provisions were not reconcilable with Germany's constitution and its domestic export control rules.[402] Here lies an unreliability factor.

Furthermore, the NFGAAE will be compared to the SDA to determine whether its provisions are more reliable when it comes to reliably licencing exports of armaments stemming from joint projects. And also, a few comments regarding potential future non-compliance or withdrawal from the agreement by Germany due to political factors (such as governmental shifts) will be made.

### 3.1.5.3. The German Perspective

The NFGAAE between Germany and France qualifies as an international agreement in accordance with Art. 2(1)(a) VCLT ('*concluded between States in written form and governed by international law*') and its provisions are therefore binding for both States.

Following the theory of (modest) dualism in international law[403], an international agreement is however not automatically part of Germany's legal order but needs to be transposed into domestic law.[404] The main legal provisions regarding the conclusion and ratification of international agreements can be found in the German constitution (the so-called "*Grundgesetz*"[405], abbreviated GG), further details are regulated in administrative regulations.

The legal basis of the NFGAAE under German constitutional law relates to the GG's provisions dealing with the conclusion of international agree-

---

401  Malcolm Shaw, *International Law* (7th edn, CUP 2014) 95.

402  Frank Schorkopf, *Staatsrecht der internationalen Beziehungen* (C.H.Beck 2017) 44–45.

403  ibid. 20–26.

404  BVerfG, Beschluss des Zweiten Senats vom 14. Oktober 2004 – 2 BvR 1481/04, at 31–37; Stefan Pieper, 'Art. 59', in Volker Epping and Christian Hillgruber (eds), *Grundgesetz* (3rd edn, C.H.Beck 2020) 1327–1329; Schweitzer and Dederer (n 381) 16–18; Torsten Stein et al., *Völkerrecht* (14th edn, Franz Vahlen 2017) 58.

405  1949 Basic Law (*Grundgesetz*) (GG) (current version 29 September 2020).

ments and their relationship to German export control law (namely the KrWaffKontrG and the AWG).

In Germany, an international agreement is (in practice[406]) concluded by the German federal government[407] via one of two different modes of procedure: either single-phase or multi-phase.[408] It is important to note that these modes of procedure are based on domestic provisions alone, as international law does not specify in what way an international agreement becomes domestically binding for a State. According to Art. 11 VCLT, '[t]he consent of a State to be bound by a treaty may be expressed by signature, exchange of instruments constituting a treaty, ratification, acceptance, approval or accession, or by any other means if so agreed.'

International agreements which are concluded through the multi-phase procedure become binding after approval by the competent legislative bodies (*Bundestag* and depending on the matter, also the *Bundesrat*[409]) and ratification by the *Bundespräsident* (federal president). On the other hand, so-called administrative agreements (*"Verwaltungsabkommen"*)[410] are intergovernmental and can be concluded by the federal government solely.[411] The *Bundestag* is usually not involved in the single-phase procedure, except for cases where it is mandated by the respective international agreement.[412] The NFGAAE was concluded as an administrative agreement via the single-phase procedure.

Art. 59(2) GG clarifies the competence question regarding which international agreements require the multi-phase procedure to be concluded (including legislative approval via a federal statute (called *"Vertragsgesetz"*

---

406  Formally, the competence on the federal level to conclude international agreements lies with the *Bundespräsident*, according to Art. 59(1) GG. In practice however, international agreements are concluded by the federal government, see Schweitzer and Dederer (n 381) 88–89.

407  Art. 32(1) GG; Schweitzer and Dederer (n 381) 80.

408  Schweitzer and Dederer (n 381) 92–93.

409  Stein et al. (n 404) 67.

410  Hermann Butzer et al., 'Art. 59', in Hans Hofmann and Hans-Günter Henneke (eds), *Grundgesetz* (15th edn, Carl Heymanns Verlag 2022) 1807–1809; Rudolf Streinz, 'Art. 59', in Michael Sachs (ed), *Grundgesetz* (9th edn, C.H.Beck 2021) 1235–1236; Pieper (n 404) 1329.

411  Butzer et al. (n 410) 1807–1808; Schweitzer and Dederer (n 381) 88–90.

412  However, it has been pointed out that such administrative agreements without parliamentary participation could also be concluded via the multi-phase procedure, including parliamentary approval, see Reinhard Warmke, 'Verwaltungsabkommen in der Bundesrepublik Deutschland' [1991] 24 Die Verwaltung 455, 458. Nevertheless, the NFGAAE does not provide for such parliamentary participation and approval.

or sometimes *"Zustimmungsgesetz"*)[413]) and which can be concluded by the federal government solely (via the single-phase procedure and without legislative approval). According to Art. 59(2) GG, treaties that regulate the political relations of the federal State or relate to subjects of federal legislation require the consent or participation, in the form of a federal statute, of the bodies competent in any specific case for such federal legislation. For administrative agreements, the federal administration regulations apply accordingly.

There is no clear definition regarding such "Political Treaties" (treaties that regulate the political relations of the federal State) in German constitutional law.[414] Due to the ambiguity of the term, which could theoretically encompass all international agreements that deal with public affairs, most scholars agree that the term needs to be interpreted narrowly.[415] According to the German BVerfG, a Political Treaty must therefore substantially and immediately concern the State's existence, its territorial integrity, its independence, its position and its determining importance within the community of States (*'wesentlich und unmittelbar die Existenz des Staates, seine territoriale Integrität, seine Unabhängigkeit, seine Stellung oder sein Gewicht unter den Staaten oder die Ordnung der Staatengemeinschaft betrifft'*[416]).

It has been pointed out that "Political Treaties" (often also called "*hochpolitische Verträge*", meaning "highly political Treaties"[417] to further underline their status[418]) are concluded only on rare occasions.[419] Such treaties have been concluded in areas relating to peace and security which affect the national constitutional order[420], like the aforementioned 1963 Elysée Treaty,

---

413 Schweitzer and Dederer (n 381) 107.

414 Butzer et al. (n 410) 1792.

415 Stein et al. (n 404) 66; Schweitzer and Dederer (n 381) 101; Werner Heun, 'Artikel 59', in Horst Dreier (ed), *Grundgesetz Kommentar* (3rd edn, Mohr Siebeck 2015) 1513; Butzer et al. (n 410) 1792.

416 BVerfG, Urteil des Zweiten Senats vom 29. Juli 1952 – 2 BvE 2/51, at 1; similarly BVerfG, Urteil des Zweiten Senats vom 12. Juli 1994 aufgrund der mündlichen Verhandlung vom 19. und 20. April 1994 – 2 BvE 3/92, 5/93, 7/93, 8/93, at 268.

417 BVerfG, Beschluß des Ersten Senats vom 7. Juli 1975 – 1 BvR 274/72, at 81; Butzer et al. (n 410) 1793; Schweitzer and Dederer (n 381) 101.

418 Schorkopf (n 402) 177.

419 Wissenschaftliche Dienste Deutscher Bundestag, 'Das Deutsch-Französische Abkommen vom 21. Oktober 2019 über Ausfuhrkontrollen im Rüstungsbereich im Lichte des Art. 59 Abs. 2 GG (WD 2 – 3000 – 122/19)' (*WD*, 2019) <https://www.bundestag.de/resource/blob/673972/3921230d2453e988b485aae981323a35/WD-2-122-19-pdf-data.pdf> accessed 20 October 2026.

420 Stein et al. (n 404) 66.

the 1972 *Grundlagenvertrag* between the Federal Republic of Germany and the German Democratic Republic, the 1990 Treaty on the Final Settlement with Respect to Germany (the "Two Plus Four Agreement"), or the afore-mentioned 2019 Aachen Treaty. Other "Political Treaties" are often alliance treaties and treaties of accession to international organisations.[421] Agreements relating to trade or cooperation usually do not fall in the category of "Political Treaties". Although they technically also deal with "political" issues, again, this would imply that every international agreement would need legislative approval, making the distinction mentioned in Art. 59(2) GG void.[422] The NFGAAE also clearly does not fall in the category of "Political Treaties", as it neither fulfils the criteria laid out by the BVerfG nor reaches the level of significance as similar agreements.

Besides "Political Treaties", international agreements which relate to subjects of federal legislation (*"gesetzesinhaltliche Verträge"*[423]) require the consent or participation, in the form of a federal statute, of the bodies competent in any specific case for such federal legislation (according to Art. 59(2) GG). According to the BVerfG, an international agreement relates to subjects of federal legislation if it requires a federal statute to be implemented and its obligations be fulfilled[424] (these agreements are often referred to as *"Gesetzgebungsverträge"*[425]). This is usually the case when the matter concerned is already regulated, regulates matters which would have otherwise required a legal statute, or the reservation of statutory powers comes into effect.[426] This norm serves the function of preventing the federal government from concluding international agreements without the *Bundestag's* approval, which's provisions could then – contrary to Germany's international obligations – not be implemented because the existing legislation would have needed to be changed or amended (norm

---

421  Butzer et al. (n 410) 1793; Pieper (n 404) 1324–1325.
422  Stein et al. (n 404) 66.
423  Pieper (n 404) 1326–1327.
424  BVerfG, Urteil des Zweiten Senats vom 29. Juli 1952 – 2 BvE 2/51, at 64.
425  Schorkopf (n 402) 180.
426  BVerfG, Urteil des Zweiten Senats vom 12. Juli 1994 aufgrund der mündlichen Verhandlung vom 19. und 20. April 1994 – 2 BvE 3/92, 5/93, 7/93, 8/93, at 265; Heun (n 415) 1515; Florian Becker, 'Völkerrechtliche Verträge und parlamentarische Gesetzgebungskompetenz' [2005] 3 NVwZ 289, 289- 291; Schorkopf (n 402) 179.

collision[427]).[428] Also, it is meant to prevent that domestic reservation of statutory powers is circumvented by means of international law[429].[430] As will be discussed below, it has been argued that the NFGAAE would have required such legislative approval as it allegedly relates to matters of federal legislation and is therefore unconstitutional.

Lastly, there are administrative agreements. According to the BVerfG, an international agreement does not require legislative approval if the federal government is already competent to implement the agreement's provisions on the grounds of an existing legal basis.[431] All other international agreements (agreements which are not covered by Art. 59(2) sentence 1 GG)) are automatically regarded as administrative agreements in accordance with Art. 59(2) sentence 2 GG. They are autonomously concluded by the federal government (usually without legislative participation) on the basis of administrative regulations and they do not require a federal statute to enter into force and be domestically implemented (single-phase procedure).[432] However, administrative agreements can only extend to matters which are within the competences of the federal government.[433] Such administrative agreements are usually intergovernmental agreements which have an administrative or technical focus.[434] According to the German federal government, the NFGAAE qualifies as such a (intergovernmental) administrative agreement in accordance with Art. 59(2) sentence 2 GG, which does not require the ratification by the competent legislative bodies, and has been concluded as such.[435] However, this view is contentious.

Particularly relevant are Boysen's comments in a legal assessment (commissioned by the non-governmental environmental organisation *Greenpeace*) regarding the validity of the Franco-German agreement.[436] Accord-

---

427  Schweitzer and Dederer (n 381) 66–70, 234.
428  Paulina Starski, 'Art. 59', in Jörn Kämmerer and Markus Kotzur (eds), *Grundgesetz Kommentar Band 1: Präambel bis Art. 69* (7th edn, C.H.Beck 2021) 2685; Butzer et al. (n 410) 1514 1516.
429  Heun (n 415) 1514; Schweitzer and Dederer (n 381) 100.
430  Wissenschaftliche Dienste Deutscher Bundestag (n 419) 6–7.
431  BVerfG, Urteil des Zweiten Senats vom 29. Juli 1952 – 2 BvE 2/51, at 66.
432  Butzer et al. (n 410) 1807–1809; Streinz (n 410) 1235–1236; Pieper (n 404) 1329; Schweitzer and Dederer (n 381) 98–100, 112–114.
433  Schweitzer and Dederer (n 381) 113.
434  Stein et al. (n 404) 69; Schweitzer and Dederer (n 381) 112–114.
435  Wissenschaftliche Dienste Deutscher Bundestag (n 419) 11.
436  Sigrid Boysen, *Rechtsfragen des deutsch-französischen Abkommens über Ausfuhrkontrollen im Rüstungsbereich vom 23. Oktober 2019* (Greenpeace 2020).

ing to Boysen, the German federal government is not allowed to delegate its export control competence to another government. Furthermore, such an agreement would require the approval of the *Bundestag*. And finally, the de-minimis rule is allegedly irreconcilable with the ATT (which is even referred to in the preamble of the NFGAAE) and with EU law.

The scientific service (*Wissenschaftliche Dienste*) of the German *Bundestag*[437] had come (prior to Boysen) to a different (and ultimately more convincing) conclusion and confirms the German government's position that the Franco-German agreement qualifies as a procedural arrangement regarding export licencing of armaments stemming from bilateral projects, which does not affect the German federal government's competence and authority to ultimately grant or deny such licences under Art. 26(2) GG, and that the agreement is in line with Germany's obligations under EU and international law.

### 3.1.5.3.1. The Non-Veto Principle – unconstitutional?

Boysen argues that the German federal government (and not another government) must conduct the assessment of armaments exports, which is allegedly not compatible with a de-minimis rule where all goods below the 20 percent threshold can be exported no matter their potential impact. For several goods (including war weapons under the KrWaffKontrG) not mentioned in the list of annex 2 of the NFGAAE, Germany is therefore neglecting its legal obligations under German constitutional law (according to Art. 26(2) GG, weapons of war can only be manufactured, moved, and put into circulation with the federal government's authorization).

According to Boysen, Art. 26(2) GG prohibits any circumvention of Germany's armaments export control regime. This includes bilateral agreements, which de-facto change Germany's export control rules and (like in the present case the de-minimis rule) allegedly delegate the German federal government's authority and obligation to control German armaments exports and to exercise discretion when it comes to granting licences for armaments exports (including component parts) to the French government (where the French government is responsible for the final armaments

---

437  The *Wissenschaftliche Dienste des Deutschen Bundestages* are independent from the German federal government and are meant to provide Members of the *Bundestag* with politically neutral expert knowledge.

system's export control). Therefore, the NFGAAE's "de-minimis" rule is allegedly irreconcilable with the comprehensive provision of Art. 26(2) GG.[438] It is however necessary to add in this context that both Art. 26(2) GG as well as the KrWaffKontrG (which implements Art. 26(2) GG) deal explicitly with weapons of war while the Franco-German agreement deals more broadly with armaments. Many armaments do not qualify as weapons of war and thus are not covered by Art. 26(2) GG[439] and the KrWaffKontrG[440].

Furthermore, according to Boysen, the NFGAAE likewise violates Art. 59(2) sentence 1 GG, because it would have needed parliamentary approval as it relates to subjects of federal legislation (as mentioned previously), namely §§ 2 in conjunction with 6 KrWaffKontrG (in particular § 6(3) No. 2) as well as § 5(1) No. 1 AWG, both of which regulate the export of armaments. According to Boysen, Germany's alleged waiver of its exercise of discretion for armaments exports violates these norms. Moreover, both statutes allegedly do not provide a sufficient legal basis to conclude an agreement on armaments exports without parliamentary approval, especially if the agreement's provisions (in particular the de-minimis rule) violate these statutes and therefore would demand a change in legislation.[441]

Boysen argues that while the de-minimis rule leaves the competence to issue export licences with the national authorities, it however obliges the parties to the agreement to grant the necessary export licences for the delivery of (sub-)components without delay (*"unverzüglich"*). According to Boysen, this amounts to an internationally agreed waiver of exercise of discretion. This is allegedly not reconcilable with § 6(3) KrWaffKontrG, which requires the denial of an export licence (without any margin of discretion) if the export in question would violate Germany's international legal obligations. Since the NFGAAE's annex 2 does not exclude all war weapons which are mentioned on the war weapons list of the KrWaffKontrG[442] from the de-minimis rule, it may be the case that certain armaments that would have required a discretionary decision (§ 6 KrWaffKontrG) or

---

438   Boysen (n 436) 5–21.
439   Rudolf Streinz, 'Art. 26' in Michael Sachs (ed), *Grundgesetz* (9th edn, C.H.Beck 2021) 916–926; Wolff Heintschel von Heinegg and Robert Frau, 'Art. 26' in Volker Epping and Christian Hillgruber (eds), *Grundgesetz* (3rd edn, C.H.Beck 2020) 884–895.
440   Streinz (n 439) 925–928; Heinegg and Frau (n 439) 893–894.
441   Boysen (n 436) 22–27.
442   Part B of the annex to § 1(1) KrWaffKontrG.

rather an export denial (§ 6(3) KrWaffKontrG) (*"Ermessensreduzierung auf Null"*) could be illegally exported.[443]

In a similar fashion, the NFGAAE is allegedly not reconcilable with § 5(1) No. 1 AWG in conjunction with § 8(1) AWV[444], which requires an authorization for armaments (including component parts) mentioned in annex 1 to the AWV. Therefore, the de-minimis rule also covers armaments which are subject to export authorization and are mentioned in the AWG and the AWV. The above-mentioned waiver of exercise of discretion is therefore allegedly also contrary to these statutes.

Moreover, because according to annex 1 No. 5 to the NFGAAE, no end-use certificate (*"Endverbleibserklärung"*) is required for exports covered by the de-minimis rule, this is allegedly likewise contrary to § 21(2) AWV. This norm in principle requires proves of end-user, end-use and intended purpose, however they can be waived by the German Federal Agency for Economic Affairs and Export Control (*Bundesamt für Wirtschaft und Ausfuhrkontrolle*, abbreviated BAFA), as Boysen also explains.[445] The fact that the NFGAAE completely negates the possibility for such certificates to be required allegedly further restricts the BAFA's exercise of discretion. However, because the AWV is only an administrative statute (*"Rechtsverordnung"*), its required change (to be reconcilable with the NFGAAE) does not infringe on Art. 59(2) sentence 1 GG, to which Boysen concedes.

### 3.1.5.3.2. The NFGAAE's Constitutionality

So far, most of the arguments raised by Boysen are not very convincing. It does not follow from the NFGAAE that Germany is delegating its authority to control German armaments exports and its obligation to exercise discretion when it comes to granting licences for armaments exports (including component parts) to the French government.

As has been shown above, according to Arts. 1 and 2, that armaments exports of one State Party stemming from joint projects will not be blocked by the other State Party, except in cases where it compromises the State Party's immediate interests or national security. This restriction even leaves the possibility open that armaments exports can be blocked in crucial cases

---

443  Boysen (n 436) 22–27.
444  2013 Foreign Trade Regulation (*Außenwirtschaftsverordnung*) (AWV) (current version 19 December 2022).
445  Boysen (n 436) 22–27.

and thus also shows that export control is not delegated (otherwise this provision could hardly be ensured).

As for the "de minimis" rule, the agreement states in annex 1 part 4 that for goods below the threshold of 20 percent of the final armaments system's value, required export licences are granted without delay (again, except in cases where the export concerns the State Party's immediate interests or national security). This again underlines that the respective government continues to be in control of these exports (because it still has to grant the required export licences for (sub-)components and assess the potential impact on its immediate interests or national security) and that Germany's authority and obligation to control German armaments exports and to exercise discretion when it comes to granting licences for armaments exports is therefore not delegated to the other government (i.e. France). The agreement does not stipulate a waiver of discretion agreed under international law (*'völkerrechtlich vereinbarte[r] Verzicht auf die Ermessensausübung'*)[446], but rather refers to the procedure (*'unverzüglich'*[447], meaning without delay) in which export licences are granted by the German government (and no other government). Otherwise, the agreement could have clearly stated an intentional delegation of export control to the other government or could have contained a provision stating that no export licences were required in cases of bilateral armaments projects. This is further underlined by the agreement's preamble, which explicitly refers to national export control competences, laws and procedures (paras. 2, 3, and 4). In international law, preambles are today regarded explicitly as part of the context for the purpose of treaty interpretation (Art. 31(2) VCLT) and are a normative part of international treaties.[448] Because Germany did not waive its authority to control armaments exports, there is no conflict of norms with regard to §§ 2 in conjunction with 6 KrWaffKontrG (in particular § 6(3) No. 2) as well as § 5(1) No. 1 AWG, as export licences can still be denied by the German government. Likewise, as even Boysen concedes to[449], there is no conflict with § 21(2) AWV because it allows the BAFA to waive proves of end-user, end-use and intended purpose. This is

---

446 ibid. 25.
447 Annex 1 Part 4 NFGAAE.
448 Makane Mbengue, 'Preamble' (*OPIL*, September 2006) <https://opil.ouplaw.com/view/10.1093/law:epil/9780199231690/law-9780199231690-e1456?prd=EPIL> accessed 30 October 2022.
449 Boysen (n 436) 22–27.

also argued by the *Bundestag*'s scientific service.[450] Looking closely at the NFGAAE, the objective of reducing the administrative burden (Preamble para. 6) together with the agreement's provisions which deal exclusively with further developing the modalities of export licencing procedures, and which are in fact restricted by the immediate interest or national security exceptions the agreement, ultimately has no effect on Germany's export control statutes and level of competence in deciding over armaments exports. It is difficult to imagine a case where a potential French export (of armaments stemming from joint projects and covered by annex 2 of the NFGAAE) would clearly violate Germany's armaments export control rules and not only Germany's political stance (as expressed for example in the aforementioned Political Principles), especially considering that France is also restricted in its armaments exports by its own functioning export control regime and by (shared) obligations under international law and EU law. And if there was such a case, then Germany could rely on the immediate interest exception and not grant the necessary export licence. Therefore, the NFGAAE is in line with Arts. 26(6) GG and Art. 59(2) GG.

Likewise, the *Bundestag*'s scientific service argues that the NFGAAE does not require a change or amendments to Germany's export control regime regarding exports to France and also does not relate to subjects of federal legislation. This is because the agreement largely deals with bilateral rules of procedure[451] coordinating and simplifying export control of armaments stemming from bilateral projects while taking expressly into account the respective national authority and regulations for armaments exports.[452] Therefore, the agreement does not require the *Bundestag*'s participation.

---

450 Wissenschaftliche Dienste Deutscher Bundestag (n 419) 10.

451 See duties to inform and consultation procedures in NFGAAE discussed above.

452 According to the paras. 2, 3 and 4 of the NFGAAE's preamble:
'in Anbetracht ihrer jeweiligen Zuständigkeit für die Genehmigung von Verbringungen und Ausfuhren aus ihren jeweiligen Hoheitsgebieten von Rüstungsgütern aus regierungsseitigen Gemeinschaftsprojekten und solchen, die von der deutschen und der französischen Industrie entwickelt wurden, in Anbetracht dessen, dass die Bundesrepublik Deutschland ihre nationale Ausfuhrkontrolle für Rüstungsgüter auf der Grundlage ihrer nationalen Rechtsvorschriften und der Politischen Grundsätze der Bundesregierung für den Export von Kriegswaffen und sonstigen Rüstungsgütern vom 26. Juni 2019 durchführt, in Anerkennung dessen, dass die Französische Republik ihre nationale Ausfuhrkontrolle für Rüstungsgüter auf der Grundlage ihrer nationalen Rechtsvorschriften einschließlich der einschlägigen Bestimmungen des Verteidigungsgesetzbuchs durchführt'.

The scientific service also reviews the NFGAAE's de-minimis rule against the backdrop of the KrWaffKontrG and the AWV. According to the scientific service, the de-minimis rule does not change Germany's licencing regime for armaments exports, but only further develops its modalities. Nevertheless, the scientific service recognizes the potential restrictions which the simplified licencing issuance methods for armaments components (Art. 3 NFGAAE) place on the federal government's exercise of discretion (*"Ermessensausübung"*) regarding the issuance of export licences; which in turn could potentially be irreconcilable with KrWaffKontrG and the AWV. According to the scientific service, if a change of these statutes was necessary, it would require parliamentary approval in accordance with Art. 59(2) sentence 1 GG.[453]

According to § 6 KrWaffKontrG, the German federal government enjoys of wide margin of discretion when it comes to authorising exports of war weapons, whose export is in the first instance presumed to be prohibited. However, there are restrictions (§ 6(3) KrWaffKontrG), under which armaments exports may not be authorised (at all), for instance, if these war weapons would (potentially) be used to disturb the peace (like acts of aggression) or if their export authorisation would violate Germany's obligations under international law. Yet, according to the NFGAAE, export authorisation can only be denied in cases where the State's immediate interests or national security is compromised, which allegedly is a much lower threshold in favour of armaments exports.[454]

However, according to the scientific service, a conflict between these two norms (the de-minimis rule and § 6(3) KrWaffKontrG) is precluded. The German armaments export control regime distinguishes between war weapons and other armaments. Only war weapons fall under the KrWaffKontrG, all other armaments are governed under the AWV and can be exported accordingly. Now, annex 2 of the NFGAAE completely excludes certain armaments from the de-minimis rule, almost all (but not all, as Boysen rightly points out[455]) of which are war weapons under the KrWaffKontrG. Annex 2 basically mirrors the German war weapons list as part of the EU Common Military List[456]. This means that the de-minimis rule only covers armaments that are not considered war weapons under German

---

453  Wissenschaftliche Dienste Deutscher Bundestag (n 419) 7–10.
454  ibid. 7–11.
455  Boysen (n 436) 25–26.
456  (n 395).

export control law, which in turn means that the KrWaffKontrG's procedural and discretional rules will in practice not be applied and therefore not collide with the de-minimis rule.[457]

Other armaments (that are not war weapons and thus not covered by the KrWaffKontrG) can principally be exported without restrictions (under the so-called principle of external trade freedom, *"Prinzip der Außenhandelsfreiheit"*). While the AWV partially still requires export licences for certain armaments, such licences are usually granted. Any denial of an export licence must by justified by the federal government / BAFA and expressly prohibited by an administrative act. A reduction of discretion of the federal government's competence (so that certain armaments can never be exported, similar to § 6(3) KrWaffKontrG) does not exist under the AWV.[458]

Lastly, the scientific services argues that even if the NFGAAE would require a change in the AWV, this could be easily done by the federal government without the *Bundestag's* participation, since the AWV is not a law, but a mere administrative statute (*"Rechtsverordnung"*), which is enacted by the federal government (without the approval of the *Bundestag*) under the AWG.

### 3.1.5.3.3. The NFGAAE – an ATT violation?

Boysen also argues that because of the de-minimis rule, Germany is allegedly disregarding its obligations under Art. 4 of the ATT, which requires each State to establish and maintain a national arms export control system to regulate the export of parts and components where the export is in a form that provides the capability to assemble conventional arms. The fact that the ATT also contains favouring provisions on regional armaments cooperation (according to the Preamble, Arts. 1[459], 26 ATT) does not change the requirement of national arms export control. Allegedly delegating Germany's arms export control (because of the de-minimis rule) to France (which is then responsible for the final armaments system's export

---

457 Wissenschaftliche Dienste Deutscher Bundestag (n 419) 7–11.

458 ibid.

459 'Acknowledging that regulation of the international trade in conventional arms and preventing their diversion should not hamper international cooperation and legitimate trade in materiel, equipment and technology for peaceful purposes'.

control) is therefore contrary to the ATT, which's Art. 4 aims at prohibiting the ATT's provisions' circumvention in a globalised armaments market. According to Boysen, there would have needed to be an explicit exception to this rule regarding joint projects in the ATT (which does not exist), therefore Art. 4 needs to be interpreted narrowly.[460]

Furthermore, Boysen argues that the infringement of Art. 4 ATT in turn also allegedly means that domestically, the Franco-German agreement is unlawful because it is contrary to § 6(3) No. 2 KrWaffKontrG, which requires that an export licence may not be granted, if there is reason to believe that issuing an export licence would violate Germany's international obligations.[461]

Again, these arguments are not convincing. As already stated, neither France nor Germany are obligated by their new agreement to refrain from establishing and maintaining their respective arms export control systems as obligated by the ATT, since export licences continue to require governmental authorization (only the procedure needs to be swift, according to annex 1 part 4). Since the NFGAAE primarily deals with the modalities and procedures of export licence issuance, the export of armaments parts and components continues to be nationally controlled and exports can be blocked when immediate interests are concerned. Such immediate interests are likely concerned if a potential armaments export violates international (or national) law and would thus allow the parties to the armaments export agreement to deny an export licence. Thereby, the agreement is also in line with Arts. 6 and 7 of the ATT, which obligate the State parties to take international peace and security law obligations (including international humanitarian law and human rights law) into account when authorizing arms transfers. It is also relevant to add that the ATT is also considered in the preamble of the NFGAAE and that both Germany and France are parties to the ATT and therefore bound by its provisions. Since there is no infringement on Art. 4 ATT and Germany continues to maintain its national export control system, there is also no conflict in regards to § 6(3) No. 2 KrWaffKontrG.

---

460  Boysen (n 436) 32–34.
461  Ibid. 34–36.

3.1.5.3.4. The NFGAAE – a violation of the EU's Common Position?

Boysen also argues that the NFGAAE deviates from the EU's CP[462] on armaments exports (which is legally binding[463] in accordance with Art. 288(4) TFEU[464] as a decision in accordance with Art. 25(b)(ii)[465] in conjunction with Art. 29 TEU[466], see part *3.2.1.4. Towards a Comprehensive European Arms Export Regime?*), which does not provide for a de-minimis rule when it comes to armaments exports, but according to Art. 1 requires each Member State to assess export licence applications made to it for items (common standards) on the EU Common Military List[467] and according to Art. 5 to only grant export licences on the basis of reliable prior knowledge of end use in the country of final destination, which for example generally requires a thoroughly checked end-user certificate. This contrasts the NFGAAE's annex 1 part 5 provision, according to which no end-use certificate (*"Endverbleibserklärung"*) regarding Franco-German export licences (*"Verbringungsgenehmigung"*) is required.

However, since both Germany and France are bound by the EU's CP, this legally implies the same level of care regarding armaments exports. Although the waiver of end-use certificates might seem irreconcilable with Art. 5 of the EU's CP, it is EU-wide practice regarding multilateral armaments projects that the State party from which's territory the final system is exported is solely responsible to assess conformity with the international and European legal obligations of the parties to the agreement (see for example Art. 13(4) FFA, discussed in part *3.3.1. Multilateral European Armaments Cooperation*).[468] Even Boysen explains how the CFSP promotes common approaches and does not preclude a Member State to implement further measures which 'it considers necessary for the protection of the

---

462  (n 61).

463  Pechstein (n 59) 427.

464  Matthias Ruffert, 'Art. 288' in Christian Calliess and Matthias Ruffert (eds), *EUV/ AEUV* (6th edn, C.H.Beck 2022) 2400–2402; Bernd Biervert, 'Artikel 288' in Jürgen Schwarze et al. (eds), *EU-Kommentar* (4th edn, Nomos 2018) 3011–3029.

465  Hans-Joachim Cremer, 'Art. 25' in Christian Calliess and Matthias Ruffert (eds), *EUV/AEUV* (6th edn, C.H.Beck 2022) 367–372; Jörg Terhechte, 'Artikel 25' in Jürgen Schwarze et al. (eds), *EU-Kommentar* (4th edn, Nomos 2018) 333–335.

466  Hans-Joachim Cremer, 'Art. 29' in Christian Calliess and Matthias Ruffert (eds), *EUV/AEUV* (6th edn, C.H.Beck 2022) 385–390; Jörg Philipp Terhechte, 'Artikel 29' in Jürgen Schwarze et al. (eds), *EU-Kommentar* (4th edn, Nomos 2018) 344–348.

467  (n 395).

468  Wissenschaftliche Dienste Deutscher Bundestag (n 419).

essential interests of its security which are connected with the production of or trade in arms, munitions and war material' (Art. 346(1)(b) TFEU). The CP also does not explicitly state an obligation for each Member State to assess and authorize armaments exports solely.[469] Consequently, it cannot be said that the NFGAAE violates the EU's CP on armaments exports and is thus unconstitutional.

### 3.1.5.3.5. Further Thoughts

Ultimately, the NFGAAE therefore appears to be in line with Germany's constitution and its rules on armaments exports. Under the presumption that the agreement has been concluded formally correct[470], potentially still occurring norm collisions between the NFGAAE and German rules on armaments exports (namely the KrWaffKontrG and the AWG) could also be solved by hierarchy rules on the basis of the GG's and the BVerfG's friendliness towards international law (*"Völkerrechtsfreundlichkeit des Bundesverfassungsgerichts"*[471]).

Art. 25 GG places international law between constitutional law and ordinary domestic law. As a consequence, in case of norm conflicts between the general rules of international law and domestic law, ordinary domestic law has to interpreted and applied in conformity with international law as much as possible[472] or not be applied (*"Anwendungsvorrang der allgemeinen Regeln des Völkerrechts"*[473]) to avoid conflicts with Germany's international obligations.[474]

According to the BVerfG, it cannot be assumed that the legislator, provided he did not explicitly expressed to that effect, wants to deviate from

---

469  Boysen (n 436) 30.
470  Schorkopf (n 402) 43.
471  BVerfG, Urteil des Zweiten Senats vom 26. Marz 1957 – 2 BvG 1/55, at 195; Frank Schorkopf, 'Völkerrechtsfreundlichkeit und Völkerrechtsskepsis in der Rechtsprechung des Bundesverfassungsgerichts' in Thomas Giegerich (ed), *Der „offene Verfassungsstaat" des Grundgesetzes nach 60 Jahren* (Duncker&Humblot 2010) 131–157; Stefan Talmon, 'Die Grenzen der Anwendung des Völkerrechts im deutschen Recht' [2013] 68(1) JuristenZeitung 12; Tobias Hofmann, 'Der Grundsatz der völkerrechtsfreundlichen Auslegung' [2013] 4 JURA 326, 326–333; Daniel Knop, *Völker- und Europarechtsfreundlichkeit als Verfassungsgrundsätze* (Mohr Siebeck 2013) 9.
472  Schorkopf (n 402) 26, 40.
473  Christian Calliess, *Staatsrecht III* (4th edn, C.H.Beck 2022) 128.
474  Schweitzer and Dederer (n 381) 66–67; Schorkopf (n 402) 40.

the Federal Republic of Germany's international obligations or wants to enable a violation of such obligations ('*Es ist nicht anzunehmen, dass der Gesetzgeber, sofern er dies nicht klar bekundet hat, von völkerrechtlichen Verpflichtungen der Bundesrepublik Deutschland abweichen oder die Verletzung solcher Verpflichtungen ermöglichen will.*').[475]

The principle of conformity with international law ("*Gebot der völkerrechtskonformen Auslegung*") also has consequences for potential future legislation, which needs to be in line with Germany's international legal obligations[476] to avoid divergence between international and domestic law.[477] Potential stricter future German legislation on armaments exports would then perhaps also need to consider the NFGAAE, which in turn might lead again to issues regarding compliance with the NFGAAE (see also further discussion below).

On the other hand, it has been pointed out that conflicts between domestic law and international obligations can in some cases also be solved by withdrawing from an agreement.[478] In the case of a bilateral agreement (like the NFGAAE) which has been concluded as an administrative agreement and thus domestically is on the same level as an administrative statute[479], conflicts between the agreement and parliamentary statutes would likely require the German federal government to withdraw from the agreement. This means that if the NFGAAE was considered to be unconstitutional by the German BVerfG (contrary to the findings of this thesis), Germany would be forced to withdraw from the agreement, which in turn would have serious adverse consequences for Franco-German armaments cooperation. As already mentioned, if France cannot rely on Germany to not block French exports of armaments stemming from joint projects, France will refuse to collaborate with Germany in armaments production.

### 3.1.5.4. The French Perspective

In France, a similar discussion of the NFGAAE's constitutionality and its compatibility with domestic law has not arisen. This has undoubtedly political reasons (as armaments exports are – compared to Germany – a

---

475   BVerfG, Beschluß des Zweiten Senats vom 26. März 1987 – 2 BvR 589/79, at 39.
476   Schweitzer and Dederer (n 381) 66–67.
477   Schorkopf (n 402) 26; BVerfG (n 404) at 31–37; Schorkopf (n 471) 131–157.
478   Schorkopf (n 402) 44.
479   ibid. 44–45.

less controversial issue[480], see also part *2.2.2. Franco-German Armaments Cooperation today*), but certainly France's different legal system vis-à-vis the ratification of international agreements and their standing within the national legal order also plays an important role.

France follows the monist theory of international law.[481] The executive power is the only authority capable of ratifying and approving an international commitment. It negotiates and signs these commitments[482] of which only a few (relating to core issues of sovereignty and exhaustively listed by the French constitution) require an authorization by the French parliament to be ratified,[483] which is therefore limited to a simple oversight function. After an international commitment has been properly ratified and published, the French parliament cannot object to its application.[484] According to Art. 55 of the 1958 *Constitution française*, treaties or agreements duly ratified or approved shall, upon publication, prevail over acts of parliament.

The NFGAAE has been concluded as an executive agreement ("*accord*")[485] by the French government not subject to ratification by the French parliament in accordance with Art. 52 of the French constitution and Arts. 1, 3(1) Décret n°53–192[486]. Because the NFGAAE does not fall in any of the categories listed in Art. 53 of the French constitution, it only required approval by the executive (government and president) to be ratified and enter into force after publication in the *Journal Officiel de la République Française*. Because it prevails over acts of parliament, a conflict between the agreement and the French rules on armaments exports does not arise. The NFGAAE is therefore also constitutional under French law.

---

480  Béraud-Sudreau (n 128) 85–86.

481  Art. 55 *Constitution française* (1958); Renoux and Villiers (n 375) 1215–1224.

482  Art. 52 in conjunction with Arts. 5 and 20 of the *Constitution française* (1958); Renoux and Villiers (n 375) 1194–1195.

483  Art. 53 *Constitution française* (1958); Renoux and Villiers (n 375) 1195–1199.

484  Francois Luchaire, 'The Participation of Parliament in the Elaboration and Application of Treaties' (1991) 67(2) Chicago-Kent Law Review 341; Michel Verpeaux, *Droit constitutionnel français* (2nd edn, PUF 2015) 535–546; Elisabeth Zoller, *Droit des relations extérieures* (PUF 1992) 176–234; Renoux and Villiers (n 375) 1194; Jean Dhommeaux, 'Le rôle du parlement dans l'élaboration des engagements internationaux: continuité et changement' [1987] RDP 1448, 1448–1478.

485  *Décret n° 2019–1168* (n 392); see also Renoux and Villiers (n 375) 1194–1195.

486  1953 International Commitments Implementation Law (*Décret n° 53–192 du 14 mars 1953 relatif à la ratification et à la publication des engagements internationaux souscrits par la France*) (current version 11 April 1986).

Similar to Germany, France's export-control procedure is executed at an administrative, inter-ministerial level. In France, armaments exports are approved (or denied) by the Inter-Ministerial Commission for the Study of the Export of War Materials (*Commission interministérielle pour l'étude des exportations de matériels de guerre*, abbreviated CIEEMG). The CIEEMG renders its export decisions based on legal and national security considerations.[487] Since the NFGAAE is line with French domestic law, international law, and EU law, the CIEEMG process is compatible with the NFGAAE. Therefore, the legal unreliabilities of the NFGAAE are (again) exclusively rooted in German political controversy and lacking constitutional reliability.

### 3.1.5.5. Lasting Unreliabilities

Again, this thesis operates under the premise that to be reliable – meaning large-scale collaborative armaments projects will be consistently realised – Franco-German armaments collaboration requires convergence and reliable rules on exports of armaments stemming from joint programmes. This is because France will not collaborate with Germany on armaments production if there are no common rules on armaments exports that ensure reliability and predictability in German export decisions so that France can conduct its armaments exports (mostly) free from German impediments. Problematically, legal and political unreliability risks remain, ultimately endangering the bilateral armaments cooperation's success as a whole.

As discussed in the previous parts, it is not entirely clear at this point whether the NFGAAE is legally reliable as several questions regarding the agreement's compatibility with Germany's constitutional law and its rules on armaments exports have not been conclusively answered. Potentially, Germany might be forced in the future to withdraw from the agreement if for example the BVerfG would rule that the agreement is incompatible with the GG or has not been concluded formally correct.

It also remains to be seen whether the NFGAAE sufficiently and reliably regulates the issue of armaments exports stemming from joint programmes in the long term. The NFGAAE resembles in many regards the failed SDA. For example, there is again no enforcement mechanism for compliance. However, the NFGAAE has at least been published by both States (unlike the SDA). This transparency will hopefully make the new agreement more

---

487  Béraud-Sudreau (n 128) 82.

reliable from a political perspective. On the other hand, the fact that the NFGAAE has not been concluded as a "Political Treaty" by Germany (like the Aachen Treaty) or its provisions been made part of the Aachen Treaty, and instead has been concluded as a mere administrative agreement is peculiar and entails the risk that the NFGAAE is at least politically regarded as legally less binding.

Furthermore, both agreements (SDA and NFGAAE) feature a general and similar non-veto principle for armaments exports, an exception rule from that principle and a consultation mechanism in case of conflicts over export authorization denials. The only major difference between the two agreements is the NFGAAE's de-minimis rule, which also features the same exception provision as mentioned in Arts. 1 and 2 of the NFGAAE. While the SDA's exception rule is general ('*Il ne pourra être fait usage qu'exceptionnellement de la possibilité de refuser l'autorisation d'exporter les composants d'un projet commun*'), the NFGAAE only allows for refusing an export licence if a State party's immediate interests or national security are compromised. However, this again entails legal ambiguity and it remains to be seen to which margin of discretion the term "immediate interests" will be interpreted in the future. It however has the potential of being more far-reaching than the SDA's exception provision.

The ambiguous "immediate interests" exception is likely a French concession towards Germany's restrictive stance on armaments exports, however it therefore also increases the risk that exports of armaments stemming from joint projects will be blocked by future German governments on the basis of that exception. This leaves Germany's armaments licencing regime unpredictable (and therefore unreliable) for France. In the end, whether an export denial can be justified by the NFGAAE or not will come down to how both States deal with and resolve potential conflicts, which is impossible to predict from a present-day perspective. At least there is a consultation mechanism to deal with such conflicts in the NFGAAE. However, again, considering that FCAS's projected development period is until 2040 and potential export issues will only arise afterwards, politically a lot can change until then, including legal interpretations of the new agreement's provisions, potentially to the disadvantage of reliable Franco-German armaments cooperation.

Furthermore, the ambiguous term "without delay" in licencing decisions (that was also featured in the SDA) is also repeated in the NFGAAE, again entailing legal and political unreliability. And again, the consultation mechanism only comes into effect in case of an export licence denial, not if the licencing process was (at least perceived as being) delayed, entailing the potential for conflicts. And again, this lack of a more effective mechanism for dispute settlement makes Franco-German armaments collaboration further unreliable, because potentially arising future conflicts might not be solved and Franco-German armaments cooperation might then be terminated (again).

From a legal standpoint, the NFGAAE therefore does not appear to be more reliable than the SDA and thus does not sufficiently ensure that the Franco-German armaments collaboration will ultimately succeed. This of course remains to be seen over the next two to three decades, however it is not a satisfactory situation that Franco-German armaments cooperation continues to be at a constant risk of failure due to an insufficient and unreliable legal framework for armaments exports.

Besides open legal reliability questions, political unreliability risks also remain. Currently, it remains questionable to which margin of discretion future German governments (which potentially favour an even more restrictive armaments export policy) might interpret its "immediate interests" in the future to potentially block the export of jointly produced armaments, even if that meant adverse consequences for Franco-German armaments cooperation. As mentioned earlier, Franco-German armaments cooperation failed before after a political shift in Germany's government lead to a more restrictive armaments export policy (despite the SDA), which ultimately caused France to refrain from further armaments collaboration with Germany. There is a possibility that in the future, Germany's armaments export policy will get even more restrictive than it is today.[488] France reserves the constitutional right to suspend its obligations from the bilateral agreement (similar to how it treated the SDA) if it views that Germany does not fully comply with the NFGAAE.[489] France would then also most likely refrain from bilateral armaments collaboration with Germany for decades to come.[490]

Yet the political unreliability risks not only concern Germany's potential future licencing conduct (whether actually in line with the NFGAAE or not). Also, both parties can withdraw from / terminate the agreement at a six-month notice (Art. 5(1)); while prior obligations, i.e. export licences,

---

488  Bundesregierung (239); Béraud-Sudreau (n 141).
489  According to Art. 55 of the *Constitution française* (1958), agreements are subject to the application by the other party (principle of *réceprocité*), see Renoux and Villiers (n 375) 1222–1223; Dinh (n 375) 557.
490  Descôtes (n 141).

continue to be upheld (Art. 5(2)). A political shift in government could therefore easily lead to a unilateral termination of the agreement and thus also seriously disrupt Franco-German armaments cooperation in the future. If the NFGAAE fails (like the SDA has) either due to non-compliance (actual or perceived) or due to a potential withdrawal by Germany, Franco-German armaments cooperation as a whole would fail for the foreseeable future. This has been made clear by France as stated above and is further underlined by the decades of non-collaboration after the failure of the SDA.

A few months before concluding the NFGAAE, the (now former) German federal government updated its Political Principles, which refers to bilateral and European armaments cooperation (Preamble and section II(2) of the 2019 Political Principles).[491] This serves as important guidance for the context of the NFGAAE's conclusion and as to how Germany will interpret and apply the NFGAAE's provisions on armaments exports in the near future.

On the one hand, the 2019 Political Principles stress the intent to further European armaments cooperation and to further convergence of armaments export matters by developing common approaches on the European level. This is expressly considered with regard to the CFSP, strengthening the EDTIB, and enhancing defence cooperation in the context of the EDU (Preamble 2019 Political Principles). PESCO is also mentioned in particular. In cases of exports of armaments to EU Member States, NATO-allies and NATO-equivalent countries, these exports are therefore principally unrestricted to enable trans-European armaments cooperation (section II(1) of the 2019 Political Principles).

On the other hand, according to the Preamble of the 2019 Political Principles, Germany intends to continue to pursue a restrictive armaments export policy, where the armaments export decisions are made by the federal government on the basis of the KrWaffKontrG, the AWG, the EU's CP on armaments exports and the ATT (section I(1) 2019 Political Principles).[492] While the export of armaments to EU Member States, NATO-allies and NATO-equivalent countries is principally unrestricted, armaments export to third countries will continue to be heavily restricted (section III 2019 Political Principles).

---

491  Bundesregierung (n 317).
492  On a related note, this also further underlines that – contrary to Boysen's claims – the German federal government does not delegate its export competence to France.

Furthermore, the 2019 Political Principles also state that the German federal government will not waive the possibility to intervene in export plans of the cooperation partner and, to enforce its Political Principles, reserves the right in any case to oppose certain export plans of the cooperation partner in a consultation procedure (section II(3) 2019 Political Principles).

This was the central point of contention between Germany and France regarding the treatment of exports of armaments stemming from joint projects in the past. The fact that Germany was able to block (and then blocked) French exports of armaments stemming from joint projects made their armaments collaboration unreliable, and problematically, this unreliability factor continues to persist. While the NFGAAE's consultation mechanism takes this unreliability factor into account in Arts. 1(3) and 2(2) and attempts to lessen its effects by requiring to "identify appropriate solutions" in case of export vetoes, it nevertheless remains an unreliability risk in Franco-German armaments collaboration due to a lack of predictability regarding future German government's armaments export practice.

Furthermore, the current "traffic light" German government coalition has agreed to pass a new national arms export act which is also meant to implement the EU's CP[493] on armaments exports, the German federal government's aforementioned (restrictive) Political Principles, and is set to extent post-shipment controls for armaments exports. This new German arms export act is meant to serve the purpose of furthering a restrictive armaments export policy. Furthermore, export licences for armaments exports to countries directly involved in the Yemen conflict will be principally denied.[494] It is to be expected that the anticipated new German arms export act will in practice entail more restrictions for armaments exports to third countries (non-EU, non-NATO and non-NATO-equivalent countries). This in turn will likely weaken the EDTIB[495] and might potentially have adverse effects on the current Franco-German armaments collaboration as it might infringe the NFGAAE's provisions on armaments exports or alter Germany's interpretation or implementation of the agreement.

For now, there have been no disagreements regarding the implementation of the NFGAAE. Both States seem to be eager to facilitate their bilateral collaboration, in particular after the 2022 Russian invasion in Ukraine, which led to a historical turning point (*'Zeitenwende'*) in Germany's de-

---

493  (n 61).
494  Bundesregierung (239).
495  FAZ (n 340).

fence priorities, including smoothly realising FCAS in particular.[496] However, the German government's position may change again, the (legally non-binding) coalition agreement which sets out objectives for more restrictive rules on armaments exports is still in force, and FCAS will not be exported before 2040 (when it is supposed to be fully developed). A lot can politically change over a period of twenty years, which is why reliable rules for the current Franco-German collaboration would have been essential.

### 3.1.6. Intermediate Conclusions – need for a different approach

In light of the foregoing analysis, it appears to be a recurring problem in Franco-German armaments collaboration that the bilateral intergovernmental agreements, which are intended to enable that collaboration by finding sufficient and long-term convergence of the differing armaments export policies regarding the treatment of exports of armaments stemming from joint projects, are unreliable in that regard. Especially the failure to ensure (Germany's) consistent compliance is a lasting unreliability risk.

The unreliabilities in the bilateral legal framework for Franco-German armaments cooperation in turn make Franco-German armaments collaboration unreliable, meaning joint projects cannot be consistently realised. This is because France will not collaborate with Germany in armaments production if it cannot rely on Germany to not impede French armaments exports. This has been the case for two decades after the failure of the SDA and has been made clear by France in the preparation phases leading to the current large-scale armaments projects (FCAS and MGCS in particular) and to the signings of the Aachen Treaty and the NFGAAE.

The lack of reliability in the bilateral framework and the resulting continuous risk of failure of Franco-German armaments collaboration is concerning. Another failure of Franco-German armaments collaboration would have serious adverse consequences for European defence capability development. Firstly, these large-scale armaments projects, which are urgently

---

496 Tobias Heimbach, '"Future Combat Air System": Das steckt hinter dem Milliarden-Projekt der Bundeswehr, das den Luftkampf revolutionieren soll' (*Business Insider*, 27 March 2022) <https://www.businessinsider.de/politik/deutschland/future-comb at-air-system-das-steckt-hinter-dem-milliarden-projekt-der-bundeswehr-das-den-lu ftkampf-revolutionieren-sollltet/> accessed 28 March 2022; Bundesministerium der Verteidigung, 'Future Combat Air System: Kampfjet-Entwicklung schreitet voran' (*BMWG*, 28 April 2023) <https://www.bmvg.de/de/aktuelles/future-combat-air-syst em-kampfjet-entwicklung-schreitet-voran-5614922> accessed 5 May 2023.

required for European strategic autonomy and Europe's ability to defend itself, would then not be realised.

Furthermore, it is to be expected that France would refrain from a third attempt to substantially collaborate with Germany in armaments production for decades to come if the current Franco-German armaments collaboration failed again due to lack of sufficient convergence of armaments exports policies. This would likewise significantly undermine any current and future efforts to make Europe more resilient against geopolitical threats.

Due to the lack of reliability of Franco-German armaments collaboration on the basis of bilateral intergovernmental agreements and the need for reliable defence capability development, there is a need for a different, more reliable approach to armaments cooperation and harmonised export rules. Such a different approach is potentially offered by EU law as an alternative, potentially more reliable legal framework for armaments cooperation. This will now be discussed.

### 3.2. European Union Law – a more reliable legal framework for Armaments Collaboration?

Since Franco-German intergovernmental agreements are apparently too unreliable to ensure that Franco-German armaments collaboration is reliable (now and in the future) and large-scale joint armaments projects will be consistently realised, it is appropriate to consider a different approach.

In this part, it will be discussed whether EU law provides for a more reliable legal framework to ensure the consistent realisation of such large-scale armaments projects and what would need to change to potentially make it reliable.

European defence integration has immensely accelerated over the last years (see *part 2.2.1. European Defence and Armaments Integration today*) and most of the EU Member States are increasingly cooperating in security and defence matters, armaments in particular. While the EU's CSDP is still almost exclusively of an intergovernmental character, meaning security and defence matters are mainly the Member States' concern, the European Commission has nevertheless become more and more active in defence and security matters, mostly via its Internal Market competence, and aims at facilitating further European armament cooperation.

Both the intergovernmental character of the CFSP/CSDP due to the traditional domaine réservé of the Member States in the areas of foreign policy, security, and defence as well as the EU's recent activism in these policy areas have led to fragmented and partially conflicting legal frameworks of European and national security and defence (including armaments) policies, to dysfunctional governance systems and partially contrasting integration approaches in the aforementioned policy areas. As will be discussed in the following parts, this again raises reliability and efficiency questions for European armaments cooperation.

Nevertheless, while European defence and armaments integration is still fragmented, the EU's increasingly challenging geopolitical environment has put pressure on the EU and its Member States to close the existing capability gaps and increase coherence in the area of security and defence. Outcomes like PESCO and the EDF are proof that deeper defence integration is possible provided the necessary political will by the Member States.

### 3.2.1. European Armaments Cooperation – torn between intergovernmentalism and supranationalism

As shown in part *2.1.1. Historical Evolution of European Defence and Armaments Integration*, CFSP and CSDP were originally and much later designed as frameworks separate from the economic and social framework of the EU. Out of respect for national sovereignty[497], they are to this day arranged in an intergovernmental manner[498] and in this regard are very different from the other supranational parts of EU law. Traditionally, this means that security and defence matters are mainly the (individual) Member States' concern and that the European Commission has no competence in these matters. This is further underlined by the CFSP's unanimity principle and with regard to armaments by the TFEU's far-reaching armaments exception (Art. 346(1)(b) TFEU), which undermines coherence and consistency in the ECAP.[499]

Despite the European Treaties' clear competence attributions, the Commission has nevertheless become more and more active in defence matters since the 1990s, including armaments in particular, through the backdoor of its Internal Market competences. Beside their defence dimension, armaments have an economic and social dimension and have thus not been

---

497   Pechstein (n 59) 426.
498   ibid. 425–432.
499   Trybus (n 34) 160.

immune to the Commission's gradual defence policy mission creep.[500] In a step-by-step process since the St Malo summit, the Commission has increasingly engaged in armaments policy and integrated armaments matters into EU competences.[501] Besides supranationally promoting intergovernmental armaments cooperation in Europe, by now this also concerns in particular supranational regulation (most notably via the Defence Package) to improve the EU's regulatory framework of the European Defence Equipment Market (EDEM).[502]

The Commission's harmonisation activism to achieve more coherence and consistency was accompanied by the Member States' objective need for a strong, competitive and innovative EDTIB as part of an effective CSDP, but also their continuing sovereignty concerns partially obstructing said activism.[503]

In its regulatory activism, the Commission has been considerably supported by the CJEU over the last decades, which significantly constricted the armaments exception and thus Member State sovereignty to a degree. This is insofar relevant as that CFSP/CSDP actions and decisions are principally not subject to judicial review by the CJEU, due to their intergovernmental nature, except where they borderline with Internal Market issues. This is frequently the case with armaments, thus opening the door for the EU's supranational institutions to become active in this area.

Furthermore, within the framework of the EU, the Member States themselves have also created capacities to facilitate armaments cooperation, such as EDA, which has however, due to its intergovernmental design, remained under strict national control.[504]

As a result, the CSDP is today an intergovernmental arrangement which has been partly supranationalised, especially in the area of armaments cooperation, although this is not expressly reflected in the Treaties. The result is a fragmented legal framework for European armaments cooperation, where the various legal instruments are based partly on intergovernmental

---

500 Hoeffler (n 46) 45.
501 Lavallée (n 104) 371–389.
502 Mörth (n 106) 173–189; Sophia Besch, 'Can the European Commission develop Europe's defence industry?' (*Centre for European Reform*, 18 November 2019) <https://www.cer.eu/insights/can-european-commission-develop-europes-defence-industry> accessed 23 June 2020.
503 Dyson and Konstadinides (n 91) 88; Kielmansegg (n 27); Hoeffler (n 46) 55; Fiott (n 103).
504 Biermann and Weiss (n 211) 228.

law and partly on supranational competences. This makes legal discussions and proposals regarding this subject quite challenging and entails the potential for competence conflicts.

The currently most prominent example for the CSDP's partial supranationalisation via Internal Market law is the EDF. In short, there is now supranational funding for intergovernmental armaments cooperation, thus bridging the traditional supranational-intergovernmental divide in European armaments cooperation since the failure of the EDC, which would have included supranational defence procurement. Yet, the Commission, which administers the EDF, has neither a mandate to determine the development of certain defence capabilities nor any control over potential exports of armaments developed with EU funding, due to rigorous Member State opposition against such proposals. Ultimately, European armaments cooperation as such remains intergovernmental and based on the principle of voluntariness,[505] but it is today nevertheless significantly promoted by the Commission.

This is further underlined by the fact that despite the Commission's promotional activities in the field of armaments, EDA remains primarily responsible to facilitate armaments cooperation under EU primary law. Consequently, the intergovernmentally arranged European Defence (or rather armaments) Agency also operates in an area concerned with the economic aspects of defence close to and potentially overlapping with supranational Single Market matters.[506] EDA has played a significant part in facilitating European capability development[507] and contributing to the creation of an EDEM,[508] which as mentioned earlier is today the Commission's main playground in defence matters. Interestingly, this intergovernmental-supranational overlap is also recognised by the TEU, which tasks EDA to cooperate with the Commission (Art. 45(2) TEU[509]) and thus links intergovernmental (CSDP) and supranational (Internal Market) policy areas under EU primary law.

Another armaments policy area where intergovernmental and supranational law borderline are armaments exports. Conventional armaments exports do not fall under the EU's regulatory competences. Instead, there is only some rudimentary EU-wide intergovernmental convergence between

---

505  Faure (n 113) 1–25.
506  Trybus (n 45) 186–187.
507  Dyson and Konstadinides (n 91) 100.
508  Terhechte (n 259) 388.
509  Consolidated version of the Treaty on European Union (TEU) [2012] OJ C326/01.

the competent Member States via common export criteria. However, dual-use goods qualify as goods under EU law due to their partial civilian nature and their export has by now been supranationally harmonised. This could be the starting point for a supranational armaments export regime, provided the necessary political will by the Member States.

In parallel to the supranational developments mentioned above, the ECAP has over the past two decades also been further developed in an intergovernmental manner (PESCO being the most noteworthy example), and then partially linked to the supranational institutional (EDA-Commission link) and regulatory (Defence Package) parts of EU law. While the CSDP's fundamental intergovernmental arrangement will likely remain immune to change, it can be expected that the CSDP's industrial dimension incrementally becomes more supranationalised in the future, due to the EU's increasingly challenging geopolitical environment and the 'geopolitical'[510] Commission's increased activism. Consequently, European armaments cooperation can increasingly be characterised by this peculiar intergovernmental-supranational hybrid.

In addition to the intra-EU intergovernmental-supranational divide, European armaments cooperation is also characterised by the extra-EU-intra-EU institutional divide (OCCAR, FFA, EDA), where despite EU structures for armaments cooperation, such cooperation continues to take place in intergovernmental formats outside the framework of the EU, furthering legal fragmentation. However, it is relevant to note that such cooperation now largely takes place within the structures of the EU, namely EDA and PESCO.

In the following parts, the intergovernmental-supranational divide will be a recurring issue when analysing the current (unreliable) state of European armaments cooperation and making proposals for legal change and development. This divide has led to significant fragmentation of the underlying framework, entail reliability and efficiency deficits, and it will therefore also be discussed, whether and to what degree the intergovernmental and the supranational parts of EU defence integration law can potentially be reconciled to make European armaments cooperation more reliable.

The dawn of supranational activities in the CSDP sphere, while currently posing a challenge in understanding and further developing European armaments integration, also shows the first beginnings of a more coherent and common European approach in this matter, which would be urgently

---

510  European Commission (n 246).

required for consistent and reliable capability development in the face of the EU's increasingly challenging geopolitical environment.

### 3.2.1.1. Towards a European Defence Union and potential consequences for European Armaments Cooperation

Most of the current political and legal discussions around further European defence integration revolve around the concept of a European Defence Union (EDU). However, the term is ambiguous and there is much political and scholarly controversy regarding its meaning, concept and necessity.[511] Before discussing the role of European armaments cooperation in a potential EDU and legal options as to how to make it more reliable and successful in that context, in the following part, the ambiguous term will therefore be contextually, politically and legally clarified first.

### 3.2.1.1.1. Context and Need for deeper Defence Integration

As discussed in *part 2.1.1. Historical Evolution of European Defence and Armaments Integration*, thoughts on how to develop a European Security and Defence Policy have existed for a long time.[512] Military integration was a central objective of early European integration after World War II. However, attempts to create a (supranational) EDC failed in the 1950s. As a consequence, NATO and WEU subsequently provided the main pillars for European Security and Defence and it took the European Member States until the 1990s to put European defence integration effectively back on the agenda and to successively develop what is today known as the CSDP under the Lisbon Treaty (Arts. 42–46 TEU).

European defence integration to this day remains an ongoing process towards the ultimate (and unclarified) goal of "common defence".[513] This process has been and remains highly complex and challenging due to Member State sovereignty concerns and divergence of national strategic cultures.

---

511 Laura Wolfstädter, „Europäische Verteidigungsunion": eine rechtliche Einordnung' (*Hertie School Jacques Delors Centre*, 1 August 2018) <https://www.delorscentre.eu/de/publikationen/detail/publication/europaeische-verteidigungsunion-eine-rechtliche-einordnung> accessed 21 June 2020; Sven Biscop, 'European Defence: Give PESCO a Chance' [2018] 60(3) Survival 161.

512 Kielmansegg (n 27); Terhechte (n 27) 373.

513 Trybus (n 34) 395.

Considering the early beginnings of the CSDP since the St Malo summit and its successive and gradual development in EU primary law, the CSDP has by now been significantly developed and consolidated under the Lisbon Treaty. Yet, compared to the supranationally far-reaching scope of the failed EDC or even certain ambitious defence integration proposals (to establish a European Security and Defence Union (ESDU), see below) during the preparations for the failed European Constitutional Treaty[514], the tasks of the CSDP remain primarily limited to crises management and to facilitate armaments cooperation. Furthermore, despite the Lisbon Treaty's mutual assistance clause (Art. 42(7) TEU, see below), the EU (or rather its Member States) remains dependent on NATO in defence matters for the foreseeable future.[515]

However, due to the EU's increasingly challenging geopolitical environment and the resulting calls for more European defence cooperation and European strategic autonomy, the EU and its Member States are currently working towards further developing the CSDP to make it more effective (see part *2.2.1. European Defence and Armaments Integration today*). The EU's recent Strategic Compass[516] for example provides a shared assessment of the EU's strategic environment and particularly stresses the need for capability development by the Member States and armaments cooperation to meet the current threats and challenges.

The reasons for the specific focus on capability development and armaments cooperation are to close Europe's capability gap. Closing Europe's capability gap is meant to make the EU and its Members States less dependent on the US's defence capabilities and rather enable them to effectively provide for their own defence and carry out CSDP tasks effectively. At least until the 2022 Russian invasion of Ukraine, the Member States' defence policies were generally characterised by low defence budgets and low spending

---

514  German-French Contribution, CONV 422/02 of 22 November 2002, further developed in the communiqué of the summit meeting between Belgium, France, Germany and Luxembourg of 29 April 2003, reproduced in Antonio Missiroli (ed), 'From Copenhagen to Brussels' [2003] 67 Chaillot Papers 1, 76–80.

515  Terhechte (n 27) 374; Eric dell'Aria, 'L'UE dans sa relation avec l'OTAN et quelques autres acteurs: bilan et perspectives', in Aurélien Raccah (ed), *Le traité de Lisbonne De nouvelles compétences pour l'Union européene?* (L'Harmattan 2012) 193–207; European Commission (n 43).

516  EEAS (n 75); the Strategic Compass was endorsed by the European Council on 25 March 2022, see European Council (n 262).

for R&D.[517] Since strengthening defence capabilities is a tedious and costly process, (for now intergovernmental) armaments cooperation between the Member States plays a crucial role in order to lower costs for R&D of defence systems through shared and more efficient spending and to facilitate their interoperability to enable the cooperation of the Member States' armed forces in multinational units (including the EU Battlegroups).[518] In 2013, it was estimated that the cost of non-Europe in security and defence matters was at least 26 billion euro a year.[519] Other estimations determine the costs to be between 20 billion to 120 billion euro annually.[520] According to EDA, in 2020, the EU Member States conducted just 11 % of their total equipment procurement in cooperation with other Member States, falling well short of the 35 % collective PESCO benchmark.[521] Intergovernmental European initiatives such as PESCO, CARD, the EDF, and EDA are intended to overcome these shortcomings and are regarded as first steps towards an EDU. They will also be further discussed in the following parts (see parts *3.2.1.2. The Future of European Armaments Cooperation* and PESCO and *3.2.1.3. The European Armaments Policy*).

Besides facilitating armaments cooperation, the EU is also currently working towards adjusting the regulatory environment of defence-related goods, likewise with the overall objective of creating an EDU. These efforts include creating an EDEM, consolidating the European defence industry and potentially harmonising armaments export control by supranational legislation. Noteworthy in this context are the Commission's Defence Package[522], the Council's dual-use regulation[523] and its regulation establishing the EDF[524]. They will likewise be discussed in the following parts (see especially part *3.2.1.3. The European Armaments Policy and its future*).

Armaments integration thus apparently plays a central role in current European defence integration and in the process of creating an EDU.[525]

---

517 Rogers and Gilli (n 205) 10; European Commission (n 43).

518 Kielmansegg (n 170) 286.

519 European Parliamentary Research Service (n 231).

520 Valerio Briani, 'The Costs of non-Erope in the Defence Field' (*Istituto Affari Internazionali*, April 2013) <https://www.iai.it/sites/default/files/CSF-IAI_noneuropedef ence_april2013.pdf> accessed 26 October 2022.

521 EDA (n 110).

522 (n 111); (n 112).

523 (n 253).

524 Regulation (EU) 2021/697 (n 186).

525 Biermann and Weiss (n 211) 229.

It is today generally agreed that the creation of an EDU and further de-fence integration must start with the integration of the Member States' defence industries and the EDEM.[526] EDA will oversee this process as per Art. 42(3) para. 2 TEU (for EDA's tasks see also part *3.2.1.2. The European Armaments Policy and its future*). What role the European Commission will play however remains contentious. The centrality of European armaments integration to further European defence integration and creating an EDU is why the initiation of PESCO and the creation of the EDF in 2017 were heralded as the starting points of the EDU.[527]

### 3.2.1.1.2. Political Notions of EDU

Interestingly, while the term EDU (or its variations) is mentioned by politi-cians and EU documents surrounding the creation of PESCO and the EDF, it is not conceptionally mentioned in the PESCO[528] or EDF[529] decisions, it does not appear in EU primary or secondary law and overall remains substantially ambiguous. In the following part, the concept of EDU will therefore be politically and legally clarified.

As mentioned above, the concept of what at the time was called a European Security and Defence Union (ESDU) was addressed during the preparations for the failed European Constitutional Treaty by Franco-Ger-man proposals[530], which was intended to further European defence integra-tion by closer and more structured cooperation of those Member States willing to make further substantial military commitments.[531] These propos-als went beyond the limits of the current CSDP that was then set out in the Lisbon Treaty. They included developing the EU into a system of collective defence by forming a mutual defence pact between the Member States

---

526  Bundesministerium der Verteidigung (n 191); EDA (n 191); European Commission (n 191).
527  Bundesministerium der Verteidigung (n 191); E EDA (n 191); European Commission (n 191).
528  (n 168).
529  Regulation (EU) 2021/697 (n 186); Regulation (EU) 2018/1092 (n 186).
530  (n 514).
531  Président du Groupe de travail VIII "Défense" à la Convention, 'Rapport final du Group de travail VIII "Défense CONV 461/02" (*cvce*, 16 December 2002) <https://www.cvce.eu/en/obj/rapport_final_du_groupe_de_travail_viii_defense_16_dece mbre_2002-fr-71dbaa92-ac9e-4556-a639-3c7665fd0812.html> accessed 22 October 2022.

joining the ESDU. Furthermore, it was envisaged that the Member States would systematically harmonize their security and defence policies[532], including enhanced armaments cooperation and capability development by harmonising armaments and procurement policies.[533] Due to the failure of the European Constitutional Treaty, these plans were never realised. However, partially, they have found their way into the Lisbon Treaty.[534] Current developments, such as the initiation of PESCO and potentially that of the EDU can be traced back to these ESDU proposals. PESCO (Arts. 42(6), 46 and Protocol No. 10 TEU) features such closer and more structured cooperation and substantial commitments. Although PESCO is a framework exclusively designed for capability development and armaments cooperation and not for collective defence. Nevertheless, such a system for collective defence exists today to some extent on the basis of the Lisbon Treaty's mutual assistance clause (Art. 42(7) TEU), but a common defence system on the basis of the evolutive clause in Art. 42(2) TEU has not been realised yet. This will be relevant later.

In 2016, the EU parliament passed a resolution[535] calling for the creation of an EDU (and PESCO in that context) by further developing the CSDP. Since then, the concept of EDU has been frequently referenced by European politicians in various contexts and with various meanings. Noteworthy in particular is Commission president von der Leyen's 2021 speech[536] on the state of the Union where she explicitly addressed the necessity for the EU to work towards an EDU.

Furthermore, the term EDU (or its variations, which furthers shows to ambiguity of the term) is increasingly mentioned in several EU documents. In 2017, in response the EU's more challenging geopolitical environment and the resulting calls for European strategic autonomy, the EU Commis-

---

532 Jolyon Howorth, 'The European Draft Constitutional Treaty and the Future of the European Defence Initiative: A Question of Flexibility' [2004] 9 European Foreign Affairs Review 1, 6–11.

533 Kielmansegg (n 170) 279; Kielmanssegg (n 174) 147.

534 Kielmansegg (n 170) 291; Kielmanssegg (n 174) 146; Howorth (n 532) 6.

535 European Parliament Resolution 2016/2052(INI) of 22 November 2016 on the European Defence Union [2016] OJ C224/18; this resolution is not legally binding. Nevertheless, it has been referenced by the European Commission in its 2017 Reflection paper on the Future of European Defence, see European Commission, Reflection paper on the Future of European Defence, COM/2017/315, 7 June 2017.

536 Ursula von der Leyen, 'Strengthening the Soul of our Union' (*European Commission*, 15 September 2021) <https://ec.europa.eu/commission/presscorner/detail/en/SPEECH_21_4701> accessed 28 September 2021.

sion presented the Reflection Paper on the Future of European Defence[537]. In this paper, the Commission outlined three possible scenarios for increased European security and defence cooperation which was conceptionally termed a Security and Defence Union (SDU). All three scenarios include increasing levels of European defence (and particularly armaments) cooperation, either primarily outside EU structures (scenario a) or within (scenarios b and c). Which scenario will be realised is a political decision by the Member States and depends on their future convergence of national strategic cultures. As will discussed below and in the following parts, all scenarios can be reconciled with current EU primary law.

Scenario a provides the least level of defence integration. The Member States would continue to decide on selective security and defence cooperation on a voluntary and ad hoc basis, while the EU would continue to only complement the Member States' efforts. In this approach, defence cooperation between the Member States would be strengthened, but the EU's involvement in defence matters would be significantly limited. Certain key defence capabilities would be developed jointly through EDF assistance, but most defence projects would be developed and procured exclusively by the Member States. Consequently, Europe's strategic autonomy in selected critical defence capabilities would be principally enhanced and their costs for R%D would be lower due to increased cooperation. However, European defence cooperation would remain fragmented. This in turn would entail the aforementioned problems of multilateral defence cooperation regarding cost-inefficiencies, lack of interoperability between defence systems and legal unreliability (see parts *2.2.1. European Defence and Armaments Integration today* and *2.2.2. Franco-German Armaments Cooperation today*). Furthermore, only the largest Member States would be financially able to retain the full spectrum of defence capabilities. CSDP actions would continue to rely on voluntary national contributions and the EU-NATO relationship would remain unchanged.

Scenario b is more ambitious. It sets out how the Member States would pool together certain financial and operational assets to increase solidarity in defence. Defence cooperation between Member States would become the norm rather than the exception. This extends to armaments in particular. National defence planning would be far more aligned and armaments cooperation increased to facilitate R&D, procurement, and interoperability of defence systems and reduce costly duplications. The European defence

---

537  European Commission (n 535).

industry would be consolidated and operating in a harmonised EDEM. The EDF and other future European programmes would play a central role in assisting the Member States to systematically develop a wide range of multinational capabilities. The EU would also become more active in defence matters. These multinational capabilities would be supported by joint planning and command structures at EU-level and standby multinational force components. The EU's military power would thus be enhanced so it could fully engage in external crisis management (meaning civilian and military missions and operations). EU and NATO would increase their mutual cooperation and coordination in defence matters.

Scenario c is the most ambitious scenario. It foresees the progressive framing of a common Union defence policy leading to a common defence on the basis of the aforementioned Art. 42(2) TEU and through comprehensive convergence of national strategic cultures. Under this scenario, the Member States would undertake significant commitments in the area of collective defence, making Europe's protection a shared responsibility of the EU and NATO and solidarity and mutual assistance the norm in European collective defence. Moreover, the EU would be able to conduct military operations by relying on integrated Member State defence forces in multinational units which can be rapidly deployed. Importantly, even this most ambitious scenario does not set out supranational defence forces under the EU's command. Armaments cooperation however would be significantly consolidated. The EU would support joint defence programmes with the EDF and set up a dedicated European Defence Research Agency. Furthermore, the EU would foster the creation of a fully harmonised EDEM. The Member States' defence planning would become fully synchronized and capability development be aligned with agreed European priorities. Such capabilities would be developed based on close cooperation and even integration or specialisation. This scenario largely reflects the aforementioned 2016 EU parliament resolution calling for the creation of an EDU.

Neither scenario nor any other official EU document mentions the potential of creating a "European army" in the context of EDU. As will be discussed below, this is because current EU law does not provide a basis for that. It is nevertheless noteworthy that the term EDU is often used interchangeably with "European army" in various contexts[538], implying armed forces under the supranational command of the EU similar to the afore-

---

538  Leyen (n 536); Maïa De la Baume and David Herszenhorn, 'Merkel Joins Macron in Calling for EU Army to Complement NATO' (*Politico*, 14 November 2018) <https://

mentioned EDC. This reflects the larger and traditional political divide between European centralists, who stress the need for further supranational defence integration and the creation of a European army, and scepticists, who intent to safeguard Member State sovereignty in security and defence matters, prefer the transatlantic defence framework and further military integration only on an intergovernmental level.

The terms ESDU or SDU have today been replaced by the term EDU.[539] Yet as mentioned before, neither of these terms as such are conceptionally mentioned in EU primary (or secondary) law. Instead, the relevant CSDP provisions (Arts. 42–46 TEU) in the Lisbon Treaty rather refer to a potential 'common defence' (Art. 42(2) TEU), a peculiar evolutive clause that has yet to be realised. In the following, the political notions of EDU will be linked and clarified in the context of EU law.

### 3.2.1.1.3. EDU and Common Defence (Art. 42(2) TEU)

The principle of conferral (Arts. 4(1), 5(1), (2) TEU) sets out that the EU may only act in any policy area, including security and defence matters, if the Treaties provide a competence for the EU to act in that policy area. Other competences remain with the Member States. For security and defence matters, the respective provisions have become successively more extensive since the Maastricht Treaty (Art. J.4(1) TEU-Maastricht) to the Amsterdam Treaty (Art. 17 TEU-Amsterdam) and finally to Arts. 42–46 TEU-Lisbon (see also part *2.1.1. Historical Evolution of European Defence and Armaments Integration*).

Under the Lisbon Treaty and its Art. 42(1) TEU, the CSDP is an integral part of the intergovernmental CFSP. The aforementioned more ambitious and highly controversial defence integration approaches (the concept of an ESDU in the context of the failed European Constitutional Treaty) have become less ambitious and controversial under the Lisbon Treaty, as the TEU only provides that the CSDP includes 'the progressive framing of a common Union defence policy' that will lead to a 'common defence, when the European Council, acting unanimously, so decides' (Art. 42(2) subpara. 1 TEU). This is the central provision for European defence integration since the Maastricht Treaty, although it has slightly changed since then and has

---

www.politico.eu/article/angela-merkel-emmanuel-macron-eu-army-to-complement -nato/> accessed 22 April 2022.
539  Wolfstädter (n 511).

become more defence-integration-committed. Under the Maastricht Treaty (Art. J.4(1) TEU-Maastricht), the provision set out the 'eventual framing of a common defence policy, which might in time lead to a common defence'. The wording was then changed in the Amsterdam Treaty to the 'progressive framing of a common defence policy, [...] which might lead to a common defence' provision (Art. J.7(1) TEU-Amsterdam) and then to 'progressive framing of a common Union defence policy' which 'will lead to a common defence, when the European Council, acting unanimously, so decides.' (Art. 42(2) subpara. 1 TEU).

The core of European defence integration under the CSDP thus is twofold. First, there is the 'progressive framing of a common Union defence policy' and secondly, the potential Union 'common defence'. The common Union defence policy is the basis for European defence integration and cooperation. It is intergovernmental and a parallel competence of EU and Member States. A common defence by contrast is currently not part of European defence integration and cooperation. It is presented as an optional evolutive clause that can be realised when the European Council so decides unanimously. This reflects the wider sovereignty concerns of the EU Member States in the area of security and defence, which is why participation in the CSDP and cessation of defence competences is always voluntary and requires consent.[540] For now, the EU does not have a competence for common defence (only for a Union defence policy).[541] With regard to creating a potential EDU, it will be decisive whether the Member States activate this far-reaching option. What makes the evolutive clause peculiar is that it can be activated by a simplified treaty revision procedure (Art. 48(6), (7) TEU) through rather simple European Council ratification. It does not require the ordinary treaty revision procedure in accordance with Art. 48(2)–(5) TEU, which by comparison is much more extensive and politically incalculable (see below and also part *3.2.2. Making European Armaments Cooperation reliable?*).

Differentiating between the concepts and contents of the EU's current defence policy and a potential common defence is difficult. The term is intentionally "constructively ambiguous" and not defined in EU primary law. It is the result of a political compromise between the eurocentrists

---

540  Fortunato (n 94) 1175–1186; Mattias Fischer and Daniel Thym, 'Article 42 CSDP: Goals and Objectives; Mutual Defence' in Hermann-Josef Blanke and Stelio Mangiameli (eds), *The Treaty on European Union (TEU) A Commentary* (Springer 2013) 1212–1231.

541  Kielmansegg (n 170) 268–269.

and the eurosceptists in the area of defence integration. Significant divergence of the manner of defence integration has existed since the St Malo summit and is apparent in EU primary law since the Maastricht Treaty. It is rooted in the Member States' respective concerns over duplicating NATO structures and the potentially resulting adverse effects for their defence readiness, certain Member States' neutrality policies (reflected in the so-called "Irish clause" of Art. 42(7) TEU), and traditional concerns over ceding core sovereignty rights in the area of security and defence. This divide characterizes European defence integration to this day.

Since "defence" is not defined in the Treaties, it is subject to ad hoc interpretation in the context of the CSDP.[542] It has been pointed out that the term is thus also capable of acquiring new connotations that reflect the EU's state of defence integration.[543] Furthermore, the Member States as "Masters of the Treaties" are not subject to the jurisdiction of the CJEU in the intergovernmental CSDP (Arts. 24(1) TEU, 275 TFEU), which leaves the possibility open for authentic and dynamic treaty interpretation.[544] Kielmansegg[545] convincingly argues that the term defence policy can be understood as an operative policy configuration for the current CSDP while common defence rather refers to a (more ambiguous) state of defence in the future. They can be distinguished by their different levels of structural and institutional arrangement.[546] In other words, they determine the boundaries of the EU's current competences in the field of defence in contrast to potential future competences. The current CSDP is meant to provide the EU with an operational capacity drawing on civilian and military assets (Art. 42(1) TEU) to fulfil the so-called "Petersberg tasks" (specified in Art. 43(1) TEU) for crises management and limited by its intergovernmental structure and the principles of unanimity (Arts. 31(1), 42(4) TEU), voluntariness (Arts. 31(4), 44 TEU), and recourse (Arts. 42(1), 42(3) TEU), which strictly safeguard national sovereignty.

Under the principle of voluntariness, the Member States are not (and cannot be) obligated to provide the EU with civilian or military capabilities to conduct CSDP tasks. This further extends to otherwise legally binding[547]

---

542 Kielmansegg (n 38) 182.
543 Dyson and Konstadinides (n 91) 60.
544 Kielmansegg (n 55) 80.
545 Kielmansegg (n 170) 270.
546 ibid. 271.
547 Pechstein (n 59) 427.

Council decisions, which are taken in the form of common actions under Art. 25(b) TEU in conjunction with Art. 28(2) TEU), where decisions having military or defence implications are explicitly excluded (Arts. 31(4), 44 TEU).[548] Under the recourse principle, the EU must rely on the Member States' voluntary capability contributions to EU operations. It cannot establish its own military forces. This is intentionally in contrast to supranational configurations like the aforementioned EDC (see part *2.1.1. Historical Evolution of European Defence and Armaments Integration*), meaning the Member States remain exclusively in control over their defence policies, including their armed forces, thereby safeguarding their sovereign interests.[549] This limits the CSDP in its current form to crises management, mutual assistance, and armaments cooperation.

By contrast, a common defence in accordance with Art. 42(2) TEU would need to go beyond these limits, which are based in particular on the principle of voluntariness. This principle is potentially already partially restricted through the TEU's mutual assistance clause (Art. 42(7) TEU), which has only been introduced with the Lisbon Treaty and has been activated by France following the 2015 Paris terrorist attacks. According to the mutual assistance clause, which closely resembles Art. 5 North Atlantic Treaty[550], in case of an armed aggression against a Member State, the other Member States are obligated to provide 'aid and assistance by all means in their power, in accordance with Art. 51 of the United Nations Charter'.

It is however controversial whether this clause entails an obligation to provide military assistance and thus limits the principle of voluntariness. According to Terhechte[551], it is to be regarded as an obligation to provide military assistance due to the reference to Art. 51 UN Charter. Kielmansegg[552] by contrast argues that the clause is flexible regarding the means to provide aid and assistance and thus does not entail an automatic

---

548  Hans-Joachim Cremer, 'Art. 42' in Christian Calliess and Matthias Ruffert (eds), *EUV/AEUV* (6th edn, C.H.Beck 2022) 428–431; Pechstein (n 59) 427.

549  Fortunato (n 94) 1175–1186; Mattias Fischer and Daniel Thym, 'Article 42 CSDP: Goals and Objectives; Mutual Defence' in Hermann-Josef Blanke and Stelio Mangiameli (eds), *The Treaty on European Union (TEU) A Commentary* (Springer 2013) 1212–1231.

550  North Atlantic Treaty (signed 4 April 1949, entered into force 24 August 1949) 610 UNTS 205.

551  Terhechte (n 27) 378.

552  Kielmansegg (n 170) 272–273.

obligation to provide military assistance. On the other hand, Terhechte[553] also argues that the mutual assistance clause cannot be regarded as a legal obligation due to the aforementioned "Irish clause", which safeguards the neutrality policy of certain Member States and is also mentioned in Art. 42(7) TEU, as well as in case law by the German BVerfG in its "Lisbon judgement"[554], which also negates any principal legal obligation to provide military assistance due to national sovereignty.

Consequently, the mutual assistance clause in the TEU only means the partial introduction of a common defence, since it does not fully override the principle of voluntariness and thus does not entail a legal obligation to provide military mutual assistance. Herein lies the difference between the mutual assistance clause and a comprehensive common defence. Activating the common defence provision would mean obligatory military assistance and thus the abolition of the principle of voluntariness through the simplified treaty revision procedure in Art. 42(2) TEU.[555] This has its basis in current CSDP law, as it would further develop the current mutual assistance clause and can also be concluded from the European Treaties negotiations.[556] It is however limited by national constitutional law. The German BVerfG for example has ruled in its aforementioned "Lisbon judgement" that only the German *Bundestag* is competent to make deployment decisions for Germany's armed forces (based on Arts. 23, 24(2) GG). Although it has been pointed out that the German constitutional parliamentary reservation (*'wehrverfassungsrechtlicher Parlamentsvorbehalt'*) regarding the deployment of German armed forces is changeable and thus not immune to European integration.[557]

Besides the principle of voluntariness, the CSDP in its current form is restricted by the recourse principle. It has been debated whether the recourse principle could (like the principle of voluntariness) be abolished via activating the common defence provision in Art. 42(2) TEU. This would open EU law up to the possibility of supranational armed forces (an "EU army"). However, based on the intentional intergovernmental structure of the CSDP with its significant consideration for Member State sovereignty and due to the fact that the creation of supranational armed forces have

---

553  Terhechte (n 27) 378; BVerfG (n 102) at 386.

554  BVerfG (n 102) at 386.

555  Kielmansegg (n 170) 273.

556  Kielmansegg (n 55) 72–73.

557  Kielmansegg (n 170) 292.

not played any role in the EU Treaties negotiations since the failure of the EDC, it can be assumed that by activating the common defence clause, the recourse principle cannot be overridden.[558] Introducing (supranational) EU armed forces similar to the EDC model is therefore not provided under current EU law and could therefore only be achieved by an ordinary treaty revision procedure (Art. 48(2)–(5) TEU) beyond the evolutive clause in Art. 42(2) TEU.[559] Such an ordinary treaty revision procedure is politically highly unlikely, due to the extensive process of participating actors (mentioned in Art. 48(3) TEU) and national ratification requirement (Art. 48(4) TEU), which makes this process highly incalculable.

This is because besides legal limits, there are also continuing, serious political and defence-strategic reservations against the creation of a European army on the Member State level, which is why the Member States have legally opted for an intergovernmentally structured CSDP and are unlikely to change this arrangement via treaty revision.

These reservations are first and foremost deeply rooted in sovereignty concerns when it comes to ceding national powers over security and defence matters (see *part 2.1.1. Historical Evolution of European Defence and Armaments Integration*). The CSDP has therefore been arranged in a manner to allow wide margins of flexibility[560] (however at the cost of reliability, see also part *3.2.1.2. The Future of European Armaments Cooperation and PESCO*). This is why Denmark for example has opted-out of the CSDP[561] (including PESCO[562] and EDA[563]) for thirty years[564] and why Malta participates in the CSDP but not in PESCO. It is also due to the different strategic cultures of the Member States regarding military action, defence spending and the role of the armaments industry. France for example participates in the CSDP and PESCO but would not integrate its armed forces into supranational defence structures, as it wants to retain its global military

---

558   ibid. 274.

559   Fortunato (n 94) 1175–1186.

560   Kielmanssegg (n 174) 145; Aurélien Raccah, 'Le traité de Lisbonne: de nouvelles compétences pour l'Union européene?', in Aurélien Raccah (ed), *Le traité de Lisbonne De nouvelles compétences pour l'Union européene?* (L'Harmattan 2012) 31.

561   Art. 5 of Protocol No. 22 Lisbon Treaty.

562   Denmark has by now joined PESCO, see Council of the EU (n 173).

563   Denmark has by now joined EDA, see EDA (n 260).

564   Following a recent referendum on 1 June 2022, Denmark has decided to participate in all aspects of CSDP, see EEAS (n 173).

ability to act to protect France's geopolitical interests.[565] Instead, France has therefore proposed to strengthen defence cooperation within the EU framework on an intergovernmental basis (which is why it has initiated PESCO with Germany, see part *3.2.1.2. The Future of European Armaments Cooperation and PESCO*), but also outside EU structures (EI2, see part *2.2.1. European Defence and Armaments Integration today*) if it considers such arrangements more effective.

The other EU Member States are generally also sceptical of surrendering national armed forces to supranational control due to sovereignty concerns or due to defence-strategic concerns, particularly the feasibility of supranationally integrating the armed forces of the Member States and the potentially adverse consequences for Europe's and their own defence capabilities if that project is unsuccessful.[566] For the foreseeable future, NATO will remain central for European collective defence.[567] These concerns are paired with traditional fears of duplicating (functioning) NATO structures and thereby undermining existing defence structures. The CSDP has thus been designed to complement but not to replace NATO (in accordance with the principles of no de-linking and no unnecessary duplications). This is also why Art. 42(2) subpara. 2 TEU explicitly confirms that the CSDP is compatible with NATO policies and obligations. In operational practice, this means that the CSDP remains limited to small military operations while large operations and collective self-defence remain with NATO.[568]

For other Member States, like Ireland and Austria, neutrality considerations play an important role. This is why TEU takes the special role of neutral States into account in its "Irish-clause" (also Art. 42(2) para. 2 TEU). These political and defence strategic reservations are the reason why the Member States politically adhere to the intergovernmentally structured CSDP, which safeguards national control over defence (and armaments) policy but is also inhibits significant and costly defence cooperation fragmentation.[569]

---

565  Ronja Kempin, 'Frankreichs Außen- und Sicherheitspolitik unter Präsident Macron' [2021] 4 SWP 1; Levêque (209) 186.

566  Maxwell Zhu, 'Obstacles to Macron's "true European army"' (*Harvard Political Review*, 19 April 2020) <https://harvardpolitics.com/european-security/> accessed 27 October 2022.

567  Terhechte (n 27) 374; dell'Aria (n 515) 193–207.

568  Kielmansegg (n 27).

569  Kielmansegg (n 170) 284.

Legally, the Member States' adverse stance against supranational armed forces is further underlined by national constitutional reservations. The creation of supranational armed forces is irreconcilable with the constitutional law of certain Member States. In particular, the German BVerfG has ruled that it would violate Germany's constitution if Germany would participate in such an amendment of the Lisbon Treaty that would abolish the German constitutional parliamentary reservation regarding the deployment of German armed forces.[570] Although again (see above), it has been pointed out that the German constitutional parliamentary reservation regarding the deployment of German armed forces is changeable and thus not immune to European integration.[571]

The incompatibility with EU law and national constitutional law is likely the reason why the creation of supranational armed forces is not mentioned in any official documents surrounding the EDU concepts, while the long-term possibility of common defence via ever-closer convergence of national strategic cultures and defence policies and European armaments cooperation is prioritized. Although the terms "European army" and EDU are often used interchangeably in political contexts[572], an EDU does not provide for the creation of supranational defence forces similar to the failed EDC project under current EU law (including the evolutive clause in Art. 42(2) TEU) because it has no legal basis. From a legal and political perspective, using a term like "European army" is problematic since it insinuates a wrong (supranational idea) about European defence integration, which is much less ambitious in reality.

A revolutionary defence integration is simply not provided for in the current progression of the CSDP and is instead restricted by the narrow limits of current EU primary law. In the Treaties and the current defence (and armaments) cooperation formats, the Member States have opted for the intergovernmental (and thus fragmented) solution, meaning selective cooperation and integration of their national armed forces and defence industries without making significant supranational commitments. Again, the CFSP is the only policy area in the Lisbon Treaty that is exclusively inter-governmental. Partial supranational funding for defence projects through the EDF is rooted in the Commission's mission creep in the field of defence (see part *3.2.1.3. The European Armaments Policy and its future*). The CSDP

---

570   BVerfG (n 102) at 388.
571   Kielmansegg (n 170) 292.
572   Leyen (n 536); Baume and Herszenhorn (n 538).

in its current form is primarily concerned with closing Europe's capability gap[573], today in particular in the context of achieving strategic autonomy, through enhancement of the Member States' military capabilities and by making them available to the EU. This is why the EU fosters military integration between Member States through different formats like Pooling[574] & Sharing[575], PESCO, CARD and the EDF. This takes place within the concept of EDU that has ambitious connotations in public discourse but is less ambitious in reality. This is also why the above-mentioned Reflection Paper scenarios remain within the narrow limits of current EU primary law and are particularly concerned with capability development and armaments cooperation. Even the farthest-reaching scenario c only goes so far as setting out the activation of Art. 42(2) TEU's common defence clause without mentioning treaty revision.

### 3.2.1.1.4. EDU and the Central Role of Armaments Cooperation

From this perspective, it appears relevant to further analyse the role of armaments cooperation within EDU and the potential activation of the common defence evolutive clause.

Initiating the European frameworks for increased armaments cooperation has been a tedious process due to the sensitivity of security and defence matters. European defence planning and military integration remain a fragmented puzzle of several individual (mainly intergovernmental) projects (some continue to exist outside EU structures, such as OCCAR or EI2, see part *2.2.1. European Defence and Armaments Integration today*), although with PESCO, several defence (including armaments) projects are now developed within a common framework. Furthermore, the EDF now provides supranational funding for these projects (see part *3.2.1.3. The European Armaments Policy and its future*), which is seen as a first step towards EDU and common defence.[576] However, whether these initiatives,

---

573  Kielmansegg (n 55) 80–81.
574  Certain capabilities or logistical components are pooled by several Member States for common usage.
575  Certain capabilities or logistical components are provided by certain Member States and made available to the others.
576  Bundesministerium der Verteidigung (n 191); EDA (n 191); European Commission (n 191); Luigi Lonardo, 'Integration in European Defence: Some Legal Considerations' [2017] 2(3) European Papers 887, 887.

which currently primarily facilitate armaments cooperation, will ultimately amount to EDU or "common defence" remains questionable. In PESCO for example, not all Member States even participate. Further European defence integration remains dependent on further convergence of national strategic cultures.[577]

These initiatives however underline the relevance of armaments cooperation in current EU defence integration efforts, including EDU. The TEU places a particular focus on strengthening the operative capabilities of the EU, including through armaments cooperation. This has been a central objective of European defence integration ever since the 1998 British-Franco summit at St Malo. Art. 42(3) subpara. 2 TEU obliges the MS to progressively improve their military capabilities, including through armaments cooperation. EDA oversees this process as per Art. 42(3) subpara. 2 TEU (for EDA's tasks see also part *3.2.1.2. The European Armaments Policy and its future*),[578] although it remains limited to a primarily coordinating role to facilitate armaments cooperation, as Art. 346(1)(b) TFEU (which will be discussed at length in the following parts) prevents any supranational harmonisation against the interests of the Member States and thus also limits further defence integration in the context of EDU.

Again, it is today generally agreed that the creation of an EDU and further defence integration must start with the integration of the Member States' defence industries and the EDEM.[579] The need for increased armaments cooperation in the context of EDU is born out of the previously discussed European capability gaps (see parts *2.1.1. Historical Evolution of European Defence and Armaments Integration* and *2.2.1. European Defence and Armaments Integration today*) which present an ongoing obstacle to European strategic autonomy and the effective execution of CSDP tasks.

The centrality of European armaments integration to further European defence integration and the EDU is why the initiation of PESCO (see part *3.2.1.1. The Common Security and Defence Policy and its future*) and the creation of the EDF (see part *3.2.1.2. The European Armaments Policy and its future*) in 2017 were heralded as the starting point of the EDU

---

577  Blockmans and Faleg (n 176) 14; Kielmansegg (n 170) 284.
578  Terhechte (n 27) 374.
579  Bundesministerium der Verteidigung (n 191); EDA (n 191); European Commission (n 191).

initiation.[580] Interestingly, while the term EDU (or its variations, see above) is mentioned by politicians and EU documents surrounding the creation of PESCO and the EDF, it is not mentioned in the PESCO[581] or EDF[582] decisions. This likely has legal reasons.

As mentioned above, PESCO has its roots in the ESDU concepts surrounding the preparation of the failed European Constitutional Treaty, which was intended to further European defence integration by closer and more structured cooperation of those Member States willing to make further substantial military commitments. The proposals went beyond the limits of the current CSDP that was then arranged in the Lisbon Treaty. They included developing the EU into a system of collective defence by forming a mutual defence pact between the Member States joining the ESDU. Furthermore, it was envisaged that the Member States would systematically harmonize their security and defence policies, including enhanced armaments cooperation and capability development by harmonising armaments and procurement policies. Due to the failure of the European Constitutional Treaty, these plans were never realised. However, partially, they have found their way into the Lisbon Treaty.[583]

While the idea to create a system of collective defence is today expressed in the aforementioned mutual assistance clause of Art. 42(7) TEU and could be further developed when the common defence provision of Art. 42(2) TEU is activated, enhanced armaments cooperation now takes place within PESCO (Arts. 42(6), 46 and Protocol No. 10 TEU). Legally, mutual assistance, common defence and enhanced armaments cooperation are today separated in different TEU provisions. Potentially, this reflects how armaments cooperation is thus excluded from common defence.

The political context however suggests a strong link between armaments integration and EDU (see all three Reflection Paper scenarios mentioned above), which in turn is legally strongly linked to common defence[584]. Through the initiation of PESCO, it appears that the enhanced armaments cooperation aspect of the original ESDU common defence conception has now been realised. The potential future activation of the common defence evolutive clause in Art. 42(2) TEU would therefore have no direct influence

---

580  Bundesministerium der Verteidigung (n 191); EDA (n 191); European Commission (n 191).
581  (n 168).
582  Regulation (EU) 2021/697 (n 186); Regulation (EU) 2018/1092 (n 186).
583  Kielmansegg (n 170) 291 Kielmanssegg (n 174) 146; Howorth (n 532) 6.
584  Lonardo (n 576) 887.

on the structure of current European armaments cooperation, since this part of EDU has already been introduced. Instead, the main aspect of introducing common defence thus remains the abolishment of the principle of voluntariness when it comes to mutual defence.

When it comes to the EDF, the lack of reference to EDU could be legally based on the fact that the Commission's competence to be active in the field of defence is contentious. The concept of EDU is strongly linked to the CSDP, as can be derived from the preparatory works surrounding the failed European Constitutional Treaty. In this area, the Commission has no competence. This is why its actions in the field of defence are based on its Internal Market competences (Arts. 173, 182(4), 183, 188(2) TFEU), which is legally disputed.[585] This is also why they only extend to supporting the European defence industry and introduce only little supranational harmonisation in the defence market, since Art. 346(1)(b) TFEU provides a strong national security exception for Member States to protect their domestic defence industries from supranational harmonisation.[586] The role of the Commission in defence and armaments will be further discussed in part *3.2.1.3. The European Armaments Policy and its future.*

The term EDU as a political concept thus refers to the advancement of the current (intergovernmentally arranged) CSDP through closer European cooperation in security and defence matters on the basis of the TEU[587], even including a potential European "common defence" in line with Art. 42(2) TEU[588]. It does however not entail the creation of a European army, although this is sometimes insinuated.

Armaments integration by contrast plays a central role and is seen as a first step towards EDU.[589] Most noteworthy in this context is PESCO, which reflects the armaments aspect of EDU and has been activated in 2017. Since European defence and armaments cooperation will nevertheless remain intergovernmental within EDU (although partial supranational support for the EDTIB is possible, see EDF), increasing efficiency and reliability of European armaments cooperation has its limits due to a lack of structural change.

---

585  Terhechte (n 27) 373.
586  Kingreen and Wegener (n 31) 2619; Dittert (n 31) 1995; Luc Weitzel, 'Article 296 CE' in Isabelle Pingel (ed), *Commentaire Article par Article des Traités UE et CU* (2nd edn, Helbing Lichtenhahn 2010) 1822–1826.
587  Wolfstädter (n 511).
588  Lonardo (n 576) 887.
589  ibid.

The centrality of armaments cooperation for EDU also underlines the need for convergence of armaments export policies in Europe. As discussed above, an EDU (meaning closer European security and defence cooperation on the basis of the Commission's Reflection Paper) and especially a potential ultimate "common defence" are inconceivable without further armaments cooperation to increase interoperability of shared defence system through standardisation and reduce costs for R&D to make defence capabilities more effective (see also part *2.2.1. European Defence and Armaments Integration today*). In Commission president von der Leyen's aforementioned 2021 speech[590] on the state of the Union, where she stressed the need to work towards an EDU, she therefore also explicitly addressed the issue of armaments cooperation. This is why she mentioned in particular the need to improve interoperability, reduce dependencies on other countries, and to find new ways for synergies, for example by waiving value added taxes when buying defence equipment that was developed and produced in the EU.

Closer European armaments cooperation in turn is inconceivable without further convergence of European armaments export policies. On that basis, there are several options for legal development.

Further harmonisation on the EU level, could potentially be achieved on the intergovernmental or even on the supranational level, especially if European armaments cooperation is increasingly conducted within EU structures (PESCO and EDF being the most noteworthy) in the context of EDU. To some extent, such harmonisation partially already exists in the form of the EU's dual-use regulation[591] or the EU's CP[592] on armaments exports, which will be further discussed in part *3.2.1.4. Towards a Comprehensive European Arms Export Regime?*.

Although, this topic is politically highly controversial. The EDF Regulation[593] makes it clear that its funding shall not have any influence on the Member States' export decisions over those armaments that were developed with EDF funding (see Arts. 20(9), 23(3) EDF Regulation). This was the result of rigid opposition by the Member States (France in particular) against any EU authority over armaments exports.[594]

---

590 Leyen (n 536).
591 (n 253).
592 (n 61).
593 Regulation (EU) 2021/697 (n 186).
594 Besch (n 190).

And generally, it is also relevant to note that all harmonisation efforts can potentially be undermined if Member States invoke Art. 346(1)(b) TFEU. As will be shown in the following parts (see especially part *3.2.2. Making European Armaments Cooperation reliable?*), further enhancing European defence integration through supranational measures would require amending or abolishing this provision. However, this in turn would require an ordinary treaty revision procedure in accordance with Art. 48(2)–(5) TEU, which is politically not feasible due to the continuing diverging strategic cultures of the Member States and their sovereignty concerns.

Alternatively (and this will be discussed more in parts *3.3. Multilateral European Armaments Cooperation – unreliable but effective?* and *3.3.3. A Future for Multilateral European Armaments Cooperation?*), further armaments export convergence could also be found on an intergovernmental level outside EU structures, despite EDU. This is more in line with scenario c of the above-mentioned EU Reflection Paper. In that regard, the NFGAAE (see part *3.1.5. Mistakes were remade? – the New Franco-German Agreement on Armaments Exports*) could potentially provide a blueprint for such future multilateral convergence outside EU structures to enable more reliable armaments cooperation, although its own unreliability also demonstrates the potential limits and risks of such approaches. Furthermore, such approaches would also lead to even more fragmentation in European defence cooperation, making European defence capability development less efficient.


### 3.2.1.1.5. Assessment and Outlook – many open questions

It remains to be seen how much of the plans for an EDU (including closer armaments cooperation) will be implemented or whether they will remain largely symbolical. Within the EU, the Commission's plans are relatively uncontroversial and supported by France and Germany, as these proposals are in line with both States' plans for deeper European defence integration, but also respect for national sovereignty. Moreover, after the 2022 Russian invasion in Ukraine, the realisation of EDU has become even more pressing and a political priority. Further defence integration has already been announced[595], in particular with regard to strategic autonomy, capability development and armaments cooperation.[596]

However, the political rhetoric surrounding the initiation of the EDF, CARD, and PESCO has raised expectations that the EU may not be able to meet due to political and legal restrictions. The Commission has gone as far as the Treaties allow it to go in defence matters through the creation of the EDF and the introduction of its Defence Package to strengthen the CSDP and the EDTIB (this will be discussed in more detail in part *3.2.1.3. The European Armaments Policy and its future*), some authors[597] have even pointed out that the Commission has overstepped its competences.

On the more general level, the Treaties do not provide for any far-reaching commitments unless the evolutive clause in Art. 42(2) TEU is activated. And even then, this does not provide for additional legal armaments integration momentum, since PESCO has already been activated and Art. 346(1)(b) TFEU prevents further supranational defence-related harmonisation. This is concerning against the backdrop of continuing defence capability gaps in Europe and fragmentations in the EDEM and the EDTIB. From a defence-strategic and politico-economic perspective, increased armaments cooperation is crucial.[598]

Also, misconceptions about the legal nature and enforceability of PESCO's alleged binding commitments and its lack of coherence and inclusivity (for example the exclusion of Poland to participate in the MGCS project, see part *3.2.1.2. The Future of European Armaments Cooperation and PESCO*) further the problem of overestimating the potential of the current cooperation frameworks.[599] PESCO remains on intergovernmental framework for armaments cooperation restricted by the CSDP's underlying principle of voluntariness. Going beyond the limits of the CSDP in its current form would require an ordinary treaty revision in accordance with Art. 48(2)–(5) TEU, since only the common defence provision in Art. 42(2) TEU features a simplified treaty revision option. An ordinary treaty revi-

---

595  EEAS (n 75); the Strategic Compass was endorsed by the European Council on 25 March 2022, see European Council (n 262); Scholz (n 1).

596  European Council (n 265).

597  Terhechte (n 27) 380.

598  Anh Nguyen, 'Macron's Call for a European Army: Still Echoing or Forgotten?' (*European Law Blog*, 22 June 2020) <https://europeanlawblog.eu/2020/06/22/ma crons-call-for-a-european-army-still-echoing-or-forgotten/> accessed 3 December 2021.

599  Blockmans (n 243) 1785.

sion (especially in the area of defence) is politically not feasible due to the principle of unanimity and Member State sovereignty concerns.

Considering the different Reflection Paper scenarios and their different levels of armaments integration, it remains to be seen whether and if so how the fragmented European armaments initiatives and frameworks will be comprehensively integrated into the concept of EDU. EDU has been initiated by closer armaments integration via PESCO, the EDF and CARD, thus European armaments cooperation increasingly takes place within common frameworks. However, trans-European armaments cooperation continues to persist outside these structures (such as the current Franco-German armaments collaboration) and it will be difficult to integrate the different formats into EU structures and thus overcome Europe's costly armaments fragmentation.

Due to the fragmentation in European armaments cooperation and the intergovernmental arrangements, which prevent deeper and more binding commitments by the Member States in this area, it also remains questionable whether European armaments cooperation is thus more reliable and efficient (in terms of consistently realising joint armaments projects) than bi- or multilateral cooperation between the Member States outside EU structures. Considering the problematic unreliability issues of the current Franco-German armaments cooperation, this question needs to be clarified. This follows now.

### 3.2.1.2. The Future of European Armaments Cooperation and PESCO

The need for closer, common European armaments cooperation because of economic and defence-strategic imperatives has been discussed in parts *2.2.1. European Defence and Armaments Integration today* and *3.2.1.1. Towards a European Defence Union and potential consequences for European Armaments Cooperation.* In this part, the challenges and shortcomings of European armaments cooperation will be discussed, in particular with regard to EDA and PESCO, which form the main frameworks in this area.

Prior to that, it is necessary to repeat again that European armaments cooperation today continues to take place within and outside the framework of the EU. This part will only analyse armaments cooperation within EU structures. Trans-European armaments cooperation, which takes place outside such structures, will be discussed separately in part *3.3. Multilateral European Armaments Cooperation – unreliable but effective?*. Both forms of cooperation however have in common that they are both characterised by their intergovernmental structures, which at the same time is the main challenge for the cooperations' overall goal: reliable European defence capability development.

### 3.2.1.2.1. European Capability Development – ECAP and EDA (Arts. 42(3), 45 TEU)

The European Capabilities and Armaments Policy (ECAP) is a central part of the CSDP. Since the St Malo summit, it has been a central objective to enhance the deficient defence capabilities of the Member States.[600] Under Art. 42(3) subpara. 2 TEU, the Member States have since commited to progressively improve their military capabilities. Although it has been pointed out that this is rather a political than a legal objective.[601] Moreover, as the CJEU has no jurisdiction in CSDP matters (Art. 24(1) subpara. 2 TEU), this would not be enforceable anyway.

A key aspect of achieving the objective of enhancing the Member States' deficient capabilities is by promoting joint capabilty development (including via armaments collaboration) and cooperation in defence planning between the Member States. Today, this is mainly the task of the so-called European Defence Agency, which forms the common institutional dimension of the ECAP and acts primarily as an armaments cooperation agency. EDA provides the EU with an active role in the area of capability development.[602] Under the same provision (Art. 42(3) subpara. 2 TEU), EDA is tasked to identify operational requirements of the CSDP, contribute to the strenghtening of the EDTIB, participate in defining an ECAP, and assist the Council in evaluating the improvement of Member State military capabilities.

Furthermore, under Art. 45(1)(a)-(c) TEU, EDA is tasked to contribute to identifying the Member States' military capability objectives and evaluating observance of the capability commitments given by the Member States, promote harmonisation of operational needs and adoption of effective, compatible procurement methods, and propose multilateral projects to fulfil the objectives in terms of military capabilities, ensure coordination of

---

600 Sebastian Graf von Kielmansegg, *Die Verteidigungspolitik der Europäischen Union* (Boorberg 2005) 93; Kielmansegg (n 170) 286.
601 Fortunato (n 94) 1220.
602 Kielmansegg (n 170) 278.

the programmes implemented by the Member States and management of specific cooperation programmes. In this regard, the functions and tasks of EDA are intended to assist Member State defence capability development in general and are not only limited to CSDP tasks.[603]

EDA's role within the CSDP is thus to support the Member States in defence planning and capability development, stimulating and coordinating their joint capability development (which includes European armaments cooperation), and strengthening the EDTIB and the EDEM. While EDA has legal personality (Art. 6 EDA Statute[604]), its policy-making powers are limited. EDA is not intended to replace but rather complement the Member States' defence procurement agencies.[605] This mere supporting role follows from the CSDP's intergovernmental arrangement, the limited role of supranational EU institutions, and the aforementioned armaments exception in Art. 346(1)(b) TFEU. Together with the principle of voluntariness regarding participation in EDA (Art. 45(2) TEU), the institutional design of EDA again reflects the larger Member State sovereignty concerns over ceding national defence competences to the supranational level.[606]

As part of that CSDP, EDA is also arranged in an intergovernmental[607] manner. In this regard, EDA continues the intergovernmental tradition of armaments cooperation in Europe,[608] previous to EDA conducted in particular by WEAG and WEAO (see *part 2.1.1. Historical Evolution of European Defence and Armament Integration*).[609] This means that the Member States ultimately remain in control over European capability development while the roles of the European Commission, the European Parliament and the CJEU are intentionally marginalised. Any resemblance to supranational decision-making in armament procurement, similar to the failed EDC (see *part 2.1.1. Historical Evolution of European Defence and Armament Integration*), is thus avoided by the Member States.

However, the TEU establishes a link for cooperation between EDA and the Commission (Art. 45(2) TEU). Under Art. 24 EDA Statute, the Com-

---

603    Trybus (n 45) 186–187.
604    Council Decision 2015/1835 (n 90).
605    Butler (n 48).
606    Hoeffler (n 46) 52.
607    According to Art. 45(1) TEU, it is subject to the authority of the Council and according to Art. 8(1) Council Decision 2015/1835 (n 90), each Member State is equally represented in EDA's steering board (EDA's decision-making body).
608    Trybus (n 45) 221–222.
609    Dyson and Konstadinides (n 91) 97.

mission is a member of EDA's Steering Board (without voting rights). This is relevant as the Commission has become increasingly involved in promoting European capability development and the EDTIB and started to harmonize the EDEM (see part *3.2.1.3. The European Armaments Policy and its future*). In this area, both institutions are active as both their respective original subject matters – defence procurement and Internal Market – are overlapping. Consequently, there is also an overlap between the intergovernmental and the supranational parts of EU law.

To this day, this competence delimitation question remains unclear. Under Arts. 45(1) TEU, 5 EDA Statute, EDA's scope of action vis-à-vis capability development is relatively precisely defined. However, the extent to which EDA should exert its competences in EDEM matters which is at the same time increasingly regulated by the Commission under Internal Market law (see part *3.2.1.3. The European Armaments Policy and its future*) remains controversial. To partially mitigate this delimitation issue, the Council has obligated EDA to respect other competences of the EU and those of its institutions when fulfilling its functions and tasks (Art. 5(1) EDA Statute).[610] Simplified, it appears today that while the Commission today focuses on defence funding and the necessary regulatory framework for defence procurement, EDA strengthens EDTIB and EDEM via promoting European standards in armaments equipment.[611]

Lastly, via EDA's statute[612] (Preamble para. 7), EDA is today also linked to the LoI Group and OCCAR (see part *3.3.1. OCCAR and LoI – unreliable and ineffective?*) and cooperates with them in various programmes and projects.

### 3.2.1.2.2. EDA's Shortcomings – lack of reliable capability development

EDA's intergovernmental nature has led to several shortcomings in European armaments cooperation.

Since EDA only plays a supporting role in armaments cooperation, its policy-making power is dependent on the Member States.[613] Arts. 42(3) subpara. 2 TEU and 2(2) EDA Statute make it clear that EDA shall 'partic-

---

610    Terpan (n 261) 1262–1263.
611    Terhechte (n 259) 388; Dyson and Konstadinides (n 91) 97–103.
612    (n 90).
613    Dyson and Konstadinides (n 91) 100–102.

ipate' in defining an ECAP, not formulate or develop it. Due to the inter-governmental structure of the CSDP and the armament exception, EDA's harmonisation and convergence efforts have remained limited to soft law measures in the form of several CoCs. In the area of defence procurement, EDA has since 2005 published a CoC on Defence Procurement[614], a CoC on Offsets[615], and a Code of Best Practices in the Supply Chain[616]. Due to their soft law nature, these CoCs were voluntary, not legally binding and relied on Member State cooperation in good faith.[617]

This system with its lack of binding and enforceable rules has proved insufficient when it comes to strengthening coherence and ensuring reliable capability development in the EU.[618] The Codes had only insufficient effects.[619] It has become apparent that simply relying on peer pressure to achieve defence procurement convergence has not significantly contributed to consolidating EDTIB and EDEM. Moreover, under Art. 24(1) subpara. 2 TEU, the CJEU has no jurisdiction in CFSP matters. This is why EDA rules are difficult to enforce and EDA suffers from a rule of law deficit.[620]

By contrast, the Commission with its supranational harmonisation efforts has been more effective (see part *3.2.1.3. The European Armament Policy and its future*). This is mostly because the Commission can rely on the CJEU to enforce its Internal Market rules. The additional and partially contrasting approach by EDA with regard to EDEM harmonisation on the other hand entails the risk of further legal fragmentation in EU defence procurement and has the potential of undermining the Commission's efforts.[621]

As shown above, the EU's armaments policy is clearly limited by the national boundaries expressed in EU primary law. Instead of an actual common approach to the development of European defence capabilities, the effects are 27 different national armament policies, which are then to some degree coordinated and evaluated under the common roof of EDA. Although a common institution like EDA, which leaves room for

---

614  EDA, The Code of Conduct on Defence Procurement of the EU Member States participating in the European Defence Agency (n 93).
615  EDA, 'Bringing Transparency into the European Defence Equipment Market: Code of Conduct on Offsets comes into force' (n 93).
616  EDA, The Code of Best Practice in the Supply Chain (n 93); EDA, 'REACH' (n 93).
617  Trybus (n 45) 191–220.
618  ibid. 221–222.
619  Martin Trybus, *Buying Defence and Security in Europe* (CUP 2014).
620  ibid. 190.
621  ibid. 221–222.

at least some convergence, is better than no armament coordination institution, ample room for fragmentation and incoherence between the Member States' armament policies remains.

More coherent coordination in Member State defence planning and joint capability development is conducted via Capability Development Plans (CDP) and CARD. Since 2008, in cooperation with the Member States, the EU Military Committee (EUMC), and the European Union Military Staff (EUMS), EDA produces CDPs to analyse Member States' defence budgets and procurement plans to identify shortfalls and recommend priorities and opportunities for collaboration (Art. 5(3)(a)(ii) EDA Statute). The CDP is since 2017 reinforced by CARD, which is designed to oversee Member State implementation of the priorities identified in the CDPs. The necessary information for EDA to assess the Member States' defence capabilities and implementation via CARD is provided by the Member States on a voluntary basis.[622] The CDP is also the reference point for PESCO and EDF.[623] PESCO is also monitored by CARD.

Generally, the CSDP is characterised by its various flexibility modes.[624] EDA as a specific flexibility tool to enable European capability development in this regard is characterised by a particular biplane mode of flexibility. First, membership in EDA is voluntary (Arts. 45(2) TEU, 1(3) EDA Statute). Secondly, EDA also functions as an umbrella for individual programmes and projects of the Member States, where EDA members are then free to choose whether they participate in these various programmes and projects managed by EDA on behalf and at the discretion of the Member States (Recital 17, Arts. 19(1), 20(4) EDA Statute).[625]

Consequently, EDA features a great variability of different groups of Member States participating in various programmes and ad hoc projects.[626] While it is to a degree adequate in terms of overall European capability development that there is joint capability development within EU structures at all, this lack of coherence and reliability contrasts an actual common European approach to capability development and entails the risk of economic and defence-strategic inefficiencies. This resembles the disadvantages

---

622 Council (n 193).
623 EDA, 'Capability Development Plan' (*EDA*, 2008) <https://eda.europa.eu/what-w e-do/all-activities/activities-search/capability-development-plan> accessed 19 December 2022.
624 Kielmanssegg (n 174) 139.
625 Terpan (n 261) 1269.
626 Kielmanssegg (n 174) 156.

of ad hoc collaborations outside EU structures mentioned in previous parts (see parts *2. The Context: Franco-German Armaments Collaboration and European Armaments Cooperation, 3.1. Unreliabilities of Franco-German Armaments Collaboration in the Bilateral Framework*, and also *3.3.1. OC-CAR and LoI – unreliable and ineffective?*), which a common approach to European capability development was meant to overcome.

While some argue that EDA has played a significant part in facilitating effective cooperation in European capability development, for example with regard to Pooling & Sharing which comprises a strong feature of EDA's efforts to improve European defence capabilities,[627] others are more critical. Especially when it comes to stimulating armaments cooperation, the most urgent aspect of capability development, 'EDA has proved largely ineffective'[628].

Large-scale collaborative projects, such as the developments of the *A400M* transport aircraft (for which OCCAR is responsible) or FCAS and MGCS (which take place within the current Franco-German armaments collaboration) are organized outside EDA structures (and PESCO for that fact). In these extra-EU programmes, Member States are able to form ad hoc partnerships based on their purely national defence-strategic and industrial interests. The intended role of EDA as a common framework and the main armaments agency in Europe has consequently been marginalized.[629] The future success of EDA and PESCO in terms of furthering coherence and efficiencies in European defence cooperation will also rely on the question whether such large-scale armaments projects will be integrated (or integrable) in these frameworks. Otherwise, crucial European capability development will continue to take place outside EU structures to a large degree, entailing all disadvantages regarding incoherence and unreliability discussed in previous parts.

From a legal perspective, these projects could well be conducted under the umbrella of EDA. According to Arts. 45(1)(c) TEU and 5(3)(c) EDA Statute, EDA is competent to coordinate multilateral armaments projects on behalf of the Member States. This only requires the necessary political will by the Member States for further armaments integration.

---

627 Dyson and Konstadinides (n 91) 100.
628 Biermann and Weiss (n 211) 233.
629 ibid.

### 3.2.1.2.3. PESCO (Art. 46 TEU) – a framework for more reliable capability development?

Since 2017, another significant framework for European armaments cooperation has emerged in the form of PESCO.

As stated throughout this thesis, closer European defence cooperation is inconceivable without closer armaments cooperation. Besides economic considerations in times of low[630] defence budgets and inefficient spending, especially defence-strategic considerations (ensuring interoperability between the Member States' armed forces) play the main role.[631]

Various formats for joint efforts by interested European States to close the capability gaps have existed outside the EU since World War II (see part *2.1.1. Historical Evolution of European Defence and Armament Integration*), either on ad hoc bases or within NATO, WEU or OCCAR structures. Via EDA, these efforts had been partially transferred into the framework of the EU since 2004, although on a rather lose and flexible basis (see above). Via PESCO, these efforts have now been given a more "permanent", i.e. systematic and long-term structure.

PESCO is today the common platform for European cooperation on enhancing joint military capabilities, in particular with regard to increasing and coordinating defence spending, cooperating in armaments projects, and pooling and sharing of military capabilities and making them available to the EU in a more binding fashion. It is intended to foster more coherence, continuity, coordination, and collaboration in the area of common security and defence and thus has been long desired to make necessary resources available to the CSDP and close Europe's capability gap. To achieve this objective, PESCO has been designed in an 'inclusive and ambitious'[632] fashion. There are currently 60 PESCO projects being developed.[633] Furthermore, PESCO projects are eligible for additional EDF funding (Art. 13(3)(a) EDF Regulation[634]).

---

630 At least before Russia's 2022 invasion of Ukraine, see European Commission (n 43).
631 Sebastian Graf von Kielmansegg, 'Article 46. [Permanent Structured Cooperation]' in Hermann-Josef Blanke and Stelio Mangiameli (eds), *The Treaty on European Union (TEU) A Commentary* (Springer 2013) 1306.
632 Deutsch-Französischer Ministerrat (n 241).
633 EU, 'Permanent Structured Cooperation (PESCO)' (*EU*, 2022) <https://www.pesco.europa.eu/> accessed 21 December 2022.
634 Regulation (EU) 2021/697 (n 186).

PESCO is a rare genuine novelty[635] in the Lisbon Treaty and has only been activated in 2017[636] following an initiative[637] by the Franco-German "couple" (see part *2.2.1. European Defence and Armament Integration today*). It is legally based on Arts. 42(6), 46 and Protocol No. 10 TEU and sets out specific and ambitious legal obligations for those Member States willing to participate to enhance their defence capabilities within the EU framework. This "avantgarde mentality" is now shared by almost all Member States. Only[638] Malta does not participate.

In this regard, PESCO represents a special form of enhanced cooperation within the Lisbon Treaty's CSDP framework[639] and thus a new and additional mechanism of flexibility and differentiated integration for defence cooperation and capability development.

Enhanced cooperation as the standard mechanism of flexibility in EU law[640] used to be excluded from the CFSP if it related to military and defence matters (Art. 27(b) TEU-Nice). This was due to the UK's concerns that continentally and EU focused Member States would destabilise the transatlantic relationship (NATO structures).[641] Instead, closer cooperation in the field of defence was conducted outside EU structures. Art. J.7 TEU-Amsterdam had earlier already opened up this possibility for closer cooperation in the field covered by the defence component of the CFSP between two or more interested Member States, as long as it did not run counter to or impede the CFSP. Several multilateral defence cooperation frameworks like the Dutch-German Corps, the Euro Corps or OCCAR are examples for such multilateral cooperation outside the framework of the EU.[642]

The Lisbon Treaty finally made enhanced cooperation also available to the CFSP (including the CSDP) under the same conditions as for any other

---

635 Kielmansegg (n 631) 1279.
636 (n 168).
637 Deutsch-Französischer Ministerrat (n 249).
638 Denmark joined PESCO in 2023, see Council of the EU (n 173).
639 Jörg Philipp Terhechte, 'EUV Art. 46 [Ständige Strukturierte Zusammenarbeit]' in Ulrich Becker et al., *EU-Kommentar* (4th edn, Nomos 2019) 389–391; Fiott (n 187) 18.
640 Kielmanssegg (n 174) 139.
641 Daniel Thym, *Ungleichzeitigkeit und europäisches Verfassungsrecht* (Nomos 2004) 159; Sebastian Graf von Kielmansegg, 'Permanent Structured Cooperation: A New Mechanism of Flexibility' in Hermann-Josef Blanke and Stelio Mangiameli (eds), *The European Union after Lisbon* (Springer 2011) 553.
642 Trybus (n 34) 85.

policy field.[643] However, for European capability development, it further introduced a more special and detailed form for cooperation: PESCO. As a result of the CFSP's intergovernmental character[644] and the need for flexibility in defence policy[645], PESCO is specifically designed to close Europe's capability gap within the Union's framework. This has been a central objective of the CSDP since St Malo[646] and has become even more crucial due to the EU's increasingly challenging geopolitical environment (see part *2.2.1. European Defence and Armament Integration today*). For this reason, Recitals 6, 7, and 8 of Protocol No. 10 TEU take the need of the international community into account.

PESCO's potential for European capability development makes it a central element of the CSDP today.[647] Again, closing Europe's capability gap is only possible through Member State defence cooperation, by more efficiently merging resources and coordinating defence planning and procurement. For the longest time, such cooperation (if at all) was dealt with in flexible multilateral arrangements outside the framework of the EU, for example within NATO, WEU, OCCAR, or LoI.[648] By opening enhanced cooperation to the field of defence policy and by establishing the additional mechanism of PESCO via the Lisbon Treaty, defence cooperation and capability development can now be fully transferred to and consolidated within the common framework of the EU.[649] Furthermore, PESCO has now given the European efforts to close the capability gaps a common, 'permanent' (i.e. systematic and long-term) framework of its own, with binding commitments for all participants covering a wide area of defence capability development.[650] In this regard, it goes a lot further than most of the other CSDP-related manifestations of flexibility (EDA, participation in CSDP missions) and thus partially restricts the CSDP's generally underlying principle of voluntariness.

While Member State participation in PESCO is voluntary and thus leaves national sovereignty untouched, once participating, its obligations

---

643  Arts. 20 TEU, 326–334 TFEU.
644  Kielmanssegg (n 174) 140.
645  Kielmansegg (n 641) 555.
646  Kielmansegg (n 600) 93.
647  Kielmansegg (n 631) 1280.
648  ibid. 1291.
649  ibid. 1280.
650  ibid. 1291.

are binding under EU primary law.[651] In this regard, PESCO is the most far-reaching element of the current CSDP.

Nevertheless, also PESCO grants wide margins of flexibility and is thus a pragmatic instrument.[652] Participation in specific PESCO projects is usually also on a voluntary basis. Arts. 1(a), 2(e) Protocol No. 10 TEU provide for such participation 'where appropriate', taking the respective defence-strategic needs and financial resources of the participating Member States into account.[653] In this regard, PESCO serves rather as an umbrella framework for subsidiary capability projects (see also Art. 4(1) subpara. 2 PESCO Decision).

One of PESCO's major functions is consequently being an intermediary forum to bring together potential partners for specific projects.[654] This modular approach takes the great variability of the circle of participating Member States with their different levels of military capabilities, defence-industrial structures, and overall willingness to undertake greater defence integration efforts into account. It has therefore been thought that more substantial and ambitious progress in defence cooperation and integration within the EU framework is easier to achieve through a flexible and voluntary model like PESCO.[655]

The wide margins of flexibility regarding participation however also come at the disadvantage of questionable coherence, although certainly to a lesser degree compared to other CSDP arrangements. Although now almost all Member States participate in PESCO, the variability of participation in PESCO projects partially resembles multilateral cooperation formats outside the EU framework.

Nevertheless, the number of participants in PESCO projects is generally higher than in comparable extra-EU cooperation arrangements, allowing for more coherence through a more common approach, and PESCO projects are inclusive and thus open to all participating Member States. This in turn however entails the risk that collaborative projects thus become more complex and overly challenging with a higher number of partners and consequently more diverse interests and requirements. This is

---

651  As all protocols annexed to the Treaties, Protocol No. 10 also forms part of primary EU law (Art. 51 TEU).
652  Fiott (n 187) 18.
653  Kielmansegg (n 631) 1309–1310.
654  ibid. 1291.
655  Kielmanssegg (n 174) 141; Kielmansegg (n 641)556.

why exclusive, ambitious projects like FCAS and MGCS were intentionally not made PESCO projects (see part *2.2.2. Franco-German Armament Cooperation today*). In this regard, the contradiction between an 'inclusive and ambitious'[656] PESCO becomes apparent.

Nevertheless, PESCO represents the most far-reaching format for defence cooperation (in particular capability development, including armament collaboration) under the current CSDP. In this regard however, it is also characterised by its intergovernmental structure, which in turn entails known shortcomings.

The European Commission is not mentioned in any of the PESCO provisions (Arts 42(6), 46, Protocol No. 10 TEU, PESCO Decision[657]). It has however a direct link to PESCO via the vice president of the Commission (Art. 18(4) TEU), who is simultaneously the High Representative for CFSP and in this role assesses Member State PESCO contributions (see Annex III Nos. 1., 2.1., 4. PESCO Decision).

Furthermore, the Commission administers the EDF and thus supports PESCO projects but has no say in defining technical-operative objectives. This competence is left to the Council[658] (Arts. 46(6) TEU, 4, 5, 6 PESCO Decision), which maintains coherence and ambition of PESCO and decision-making following the unanimity rule (Art. 46(6) TEU) for the most part. Consequently, national sovereignty remains protected when Member States participate in PESCO projects.[659]

However, and this further distinguishes PESCO from conventional CSDP elements, the TEU breaks through the unanimity rule when it comes to establishing PESCO and PESCO participation (Arts. 46(2)-(5) TEU). This allows for more inclusivity and makes PESCO as a common European approach to capability development more effective, as individual Member States cannot impede this common approach due to national reservations. Nevertheless, the unanimity rule for adopting new PESCO projects (Annex III Nos. 2.1., 2.2.1. subpara. 5 PESCO Decision) persists, potentially preventing the introduction of far-reaching projects.

---

656  Deutsch-Französischer Ministerrat (n 241).

657  (n 168).

658  In accordance with Art. 46(6) TEU, only Member States participating in PESCO can participate in PESCO votings.

659  Werner Kaufmann-Bühler, 'Art. 46 EUV' in Eberhard Grabitz et al. (eds), *Das Recht der Europäischen Union Kommentar 1* (März 2011 EL 43, C.H.Beck 2022) 2–10.

Furthermore, the effects of decisions as legally binding acts for implementation of PESCO (Art. 46(6) TEU) are potentially insufficient. While being legally binding[660] on participating Member States under EU primary law (Art. 288(4)[661] TFEU in accordance with Art. 25(b)(ii)[662] in conjunction with Art. 29 TEU[663]) most commentators agree that the primacy of EU law does not apply to CFSP decisions, since they are only intergovernmental and not supranational law.[664] Except for Art. 40 TEU and fundamental rights provisions (which are concerned in case of CFSP sanction decisions)[665], this means that the CJEU has no jurisdiction in PESCO matters (Art. 24(1) subpara. 2 TEU) and thus cannot enforce its commitments.[666]

The lack of Commission involvement in PESCO despite its increasing involvement in armaments cooperation (see part *3.2.1.3. The European Armament Policy and its future*) raises questions in terms of coherence. In this regard, it has been pointed out that involving the Commission in PESCO is not generally excluded by the Treaties.[667] Furthermore, Arts. 21(3) subpara.

---

660 Pechstein (n 59) 427; Cremer (n 466) 385–390; Werner Kaufmann-Bühler, 'Art. 29 EUV' in Eberhard Grabitz et al. (eds), *Das Recht der Europäischen Union Kommentar 1* (Juli 2010 EL 41, C.H.Beck 2022) 9; a different view is offered by Elfriede Regelsberger and Dieter Kugelmann, 'Art. 24' in Rudolf Streinz (ed), *EUV/AEUV* (3rd edn, C.H. Beck 2018) 249–250, who deny direct application and supremacy of the intergovernmental CFSP law and instead argue that its effect is limited by the Member States' respective constitutional orders.

661 Ruffert (n 464) 2400–2402; Biervert (n 464) 3011–3029.

662 Cremer (n 465) 367–372; Terhechte (n 465) 333–335.

663 Cremer (n 466) 385–390; Terhechte (n 466) 344–348.

664 Terhechte (n 465) 334–335; Daniel Thym, '§ 18 GASP und äußere Sicherheit' in Andreas von Arnauld and Marc Bungenberg (eds), *Enzyklopädie Europarecht Band 12* (2nd edn, Nomos 2022) 1241; Pechstein (n 59) 427; similarly BVerfG (n 102) at 342, 390; different views are presented by Cremer (n 466) 385–390; Kaufmann-Bühler (n 660) 9.

665 Arts. 24(1) subpara. 2 TEU, 275 TFEU; Case C-72/15, Rosneft, [2017] ECLI:EU:C:2017:236.

666 Case C-455/14 P, H v Council and Others, [2016] ECLI:EU:C:2016:569; Case C-348/12 P, Council v Manufacturing Support & Procurement Kala Naft, [2013] ECLI:EU:C:2013:776.

667 Kaufmann-Bühler (n 659) 7.

2 TEU[668] and 334 TFEU[669] obligate the Council and the Commission to ensure consistency in the activities relating to external action and enhanced cooperation and to cooperate to that effect. Therefore, an involvement of the Commission in PESCO would be justifiable under EU law, in particular since it is already active in the field of armaments cooperation.[670] However, the Member States have yet to opt for that possibility.

Consequently, PESCO is characterised by a very complex organisation structure, where the Council defines technical-operative objectives and projects, the Commission financially promotes PESCO projects via the EDF, which's budget is granted by the European Parliament, and the Member States' armed forces and defence industries then realise the PESCO projects. This makes PESCO's governance system incoherent.

### 3.2.1.2.4. EDA-PESCO Relationship

PESCO and EDA are closely interlinked. According to Art. 1(a) Protocol No. 10 TEU, the Member States participating in PESCO develop their defence capacities, where appropriate, more intensely in the activity of EDA and according to Art. 2(e) take part, where appropriate, in the development of major joint or European equipment programmes in the framework of EDA. This provision is mirrored by Art. 5(3)(f)(i) EDA Statute, which states that EDA shall support PESCO in particular by facilitating major joint or European capability development initiatives.

Furthermore, according to Art. 3 Protocol No. 10 TEU, EDA shall contribute to the regular assessment of the participating Member States

---

668  Hans-Joachim Cremer, 'Art. 21' in Christian Calliess and Matthias Ruffert (eds), *EUV/AEUV* (6th edn, C.H.Beck 2022) 355–355; Jörg Philipp Terhechte, 'Artikel 21' in Jürgen Schwarze et al. (eds), *EU-Kommentar* (4th edn, Nomos 2018) 318–320; Rudolf Geiger and Lando Kirchmair, 'Art. 21' in Rudolf Geiger et al. (eds), *EUV AEUV* (7th edn, C.H.Beck 2023) 142; Elfriede Regelsberger and Dieter Kugelmann, 'Art. 21' in Rudolf Streinz (ed), *EUV/AEUV* (3rd edn, C.H.Beck 2018) 244–245; Priollaud and Siritzky (n 187) 108–109.

669  Matthias Ruffert, 'Art. 334' in Christian Calliess and Matthias Ruffert, *EUV/AEUV* (6th edn, C.H.Beck 2022) 2562; Armin Hatje, 'Artikel 334' in Jürgen Schwarze et al. (eds), *EU-Kommentar* (4th edn, Nomos 2018) 3223; Rudolf Geiger and Lando Kirchmair, 'Art. 334', in Rudolf Geiger et al. (eds), *EUV AEUV* (7th edn, C.H.Beck 2023) 1150; Matthias Pechstein, 'Art. 334', in Rudolf Streinz (ed), *EUV/AEUV* (3rd edn, C.H.Beck 2018) 2566.

670  Kielmansegg (n 631) 1303.

PESCO contributions. This provision is mirrored by Art. 5(3)(f)(ii) EDA Statute. Both are part of PESCO's special enforcement system.

### 3.2.1.2.5. PESCO's Enforcement System

PESCO encompasses regulatory instruments that normatively address the Member States' legislative and administrative defence policies. While PESCO obligations are not enforceable by the CJEU, they are however enforced by a centralized oversight regime, based on "naming and shaming" (i.e. peer pressure) by the other Member States in case of non-compliance.

The implementation of PESCO decisions is structured by a schedule and sequenced phases. Member States are obligated to report their progress, efforts, and plans regarding implementation in annual National Implementation Plans, which are then assessed by the High Representative (Art. 6 PESCO Decision). In this assessment, the High Representative is supported by EDA (Art. 7(3) PESCO Decision). PESCO further uses CARD as a monitoring system to evaluate progress against the benchmarks of the capability development priorities (see Annex – List of ambitious and more binding common commitments undertaken by participating Member States in the five areas set out by Article 2 of Protocol 10 Nos. 2, 6, 7 PESCO Decision). Ultimately, non-compliance with PESCO obligations is sanctionable by the Council's right to exclude non-complying Member States from PESCO by qualified majority vote (Art. 46(4) TEU).

Whether this sanctions regime will ensure compliance and integration in the long run[671] remains to be seen. The National Implementation Plans do not guarantee that the Member States will fulfil all their commitments. However, any failures will be observed by the other Member States as well as the public. This creates a soft-law-like enforcement system based on peer pressure.

### 3.2.1.2.6. Assessment and Outlook – high potentials

PESCO now consolidates European defence cooperation and capability development within a common framework with specific, binding (therefore more reliable) commitments. It could be a major tool of European defence

---

671  Wolfstädter (n 511).

integration towards an EDU (see part *3.2.1.1. Towards a European Defence Union and potential consequences for European Armament Cooperation*). Annex I PESCO Decision in this regard specifically refers to the possible development towards a common defence under Art. 42(2) TEU. Until then however, PESCO only remains a first step in this direction and many reliability and efficiency questions remain open.

Firstly, European defence cooperation and capability development remain legally possible outside the EU framework too,[672] entrenching fragmentation and efficiency losses. In this regard, it is again (see part *2.2.2. Franco-German Armaments Cooperation today*) noteworthy how during the 2017 Franco-German Ministerial Conference, both States decided to initiate PESCO[673] and then develop their large-scale armaments projects FCAS and MGCS outside the PESCO framework. The future success of EDA and PESCO in terms of strengthening coherence and efficiencies in European capability development will thus also depend on whether such large-scale armaments projects will be primarily integrated (or integrable) in these frameworks. Otherwise, European capability development will continue take place outside EU structures to a large degree, entailing all known disadvantages regarding incoherence and unreliability discussed in previous parts.

Furthermore, the fulfilment of PESCO's binding, but still intergovernmental commitments will be difficult to enforce and will thus be largely subject to the volatile and diverging interests of the Member States. This phenomenon can also be observed in other areas of EU law, but is a known issue especially in defence policies, because of the CSDP's intergovernmental arrangement.

In the EU's daily political business, Member State obligations under EU primary law are readily ignored on a frequent basis. The Euro convergence criteria ("Maastricht criteria", Arts. 126, 140 TFEU) for example have been largely disregarded since their introduction due to contrary political interests. Similar compliance issues could arise in PESCO. Consequently, PESCO's success will thus ultimately depend on the political will by the Member States to make it a success.

Moreover, when looking at other areas of EU law, the Internal Market in particular, successful integration has been largely dependent on the effective (supranational) sanction mechanisms implemented by the Com-

---

672  Kielmansegg (n 631) 1280.
673  Deutsch-Französischer Ministerrat (n 241).

mission and the CJEU. They do not exist for PESCO. On the other hand, since EU (intergovernmental) law leaves the possibility open for Member State margins of discretion in terms of dynamic Treaty interpretation and application, while making EU law unreliable to a degree, it also allows for rapid change if need be, for example if Europe's geopolitical environment becomes even more unstable.

Whether the European framework for armaments cooperation (at least in its current form) is consequently more suitable than extra-EU formats to reliably ensure the consistent realisation of large-scale armaments projects remains difficult to answer. In many respects, intra-EU and extra-EU forms of armaments cooperation are similar, due to their intergovernmental arrangement and the resulting reliability and enforcement deficits. Ultimately, Member States participating in EDA and PESCO remain free to withdraw from these frameworks relatively easily, just like they can in conventional multilateral armaments cooperation arrangements. However, the increasingly common approach within EU structures has the potential to lead to more coherence and reliability due to the at least rudimentary enforcement system of PESCO obligations, Member State peer pressure, and potentially the normative effect of EU law.

The advantages of a common approach to capability development in terms of economic and defence-strategic efficiencies are obvious, especially at times when Europe and its Member States are facing an increasingly challenging geopolitical environment. This might provide intra-EU armaments cooperation with a further impetus and persuade Member States to make PESCO a success.

### 3.2.1.3. The European Armaments Policy and its future

Since the mid-1990s, the EU institutions have worked towards creating an integrated European defence market and supporting the European defence industry as part of broader European defence integration (see part *2.1.1. Historical Evolution of European Defence and Armaments Integration*). In this process, the European Commission – often referred to as the "motor of integration" – has played a central role.

As discussed in part *3.2.1.2. The Future of European Armaments Cooperation and PESCO*, the objectives of promoting European capability development and armaments cooperation are primarily the task of EDA under the CSDP's ECAP, while the Commission plays virtually no role in CSDP matters. Via EDA, the EU is provided with an active role in the area of armaments cooperation,[674] but to this day has no competence to manage armaments projects (much less the necessary infrastructure that would be required for that task).

Yet, despite its limited role in CSDP matters, the Commission has increasingly started to engage in defence-related policy areas. To circumvent its limited role in the intergovernmentally arranged CSDP, the Commission placed a particular focus on harmonising the defence market on the basis of its Internal Market competences (see part *3.2.1. European Armaments Cooperation – torn between intergovernmentalism and supranationalism*) to promote collaborative defence capability development in Europe via strengthening the EDTIB. Therefore, because of the Internal Market dimension of armaments, CSDP matters have since then increasingly been linked to Internal Market law.

### 3.2.1.3.1. Towards a genuine European Market for Defence Equipment?

European armaments integration as a means to enhance the deficient defence capabilities of the Member States has been a central objective of the CSDP since the 1998 St Malo summit (see part *2.1.1. Historical Evolution of European Defence and Armaments Integration*).[675] A genuine European market for defence equipment is regarded as a central part of an effective CSDP as only through a strong and autonomous EDTIB will Europe be able to close its aforementioned capability gaps (see part *2.2.1. European Defence and Armaments Integration today*).[676]

The Commission's efforts to create a genuine EDEM were established against the Member States' sovereignty and defence-industrial concerns, legally expressed since the Rome Treaty in what is today the armaments exception provision in Art. 346(1)(b) TFEU, which principally excludes armaments from supranational regulation and consequently undermines the coherence and consistency of the ECAP.[677] Defence matters are traditionally perceived to be at the heart of national sovereignty. Armaments procurement is further considered under (national) economic aspects, in

---

674  Kielmansegg (n 170) 278.
675  Kielmansegg (n 600) 93; Kielmansegg (n 170) 286.
676  Dyson and Konstadinides (n 99) 88.
677  Trybus (n 34) 160.

particular with regard to employment or public expenditure. The Member States' protectionism of their national defence industries has led to significant economic and defence inefficiencies through costly duplications and lack of competition and to a fragmented EDEM.[678]

Even in times of financial crises, decreasing defence budgets (at least until the 2022 Russian invasion in Ukraine), and evident capability gaps, the Member States' defence procurement is characterised by capability duplications and inefficient spending. There are significant economic and defence-strategic benefits expected from the creation of a genuine EDEM, which is yet to be completed. From an economic perspective, European integration in defence procurement is expected to lead to fiscal savings because of economies of scale and competition, and to a more consolidated and globally competitive EDTIB due to a higher market power and output potential. From a defence-strategic perspective, Europe's strategic autonomy and defence capabilities would be enhanced through increased interoperability of the Member States' defence systems and advanced armaments.[679]

Despite the Member States sovereignty concerns, but as part of broader European defence integration efforts since the mid-1990s, an EDTIB has started to be consolidated and the rules of the Internal Market have started to be applied to the defence sectors through supranational legislation to overcome the defence market fragmentation in the EU and establish a globally competitive EDTIB. However, this process remains overall incomplete. In this part, it will be discussed whether the EU serves or could serve as an appropriate framework to reform the European armaments sector and further harmonise European defence procurement, to make collaborative defence procurement in Europe more reliable (such as the current Franco-German armaments collaboration) and thus also strengthen the CSDP and the Member States' defence capability development.

The defence market fragmentation in the EU is regarded as an impediment to an efficient and autonomous EDTIB.[680] Alongside the industrial fragmentation discussed in part *2.2.1. European Defence and Armaments Integration today*, the legal framework for the EDEM is likewise fragmented. Procurements, competition law, State aids, merger regulation, intra-Community transfers and exports are inconsistently regulated at the suprana-

---

678  European Commission (n 51).
679  Trybus (n 45) 2.
680  Dyson and Konstadinides (n 91) 88.

tional level and partially excluded from the Internal Market rules because of Art. 346(1)(b) TFEU.[681] This is why in recent years, the EU has taken several legislative measures to consolidate the EDTIB and thus the CSDP via defence-industrial consolidation, to promote more efficient public procurement and intra-EU transfers of defence products through legislative harmonisation, and to also harmonise armaments exports rules. These steps seek to enhance the competitiveness of the EU's defence industries and also broader resource efficiency and capability development.

However, the Commission's influence over the EDEM remains limited, and bilateral and multilateral defence-industrial procurement continues to take place mainly outside EU structures. Despite the proliferation of several collaborative procurement initiatives, the Member States remain opposed to confer any significant decision-making powers to European institutions. Besides EU law, national regulations regarding defence procurement and armaments exports continue to be predominant due to the aforementioned armaments exception in EU primary law, thus upholding the current fragmented state of the EDEM.

Many armaments issues thus continue to be addressed outside the TFEU's (supranational) scope of application. EDA was originally established (in 2004) to manage those (intergovernmental) parts of the ECAP intended to be outside the TFEU's scope by the Member States and this has changed little since then. Until the EU's 2009 Defence Package (see below) that included rules on procurement.

Today, EDA is also responsible for promoting and coordinating European armaments cooperation by opening up the Member States' defence markets and promoting competition. The TEU explicitly tasks EDA to oversee the Member States' defence capabilities development and propose armaments collaboration, to promote harmonisation of operational needs and adoption of effective, compatible procurement methods, to contribute to identify and where appropriate implement measures to strengthen the EDTIB, and to participate in the ECAP.[682] EDA thus plays the central role in European capability development within EU structures.[683]

However, due to the CSDP's intergovernmental structure, EDA has no hard law power. It is not a defence procurement agency and consequently, the responsibility for capability development remains with each individual

---

681 Trybus (n 45); Trybus (n 34).
682 Arts. 42(3), 45(1) TEU.
683 Terpan (n 261) 1266.

Member State.[684] Because of the intergovernmental structure and principle of voluntariness (deriving from Art. 45(2) TEU), the Member States remain in control and can decide over their varying levels of participation. Nevertheless, EDA provides the first systematic approach to collaborative defence capability development within the EU framework. Since its creation, EDA has started a multitude of initiatives[685] to strengthen the EDTIB, however with lacking results considering the ongoing fragmented state of the EDTIB and the European armaments market, which in turn is the result of the Member States' known sovereignty concerns. These EDA initiatives are non-binding soft law agreements, since EDA can only play a supporting role in defence matters, which partially explains the initiatives' lacking results.

Moreover, defence procurement rules in Europe also arise from organisational, intergovernmental structures outside the EU framework, partially complementing or even competing with some of the Commission's and EDA's procurement initiatives. The most relevant frameworks in this context are OCCAR and the LoI, which at the time of their establishment only included EU Member States[686] and will be further discussed in part *3.3.1. Multilateral European Armaments Cooperation*.

### 3.2.1.3.2. The Armaments Exception (Art. 346(1)(b) TFEU)

Public procurement (including for defence goods) generally falls under the scope of EU primary (and by now also secondary) law. Defence procurement is however limited by the armaments exception provision of Art. 346(1)(b) TFEU, which principally safeguards the Member States' national security interests concerning armaments against the application of the EU's Internal Market rules. Nevertheless, the CJEU has established in several cases that there is no general exclusion of procurement from the scope of EU primary law and that national practices exempting their defence contracts from EU law can be contrary to the conditions of competition in the Internal Market.

At this point, a closer look at Art. 346(1)(b) TFEU is appropriate to better understand its limiting effects on harmonising the EDEM and further promoting European armaments integration.

---

684  Biermann and Weiss (n 211) 228.
685  See for example (n 93).
686  The UK has withdrawn from the EU since then.

As discussed in detail in part *2.1.1. Historical Evolution of European Defence and Armaments Integration,* traditionally and based on EU primary law, European defence integration was regarded as an exclusively intergovernmental policy field. For armaments, this policy was legally based on what is today Art. 346(1)(b) TFEU, the extraordinary national security exception in EU law for Member States to avoid complying other provisions of EU primary law[687], including with the general Internal Market rules[688] but also the CFSP[689].

According to this provision, an EU Member State 'may take such measures as it considers necessary for the protection of the essential interests of its security which are connected with the production of or trade in arms, munitions and war material'. This self-assessment prerogative ("*Einschätzungsprerogativ*"[690]) following from 'as it considers necessary' has given the Member States a significant margin of discretion when invoking the provision. However, the provision also states that 'such measures shall not adversely affect the conditions of competition in the internal market regarding products which are not intended for specifically military purposes'.

Art. 346(1)(b) TFEU applies to armaments included in the 1958 Council List[691] in accordance with Art. 346(2) TFEU. This very general list covers all "hard" defence material (including fighter jets and tanks, which is relevant in the context of FCAS and MGCS). Different from the public security exceptions in the free movement regimes (Arts. 36, 45(3), 52(1), 65(1)(b) and 72 TFEU), which only allow derogations from their specific regimes on goods, workers, services, establishment, and capital), Art. 346(1)(b) TFEU by contrast allows derogations from the EU treaties as a whole and is subject to the special judicial review procedure of Art. 348 subpara. 2 TFEU.[692]

---

687  Art. 346(1) TFEU refers to the plural 'Treaties'.

688  Juliane Kokott, 'Art. 346' in Rudolf Streinz (ed), *EUV/AEUV* (3rd edn, C.H.Beck 2018) 2631; Dittert (n 31) 1988.

689  Dittert (n 31) 1991.

690  Kingreen and Wegener (n 31) 2618.

691  The list is based on Council Decision 255/58 of 15 April 1958. It was only published in 2008 via Council of the European Union, Extract of the Council Decision 255/58 of 15 April 1958, 14538/4/08 REV 4, 26 November 2008; the 1958 list is not to be confused with the EU's Common Military List, see (n 395).

692  Christian Calliess, 'Art. 348' in Christian Calliess and Matthias Ruffert (eds), *EUV/ AEUV* (6th edn, C.H.Beck 2022) 2626–2631; Kirsten Schmalenbach and Hans-Joachim Cremer, 'Art. 215' in Christian Calliess and Matthias Ruffert (eds), *EUV/ AEUV* (6th edn, C.H.Beck 2022) 2050–2063; Daniel Dittert, 'Artikel 348' in Hans von der Groeben et al. (eds), *Europäisches Unionsrecht* (7th edn, Nomos 2015) 2006.

Since the Rome Treaty, the Member States have interpreted the armaments exception widely and frequently made use of it, relying on the broad wording of the provision where a Member State was allowed to take 'such measures as it considers necessary'. At the same time, the Commission was reluctant to bring cases involving the armaments exception before the CJEU (which has jurisdiction in accordance with Art. 348 subpara. 2 TFEU over cases of improper use of Art. 346 TFEU leading to distorting the conditions of competition within the internal market[693]) for a long time since the defence sector was generally considered to be outside the scope of application of EU law.[694]

As discussed in part *2.1.1. Historical Evolution of European Defence and Armaments Integration*, the Rome Treaty and with it the armaments exception provision were introduced in 1957, shortly after the failure of the EDC in 1954. The EDC had failed due to the French opposition over sovereignty concerns and consequently, the subsequent European Treaties were widely considered to completely exclude defence matters and the armaments exception to be a manifestation of this general exclusion.

Furthermore, because cases involving defence matters involve secrecy, the Commission was often unable to prove or even detect abuses of the armaments exception provision in practice.[695] This exclusion of Internal Market rules to defence matters for more than thirty years has led to today's defence market fragmentation and lack of defence-industrial competition in the EU, entailing significant efficiency losses.

The Commission's reluctance to bring cases involving security exceptions before the CJEU changed in the course of the 1990s, when the Commission started to become more active in defence market matters.[696] Over the following three decades, several CJEU rulings have successively limited the application of Art. 346(1)(b) TFEU, which consequently has to be narrowly construed today.[697]

According to the CJEU, in case of derogations from Internal Market rules on the basis of Art. 346(1)(b) TFEU, Member States have to find a balance between the interests of the Internal Market (such as free movement or fair competition) and their own national security interests (such as retaining

---

693  Calliess (n 692) 2626–2631; Schmalenbach and Cremer (n 692) 2050–2063; Dittert (n 692) 2006.

694  Trybus (n 34) 151; Kingreen and Wegener (n 31) 2616–2621.

695  Trybus (n 45) 106–107.

696  Trybus (n 45) 107.

697  Trybus (n 34) 396.

defence-industrial capabilities or armed forces equipment). The CJEU thus introduced a proportionality test.

At the same time, this need for balance also limits the Commission's competences to harmonise those parts of the Internal Market with defence implications.[698] On the basis of the CJEU's rulings, the defence sector was moved into the scope of application of EU law. Consequently, defence matters have become partially supranationally harmonised – especially where they border with the Internal Market (such as procurements, competition law, State aids, merger regulation, or intra-Community transfers).

In the 1986 landmark case Marguerite Johnston v Chief Constable of the Royal Ulster Constabulary[699], the CJEU established that there is an underlying principle that all security exceptions from the Treaties are exhaustive and must be interpreted narrowly. According to the CJEU, there are no general and automatic national security exceptions from the Treaty as this might impair the effectiveness of EU law (at the time Community law). This includes Art. 346(1)(b) TFEU, which has been the centre of increased attention in subsequent cases that have been brought by the Commission as part of its increased defence policy activism.

In these cases, the CJEU had to define the limits of Member State sovereignty over their national security to interpret what is today Art. 346(1)(b) TFEU.[700] This security exception is part of the sophisticated mechanism provided in EU primary law to balance the interests of the Internal Market with the essential national security interests of the Member States. While the CJEU recognized these legitimate interests, in 1999, in its second landmark ruling concerning the armaments exception in Commission v Spain[701], it defined a narrow interpretation for Art. 346(1)(b) TFEU specifically and ruled that the provision does not represent an automatic or

---

698  Trybus (n 34) 124.
699  Case C-222/84, Marguerite Johnston v Chief Constable of the Royal Ulster Constabulary, [1986] ECR 1651.
700  Trybus (n 34) 127.
701  Case C-414/97, Commission v Spain, [1999] ECR I-5585; this position has been confirmed and further refined in subsequent rulings: Case C-615/10, Insinööritoimisto InsTiimi, [2004] ECLI:EU:C:2012:324; Case C-337/05, Commission v Italy, [2008] ECR I-2173; Case C-157/06, Commission v Italy, [2008] ECR I-7313; Case C-284/05, Commission v Finland, [2009] ECR I-11705; Case C-294/05, Commission v Sweden, [2009] ECR I-11777; Case C-387/05, Commission v Italy, [2009] ECR I-11831; Case C-409/05, Commission v Greece, [2009] ECR I-11859; Case C-461/05, Commission v Denmark, [2009] ECR I-11887; Case C-239/06, Commission v Italy [2009], ECR I-11913; Case C-38/06, Commission v Portugal, [2010] ECR I-1569; Case C-246/12

categorial exclusion of the application of EU primary law from intra-Community trade in defence products, but instead relying on the exception has to be justified on a case-by-case basis by a Member State that wants to invoke it. Otherwise, this exception could be used as a loophole that could potentially undermine the functioning of the Internal Market as a whole. Consequently, armaments cannot generally be considered to be outside the scope of application of the Treaties and defence-related derogations from general Internal Market rules are subject to judicial review by the CJEU.[702]

In 2003, in Commission v Fiocchi Munizioni[703], the CJEU shifted the balance in the favour of the Member States and affirmed that the security exception (today Art. 346(1)(b) TFEU) is meant to safeguard the Member States' sovereignty and national security interests and leaves a wide margin of discretion for the Member States in defining these interests. Furthermore, in Commission v Belgium[704] the court confirmed the exclusive national competence of the Member States to assess and define their national security interests vis-à-vis EU public procurement rules.

In 2004, in Finnish Turntable[705], it then shifted the balance back into the favour of the Internal Market by reconfirming that the armaments exception must be applied on strict conditions and on a case-by-case basis. The CJEU ruled that the burden of proof, with regard to specific procurement being indispensable and directly linked to a Member State's national security, lies with the Member State invoking the exception. As ruled in a further 2008 case in Commission v Italy[706], just because the armed forces were acquiring a defence product was not sufficient to invoke the armaments exception provision. Building on its previous case law, the court reaffirmed that the armaments exception (together with the other public security exceptions mentioned in the TFEU[707]) deals with 'exceptional and clearly defined cases'. The exception provisions in EU primary law cannot be interpreted as an 'inherent general exception excluding all measures taken for reasons of public security from the scope of' Internal Market law. Instead, they must be interpreted strictly.

---

P, Commission v Ellinika Nafpigeia, [2013] ECLI:EU:C:2013:133; Case C-474/12, Schiebel Aircraft, [2014] ECLI:EU:C:2014:2139.
702   Trybus (n 34) 162.
703   Case T-26/01, Fiocchi Munizioni SpA v Commission, [2003] ECR II-03951.
704   Case C-252/01, Commission v Belgium, [2003] ECR I-11859.
705   Case C-615/10 (n 701).
706   Case C-337/05 (n 701); Case C-157/06 (n 701).
707   Arts. 36, 45, 52, 65, 72, 346, 347 TFEU.

Following these narrow interpretations of (what is today) Art. 346(1)(b) TFEU, in the following year, the 2009 Defence Package (see below) was introduced by the EU, which aims at partially harmonising the EDEM within the limits of Art. 346(1)(b) TFEU.[708] The CJEU's line of case law on Art. 346(1)(b) TFEU thus created a legally binding and enforceable system that has subsequently allowed to (partially) open up the defence markets in the EU.

Art. 346(1)(b) TFEU is still in place today and continues to limit European defence market harmonisation as will be shown below. The very existence of the security exceptions in the TFEU underlines the significance of the Member States' security interests in EU primary law. Art. 346(1)(b) TFEU confers to the Member States relatively wide discretion in assessing its own national security interests, favouring them in the CJEU's proportionality test. However, they are limited by the narrow interpretation and judicial scrutiny of the CJEU in the interest of the Internal Market.[709] As follows from the case law discussed above, Art. 346(1)(b) TFEU deals with specific cases and it cannot be inferred from this provision that it generally excludes all measures taken for reasons of national security. The armaments exception does not lend itself to a wide interpretation and must instead by applied strictly on a case-by-case basis. It cannot be interpreted in such a way as to confer on Member States a limitless power to derogate from the Internal Market rules by simply invoking national security interests without regard to the interests of the Internal Market. These interests must be specific, essential and proven by the invoking Member State. Measures based on Art. 346(1)(b) TFEU must not exceed what is appropriate and necessary to protect the invoking Member States' essential national security interest (proportionality[710] and necessity[711]).

Following the CJEU's narrow interpretation of Art. 346(1)(b) TFEU, the EU could potentially serve as an appropriate framework to further harmonise or even coordinate defence procurement within the EU. Armaments are a central part of the CSDP and increased capability development is required to close Europe's capability gap. In the following parts (see especially parts *3.2.1.4. Towards a Comprehensive European Armaments Export Regime?* and *3.2.2. Making European Armaments Cooperation reliable?*),

---

708   Trybus (n 34) 124.
709   ibid. 126–127.
710   See also Dittert (n 31) 1994.
711   See also Kingreen and Wegener (n 31) 2617; Dittert (n 31) 1988.

the options for a comprehensive, supranational regulative approach for armaments projects will be discussed under EU law.

### 3.2.1.3.3. EDEM Regulation

The EU's 2009 Defence Package is of particular relevance for the ongoing efforts to create a genuine EDEM. Following proposals by the Commission, which were motivated[712] by the CJEU's narrow interpretations of the armaments exception discussed above, it consists of two directives designed to improve the functioning of the Single Market for defence-related products at the core. The first deals with transfers of defence-related products[713] ('Transfer Directive') and the second with defence procurement[714] (Procurement Directive). The Defence Package is the Commission's response to the frequent invocation of Art. 346(1)(b) TFEU by the Member States which ran counter to the Commission's efforts of creating a more unified defence market and consolidating the EDTIB.[715]

### 3.2.1.3.4. The Transfer Directive – lacking effects

The Transfer Directive has been described as a significant first step towards reducing barriers to intra-EU transfers of defence-related products.[716] It aims at simplifying and harmonising the (differing national) conditions and procedures for transfers of defence-related products within the EU to ensure the proper functioning of the Internal Market (Art. 1(1) Transfer Directive). Thus, the directive is firstly meant to provide for European harmonisation of the material scope for transferring defence-related goods within the EU. Secondly, the directive is intended to make the EDEM more

---

712 Trybus (n 34) 124.
713 (n 111).
714 (n 112).
715 European Commission, Communication from the Commission to the European Parliament, the Council, the European Economic and Social Committee and the Committee of the Regions – A strategy for a stronger and more competitive european defence industry, COM/2007/764 final, 5 December 2007.
716 European Parliamentary Research Service, 'EU Defence Package: Defence Procurement and Intra-Community Transfers Directives European Implementation Assessment' (*europa*, 2020) <http://www.europarl.europa.eu/RegData/etudes/STUD/2020/654171/EPRS_STU(2020)654171_EN.pdf> accessed 25 December 2023.

efficient, integrated, and competitive, by minimising administrative costs associated with transferring defence-related goods between Member States for defence companies on the basis of a harmonised and transparent European licencing system aimed at reducing the number of individual licences to the benefit of general licences thus facilitating intra-EU transfers. At the same time, the directive respects the Member States' national security and defence interests. In these respects, the directive has had some success. Specifically, it reduced the extent of fragmentation between national licencing systems and provides a framework within further harmonisation can take place.[717]

Until the introduction of the Transfer Directive, the Member States treated intra-EU transfers of defence-related products like third country armaments exports without distinction. This was regarded as a significant obstacle for the EDTIB's competitiveness and European defence (market) integration.[718] The Transfer Directive's 'fundamental innovation'[719] is to qualitatively differentiate transfers from exports. Art. 3(2) Transfer Directive defines a "transfer" as 'any transmission or movement of a defence-related product from a supplier to a recipient in another Member State'.

Under Art. 4(1) Transfer Directive, the transfer of defence-related products between Member States is subject to prior authorisation. However, it also states that no further authorisation by other Member States is required for passage through Member States or for entrance onto the territory of the Member State where the recipient of defence-related products is located, without prejudice to the application of provisions necessary on grounds of public security or public policy. This means principally only one licence in total is necessary for the whole intra-EU transfer. Transferring defence-related products within the EU is thus significantly facilitated.

Furthermore, Member States may exempt transfers from the obligation of prior authorisation under the conditions set out in Art. 4(2)(a)-(e) Transfer Directive. Transferring defence-related products within the EU is then even more liberalised. Especially relevant to point out in the context of this

---

717 European Commission, 'Evaluation of Directive 2009/43/EC on the Transfers of Defence-Related Products within the Community Final Report' (*europa*, 2016) <https://op.europa.eu/en/publication-detail/-/publication/538beabd-92af-11e7 -b92d-01aa75ed71a1/language-en> accessed 6 May 2023.

718 Martin Trybus and Luke Butler, 'The internal market and national security: Transposition, impact and reform of the EU directive on Intra-Community Transfers of Defence Products' [2017] 54(2) Common Market Law Review 403, 403–441.

719 ibid. 416.

thesis is Art. 4(2)(c), under which Member States may exempt transfers of defence-related products from the obligation of prior authorisation where the transfer is necessary for the implementation of a cooperative armament programme between Member States, thus further facilitating European armaments cooperation.

The directive sets out a binding list of defence-related products that are subject to a specific licencing requirement (general transfer licences, global transfer licences, and individual transfer licences, see below). This list (stated in the annex to the directive, see Art. 2 Transfer Directive) corresponds with the EU Common Military List.[720] The Commission had to limit the scope of equipment categories applicable under the directive to that list due to Member State pressure to exclude defence-related products deemed too sensitive.[721] Nevertheless, in this way, the material scope for transferring defence-related goods within the EU is now largely harmonised.

Under Art. 5 Transfer Directive, Member States shall publish general transfer licences directly granting authorisation to suppliers established on their territory, which fulfil the terms and conditions attached to the general transfer licence, to perform transfers of defence-related products, to be specified in the general transfer licence, to a category or categories of recipients located in another Member State. In four areas mentioned under Art. 5(2)(a)-(d) Transfer Directive, Member States are obligated to publish general transfer licences. Importantly, no request to publish a general transfer licence is needed, they are granted ex officio. A supplier meeting a general transfer licence's terms and conditions is directly authorized to transfer. Furthermore, Art. 5(3) Transfer Directive aims at further facilitating armaments cooperation and thus proposes that Member States participating in an intergovernmental cooperation programme concerning the development, production, and use of one or more defence-related products publish a general transfer licence for such transfers to other Member States which participate in that programme as are necessary for the execution of that programme.

---

720 (n 395).
721 European Commission, Evaluation of the Transfers Directive Accompanying the document Report from the Commission to the European Parliament and the Council on the evaluation of Directive 2009/43/EC of the European Parliament and of the Council of 6 May 2009 simplifying terms and conditions of transfers of defence-related products within the Community, SWD/2016/0398 final, 2 December 2016.

General transfer licences are the "new" and most relevant type of licence under the directive in terms of simplifying intra-EU transfers, as it is meant to reduce the use of individual licences (see below) and associated administrative burdens.[722] Alongside general transfer licences subject to Art. 5(1) Transfer Directive, global and individual transfer licences however continue to exist, for transfers of sensitive products (Art. 4(7), recital 18 Transfer Directive). Member States remain free to determine the appropriate type of licence (Art. 4(5) Transfer Directive).

Global transfer licences (under Art. 6 Transfer Directive) allow an individual supplier, at its request, the transfer of a type or category of products under the same licence to one or more recipients in other Member States over a period of three years (renewable).

Individual transfer licences (under Art. 7 Transfer Directive) authorise an individual supplier, at its request, one transfer of a specified quantity of specified defence-related products to one recipient in another Member State. This type of licence is now reserved for transfers where a Member State's essential security interests or public policy are concerned (Art. 7(b) Transfer Directive), where it is necessary for compliance with international obligations and commitments of Member States (Art. 7(c) Transfer Directive), or where a Member State has serious reason to believe that the supplier will not be able to comply with all the terms and conditions necessary to grant it a global transfer licence (Art. 7(d) Transfer Directive). Before the introduction of the defence directive, individual transfer licences were the most common licence and imposed significant administrative burdens and trade barriers.[723]

The Transfer Directive seeks to increase defence-industrial cooperation to generate economies of scale.[724] In this context, the certification (under Art. 9 Transfer Directive) of companies ('recipients') is a key element of the directive. Companies which are considered reliable under Art. 9(2) Transfer Directive, in particular regarding its capacity to observe export limitations of defence-related products received under a transfer licence from another Member State, are entitled to undertake transfers under the general transfer licences (Art. 9(1) in conjunction with Art. 5(2)(b) Transfer Directive). Individual licences should thereby become an exception and limited to the cases mentioned above (Arts. 7(b)-(c) Transfer Directive). Also noteworthy

---

722   Trybus and Butler (n 718) 419–423.
723   Trybus and Butler (n 718) 417.
724   European Parliamentary Research Service (n 716).

is that certification is conducted in the Member State in which the recipient is established (Art. 9(1) Transfer Directive). The certification of recipients is another 'fundamental innovation'[725]. It has the potential to further increase the level of defence-industrial cooperation and EDEM consolidation as defence manufacturers can now rely on more predictable licencing conditions within the EU.

Lastly, the Transfer Directive establishes ex-post controls on third country exports if these exports were originally received under a transfer licence from another Member State. According to its Art. 10, Member States shall ensure that recipients of defence-related products, when applying for an export licence, declare to their competent authorities, in cases where such products received under a transfer licence from another Member State have export limitations attached to them, that they have complied with the terms of those limitations, including, as the case may be, by having obtained the required consent from the originating Member State.

Despite the simplifications and harmonisation of the conditions and procedures for transfers of defence-related products within the EU, these transfers remain subject to national controls under the directive. The list of defence-related goods does not automatically replace existing national lists (Art. 1(2) Transfer Directive), but Member States are expected to make their national lists conform to the directive's list. As discussed in previous parts of this thesis, an effective CSDP is hardly imaginable without a genuine EDEM.[726] Furthermore, capability development remains less efficient. To that end, it is problematic that the Transfer Directive has not fully satisfied the expectations.

Firstly, full transposition of the directive has proved difficult. It failed to achieve the intended effects of simplifying and harmonising licencing systems/requirements and intra-EU transfers.[727] Although the number of certified companies in the EU has increased, the majority are located in

---

725  Trybus and Butler (n 718) 435.

726  Dyson and Konstadinides (n 91) 88.

727  European Commission, Evaluation of Directive 2009/43/EC of the European Parliament and of the Council of 6 May 2009 simplifying terms and conditions of transfers of defence-related products within the Community, COM/2016/760 final, 30 November 2016; Lucie Béraud-Sudreau, 'Integrated markets? – Europe's defence industry after 20 years' in Daniel Fiott (ed), *The CSDP in 2020* The EU's legacy and ambition in security and defence (EUISS 2020) 65–66; Trybus and Butler (n 718) 403–441.

only two Member States, Germany and France.[728] This is particularly disadvantageous for European armaments collaboration, which usually takes place in at least two Member States and where sub-components thus need to be frequently transferred between them – preferably unobstructed.

Furthermore, collaborative defence procurement is subject to specific provisions in the Transfer Directive (Arts. 4(2)(c), 5(3)). Member States participating in intergovernmental armaments cooperation may publish a general transfer licence to generally cover intra-EU transfers for the purpose of their cooperation. However, the possibility of using general licences for collaborative programmes is optional in the Directive (under Art. 5(3)) and has not been transposed into the legislation of all Member States, including Germany and France.[729] This is likely because under Art. 12 FFA (see *3.3.1. Multilateral European Armaments Cooperation*), such a licensing regime already exists on a multilateral (non-EU) basis.

Furthermore, the directive's application is limited because of Art. 346(1) (b) TFEU, which continues to apply, as EU primary law supersedes secondary law. Art. 1(3) of the directive thus also expressly takes this provision into account, respecting the CJEU's proportionality test by safeguarding the interests of the Internal Market without sacrificing the Member States' essential security interests vis-à-vis armaments. Consequently, the Member States can continue to invoke the armaments exception provision, although limited by the CJEU case law discussed earlier.

The Transfer Directive was adopted under Art. 114 TFEU, which enables EU legislation to harmonise relevant national laws for the establishment and functioning of the Internal Market.[730] Recital 43 of the Transfer Directive thus refers to this objective. The directive considers such harmonisation necessary because Art. 346(1)(b) TFEU limits the application of the free movement principles to the disadvantage of the Internal Market (recitals 2 and 5 Transfer Directive).

Since intra-EU transfers are regulated by the EU under Internal Market rules, including Art. 348 subpara. 2 TFEU, which extends the CJEU's jurisdiction over disputes arising from improper uses of Art. 346 TFEU,

---

728  (n 721).

729  Baudouin Heuninckx, *The Law of Collaborative Defence Procurement in the European Union* (CUP 2017) 75.

730  Stefan Korte, 'Art. 114' in Christian Calliess and Matthias Ruffert (eds), *EUV/AEUV* (6th edn, C.H.Beck 2022) 1483–1521; Hans-Holger Herrnfeld, 'Artikel 114' in Jürgen Schwarze et al. (eds), *EU-Kommentar* (4th edn, Nomos 2018) 1869–1935.

derogations from the Transfer Directive are subject to judicial review and a proportionality test. Consequently, if a Member State derogates from the directive by relying on Art. 346(1)(b) TFEU, it must demonstrate on a case-by-case basis in line with the CJEU's case law that the non-application of the directive is necessary and proportionate to safeguard its essential security interests.[731]

Nevertheless, as stated earlier, the transfer of defence-related products remains subject to national controls under the directive. Due to the limits posed by Art. 346(1)(b) TFEU, further harmonisation cannot be achieved. Instead, the Commission is therefore considering further harmonisation through soft law recommendations due to Member State resistance against further secondary law harmonisation.[732] Considering the lacking results of other soft law initiatives in this area (see EDA initiatives mentioned above), the EDEM will consequently most likely remain fragmented and inefficient for the foreseeable future.

### 3.2.1.3.5. The Procurement Directive – also lacking effects

Besides the Transfer Directive, the EU's 2009 Defence Package has also introduced the Procurement Directive. The directive is legally based on the EU's Internal Market competences (namely Arts. 53(2), 62, 114 TFEU), as this is where the Commission is competent to act in defence matters (see part *3.2.1. European Armaments Cooperation – torn between intergovernmentalism and supranationalism*).

---

731  Trybus and Butler (n 718) 403–441.
732  European Commission (n 717); European Commission, Report from the Commission to the European Parliament and the Council Evaluation of Directive 2009/43/EC of the European Parliament and of the Council of 6 May 2009 simplifying terms and conditions of transfers of defence-related products within the Community, COM/2016/0760 final, 30 November 2016; Commission Recommendation of 30 November 2016 on the harmonisation of the scope of and conditions for general transfer licences for armed forces and contracting authorities as referred to in point (a) of Article 5(2) of Directive 2009/43/EC of the European Parliament and of the Council, C/2016/7711 final, 30 November 2016; Commission Recommendation of 30 November 2016 on the harmonisation of the scope of and conditions for general transfer licences for certified recipients as referred to in Article 9 of Directive 2009/43/EC of the European Parliament and of the Council, C/2016/7728 final, 30 November 2016.

The Procurement Directive is now the basis for public and private entities buying defence-related goods and services within the Internal Market.
It sets out harmonised rules and procedures aimed at ensuring competition,
transparency and non-discrimination in Member State defence procurement by opening up national defence markets and applying EU Internal
Market law. In essence, it provides that defence contracts, which fall within
its Art. 2 scope of application are not excluded, and whose value is above
certain thresholds (Arts. 8, 9, 52 Procurement Directive), must be awarded
following competitive tendering procedures and selection criteria based on
the principles of transparency and non-discrimination (Art. 4, Titles II, III
Procurement Directive). It is supposed to promote the EDEM by providing
the Member States with specific rules and special safeguards for defence
procurement which are tailored to the specificities of defence procurement
tending to be particularly complex and sensitive. By enhancing transparency and openness in Member State defence markets, they make it easier
for defence companies to access other Member States' defence markets.
At the same time, Member States profit from lower equipment prices and
higher quality of equipment in their defence procurement due to increased
competition. In these respects, the directive has had some success.[733] While
the directive strengthens and consolidates the EDEM, it also takes the
Member States' national security and defence interests into account (recital
8, Arts. 2, 12, 13 Procurement Directive) and therefore offers a large range
of award procedures (Arts. 25–28 Procurement Directive) and 13 types of
exclusions (section 3 of the directive – excluded contracts).

The scope of the directive is large. Under its Art. 2, it applies principally
to all contracts for the procurement of military equipment, works and
services and to sensitive purchases with a security dimension and involving
classified information. At the same time, Member States have the right
under Art. 346 TFEU to exempt certain contracts from the directive when
it is necessary to protect their essential security interests. The directive's
scope is based on the 1958 Council List[734], to which the provisions of
Art. 346(1)(b) TFEU apply in accordance with Art. 346(2) TFEU.

The Commission's rationale in introducing the directive was that its
rules would limit the Member States' recourse to Art. 346(1)(b) TFEU (see

---

733 European Commission, Evaluation of Directive 2009/81/EC on public procurement
in the fields of defence and security, SWD/2016/407 final, 30 November 2016;
European Parliamentary Research Service (n 716).
734 (n 691).

recital 3 of the directive) and would thus open up the national defence markets.[735] Again, an effective CSDP is hardly imaginable without a genuine European market for defence.[736] Furthermore, capability development remains less efficient. To that end, it is problematic that similar to the Transfer Directive's shortcomings, the Procurement Directive has also not fully satisfied the expectations.

Like the Transfer Directive, above all else, the Procurement Directive's application is limited because of Art. 346(1)(b) TFEU, which continues to apply, as EU primary law supersedes secondary law. Art. 2 of the directive thus also expressly takes this provision into account, respecting the proportionality test established by the CJEU by safeguarding the interests of the Internal Market without sacrificing the Member States essential security interests vis-à-vis armaments. This has stifled the intended effects of the directive in terms of progressively establishing a genuine EDEM, because Member States can continue to rely on the armaments exception.[737]

Despite Art. 346(1)(b) TFEU, it is relevant to note that the directive has proved partially effective.[738] This has to do with the aforementioned CJEU case law, in which the application of Art. 346(1)(b) TFEU has been successively limited by several rulings (see above) and consequently Art. 346(1)(b) TFEU has been invoked less since its introduction.

Since defence procurement is regulated by the EU under Internal Market rules, including Art. 348 subpara. 2 TFEU, which extends the CJEU's jurisdiction over disputes arising from improper uses of Art. 346 TFEU, derogations from the Procurement Directive are also subject to judicial review and a proportionality test. Consequently, if a Member State derogates from the directive in defence equipment procurement by relying on Art. 346(1)(b) TFEU, it must demonstrate on a case-by-case basis in line with the CJEU's case law that the non-application of the directive is necessary and proportionate to safeguard its essential security interests. The very specific and national security-accommodating provisions of the directive, which has taken the CJEU's case law into account, have made it more challenging for Member States to prove that they cannot protect their

---

735  Butler (n 48) 1.
736  Dyson and Konstadinides (n 91) 88.
737  Trybus and Butler (n 718) 403–441; Béraud-Sudreau (n 727) 64–65.
738  European Commission, Report from the Commission to the European Parliament and the Council on the implementation of Directive 2009/81/EC on public procurement in the fields of defence and security, to comply with Article 73(2) of that Directive, COM/2016/762 final, 30 November 2016.

essential security interests within the procurement procedures set out by the directive.[739] This has evidently led to more transparent competition in the EU defence market, expressed by a higher number of publicised defence contract notices and awards.[740]

Yet, when it comes to European armaments collaboration, the Procurement Directive has left a significant gap. According to Art. 13(c) of the directive, multinational armaments projects are expressly excluded from the directive's scope of application. This exception was included in the directive by the Commission because of Member State pressure.[741] This exempts the large trans-European armaments collaborations (such as the Franco-German armaments collaboration) from the directive's scope and leaves room for frameworks outside the Internal Market, such as EDA, but also outside the EU framework altogether, such as OCCAR, LoI, or NATO.

On the one hand, this allows for "enhanced" forms of armaments co-operation (see also part *3.3.2. The Bilateral Franco-German Armaments Collaboration in the context of European Union Law – exclusive cooperation within common integration*) between Member States or even non-Member States, which leads to necessary capability development and partially jointly procured defence equipment by certain (collaborating) Member States. On the other hand, this proliferates European procurement fragmentation and resulting duplications and inefficiencies, which the Procurement Directive was intended to reduce.

The Procurement Directive was passed by the Council with all Member States voting in favour except for Poland which abstained. This suggests at first a clear Member State interest to harmonise European defence procurement and legislate against the excessive recourse to Art. 346(1)(b) TFEU in their own defence procurement. However, many Member States failed to transpose the directive within the legal deadline and the Commission had to intervene to ensure that the Member States were indeed applying the directive.[742] By now, all Member States have transposed the directive. Yet,

---

739  Trybus (n 45) 9.

740  European Commission (n 733); Kévin Martin, 'Observatoire des marchés publics de défense et de sécurité européens' (*Fondation pour la Recherche Stratégique*, October 2019) <https://www.frstrategie.org/programmes/observatoire-des-marches-publi cs-de-defense-et-de-securite-europeens/bulletins/2019/2> accessed 16 September 2022.

741  Mölling (n 44) 14.

742  European Commission, Report on the Transposition of directive 2009/81/EC on Defence and Security Procurement, COM/2012/565 final, 2 October 2012.

in 2018, the Commission opened infringement procedures for the first time against five Member States for breaches of the Procurement Directive.[743] Due to the sensitive nature of procurement decisions in terms of national security and economic considerations, the Commission and defence companies have generally proved to be reluctant to take legal actions against Member States.[744]

This shows how difficult a task it remains for the Commission to create a genuine EDEM against the Member States' continuing resistance when it comes to harmonising defence-related policies. In 2016, the Procurement Directive was reviewed by the Commission, but left unchanged.[745] Identified implementation gaps led the Commission to the aforementioned infringement procedures,[746] however ultimately, the Commission has gone as far as the Treaties allow it to go in regulating defence procurement due to the restrictions posed by Art. 346(1)(b) TFEU. Consequently, the European market for defence equipment remains fragmented and inefficient as Member States can make use of the many exceptions to derogate from the Procurement Directive.

### 3.2.1.3.6. The European Defence Fund – the start of supranational capability development?

Due to the legal limits posed by the armaments exception, further developments in the ECAP were stalled until 2017, when the EDF[747] was introduced.

The EDF represents for the first time in European defence integration a supranational budget in CSDP matters, thus bridging the traditional supranational-intergovernmental divide in European defence integration since the failure of the EDC, which would have included supranational defence procurement (see parts *2.1.1. Historical Evolution of European Defence and Armaments Integration* and *3.2.1. European Armaments Cooperation – torn between intergovernmentalism and supranationalism*).

---

743 European Commission, 'Defence Procurement: Commission opens infringement procedures against 5 Member States' (*European Commission*, 25 January 2018) <https://ec.europa.eu/commission/presscorner/detail/en/IP_18_357> accessed 10 September 2022.

744 Besch (n 502).

745 European Commission (n 738).

746 European Commission (n 743).

747 Regulation (EU) 2021/697 (n 186); Regulation (EU) 2018/1092 (n 186).

The EDF has as one of its explicit objectives the promotion of the EU's 'strategic autonomy' and to close the EU's capability gap (Recital 5 EDF Regulation). It is thus contextually closely linked to CSDP matters and the EU's overall EDU efforts (see part *3.2.1.1. Towards a European Defence Union and potential consequences for European Armaments Cooperation*).

The EDF co-finances collaborative capability projects between three (sometimes two) or more Member States or associated countries. PESCO projects are eligible to receive additional funding (Article 13 EDF Regulation). The overall objective of the EDF is to generate cost-efficiencies, reduce duplications and overcome the European defence market fragmentation (Recital 3 EDF Regulation). It thus addresses the industrial dimension of strategic autonomy by strengthening the EDTIB. The fund focuses mainly on collaborative R&D and acquisition of defence capabilities.

Despite its CSDP dimension, the fund is administered by the Commission (Recital 21, Art. 11 EDF Regulation), which conventionally has had no mandate in CSDP matters. According to Art. 41(2) TEU in particular, CFSP operating expenditures are charged to the Union's (supranational) budget, however expenditure arising from operations having military or defence implications is precluded. Conventionally, there was thus no supranational funding for defence integration.

To overcome this legal obstacle, the legal basis for the Commission's activities related to the EDF is therefore construed from the Commission's Internal Market competences (Arts. 173, 182(4), 183, 188(2) TFEU for 'Industry' and 'Research and technological development and space') instead. This is why the EDF specifically addresses the industrial dimension of defence integration by promoting the EDTIB and the Single Market for defence (Recitals 3, 4 EDF Regulation). This approach to circumvent the conventional supranational preclusion of defence matters under EU primary law via Internal Market law is not without legal questions,[748] yet the Member States (who are "Masters of the Treaties") support it and have adopted the EDF Regulation in the Council.

The EDF represents a significant step forward in European capability development. Its budget close to 8 billion Euros for 2021–2027 will significantly promote more coordinated and fiscally more efficient European armaments collaboration.[749] Legally, the EDF has opened the path for

---

748  Terhechte (n 27) 373.
749  Steven Blockmans and Dylan Macchiarini Crosson, 'Differentiated integration within PESCO – clusters and convergence in EU defence' [2019] 4 CEPS Research Re-

supranational defence capability development beyond the strict (intergovernmental) limits of the CSDP and beyond the Commission's prior mere EDEM harmonisation efforts.[750] There is currently much discussion[751] as to how the EDF could be enhanced and as a policy instrument be potentially further used to increase the EU's role in directing defence policy.[752]

However, like the Defence Package directives, the EDF inhibits several deficits when it comes to establishing comprehensive European capability development, which are also rooted in the aforementioned armaments exception provision and the intergovernmental arrangement of European defence integration. This limits its effectiveness.

Firstly, since the EDF's legal basis lies in the Commission's Internal Market competences, the Commission has no mandate to determine specific defence capabilities necessary for CSDP missions or to close Member State capability gaps.

Such a mandate would be incompatible with Art. 346(1)(b) TFEU, since the interests of the Internal Market do not extend to defence coordination, and it would thus violate the Member States' essential security interests. The award criteria for EDF funding (Art. 12 EDF Regulation) are thus also rather broad and do not set out preferences for specific defence capability development. The criteria only confer a mandate to the Commission which addresses the industrial dimension of capability development (bolstering the EDTIB), but not the strategic dimension. This competence remains with the Member States (Art. 3 EDF Regulation).

This means that the Commission has no managing powers when it comes to capability development, but rather remains reduced to a coordinating and promoting role. Through the EDF, European capability development is now partially supranationally funded, however its execution

---

port 1, 1; EDA, 'EDA study analyses defence industrial strategies' (*EDA*, 11 October 2022) <https://eda.europa.eu/news-and-events/news/2022/10/11/eda-study-analyses defence industrial-strategies> accessed 19 October 2022.

750  Hoeffler (n 46) 64.

751  European Commission (n 43); European Court of Auditors, 'The Preparatory action on defence
research' (*European Court of Auditors*, 26 April 2023) <https://www.eca.europa.eu/ECAPublications/SR-2023-10/SR-2023-10_EN.pdf> accessed 27 April 2023.

752  Jesse Peters, 'Convenient, but controversial: Why the European Defence Fund should not be expanded as the Commission becomes 'geopolitical' (*European Law Blog*, 5 July 2022) <https://europeanlawblog.eu/2022/07/05/convenient-but-controversial-why-the-european-defence-fund-should-not-be-expanded-as-the-commission-becomes-geopolitical/> accessed 2 September 2022.

remains intergovernmental and dependent on selected collaborating Member States. Consequently, European armaments collaboration remains fragmented and genuine comprehensive common armaments policy coordination continues to be non-existent.

Furthermore, the EDF does not resolve the issue of diverging armaments export policies between collaborating Member States. As discussed in parts *2.1.2. Historical Evolution of the Franco-German Armaments Collaboration* and *2.2.2. Franco-German Armaments Cooperation today*, divergences in policies of exports of armaments stemming from collaborative projects are a central obstacle to European armaments collaboration (especially when Germany participates).

The EDF regulation[753] makes it clear that its funding shall not have any influence over the Member States' export decisions over those armaments that were developed with EDF funding (see Arts. 20(9), 23(3) EDF Regulation). This was the result of rigid opposition by the Member States (France in particular) against any EU authority over armaments exports.[754] Consequently, this principal obstacle to enhanced European armaments collaboration remains under the EDF – an EU instrument that is intended to facilitate such collaboration. In particular with regard to Franco-German armaments collaboration, the EDF is thus not an instrument which provides more reliability in terms of ensuring the realisation of their large-scale projects.

### 3.2.1.3.7. Assessment and Outlook – incomplete EDEM

Since the 1990s, defence procurement in Europe has gradually moved beyond the strict intergovernmental design through increasing supranational regulation. However, 14 years after the introduction of the Defence Package, lacking effects in terms of setting-up a genuine EDEM persist. From the perspective of EU primary law, this is because defence-industrial policy has remained primarily national and intergovernmental, entailing the known unreliability and inefficiency issues (see part *2.2.2. Franco-German Armaments Cooperation today*).

---

753  Regulation (EU) 2021/697 (n 186).
754  Besch (n 190).

The Member States continue to invoke Art. 346(1)(b) TFEU and thus circumvent the directives or rely on exceptions which the directives provide.[755] According to EDA, the Member States conducted just 11 % of their total equipment procurement in cooperation with other EU Member States in 2020, falling well short of the 35 % collective benchmark, which is also a commitment under PESCO.[756]

Furthermore, through EDA, the Member States have created a supranational procurement capacity, which has however, due to its intergovernmental configuration and location within the CSDP, remained under strict Member State control.

Consequently, the EDEM continues to be fragmented. The unnecessary duplications and the uncoordinated development and procurement of defence capabilities by the Member States continue to entail cost inefficiencies and undermine the effectiveness of European defence. Furthermore, as a result of market and industrial fragmentation, defence systems lack interoperability, which in turn undermines effective cooperation between the Member States' armed forces, for example in multinational units or CSDP missions, because capabilities cannot be shared.

A potential solution to promote European armaments cooperation and European defence procurement is presented via the EDF since 2017. However, despite it being a milestone in European defence integration, its effects vis-à-vis reducing the EDEM's fragmentation nevertheless remain limited. Through the EDF, the Commission has become part of the (technically still) intergovernmental CSDP structure,[757] although within the narrow (contested) limits of the Treaties. Crucial aspects of a comprehensive and coherent ECAP, such as managing capability development or armaments exports (see part *3.2.1.4. Towards a Comprehensive European Arms Export Regime?*) remain outside its control.

The Commission is currently exploring ways to further collaborative defence procurement in Europe and thus European capability development. These proposals encompass new financing solutions like incentivizing joint Member State procurement of defence equipment, including through VAT exemptions,[758] exempting goods and services used in activities carried out

---

755  European Commission (n 738); Trybus (n 45); Trybus and Butler (n 718).
756  EDA (n 110).
757  Hoeffler (n 46) 45.
758  European Commission, Proposal for a Regulation of the European Parliament and of the Council on establishing the European defence industry Reinforcement

by the armed forces of one Member State in another Member State from VAT as part of defence efforts under the CSDP[759], and increase the size of the EDF.[760] While these (proposed) financial incentives are likely to further promote more efficient and collaborative European capability development and the EDTIB, they remain within the limits of current EU primary law and do not address the underlying intergovernmental structure of the CSDP and the armaments exception, which entrench structural industrial and legal defence market fragmentation and in turn entail fiscal and de-fence-strategic inefficiencies. The Commission's supranational EDEM har-monisation efforts within the intergovernmental limits of EU primary law have been appropriately coined 'intergovernmental supranationalism'[761].

The gradual harmonisation of defence procurement as part of broader European defence integration is an important step towards the potential creation of an EDU (see part *3.2.1.1. Towards a European Defence Union and potential consequences for European Armaments Cooperation*) in the future.[762] Yet for now, the efforts to create an integrated European defence market remain overall incomplete.

As the limits and deficits of the Defence Package and the EDF have shown, the Commission has gone as far as the Treaties allow it to go. Despite supranational legislation, the EDF and the CJEU's case law, Art. 346(1)(b) TFEU continues to significantly impede the creation of an EDEM and a comprehensive and coherent ECAP. Most major military equipment contracts continue to be awarded without an EU-wide tender as EDA data shows. Furthermore, defence procurement takes place within (PESCO, EDA, EDF) and outside (OCCAR, LoI, ad hoc multilateral co-operation formats) the framework of the EU, further contributing to the EDEM's institutional, legal and industrial fragmentation.

Within the EU framework, this fragmentation is furthered by intergov-ernmental and supranational approaches. This lack of coherence and coor-dination means that economic (costly duplications) and defence-political inefficiencies (impeded capability development) remain.

---

through common Procurement Act, COM/2022/349 final, 19 July 2022; European Commission (n 51).

759 European Commission, Proposal for a Council Implementing Regulation amending Implementing Regulation (EU) No 282/2011 as regards the update of the VAT and/or excise duty exemption certificate, COM/2022/8 final, 13 January 2022.

760 European Commission (n 43).

761 Dyson and Konstadinides (n 91) 111–112.

762 Dyson and Konstadinides (n 91) 89.

Consequently, the EU falls short of its potentials as the most appropriate framework for reliable European defence procurement, at least under current EU law. As will be discussed in the subsequent parts, whether this will change in the future is highly dependent on the Member States' political will and their adherence to national sovereignty over defence-related issues.

Since increasing (reliable and efficient) European armaments collaboration and capability development is viewed as necessary with regard to current geopolitical developments in the EU's neighbourhood, it appears necessary to discuss potential options for legal change and development against the continuing political background constraints posed by the Member States. This discussion will take place in part *3.2.2. Making European Armaments Cooperation reliable?*.

### 3.2.1.4. Towards a Comprehensive European Armaments Export Regime?

As discussed in the contextual section of this thesis (*The Context: 2. Franco-German Armaments Collaboration and European Armaments Cooperation*), the issue of divergence of armaments export policies in Europe is a central impediment to trans-European armaments collaboration. Besides (non-EU) multilateral (see part *3.3. Multilateral European Armaments Cooperation – unreliable but effective?*) and bilateral (see part *3.1. Unreliabilities of Franco-German Armaments Collaboration in the Bilateral Framework*) attempts to achieve some convergence on the intergovernmental level in recent years, there have been ongoing efforts at the EU level to strengthen and partially harmonize Member States' armaments export policies.[763] The most relevant outcomes of these efforts are the 1998 CoC, which in 2008 became the EU Common Position[764] (CP) on armaments exports, and the EU's Dual-Use Regulation[765], both of which will be discussed in this part. Worth mentioning however are also the 1998[766] and 2022[767] Council

---

763  Bromley (n 58).

764  (n 61).

765  (n 253).

766  Joint Action of 17 December 1998 adopted by the Council on the basis of Article J.3 of the Treaty on European Union on the European Union's contribution to combating the destabilising accumulation and spread of small arms and light weapons [1999] OJ L9/1.

767  Council Decision (CFSP) 2022/1965 of 17 October 2022 in support of the United Nations Programme of Action to Prevent, Combat and Eradicate the Illicit Trade in Small Arms and Light Weapons in All Its Aspects [2022] OJ L270/67.

Joint Actions on Small Arms and Light Weapons, the 2003 Council Common Position on Arms Brokering[768], the 2019 Anti-Torture Regulation[769], and the EU's arms embargos[770], which are legally binding for all Member States[771]. Furthermore, the Member States participate in most international defence-related export control regimes.[772] Despite these efforts at the EU level however, armaments export decisions ultimately remain a Member States prerogative, leading to legal and political fragmentation in the EU and impeding reliable armaments collaboration.

When it comes to armaments exports within the EU context, it is further necessary to distinguish between external and internal harmonisation of exports. Exports in the context of this thesis are to be understood as extra-EU trade in armaments. This is the focus of this part. Beginnings of such external export harmonisation can be seen in particular in the form of the CP and the Dual-Use Regulation, although their scope is limited. By contrast, intra-EU trade in armaments relates to the EDEM and has become partially regulated via the Transfer Directive. This has been discussed in detail in part *3.2.1.3. The European Armaments Policy and its future.* Both external and internal European harmonisation efforts of armaments transfers have in common that they are significantly limited by the infamous Art. 346(1)(b) TFEU, which likewise has been discussed in

---

768 Council Common Position 2003/468/CFSP of 23 June 2003 on the control of arms brokering [2003] OJ L156/79.

769 Regulation (EU) 2019/125 of the European Parliament and of the Council of 16 January 2019 concerning trade in certain goods which could be used for capital punishment, torture or other cruel, inhuman or degrading treatment or punishment (codification) [2019] OJ L30/1.

770 For an overview of the EU's global sanctions, see <https://sanctionsmap.eu/#/m ain>.

771 Marc Bungenberg, 'Artikel 215, in Hans von der Groeben et al. (eds), *Europäisches Unionsrecht* (7th edn, Nomos 2015) 426–457; Henning Schneider and Jörg Terhechte, 'Art. 215' in Eberhard Grabitz et al. (eds), *Das Recht der Europäischen Union Kommentar 2* (May 2014 EL 53, C.H.Beck 2022) 15; Juliane Kokott, 'Art. 215', Rudolf Streinz (ed), EUV/AEUV (3rd edn, C.H.Beck 2018) 1968.

772 Such as the Australia Group, the Missile Technology Control Regime, the Nuclear Suppliers' Group, the Wassenaar Arrangement, FFA, Wassenaar Arrangement (WA), Control Regime (MTCR), Nuclear Non-Proliferation Treaty (NPT), Chemical Weapons Convention (CCW), Biological & Toxin Weapons Convention (BTWC), ATT, WTO Agreements, The Hague Code of Conduct against missile proliferation (HCoC), Anti-Personnel Mine Ban Convention (APpMBC), UN Programme of Action on Small Arms (PoA), Proliferation Security Initiative (PSI), Global Initiative to Combat Nuclear Terrorism (GICNT), UN SC Resolutions, or Customary International Law.

detail in part *3.2.1.3. The European Armaments Policy and its future.* When it comes to external harmonisation of trade in armaments, the armaments exception puts armaments exports principally outside the scope of EU law. This is why the Member States continue to maintain ultimate control over their armaments export decisions and insist on their sovereignty in this area.[773] For the larger armaments-producing Member States, extra-EU exports are also significantly more relevant than intra-EU transfers. For example, it has been pointed out that between 2014 and 2018, 90 per cent of France's armaments exports and 73 per cent of Germany's were extra-EU transfers.[774]

The issue of armaments exports from the EU to third countries and their legal harmonisation on the European level continues to be politically and legally highly controversial. Continuing Member State concerns regarding sovereignty over defence policy issues and defence-industrial protectionism[775] clash with the objective multidimensional (defence policy, legal, and economic) need for convergence. Since armaments export control inhibits this transversal nature by encompassing security and defence policy matters while also relating to trade policy and Internal Market matters, the EU legislation which deals with the many aspects of armaments trade (like conventional arms, civilian fire-arms or dual-use products) is based on different EU competences and originates either from the Commission (under Single Market law) or the European Council (under CFSP law). This also entrenches fragmentation within EU law.

As discussed in part *2.1.1. Historical Evolution of European Defence and Armaments*, since the 1957 Treaty of Rome, defence policy issues, including armaments exports, were largely exempted from EC/EU law and only gradually moved within its scope. This exemption was legally expressed by what is today Art. 346(1)(b) TFEU. Consequently, the rules for armaments exports in Europe became highly fragmented while the Member States pursued widely divergent national armaments export policies. With the exception of multilateral arms embargos, until the 1990s, the Member States were reluctant to cede any national control over their respective armaments

---

773  Grebe (n 58).
774  Sophia Besch and Beth Oppenheim, 'The EU needs an effective common arms export policy' (*Centre for European Reform*, 4 June 2019) <https://www.cer.eu/publ ications/archive/bulletin-article/2019/eu-needs-effective-common-arms-export-pol icy> accessed 22 June 2020.
775  Cops et al. (n 60) 189–190.

export regimes. This reluctant stance only began to change because of several developments following the fall or the Iron Curtain. The Member States subsequently began to agree on a range of instruments to increase convergence and coherence of their national armaments export regimes. Again, as briefly discussed in part *2.1.1. Historical Evolution of European Defence and Armaments*, the emergence of the CFSP and the CSDP (ESDP at the time) provided an opportunity for common action in this area. Furthermore, the increasing consolidation and internationalisation of the EDTIB during the 1990s increased the economic need for a more coordinated approach to armaments exports on the European level. This economic need was then accompanied by a political rationale following the adverse effects of certain Member States armaments exports to repressive regimes and even embargoed countries during the 1980s and 1990s.[776]

This need for increased convergence and coherence continues to this day. The EU's efforts towards further convergence of armaments export matters are part of its broader efforts to further develop the CFSP/CSPD in the context of the EU's increasingly challenging geopolitical environment, in particular with regard to EDU, defence capability development and strengthening the EDTIB as part of the ECAP as foreseen in Art. 42(3) TEU (see part *3.2.1.1. Towards a European Defence Union and potential consequences for European Armaments Cooperation*). As discussed in parts *2.1. Historical Context: Evolution of European Defence Integration and Franco-German Armaments Cooperation* and *2.2. Current Context: State of European Defence Integration and Franco-German Armaments Cooperation*, closer European armaments cooperation and integration are inconceivable without further convergence of European armaments export policies, which is a central recurring contentious issue in European armaments cooperation. In other words, the existing heterogonous armaments export policies in Europe are an impediment to necessary European capability development.

Despite widespread consensus on the need for convergence and harmonisation of European armaments export policies, in practice, effective steps to achieve such convergence have nevertheless been stalled by the Member States, even in recent years.[777] Since the early debates on European export

---

776  Bromley (n 58).

777  Diederik Cops and Nils Duquet, 'Reviewing the EU Common Position on arms exports: Whither EU arms transfer controls?' (*Flemish Peace Institute*, 2019) <https:/ /vlaamsvredesinstituut.eu/wp-content/uploads/2019/12/VI_policy-brief_EU_ar

harmonisation in the 1990s, the divergence of Member State export regulation and notions for potential convergence and coherence have since remained an impediment for European defence and armaments integration. While Member States like France and the UK favoured more flexible and liberal export regimes, Germany has maintained its restrictive position.[778] This is why the scope of EU legislation regarding armaments exports remains limited. These different armaments export cultures in Europe must be kept in mind when it comes to making proposals for legal change, as they significantly limit the feasibility of such change due to the unanimity requirements in Council decisions or treaty revision.

### 3.2.1.4.1. The EU's Common Position on Armaments Exports – substantial convergence?

The cornerstone on the EU level towards more convergence and coherence in the Member States' armaments export policies is the 2008 Council CP on armaments exports[779] (including the 2019 updated version[780], which only features minor changes and takes into account a number of EU and international developments that have resulted in new obligations and commitments for the Member States, in particular relating to the ATT). As a CFSP decision it is intergovernmental but legally binding[781] for all Member States under Art. 288(4)[782] TFEU in accordance with Art. 25(b) (ii)[783] in conjunction with Art. 29 TEU[784]. However, because it is part of

---

ms_export_2019web.pdf> accessed 28 October 2022; Mark Bromley and Michael Brzoska, 'Towards a Common, Restrictive EU Arms Export Policy? The Impact of the EU Code of Conduct on Major Conventional Arms Exports' [2008] 13(3) European Foreign Affairs Review 333, 333–356.

778  Trybus (n 34) 255.
779  (n 61).
780  Council Decision (CFSP) 2019/1560 of 16 September 2019 amending Common Position 2008/944/CFSP defining common rules governing control of exports of military technology and equipment [2019] OJ L239/16.
781  Pechstein (n 59) 427; Cremer (n 466) 385–390; Kaufmann-Bühler (n 660) 9; a different view is offered by Regelsberger and Kugelmann (n 660) 249–250, who deny direct application and supremacy of the intergovernmental CFSP law and instead argue that its effect is limited by the Member States' respective constitutional orders.
782  Ruffert (n 464) 2400–2402; Biervert (n 464) 3011–3029.
783  Cremer (n 465) 367–372; Terhechte (n 465) 333–335.
784  Cremer (n 466) 385–390; Terhechte (n 466) 344–348.

CFSP law, the CJEU's jurisdiction is precluded (Art. 275 TFEU). The only control mechanism for Member State compliance is established through confidential information sharing among the Member States on the basis of the national exports reporting requirement in Art. 8 CP, which entails "naming and shaming"/peer pressure by the other Member States in case of non-compliance.

The CP stipulates eight (rudimentary) common criteria that the Member States should apply in their (extra-EU) armaments export decisions and creates a mechanism for consultation and information exchange. They are: 1. Respect for the international obligations and commitments of Member States, in particular the sanctions adopted by the UN Security Council or the European Union, agreements on non-proliferation and other subjects, as well as other international obligations, 2. Respect for human rights in the country of final destination as well as respect by that country of international humanitarian law, 3. Internal situation in the country of final destination, as a function of the existence of tensions or armed conflicts, 4. Preservation of regional peace, security and stability, 5. National security of the Member States and of territories whose external relations are the responsibility of a Member State, as well as that of friendly and allied countries, 6. Behaviour of the buyer country with regard to the international community, as regards in particular its attitude to terrorism, the nature of its alliances and respect for international law, 7. Existence of a risk that the military technology or equipment will be diverted within the buyer country or re-exported under undesirable conditions, and 8. Compatibility of the exports of the military technology or equipment with the technical and economic capacity of the recipient country, taking into account the desirability that states should meet their legitimate security and defence needs with the least diversion of human and economic resources for armaments.

These common criteria serve as common minimum standards (individual Member States, like Germany[785], can apply stricter principles if they wish to do) for armaments exports and apply to military goods based on the EU Common Military List[786] (Art. 12 CP). The list is almost identical to

---

785 Under its 2019 Political Principles, Germany applies stricter criteria for example with regard to the Human Rights situation in destination countries and does not grant licences under economic considerations, which Art. 10 CP expressly permits, see Bundesregierung (n 317).

786 (n 395).

the Munitions List of the Wassenaar Arrangement[787]. In this context it is important to note that according to Art. 12 CP, the EU Common Military List shall act as a reference point for the Member States' armaments export regimes and does not replace the respective national lists. Also, the CP does not establish a harmonised licencing regime similar to the Transfer Directive (see part *3.2.1.3. The European Armaments Policy and its future*). This again shows that armaments export control remains a national prerogative under EU law, which also follows from Art. 346(1)(b) TFEU, which continues to apply.[788]

Consultation and information exchange between the Member States regarding CP implementation, national export decisions, and potential for harmonisation take place on a monthly basis within COARM. While it remains questionable how much convergence can effectively be achieved in a forum like COARM, it serves a relevant purpose having practical effects. Under Art. 4 CP, if a Member State intends to grant an export licence to a country to which such a licence was denied earlier by another Member State, it is obligated to notify the other Member States and justify its decision. The purpose of this denial notification procedure is to prevent undercutting other Member States' more restrictive export policies ("export control forum shopping") when it comes to applying the Common Position criteria in licencing decisions.[789]

COARM has also developed an electronic system for information-sharing and has developed a User's Guide[790] to facilitate a more consistent interpretation and application of the CP criteria by the national export control authorities (based on Art. 13 CP). While it certainly is a step towards a more uniform interpretation and application of the CP criteria, it is not legally binding and thus only of limited reliability when it comes to overcoming European armaments export control fragmentation.

---

787  Wassenaar Arrangement Secretariat, 'Wassenaar Arrangement on Export Controls for Conventional Arms and Dual-Use Goods and Technologies, Public Documents Volume II, List of Dual-Use Goods and Technologies and Munitions List' (*WAS*, December 2022) <https://www.wassenaar.org/app/uploads/2022/12/List-of-Dual-Use-Goods-and-Technologies-Munitions-List-Dec-2022.pdf> accessed 6 December 2022.

788  Wisotzki and Mutschler (n 58) 279.

789  Cops et al. (n 60) 39.

790  Council of the European Union, User's Guide to Council Common Position 2008/944/CFSP defining common rules governing the control of exports of military technology and equipment, COARM 153, CFSP/PESC 683, 16 September 2019.

In this regard, the EU Common Military List is also of limited relevance when it comes to achieving European convergence. Indeed, the development of that list since 2000 has had an important effect on harmonising the Member States' armaments export control regimes, although ultimately the national lists remain decisive. The list serves as a common framework for determining the material scope of these regimes for both the intra-EU and extra-EU trade in armaments. Without this list, the differences among the Member States with regard to the material scope of their respective armaments control regimes would be much larger.[791] Nevertheless, the lack of the CP's enforceability also applies to the Common Military List, entrenching legal and policy fragmentation and unreliability.

The fact that the cornerstone of the efforts to achieve convergence of the Member States' armaments exports at the European level is part of the (intergovernmental) CFSP framework under the auspices of the Council is significant. This again reflects the Member States' intent to retain national sovereignty over armaments matters, which is also expressed in Art. 346(1) (b) TFEU and the intergovernmental nature of the CSDP's ECAP. Any control of the (supranational) Commission over armaments exports is consequently precluded. This is relevant to note since the Commission has become increasingly active in harmonising the EDEM and is even (co-)funding European collaborative programmes through the EDF, based on its Internal Market competence (see part *3.2.1.3. The European Armaments Policy and its future*).

Therefore, when it comes to assessing the effectiveness of the CP as a legal instrument in terms of achieving convergence of armaments export policies, much remains to be desired.[792] While the CP is legally binding, which is certainly a significant step forward from its precursory CoC (being only soft law), the enforceability of the criteria (which are minimal common standards anyway) as set out in the CP however remains very limited. Since the CP is a legal instrument under the CFSP, while binding, the CJEU (or any other independent authority or mechanism at the EU level to sanction non-compliance) has no jurisdiction to enforce it (Art. 275 TFEU). It is highly doubtful whether information exchange procedures and mechanisms are sufficient to achieve compliance with the CP criteria, never mind convergence of the Member States' export control regimes.

---

791  Cops et al. (n 60) 167.
792  Wisotzki and Mutschler (n 58) 275.

Furthermore, Art. 346(1)(b) TFEU continues to apply and enable Member States to fall short of their obligations under the CP. This has led to lack of coherence and reliability.[793] Legislative acts under the CFSP are excluded (Arts. 24(1), 31(1) TEU). Furthermore, most commentators agree that the primacy of EU law does not apply for CFSP decisions, since they are not supranational law but "only" intergovernmental law.[794] Except for Art. 40 TEU and fundamental rights provisions (which are concerned in case of CFSP sanction decisions)[795], this further underlines that the CJEU has no jurisdiction on the matter (Art. 24(1) subpara. 2 TEU).[796] While under Art. 29 TEU the Member States are obliged to adapt their own national policies in accordance with the CP,[797] they however remain exclusively competent to determine the extent to which the criteria are implemented into their national export control regimes and how they are interpreted in practice.[798] While the CP has led to some rudimentary convergence of the Member States' export control regimes, the consequence of the resulting Member States prerogative over armaments export decisions remains to be 27 (significantly different) national armaments export regimes and policies, which are often contradictory, incoherently incorporate the CP criteria,[799] and are often guided by political or defence-industrial considerations.[800] A recent example for the CP's lacking effects are the UK's armaments export to Saudi Arabia during the Yemen conflict.[801]

Consequently, the CP's primary effect has been creating a mechanism for the Member States to exchange information and enhance transparency regarding export decisions. This is insufficient from an armaments integration perspective under which further convergence and coherence in national armaments export policies are urgently required to ensure reliable European armaments cooperation.

---

793  Wisotzki and Mutschler (n 58).
794  Terhechte (n 465) 334–335; Thym (n 664) 1241; Pechstein (n 59) 427; similarly BVerfG (n 102) at 342, 390; different views are presented by Cremer (n 466) 385–390; Kaufmann-Bühler (n 660) 9.
795  Arts. 24(1) subpara. 2 TEU, 275 TFEU; Case C-72/15 (n 665).
796  Case C-455/14 P (n 666); Case C-348/12 P (n 666).
797  Cremer (n 466) 385–390; Terhechte (n 466) 344–348.
798  Cops et al. (n 60) 41–42.
799  Hansen (n 58) 211; Cops et al. (n 60) 161.
800  Wisotzki and Mutschler (n 58) 279; Besch and Oppenheim (n 774).
801  Niall McCarthy, 'UK arms exports to Saudi Arabia fuel Yemen conflict' (*Statista*, 28 March 2017) <https://www.statista.com/chart/8708/uk-arms-exports-to-saudi-arabi a-fuel-yemen-conflict/> accessed 2 December 2022.

### 3.2.1.4.2. The Dual-Use Regulation – a starting point for EU-wide armaments export harmonisation?

Besides the CP, further convergence with regard to defence-related exports has been achieved on the EU level via the Dual-Use Regulation. Again, since the early beginnings of European integration, the debate as to whether and to what extent national competences over export control should be ceded to the supranational level is highly contentious due to sovereignty concerns. Consequently, comprehensive regulation in this area is still not achieved, in particular with regard to armaments exports, which remain under national control on the basis of Art. 346(1)(b) TFEU (see above).

With regard to dual-use goods however, the armaments exception does not apply, since they are not mentioned in the 1958 Council List[802] to which the provisions of Art. 346(1)(b) TFEU apply in accordance with Art. 346(2) TFEU.[803] This has opened the path for supranational harmonisation, starting in 2009 with the Dual-Use Regulation[804] which was recast in 2021[805] to align it with Member States' international commitments stemming from non-proliferation regimes (in particular the Wassenaar Arrangement and the Missile Technology Control Regime). Simultaneously, the Commission's powers to oversee export control have increased. The legal basis for the Dual-Use Regulation thus does not stem from CFSP law but from Art. 207(2) TFEU, i.e. the Commission's (exclusive) Common Commercial Policy (CCP) competence, which gives the Commission regulatory power.

Consequently, as part of the CCP, the Dual-Use Regulation is binding and directly applicable throughout the EU. Nevertheless, the competence for implementation of the regulation's provisions in their national export control regimes lies with the Member States, which therefore continue to be ultimately responsible for export decisions. However, since the Dual-Use Regulation is part of supranational law, the Commission is able to sanction Member State infringements by relying on the CJEU.

The Dual-Use Regulation includes common export control rules, including a common set of assessment criteria (for example relating to the CP and international obligations stemming from non-proliferation regimes),

---

802   (n 691).
803   Dittert (n 31) 1993; Trybus (n 34) 149; Case C-337/05 (n 701); Case C-157/06 (n 701); Case C-615/10 (n 701).
804   (n 114).
805   (n 253).

common types of export authorisations (individual, global and general authorisations, corresponding to the licencing regime under the Transfer Directive), a common EU list of dual-use items, common provisions for end-use controls on non-listed items which could be used for example in connection with a WMD programme or for Human Rights violations, controls on brokering and technical assistance relating to dual-use items and their transit through the EU, specific control measures and compliance to be introduced by exporters, such as record-keeping and registers, and provisions setting up a network of competent authorities supporting the exchange of information to ensure the consistent implementation and enforcement of controls throughout the EU.

The EU's dual-use export regime is highly sophisticated. Encompassing a very detailed licencing regime (Art. 12 Dual-Use Regulation) and strict end-use control (Arts. 12(4), 16, 27(1)(d) Dual-Use Regulation), it has the potential to be expanded to also cover the export of European armaments or serve as a reference point for an EU armaments export regulation, provided the necessary political will by the Member States.

While the Member States are responsible to implement the Dual-Use Regulation, it is administered and overseen by the Commission. Under Chapter IV of the regulation, the Commission is responsible for amendments to the lists of dual-use items and destinations, under Chapter VI for administrative cooperation, implementation and enforcement. Considering the overall success of the Dual-Use Regulation in harmonising the export of dual-use goods and the Commission's overall successful administration of that regime, it seems plausible that the Commission would be able to expand its export control regime potentially further to also cover the export of armaments which are currently covered by the 1958 Council List. The feasibility of creating such a supranational regime for European armaments exports will be discussed in part *3.2.2. Making European Armaments Cooperation reliable?*.

### 3.2.1.4.3. Addendum

In addition to the CP and the Dual-Use Regulation, the EU has introduced legally binding embargo measures[806] as part of its CFSP, which thus also

---

806 For an overview of the EU's global sanctions, see <https://sanctionsmap.eu/#/m ain>.

form part of the EU's efforts of forming a more comprehensive approach to armaments exports. The EU's embargo regimes are administered by the Council, but then again implemented through national measures.

Lastly, besides introducing its own legislation, the EU is a relevant global policy actor when it comes to conventional arms control. As part of its CFSP, it is actively promoting its standards in global forums and regional outreach initiatives, and it also lobbied for the ATT's adoption, widespread acceptance and effective implementation.[807]

### 3.2.1.4.4. Assessment and Outlook – incomplete harmonisation

Since the 1990s, the EU has developed several regulatory initiatives to harmonise the Member States' armaments export control regimes. However, their effects with regard to sufficient convergence are lacking, leaving ample room for national application and interpretation. The ultimate Member States prerogative over armaments export decisions upholds legal fragmentation. The lack of European convergence impedes harmonisation on the European level and entrenches national sovereignty reservations. Germany for example favours further harmonisation on the European level[808], however its highly restrictive ideas are not supported by the majority of the other Member States.[809] Especially France remains unconvinced and wants to retain armaments export control as an exclusive national competence.[810] This is why proposals for a more coherent system for armaments cooperation and export control on the European level by expanding EU competences over armaments export control were actively prevented in the recent years.[811] For example, in the EDF precursor programme European Defence Industrial Development Programme (EDIDP)[812], a French intervention prevented a compromise between the Council, the Commission and the

---

807  Cops and Duquet (n 777).
808  Bundesregierung (239), see page 146; Federal Government of Germany, 'White Paper on German Security Policy and the Future of the Bundeswehr' (*Bundeswehr*, July 2016) <https://www.bundeswehr.de/resource/blob/4800140/fe103a80d8576b 2cd7a135a5a8a86dde/download-white-paper-2016-data.pdf> accessed 25 October 2022.
809  Jungholt (n 163).
810  Descôtes (n 141); Béraud-Sudreau (n 128) 90–91.
811  Cops et al. (n 60) 211.
812  Regulation (EU) 2018/1092 (n 186).

Parliament which was designed so that the Commission had control pow-ers in the case of exports of EU-financed armaments to third countries, including a veto right. This is why the EDIDP Regulation made it clear that its funding should not have any influence over the Member States' export decisions over those armaments that were developed with EU funding (para 10 EDIDP Regulation). The Commission then faced similar oppo-sition during the EDF negotiations (see part *3.2.1.3. The European Arma-ments Policy and its future*).[813] The opportunity for potential further export harmonisation on the EU level has thus been missed. And if Member States oppose any EU control over exports of EU-financed armaments exports, EU control over non-EU-financed armaments is even more inconceivable.

The CP has been reviewed thrice (in 2012, 2015 and 2019) by the Council and this process has revealed the Member States' general unwillingness to further develop it (i.e. further harmonise their export control regimes). France was particularly reserved, but Germany also.[814] Concluding the 2012 review and while recognising the lack of sufficient implementation and convergence regarding the CP, the Council also stated that 'the provisions of the Common Position, and the instruments it provides for, continue to properly serve the objectives set in 2008 and to provide a solid basis for the coordination of Member States' arms export policies.'[815] Following the 2012 review process and to achieve further convergence, the User's Guide (see above) was adapted to achieve a more uniform interpretation and application of the CP criteria and an electronic system was introduced to enhance the sharing of information of export licence denials.[816] This of course did not entail any structural change from a legal perspective to overcome the CP's insufficiencies.

The 2015 review conclusion[817] likewise (rather implicitly) recognized that further convergence is possible, but only led to minor improvements. In this regard, the Council welcomed the amended User's Guide to the CP as a

---

813 Besch (n 190); Keul and Bütikofer (n 127).
814 Hansen (n 58) 211.
815 Council of the European Union, Council conclusions on the review of Council Common Position 2008/944/CFSP defining common rules governing control of ex-ports of military technology and Equipment, COARM 245 PESC 1404, 19 Novem-ber 2012.
816 Wisotzki and Mutschler (n 58) 280.
817 Council of the European Union, Council conclusions relating to the review of Common Position 2008/944/CFSP on arms exports and the implementation of the Arms Trade treaty (ATT), COARM 174 CFSP/PESC 401, July 2015.

tool for further convergence, but the fundamental insufficiencies of the CP as a legal instrument were again not addressed.

The third review in 2019 primarily revolved around the CP's update to include new instruments to be in line with the ATT. The User's Guide was therefore amended to further operationalise the risk assessment criteria laid down by the CP. Furthermore, the objective need for further European convergence of armaments export matters was also recognised by the Member States. The 2019 review conclusions note that 'the strengthening of a European defence technological and industrial base, which contributes to the implementation of the Common Foreign and Security Policy, in particular the Common European Security and Defence Policy, should be accompanied by closer cooperation and convergence in the field of export control of military technology and equipment.'[818] This contradiction between pro-harmonisation declarations and contra-harmonisation practice makes the Member States' stance vis-à-vis further export harmonisation somewhat ambiguous. It is also important to note in this context again that this statement by the intergovernmental Council does not propose any structural legal change, never mind the cessation of additional competences to the supranational level.

Despite Member State reluctance, the EU's involvement in armaments exports has gradually developed since the 1990s, encompassing more and more aspects of armaments export control and increasing the level of bindingness of the various convergence initiatives. The most relevant outcomes of these efforts are the EU CP and the EU's Dual-Use Regulation. As a consequence, the Member States' armaments export control systems have to a certain extent been harmonised.

Nevertheless, this process remains overall incomplete. Considering that the beginnings of European convergence of armaments export matters date back to the 1990s, it is concerning that the lack of sufficient convergence of armaments export policies continues to endanger reliable European armaments cooperation to this day, as the Franco-German disputes surrounding the Aachen Treaty demonstrate (see part *2.2.2. Franco-German Armaments Cooperation today*).

While the CP has led to some convergence of the Member States' armaments export regimes, enforceability remains lacking, since applying the

---

818 Council of the European Union, Council conclusions on the review of Council Common Position 2008/944/CFSP of 8 December 2008 on the control of arms exports, COARM 154 CFSP/PESC 684, 16 September 2019.

CP's criteria remains an exclusive Member States competence. The CJEU has no jurisdiction in CFSP matters and Art. 346(1)(b) TFEU remains fully preserved. This likewise applies to the EU Common Military List, which is today legally binding for both intra- and extra-EU trade in defence-related goods.

The Dual-Use Regulation has furthermore led to some convergence of the Member States' export control regimes, however while being enforceable as part of supranational law, it does not apply to "hard defence" goods, which are central to European capability development.

Ultimately, despite the EU's growing efforts to harmonise the Member States' armaments export regimes, it is the Member States which remain in control over their armaments export policies, control systems and licencing decisions. The consequence of the resulting Member State prerogative over armaments export decisions remains to be 27 (significantly different) national armaments export regimes and policies, which are often contradictory and incoherent. A comprehensive European armaments export regime is currently not underway.

This is turn continues to undermine reliable European armaments cooperation, which requires sufficient convergence of armaments export matters. Seeing that European armaments cooperation increasingly takes place within EU structures (PESCO and EDF being the most noteworthy) and potentially within an EDU, a coherent and coordinated European armaments export control regime is needed and has the potential to strengthen European armaments cooperation and integration by overcoming the export issue.[819] PESCO already demonstrates the challenges that arise from a multitude of project partners and complex interests which increase the risk of dysfunctionality (see part *3.2.1.2. The Future of European Armaments Cooperation and PESCO*). In this regard, it is concerning that the Member States insist on their national sovereignty in this policy area and remain primarily in control over their respective armaments export regimes.[820]

This again makes it questionable whether EU law (at least in its current form) provides for a more reliable framework for armaments cooperation in Europe than multilateral frameworks. However, the EU's increasingly challenging geopolitical environment and the defence integration momentum since 2017 (PESCO, EDF, CARD) and especially since February 2022 however could provide a window of opportunity for further European

---

819   Atzpodien (n 136).
820   Grebe (n 66).

convergence of armaments export matters. This could then lead to more coherence and reliability.

There is an objective need for further European convergence vis-à-vis armaments exports, as this is a recurring issue in European armaments cooperation. On that basis, there are several options for legal development. Provided the necessary political will, further harmonisation on the EU level could potentially be achieved on the intergovernmental or even on the supranational level, especially if European armaments cooperation increasingly takes place within EU structures in the context of EDU. However, this issue is politically highly controversial, but will nevertheless be further discussed in the subsequent part *3.2.2. Making European Armaments Cooperation reliable?*).

Furthermore, considering the impediments which current EU law and lacking Member State support with regard to Europeanising national armaments export regimes continue to pose, there is also increased scepticism regarding the feasibility of a converged and coherent European armaments export regime.[821] This is why potential further extra-EU intergovernmental convergence will subsequently also be discussed (see part *3.3.3. A Future for Multilateral European Armaments Cooperation?*).

3.2.2. Making European Armaments Cooperation reliable?

To overcome the lasting deficits of European defence procurement and capability development, a comprehensive regulative approach could increase efficiency and reliability. Building on the various legal initiatives discussed in the previous parts, this could encompass a general, exceptionless EU-wide procurement regime for armaments, potentially setting common standards and technical norms, or even confer on EDA or the European Commission a competence to identify capability gaps (which EDA already possesses) and consequently fund or even manage necessary European armaments projects to close these gaps as part of wider EDU efforts. Furthermore, the CJEU's jurisdiction over the ECAP could be expanded to ensure consistent enforcement.

The lack of coherence and convergence of the Member States' armaments export regimes is a central obstacle to reliable European armaments cooperation. Building on the already existing legal initiatives of European armaments export control and the increasing activism of the Commission in the field of armaments cooperation, such a comprehensive regulative approach could further encompass the further development of the CP as

---

821 Cops and Duquet (n 777).

the intergovernmental way forward to achieve more convergence or potentially even further supranationalisation of export control, which partially already exists in the form of the Dual-Use Regulation and could confer on the Commission the competence to establish common rules for armaments exports.

Furthermore, to overcome the institutional EU-multilateral and intra-EU intergovernmental-supranational divide, merging these various frameworks and policies into a coherent ECAP appears appropriate. The legal feasibility of realising these proposals will be discussed in this part.

### 3.2.2.1. Legal Change – a question of competence (Arts. 5(1), (2) TEU, 352 TFEU)

Central to the subsequent discussion is the so-called principle of conferral. Set out in Art. 5(1), (2) TEU, it states that the EU shall only act 'within the limits of the competences conferred upon it by the Member States in the Treaties.' Competences not conferred upon the EU in the Treaties remain with the Member States. Consequently, the EU can only operate and adopt secondary measures in designated policy fields within the limits of conferred competences. However, as apparent in the Commission's defence policy mission-creep, there are examples for creative workarounds.

Also relevant for the subsequent discussion is the principle of *effet utile*. The CJEU has established the principle of *effet utile* in several rulings[822], under which legal interpretation of primary law norms is to be made in a manner which ensures the norms' most effective application.[823] This is relevant to explain the CJEU's narrow interpretation of the armaments exception to protect the interests of the Internal Market (see above) and has allowed the Commission to regulate the EDEM and promote the EDTIB as part of its Internal Market competences.

Furthermore, EU primary law offers some flexibility for potentially extending competences via the implied powers clause of Art. 352 TFEU. The provision provides for cases in which the Treaties have not sufficiently and

---

822 Starting with the famous cases van Gend en Loos and Costa v ENEL, see Case C-26/62, NV Algemene Transport-en Expeditie Onderneming van Gend en Loos v Nederlandse Administratie der Belastigen, [1963] ECR 1; Case C-6-/64, Flaminio Costa v E.N.E.L., [1964] ECR 585.

823 Michael Potacs, 'Effet utile als Auslegungsgrundsatz' [2009] 4 Zeitschrift Europarecht 465, 467; Schorkopf (n 402) 13.

explicitly provided the EU with the necessary powers to attain one of the objectives set out in the Treaties and therefore allows for the conferral of additional competences to the EU. This requires unanimity by the Council (Art. 352(1) TFEU), thus ensuring Member State consent. It is part of the same national sovereignty safeguard system that also protects the Member States sovereignty interests in CSDP matters (Arts. 31(1) subpara. 1, 42(4) TEU) or treaty revisions (in particular Art. 48(1)–(5) TEU for ordinary and Art. 48(6), (7) TEU for simplified revision procedures, such as Art. 42(2) TEU).[824]

However, Art. 352 TFEU is only of limited usefulness when it comes to EDEM harmonisation or armaments integration. While the unanimity requirement in the Council already provides for a high legal hurdle, Art. 352(3) TFEU further states that measures based on Art. 352 TFEU 'shall not entail harmonisation of Member States' laws or regulations in cases where the Treaties exclude such harmonisation'. This is particularly relevant in the context of this thesis because of the armaments exception in Art. 346(1)(b) TFEU, which specifically prevents supranational harmonisation. Furthermore, CSDP matters were intentionally left out of the supranational scope of EU law (see part *2.1.1. Historical Evolution of European Defence and Armaments Integration*) and are not part of the EU's objectives mentioned in Art. 3 TEU. This is ultimately underlined by Art. 352(4) TFEU, which excludes the utilization of Art. 352 TFEU as a basis for attaining CFSP (which – again – includes the CSDP) objectives.[825]

These legal limits together with the aforementioned armaments exception provision prevent a comprehensive regulative approach for European defence procurement and export control. The EU does not have a competence to determine its own competences and its institutions cannot expand their mandate in defence matters beyond their competences under current EU primary law.

---

824 Eileen Denza, 'Article 48 Treaty Revision Procedures' in Hermann-Josef Blanke and Stelio Mangiameli (eds), *The Treaty on European Union (TEU) A Commentary* (Springer 2013) 1331–1355.

825 Patrizia De Pasquale, 'Article 25 The Instruments for the Conduct of the CFSP' in Hermann-Josef Blanke and Stelio Mangiameli (eds), T*he Treaty on European Union (TEU) A Commentary* (Springer 2013) 930–931.

### 3.2.2.2. Legal Change by Treaty Revision (Art. 48 TEU)

This only leaves treaty revision as an option for provide for further EDEM integration and integrated capability development by conferring additional competences to the EU. Treaty revision procedures are set out in Art. 48 TEU. The TEU distinguishes between the ordinary revision procedure[826] (Art. 48(1)–(5) TEU) and the simplified revision procedure[827] (Art. 48(6), (7) TEU). They are both relevant for discussing potential legal options facilitating further armaments integration in Europe and primarily differ in the level of competent institutions required to approve.

The ordinary revision procedure requires consensus by a 'Convention composed of representatives of the national Parliaments, of the Heads of State or Government of the Member States, of the European Parliament and of the Commission' which 'shall adopt by consensus a recommendation to a conference of representatives of the governments of the Member States' in accordance with Art. 48(3) TEU.

By contrast, the simplified treaty revision procedure principally only requires a unanimous decision by the European Council in accordance with Art. 48(6) subpara. 2 TEU.

Consequently, only the Member States have the power to establish, amend or terminate EU competences by unanimous consent, which is a significant obstacle. It is also relevant to note in this context that EU law does not principally exclude any Member State competence from being transferred to the EU. Therefore, far-reaching defence competences could be theoretically conferred upon the EU.[828]

As discussed above, the central legal obstacles to further harmonisation of the EDEM and capability development arise from the intergovernmental arrangement of the CSDP (the principle of unanimity and the marginal role of the Commission in particular) and the armaments exception in the TFEU (limiting the application of Internal Market law to armaments matters), which prevent further supranational harmonisation and even more so farther-reaching proposals like managing powers for capability de-

---

826 Hans-Holger Herrnfeld, 'Artikel 48' in Jürgen Schwarze et al. (eds), *EU-Kommentar* (4th edn, Nomos 2018) 405–408; Matthieu Poujol, 'Article 48 UE' in Isabelle Pingel (ed), *Commentaire Article par Article des Traités UE et CU* (2nd edn, Helbing Lichtenhahn 2010) 232–235; Priollaud and Siritzky (n 187) 138–140.

827 Herrnfeld (n 826) 408–410; Poujol (n 826) 235–236; Priollaud and Siritzky (n 187) 140.

828 Denza (n 824) 1331–1355.

velopment. Discussing potential legal options facilitating further European armaments integration must therefore begin here.

EU primary law does not offer a specific competence title for EDEM integration nor an evolutive clause similar to Art. 42(2) TEU for a common defence (see part *3.2.1.1. Towards a European Defence Union and potential consequences for European Armaments Cooperation*). The simplified revision procedure in Art. 48(6) subpara. 2 TEU however does offer the possibility that the European Council adopts 'a decision amending all or part of the provisions of Part Three' of the TFEU, which relates to the internal policies and action of the EU. The legal basis for the 2009 Defence Package and the EDF was construed from that Part Three of the TFEU and thus it could appear that Art. 48(6) subpara. 2 TEU could potentially serve as a basis to increase the EU's competences for EDEM harmonisation.

However, there are several reasons why this provision must be ruled out in this regard. First, as per Art. 15(4) TEU, 'decisions of the European Council shall be taken by consensus.' This again reflects the respect for the Member States' sovereignty and is a significant obstacle to European defence integration as demonstrated throughout this thesis. But even if there was consensus, according to Art. 48(6) subpara. 3 TEU, such a decision 'shall not increase the competences conferred on the Union in the Treaties'. In the context of the CSDP, the EU institutions are thus prevented from endowing themselves with additional competences not conferred by the Treaties. A flexibility device parallel to the mechanism set by Art. 352 TFEU does not exist.[829] And lastly, Part Three of the TFEU does not cover the armaments exception of Art. 346(1)(b) TFEU (which is part of Part Seven of the TFEU), which therefore cannot be amended via simplified treaty revision and thus continues to apply regardless and ultimately impede defence market harmonisation. Therefore, Art. 48(6) TEU cannot serve as a basis to confer additional competences to the EU for defence market harmonisation.

Of similar interest for enhancing EDEM integration is potentially Art. 48(7) TEU, which reads that where Title V of the TEU 'provides for the Council to act by unanimity in a given area or case, the European Council may adopt a decision authorising the Council to act by a qualified majority in that area or in that case.' Title V of the TEU covers the CFSP and thus principally the ECAP. Qualified majority voting generally has the potential to facilitate decision-making processes on the European

---

829  Pasquale (n 825) 930–931.

level, since the unanimity requirement by contrast is an often near unsurmountable obstacle. This could potentially significantly facilitate a treaty amendment with regard to further harmonising European defence procurement. However, amending the ratification requirement from unanimity to qualified majority voting under Art. 48(7) TEU likewise requires consensus by the European Council and thus Member State unanimity. The near unsurmountable obstacle therefore remains in place. Secondly, Art. 48(7) TEU does 'not apply to decisions with military implications or those in the area of defence.' The CSDP is therefore excluded from simplified treaty revision under Art. 48(7) TEU, which again demonstrates the Treaties' respect for national sovereignty over defence matters. Consequently, Art. 48(7) TEU likewise cannot serve as a basis to enhance the ECAP.

The ratification requirement to increase the EU's competences for EDEM harmonisation and capability development therefore can only be based on the ordinary treaty revision procedure (Art. 48(1)–(5) TEU), which explicitly provides for amendment proposals to increase EU competences.

### 3.2.2.3. Changing the Armaments Exception Provision (Art. 346(1)(b) TFEU)

Discussions concerning the revision of the legal framework for European defence integration are not new. As discussed in parts *2.1.1. Historical Evolution of European Defence and Armaments Integration* and *2.2.1. European Defence and Armaments Integration today*, the legal framework for European defence cooperation, including the ECAP, is the result of a decade-long integration process that has always been impeded by national sovereignty concerns which last to this day. This is reflected in the intentionally intergovernmentally arranged CSDP and the highly restricted role of the Commission in defence matters. Any proposals for legal change and development need to consider this background.

As discussed above, Art. 346(1)(b) TFEU continues to be the main obstacle to further EDEM and export control harmonisation, as it very broadly offers Member States the possibility to opt-out of harmonisation efforts. It has long been recognized that the armaments exception therefore needs to be either refined in light of today's CSDP objectives to progressively develop a common defence policy (including an ECAP) or outright abolished.[830] There are several options in this regard.

First, the armaments exception could be amended or abolished to allow further EDEM and export control harmonisation via ordinary treaty revision procedure. However, the political obstacles are considerably high. Attempts to amend or abolish the armaments exception have not been successful in the past due to national sovereignty concerns, which continue to apply today.[831] The exception has remained untouched in EU primary law since the Rome Treaty. Despite the EU's increasingly challenging geopolitical environment, which has increased the need for European armaments collaboration (see part *2.2.1. European Defence and Armaments Integration today*) and the discussions around creating an EDU (see part *3.2.1.1. Towards a European Defence Union and potential consequences for European Armaments Cooperation*), there is currently no political debate on the EU level on amending or abolishing Art. 346(1)(b) TFEU due to ongoing national sovereignty concerns[832].

Yet, for an ordinary treaty revision procedure, unanimous, Member State-wide support is particularly necessary. Different to the simplified treaty revision procedure, which only requires the Member States' governments to consent in the European Council, because of the Convention requirement the ordinary treaty revision procedure is far more comprehensive in terms participating actors who need to approve, making the process of ordinary treaty revision generally politically incalculable. In the politically highly sensitive field of armaments, such unanimous consent is currently inconceivable.

Since Treaty revision appears to be politically unfeasible at the moment, there are potentially further options as to how to work past the impediment of the armaments exception and make EU law more reliable to promote European defence capability development.

Amending Art. 346(1)(b) TFEU is also possible by redrafting the aforementioned 1958 Council list[833], to which the armaments exception applies under Art. 346(2) TFEU. Again, this requires unanimity in the Council, which is a considerable (political) obstacle to any proposal for legal change and development. Considering that the list has never been amended since

---

830 Dyson and Konstadinides (n 91) 88.
831 Trybus (n 34) 151; Hansen (n 58) 201; Kingreen and Wegener (n 31) 2616–2621.
832 Descôtes (n 141).
833 (n 691).

its introduction (due to political reasons) and is generally considered to be outdated[834], redrafting it in light of current defence integration needs seems appropriate. In the past, there have been proposals[835] to limit the list to the most sensitive weapons which would subject most conventional armaments to Internal Market law and thus the CJEU's jurisdiction. This in turn would likely have positive effects regarding defence procurement regime compliance by the Member States, making the EDEM more efficient. European armaments collaboration however usually concerns highly sensitive weapon systems. The current Franco-German armaments collaboration and its highly advanced FCAS and MGCS projects are prominent examples of that. Making the ECAP sufficiently effective under current EDEM needs and reduce defence-industrial fragmentation would thus require redrafting the list in a way as to also cover such highly sensitive weapon systems, which would ultimately equal the abolishment of the armaments exception. Again, due to national sovereignty concerns, this is politically inconceivable.

### 3.2.2.4. Transferring Multilateral Armaments Cooperation into EU Frameworks

When it comes to the multitude and, arguably, congestion of multilateral defence procurement initiatives and frameworks outside the EU's frameworks, such as OCCAR, LoI, or the Franco-German armaments collaboration as an example of ad hoc multilateral cooperation, this fragmentation and the resulting inefficiencies could be overcome by gradually transferring these structures into PESCO and EDA, to which in EDA's case they are already linked (see parts *3.3.1. Multilateral European Armaments Cooperation* and *3.3.2. The bilateral Franco-German Armaments Collaboration in the context of European Union Law*). This would certainly strengthen the legal coherence of European armaments cooperation and avoid further entrenching the fragmentation of the so-called Common (!) Security and Defence Policy.

Whether this would lead to more consistent armaments collaboration is questionable however, since the Member States have shown to be more receptive to intergovernmental and exclusive collaboration formats in the past (see parts *2.2.1. European Defence and Armaments Integration today,*

---

834  Trybus (n 34) 143; Kingreen and Wegener (n 31) 2616–2621.
835  Kokott (n 688) 2631; Trybus (n 34) 398.

*2.2.2. Franco-German Armaments Cooperation today* and *3.3.2. The bilateral Franco-German Armaments Collaboration in the context of European Union Law*). Furthermore, the UK's withdrawal from the EU has made it more difficult to incorporate OCCAR and LoI into EDA, since the UK is now a third country to EDA, but an equal member to OCCAR and LoI. Incorporating OCCAR and LoI into EDA would thus require an EDA-UK administrative agreement similar to agreements EDA signed with Norway, Switzerland, Serbia, and Ukraine to enable EDA-UK cooperation. Nevertheless, EDA and especially PESCO (see part *3.2.1.2. The Future of European Armaments Cooperation and PESCO*) have shown that intra-EU defence procurement formats are also a viable option for the EU Member States. Ultimately, this again depends on the Member States' political will regarding (partial) cessation of national powers over armaments.

### 3.2.2.5. Harmonising Armaments Exports – the "gretchenfrage"

When it comes to finding further European convergence of armaments export matters, there are three fundamental options on how to proceed. 1. Intergovernmental harmonisation within the framework of the EU, 2. Supranational harmonisation within the framework of the EU, and 3. Intergovernmental harmonisations outside the framework of the EU on the basis of ad hoc agreements. The first two options will be discussed below, the third in part *3.3.3. A Future for Multilateral European Armaments Cooperation?*.

Intergovernmental EU harmonisation has been partly achieved through the CP. Beginnings of supranational harmonisation can be found in the Dual-Use Regulation. An example for intergovernmental non-EU harmonisation is the NFGAAE.

Intergovernmental EU harmonisation has had limited effects in terms of sufficient convergence, as the shortcomings of the CP have shown. Considering the positive impact of the Dual-Use Regulation and the consequential potential of supranational harmonisation of European armaments exports as part of the EU's CCP, it is worth discussing the legal feasibility of introducing such supranational harmonisation, even if it goes beyond the limits of current EU law.

In this context, it is important to first note the political backdrop again. The limited effects of the CP have resulted from lacking Member State support to further develop the system of European armaments export control. The CP as a Council decision could legally be further developed relatively easily, however this requires unanimous Member State consent (Arts. 31(1) subpara. 1 TEU). In this regard, continuing Member State disparities with regard to harmonising armaments export control rules (in particular Franco-German divergence) is a significant impediment to making proposals for legal change and development, due to the unanimity requirements in Council decisions or treaty revision.

Legal armaments export harmonisation can only follow political convergence on the national and European level regarding strategic interests and export policies. Specifically Germany and France as the European tandem of integration need to agree on a common approach for any progress to be made at the EU level.[836] The increasingly challenging geopolitical environment provides a window of opportunity to find the necessary common ground. Again, European convergence of armaments exports is a central condition to improve European armaments cooperation which in turn is urgently required to close the European defence capability gaps.

Furthermore, the Europeanisation of armaments export control has the potential to withdraw it as an issue of political divergence from the national debates and consequently facilitate European armaments cooperation based on common rules.

Germany has long favoured greater European harmonisation of export controls, reiterating this preference in its 2016 Defence White Paper[837] and in the 2021 coalition treaty of the federal government.[838] In this regard, Germany aims at "Europeanising" its own restrictive standards – a policy that is not supported by the majority of the other Member States.[839]

This continuing divergence makes it unlikely that the Member States will cede national control over their armaments exports to the EU. Particularly France regards supranational control over armaments exports as disadvantageous for its defence industry (see parts *2. The Context: Franco-German Armaments Collaboration and European Armaments Cooperation* and *3.2.1.4. Towards a Comprehensive European Armaments Export Regime?*).

On the other hand, a more Europeanised approach to armaments exports could hold defence-industrial advantages for France (and the EDTIB by extension), as a central impediment to European armaments cooperation would be diminished. Furthermore, France itself has long been calling

---

836   Béraud-Sudreau (n 141).
837   Federal Government of Germany (n 808).
838   Bundesregierung (239), see page 146.
839   Jungholt (n 163).

for "*l'Europe de la défense*"[840], which is inconceivable without further convergence of armaments exports. This is of course known to France, under which's Council presidency the CP was adopted in 2008. Consequently, the important question is how further European convergence can be achieved. For France, further convergence on an intergovernmental basis might be feasible, as long as it does not infringe on its sovereign interests, in particular by applying (at least perceived) overly restrictive German export standards.

Furthermore, the ongoing consolidation of the EDTIB means that there is a commercial interest for a level playing field for the Member States' armaments manufacturers and exporters, as this would reduce uncertainties regarding unpredictable licence denials, decrease costs for compliance and licence application throughout the EU, and prevent "export control forum shopping" (i.e. undercutting certain Member States' more restrictive export policies by industrial relocation) within the EU. The EU is home to some of the largest armaments exporters globally.[841] Over the last years, armaments exports from the EU have risen significantly, partly also due to decreasing defence budgets in the EU and a consequential internationalisation of the Member States' defence industries to sustain themselves.[842] Moreover, as shown during the 1980s and 1990s, arms control is more effective the more it is harmonized within the EU. Armaments export policy fragmentation increases the risk for lacking Human Rights and International Humanitarian Law protection and that armaments fall into the wrong hands. The fragmentation and ineffectiveness of European armaments export control entail the risk that in the Single Market, defence-related goods could be exported through the Member States with the least restrictive export control standards and thus compromise security interests of others.[843]

Now, how could further legal convergence on the European level look like? Considering the increasing relevance of European armaments cooperation, in particular within the frameworks of PESCO and the EDF, it would make sense to update the CP to include common rules for exports of armaments that were developed within these frameworks, which take into account the different national export cultures and the adverse consequences of overly restrictive armaments export policies. This would also enhance

---

840  Levêque (209) 185–191.
841  Wezeman et al. (n 222).
842  Besch and Oppenheim (n 774)
843  Hansen (n 58) 199; Wisotzki and Mutschler (n 58) 277.

PESCO as a platform for European armaments collaboration. Such proposals have not been genuinely discussed however.

More concrete proposals have been made by the European Parliament, in particular suggesting to establish a peer-review process for licencing decisions and procedures, similar to existing practices for dual-use goods.[844] It has also been proposed to establish 'whitelists' of recipient countries agreed by partners of joint armaments projects, similar to the FFA (see part *3.3.1. OCCAR and LoI – unreliable and ineffective?,* where the lacking effectiveness of the FFA's whitelists will also be discussed) for example, or to institutionalise licencing procedures within EU entities, such as EDA.[845] These proposals remain within the intergovernmental structure of the CP and do not fundamentally solve the issue of diverging armaments export cultures and incoherent export control systems in Europe. Their advantage is however that their implementation might be politically more feasible than supranational competence cessation, since it allows Member States to protect their sovereignty interests in armaments matters.

Proposals meant to overcome these fundamental issues with regard to updating the CP remain out of sight for now due to lacking Member State support. Updating the CP requires unanimity in the Council (Art. 31(1) subpara. 1 TEU), which makes significant changes of the status quo regarding Member State control over armaments exports very unlikely (see above).

Furthermore, as long as armaments exports are harmonised under CFSP law, the CJEU has no jurisdiction. Sufficient mechanisms to enforce the (potentially further developed) CP and sanction non-compliance thus remain precluded.

This puts the suitability of CFSP law with regard to harmonising armaments exports into question. Instead, the supranationalisation of armaments export control by expanding the CP or building on the Dual-Use Regulation could be more effective.

The biggest faults of the CP are its limited scope and its lack of enforceability. The expansion of the CP's scope has been discussed above. Another discussion relates to whether the Commission could be provided with the necessary competences to ensure CP coherence and compliance. This could

---

844 Sibylle Bauer et al., 'The further development of the Common Position 944/2008/ CFSP on Arms Exports Control' (*European Parliament,* July 2018) <https:// www.europarl.europa.eu/RegData/etudes/STUD/2018/603876/EXPO_ STU(2018)603876_EN.pdf> accessed 25 October 2022.

845 Béraud-Sudreau (n 128) 91.

mean a supervisory role with the power to impose sanctions in case of non-compliance and even direct decision-making powers. In this regard, it can be further discussed that if the Commission would obtain such far-reaching powers, why not go further and establish a comprehensive regime for European armaments exports, administered by the Commission under the CCP.

Corresponding proposals have already been made. A 2015 report by the European Parliament has mentioned a 'European Arms Control Authority'.[846] The Commission could establish its own armaments export control agency. At least, it would need sanction powers in case of non-compliance with the potential EU armaments export rules by relying on the CJEU when instigating infringement procedures. In this regard, the Dual-Use Regulation has the potential so serve as a valuable basis for such a comprehensive regime. The Dual-Use Regulation already encompasses very detailed rules for exports, including a licencing regime (Art. 12) and end-use controls (Art. 12 in particular, but also Arts. 4, 10, 27), which could possibly be expanded to serve armaments specific and Member State needs. Provided the necessary political will by the Member States, the Dual-Use Regulation could serve as model for a potential European Armaments Export Regulation.

Again, as discussed above, this would require changing or abolishing Art. 346(1)(b) TFEU due to the principle of conferral, which in turn is legally challenging and politically unlikely due the continuing Member State sovereignty concerns, as their fierce opposition against any EU authority over armaments exports has shown during the EDF negotiations. This is why armaments policy and cooperation have been part of intergovernmental law (today in the TEU) since the St Malo summit, because Member States intended to protect their sovereign interests in defence matters.[847]

Also, it is necessary in this context to point out potential national constitutional obstacles to potential supranational armaments export harmonisation. Changing these national constitutional obstacles would likewise require significant political capital. In Germany for example, Art. 26(2) GG clearly states that armaments exports require an authorisation by the German federal government (see discussion around constitutionality of

---

846   Bodil Valero, 'Arms export: implementation of Common Position 2008/944/CFSP' <https://oeil.secure.europarl.europa.eu/oeil/popups/ficheprocedure.do?lang=en&r eference=2015/2114(INI)> (*European Parliament*, 2015) accessed 25 October 2022.

847   Kielmansegg (n 55) 70.

alien export control for domestic armaments in part *3.1.5. Mistakes were remade? – the New Franco-German Agreement on Armaments Exports*). Furthermore, the German BVerfG has made it clear in its Lisbon judgement that EU harmonisation must not infringe on the unimpeachable core of the constitutional identity.[848] This core of the constitutional identity would likely not be concerned however, since Art. 26(2) GG is not an unimpeachable principle of the GG.[849] Furthermore, the German constitutional order is generally highly receptive to European integration (under Art. 23 GG).[850] Provided the necessary political will to amend the German constitution, which however appears unfeasible under the current political climate in Germany and the majority situation in the *Bundestag*, it is up to the competent German legislator's discretion to amend Art. 26(2) GG in order to take into account a changing European defence architecture.

A proposal to reconcile the intergovernmental-supranational divide in armaments export matters has been made by Trybus[851]. Considering the likely scenario that the armaments exception will prevail, the CFSP will stay relevant in armaments export matters, even with more comprehensive harmonisation. Trybus proposes that armaments exports would be covered by a supranational regulation based on Internal Market law, which would take into account Art. 346(1)(b) TFEU. This strongly resembles the EU's approach in its 2009 Defence Package. If a Member State were then to invoke the armaments exception in its licencing decision in cases where its essential security interests were concerned, the licencing decision would fall under CFSP law. The CFSP would therefore have to provide a CoC to deal with such cases. Trybus concedes that this approach would entrench the fragmentation of the intergovernmental-supranational divide, which could potentially undermine the effectiveness of his proposal. However, he argues that such a single export regime would contribute to more coherence in the European armaments export policy, as Member States would have to follow uniform procedures.

While such a single European export regime based on Trybus' proposals would certainly contribute to more coherence and reliability to a degree, the overall issue of lacking enforceability in CFSP armaments export law, especially with regard to a CoC (being only soft law) and further reinforced

---

848  BVerfG (n 102) at 240.
849  According to Art. 79(3) GG, only Arts. 1 and 20 GG are unalterable.
850  BVerfG (n 471), at 195; Schorkopf (n 471) 131–157; Talmon (n 471) 12; Hofmann (n 471) 9.
851  Trybus (n 45) 165–166.

by a fully preserved armaments exception remains. This makes it questionable whether Trybus' proposals are sufficiently suited to ensure more reliability of European armaments collaboration. From a political perspective however, Trybus' proposals appear more feasible than the far-reaching supranational proposals made in this thesis.

Nevertheless, PESCO already shows the challenges that a multitude of project partners and correspondingly complex interests and requirements entail for armaments collaborations. In this regard, it appears that comprehensive supranational harmonisation would be more effective to avoid legal fragmentation and resulting dysfunctionalities.

The Member States' overall opposition to supranational harmonisation is again relevant to note in this regard because all EU harmonisation efforts can potentially be undermined if Member States invoke Art. 346(1)(b) TFEU to substantiate their claims to their exclusive competence to control the armaments export licensing process. Enhancing the EDTIB trough supranational measures would thus again require amending or abolishing the armaments exception provision, which is politically not feasible (see above).

Nevertheless, it is also important to note again that the CJEU case law on Art. 346(1)(b) TFEU has made it clear that the armaments exception provision does not automatically exempt all defence-related matters from EU law. Instead, the armaments exception must be interpreted strictly and derogations from the EU's Single Market rules must be justified on a case-by-case basis by the invoking Member State (see part *3.2.1.3. The European Armaments Policy and its future*).

Similar to its attempts to harmonise the EDEM (see part *3.2.1.3. The European Armaments Policy and its future*), it could be that the Commission will try to increase its competence over armaments export control in the future by relying on the CJEU's Art. 346(1)(b) TFEU case law and on its competences for the EU's CCP (Art. 207 TFEU), especially since it is today active in financing European armaments collaborations. Art. 207 TFEU expressly refers to a uniformity in export policy and that the CCP be conducted in the context of the principles and objectives of the EU's external action. Whether this argumentation will hold against the strong armaments exception in the TFEU and could be asserted against Member

State opposition remains to be seen.[852] Different from CFSP law, the CJEU has jurisdiction (and thus enforcement powers) in CCP matters.

In EU law debates, it remains controversial whether the EU has a competence to regulate armaments exports. Under Art. 3(1)(e) TFEU, the EU has an exclusive competence for the CCP,[853] which is then further developed in Art. 207 TFEU, including regulating (and restricting) the trade in goods (Art. 207(1) TFEU).[854] Whether this includes armaments (as goods) is controversial. Several commentators have pointed out that because of Art. 346(1)(b) TFEU, while principally being goods, armaments are excluded from the CCP because of the armaments exception's far-reaching scope.[855] Art. 10 of the EU's Exports Regulation[856] also implicitly supports this position by allowing Member States to apply (additional) quantitative export restrictions based on public policy or public security considerations. In this context it is interesting to note that despite their security dimension, dual-use goods on the other hand fall exclusively under the scope of Art. 207 TFEU as the CJEU has clarified in several rulings[857], which is why the EU was able to introduce the Dual-Use Regulation.

Some other commentators have pointed out that the EU already has a competence to control armaments exports because of its CFSP embargo regime (Art. 215 TFEU),[858] and that the armaments exception must be interpreted narrowly in this context when Member States intend to invoke it.[859] However, such embargo measures are taken by unanimous consent in the Council and on a case-by-case basis, are then applied nationally and

---

852  Cops and Duquet (n 777).
853  Christian Calliess, 'Art. 3' in Christian Calliess and Matthias Ruffert (eds), *EUV/ AEUV* (6th edn, C.H.Beck 2022) 515–516; Sascha Pelka, 'Artikel 4' in Jürgen Schwarze et al. (eds), *EU-Kommentar* (4th ed, Nomos 2018) 452.
854  Case C-83/94, Criminal Proceedings against Peter Leifer [1995] ECR I-3231; Kingreen and Wegener (n 31) 2616–2621.
855  Martin Nettesheim, 'Art. 207' in Rudolf Streinz (ed), *EUV/AEUV* (3rd edn, C.H.Beck 2018) 1898–1899; Walter Frenz, 'Artikel 346' in Matthias Pechstein et al., *Frankfurter Kommentare Band IV AEUV Artikel 216–358* (Mohr Siebeck 2017) 1507–1508; Kokott (n 688) 2631; Dittert (n 31) 1988.
856  Regulation (EU) 2015/479 of the European Parliament and of the Council of 11 March 2015 on common rules for exports (codification) [2015] OJ L83/34.
857  Case C-70/94, Fritz Werner Industrie-Ausrüstungen GmbH v Federal Republic of Germany, [1995] ECR I-3189; Case C-83/94 (n 854); Dittert (n 31) 1993; Case C-337/05 (n 701); Case C-157/06 (n 701); Case C-615/10 (n 701).
858  Bungenberg (n 771) 426–457.; Schneider and Terhechte (n 771) 15; Kokott (n 771) 1968.
859  Bungenberg (n 771) 454.

thus give Member States the opportunity to protect their essential security interest without handing the Commission a broad mandate establish a comprehensive European export control regime.

In this regard, it should be stressed again how much Art. 346(1)(b) TFEU continues to prevent any substantial reform of European armaments integration. Due to its continuing broad application, there will always be the danger that Member States will not or only insufficiently apply (future) EU law, as long as the armaments exception exists.[860] Indeed, Art. 348 subpara. 2 TFEU offers the possibility that the CJEU can act in cases of 'improper use' of Art. 346(1)(b) TFEU, however this only applies to Internal Market violations and for now, armaments exports remain part of CFSP law, where the CJEU's jurisdiction is expressly precluded. This further underlines the need to overcome the intergovernmental-supranational divide in European armaments integration, which entails significant legal fragmentation and resulting unreliability issues.

Indeed, commentators like Dittert[861] have argued that Art. 346(1)(b) TFEU does not apply in cases of EU regulation for armaments exports (for example the CP, Dual-Use Regulation, or embargos[862]). Derivations from EU law in such cases were difficult to justify. Essential national security interests must be concerned while simple foreign policy preferences are not justifiable.[863] On the other hand, such regulation cannot be introduced against Member State consent, which is only possible if the Member States do not see their policy interests concerned, which is of even greater than usual significance in case of armaments exports. Moreover, the shortcomings of the CP in practice have shown that incoherent application is certainly possible due to lack of enforcement even if it was legally not justifiable.

The best thing for European armaments cooperation in terms of efficiency and reliability would be a common European approach to defence procurement and armaments exports. However, this requires unanimous Member State consensus, which despite current geopolitical challenges, even an all-out war in Europe, remains unidentifiable for the foreseeable future.

---

860  Trybus (n 34) 161.
861  Dittert (n 31) 1996.
862  Bungenberg argues that Art. 346 TFEU must be applied narrowly if Member States invoke it in the context of EU embargos, see Bungenberg (n 771) 454.
863  Kingreen and Wegener (n 31) 2620–2621; Dittert (n 31) 1996.

The remaining alternative due to the lack of Member State willingness to take substantial steps towards more European convergence of armaments export regimes within the framework of the EU is a refocus on national competences and ad hoc intergovernmental convergence outside the framework of the EU. In this regard, the NFGAAE indicates a practical way forward. This will be discussed in part *3.3.3. A Future for Multilateral European Armaments Cooperation?*. However, it relevant to point out that significant legal fragmentation and resulting inefficiencies would consequently persist.

### 3.2.3. Europeanising Franco-German Armaments Collaboration?

Part *3.2. European Union Law – a more reliable legal framework for Armaments Collaboration?* started out by asking whether EU law provides for a more reliable legal framework to ensure the consistent realisation of large-scale armaments projects such as FCAS or MGCS than the current bilateral Franco-German framework for armaments cooperation.

From a legal standpoint, such projects could well be realised within EU structures, such as EDA or PESCO. There are no provisions in EU law prohibiting the realisation of such projects within the framework of the EU. By contrast, as shown in parts *3.2.1.2. The Future of European Armaments Cooperation and PESCO* and *3.2.1.3. The European Armaments Policy and its future*, EDA or PESCO are very accessible and designed for such collaborative projects. The fact that FCAS and MGCS (for now at least) are developed in multilateral extra-EU formats is a political decision based on national defence-industrial and feasibility considerations (see part *2.2.2. Franco-German Armaments Cooperation today*). It goes to show how the Member States (France and Germany in particular) still largely perceive collaborative defence procurement within EU structures: as ineffective and obstructive to their national defence(-industrial) interests.

It is another question however whether projects such as FCAS or MGCS should be realised within EU structures to ensure more reliable capability development. In light of the previous analysis, it remains legally and politically doubtful whether the (current) European frameworks for armaments cooperation are sufficiently more reliable than extra-EU formats. In many respects, intra-EU and extra-EU forms of armaments cooperation are similar, due to their intergovernmental arrangement and the resulting reliability and enforcement deficits. Ultimately, Member States participating in EDA and PESCO remain free to withdraw from these frameworks and their projects relatively easily, just like they can in conventional multilateral armaments cooperation arrangements. However, it has also been shown in the previous analysis how defence procurement within EU structures has the potential to lead to more efficiency, coherence and reliability due to the at least rudimentary enforcement system of PESCO obligations, Member State peer pressure, and potentially the normative effect of EU law.

The ECAP in its current form is limited to facilitating capability development between the Member States through providing common structures like EDA or PESCO and financial incentives like the EDF. An EU competence for managing armaments projects does not exist under EU law. Furthermore, even if such a competence existed (which is unlikely for the foreseeable future because of the Member States' continuing sovereignty concerns), it is questionable whether the EU would be more appropriate to oversee capability development than the Member States, considering it does not have armed forces of its own and has an only limited understanding of the needs of the Member States' armed forces and defence interests. EDF funding is also available for capability development projects that are realised outside EDA or PESCO, for example for FCAS.

It has also been demonstrated how finding convergence of armaments export policies is central to Franco-German armaments cooperation. Problematically, when it comes to harmonising armament exports on the EU level, further supranational harmonisation is precluded under current EU law. Further intergovernmental harmonisation is possible, however this requires unanimity in the Council and could not be achieved in a noteworthy fashion since the introduction of the CP.

EU law in its current form is therefore not a more reliable alternative to ensure the consistent realisation of large-scale joint armaments projects in this regard. Despite options to ensure more reliability, their implementation remains unfeasible for the foreseeable future. Consequently, it appears more effective for now to attempt further convergence of armaments export policies on an ad hoc basis within multilateral arrangements, where lesser participating States makes reaching agreements more likely and agreements can be better tailored to the needs of the respective ad hoc partnerships (see also part 3.3.3. *A Future for Multilateral European Armaments Cooperation?*). The Franco-German armaments cooperation has shown the difficulties which convergence on a bilateral/multilateral level also inhibit. This however has primarily political reasons which are easier to overcome than the significant legal obstacles to harmonisation in EU primary law.

Under the premise that the EU framework is not significantly more reliable than multilateral formats, which are usually more flexible at least, it is understandable that Member States pursue their capability development (also) outside EU structures and often view them as more appropriate. The analysis above has shown that the European frameworks for armaments cooperation are ultimately not sufficiently more reliable to ensure the realisation of projects such as FCAS or MGCS if they were transferred into EU structures.

From the perspective of the CSDP and European defence capability development overall, the problem of legal, political, and defence-strategic fragmentation and the resulting adverse effects in terms of inefficiencies and lacking defence autonomy however still remain. Several proposals on how to enhance lacking reliability within the framework of the EU have been discussed in the previous part. Were they implemented, Europeanising Franco-German armaments collaboration would be a more viable alternative. However, these proposals likewise remain politically unfeasible for the foreseeable future due to the Member States' sovereignty concerns and diverging defence-political interests.

## 3.3. Multilateral European Armaments Cooperation – unreliable but effective?

European armaments cooperation today continues to take place within and outside the framework of the EU (see part *2.2.1. European Defence and Armaments Integration today*). European armaments cooperation within the EU framework and its unreliabilities and potentials have been discussed in parts *3.2.1.2. The Future of European Armaments Cooperation and PESCO* and *3.2.2. Making European Armaments Cooperation reliable?*. As a consequence of the lasting unreliability issues which EU law features when it comes to ensuring consistent and efficient defence capability development in the EU and due to the general political unwillingness to make the necessary changes discussed in the previous parts, this thesis will now return to the subject of multilateral (meaning non-EU or trans-) European armaments cooperation (of which the Franco-German collaboration is a part), which consequently might provide for more effective frameworks for capability development after all. Similar to previous parts, potential deficits of multilateral European armaments cooperation and options to make it more reliable in terms of realising large-scale armaments projects will be discussed. A particular focus will again be placed on the central and contentious issue of armaments exports and on the relationship between the multilateral frameworks and EU law.

### 3.3.1. OCCAR and LoI – unreliable and ineffective?

The most relevant frameworks for European multilateral armaments cooperation are the *Organisation Conjointe de Coopération en matière d'Armement* (OCCAR) and the Letter of Intent (LoI) Group. The context of their creation are – same es for broader European defence integration since the mid-1990s – the lessons from the Yugoslav Wars and Europe's self-perceived inability to act in security and defence matters. Both frameworks were created in 1998, the same year as the aforementioned St Malo summit took place (see part *2.1.1. Historical Evolution of European Defence and Armaments Integration*). At the time and to some degree until today, the exclusive and intergovernmental character of both frameworks reflects the interest of certain EU Member States to seek progress in European defence integration through smaller multilateral initiatives which are (at least perceived as) more flexible and efficient than initiatives on the common EU level (such as also EI2 for example, see part *2.2.1. European Defence and Armaments Integration today*). They come at the cost of institutional and legal fragmentation and thus efficiency losses. However, this "avant-garde mentality" can also be observed in PESCO's arrangement ('higher criteria' according to Art. 42(6) TEU, see part *3.2.1.2. The Future of European Armaments Cooperation and PESCO*) and therefore within the framework of the EU.

### 3.3.1.1. OCCAR

OCCAR was established in 1998 by France, Germany, Italy, and the UK. Belgium joined in 2003, Spain in 2005. At the time, all six OCCAR members were EU Member States. OCCAR constitutes the main European non-EU management agency of defence collaborative projects. Relevant large-scale armaments projects that were realised within the OCCAR framework are for example the *A400M* transport aircraft, the *Tiger* and *Cobra* attack helicopters, and the *Boxer* armoured fighting vehicle. The organisation's legal basis is the multilateral OCCAR Convention[864]. OCCAR's objectives are primarily to improve efficiency and reduce costs of collaborative armaments projects and thus also to enhance the EDTIB (Preamble OCCAR Convention). In this context, two aspects are noteworthy.

First, under Art. 5 OCCAR Convention, all Member States renounce the aforementioned *juste retour* principle, which is traditionally – besides the issue of armaments exports – a central obstacle to efficient European armaments collaboration (see part *2.1.1. Historical Evolution of European Defence and Armaments Integration*). Secondly, OCCAR does not address the issue of armaments exports and thus does not provide for any harmonisation of its Member States' armaments export regimes. As stated in previous parts, the diverging armaments export policies in Europe are a central obstacle for reliable European armaments cooperation (see part *2.2.1. European Defence and Armaments Integration today*). Consequently, while the renunciation of *juste retour* at the time represented a significant step forward to improve the efficiency of the Member States' armaments cooperation, lacking political will to also find sufficient consensus on dealing with the contentious issue of armaments exports makes it questionable whether such intergovernmental cooperation formats outside the EU frameworks are principally more reliable than organising EU armaments cooperation within EDA and PESCO. Nevertheless, as mentioned above, several large-scale joint armaments programmes were successfully realised within OCCAR.

Another of OCCAR's objectives mentioned in the preamble of the OCCAR Convention is to pave the way for a 'European Armaments Agency' by strengthening cooperative defence procurement. In this context, the relationship between OCCAR and EDA is noteworthy.

Firstly, OCCAR resembles EDA in many ways. Like EDA, it is intergovernmental, meaning the Member States retain ultimate control. Neither OCCAR nor EDA have a mandate to determine specific armaments projects and thus depend on projects assigned to them by the Member States. Yet both OCCAR (Art. 39 OCCAR Convention) and EDA (Art. 6 EDA Statute[865]) have legal personality, including the capacity to contract and be a party to legal proceedings. Also like EDA (Art. 45 TEU), OCCAR is a management agency for collaborative armaments projects, aiming at greater efficiency in the management of collaborative defence equipment

---

864 Convention on the establishment of the Organisation for Joint Armaments Cooperation (United Kingdom, France, Germany, Italy) (9 September 1998).
865 Council Decision 2015/1835 (n 90).

programmes by coordinating, controlling and implementing collaborative armaments projects assigned to the organisation by the Member States and by promoting future joint activities (Arts. 7, 9 OCCAR Convention). Apart from the UK, all Member States of OCCAR are EDA members.

Secondly, given the similarities in tasks, to overcome the fragmentation in European defence procurement and ensure the coherence of the CSDP, it has been discussed since the creation of EDA whether OCCAR's functions should be incorporated into EDA.[866] The preamble of OCCAR thus also refers to the potential 'creation of a European Armaments Agency'. In that sense, Art. 26(2) EDA Statute, which sets out the relationship between EDA and third countries, organisations and entities, further stipulates that EDA 'shall pursue close working relations with the relevant elements of OCCAR and with those established under the LoI Framework Agreement, with a view to incorporating those elements or assimilating their principles and practices in due course, as appropriate and by mutual agreement.' However, this incorporation has not been realised to this day. Instead, EDA and OCCAR have established a working relationship based on an administrative arrangement[867]. Moreover, since 2022, two OCCAR projects receive EDF funding,[868] further institutionally linking (but not integrating) OCCAR to the EU and the Commission's efforts for European capability development.

Furthermore, the EU's Procurement Directive intentionally leaves legal gaps for multilateral armaments frameworks (see part *3.2.1.3. The European Armaments Policy and its future*). This ensures compatibility between the EU's defence procurement regime and Art. 6 OCCAR Convention, which stipulates that OCCAR Member States shall give preference in their procurement to defence equipment developed within the OCCAR framework, which otherwise would violate the EU Internal Market's principle of non-discrimination without such an exception in the Procurement Directive. This in turn entrenches the EU-multilateral divide and fragmentation in European defence procurement.

---

866   Butler (n 48).

867   Administrative Arrangement between the European Defence Agency and the Organisation for Joint Armaments Cooperation (OCCAR) (EDA-OCCAR) (27 July 2012).

868   EDA, 'EU Commission, EDA and OCCAR sign European Defence Fund agreements' (*EDA*, 14 December 2022) <https://eda.europa.eu/news-and-events/news/20 22/12/14/european-commission-signs-european-defence-fund-agreement-with-eda -and-occar> accessed 14 March 2023.

3.3.1.2. LoI

Besides OCCAR, in 1998, France, Germany, Italy, Spain, Sweden and the UK signed the Letter of Intent (LoI), which by 2000 became the Farnborough Framework Agreement (FFA). At the time, all State parties to the FFA were EU Member States. Furthermore, it is noteworthy that Sweden is part of the LoI Group, but not OCCAR, and Belgium part of OCCAR but not the LoI, further underlining the institutional fragmentation in European defence procurement.

The LoI aims at creating the political and legal framework necessary to facilitate defence-industrial cross-border restructuring in Europe to promote a more competitive and robust EDTIB in the global defence market (Preamble FFA). Different from OCCAR, the LoI does not institute an independent agency with separate legal personality but rather a forum for information exchange and cooperation in the following areas: security of supply, transfer and export procedures, security of classified information, defence-related research and technology, treatment of technical information, harmonisation of military requirements, and protection of commercially sensitive information.

Part 3 of the FFA, which deals extensively with transfer and export procedures is particularly noteworthy with regard to trans-European armaments cooperation as it addresses – different from the OCCAR Convention – the contentious issue of diverging national armaments export regimes and procedures and attempts a certain degree of harmonisation.

The FFA distinguishes between transfers between parties to the agreement (Art. 12) and exports to non-parties (Art. 13). For transfers between parties, Arts. 12(2), (3) FFA stipulate the issuance of so-called Global Project Licences for cooperative armaments programmes to be used as the necessary export authorisation between the parties and thus remove the need for specific authorisation. This constitutes a simplified licencing issuance method, which is in different variations used for collaborative armaments projects in Europe by default to facilitate the transfer of defence-related goods and services and of sub-components (see also part *3.1.5. Mistakes were remade? – the New Franco-German Agreement on Armaments Exports*).

At the same time, ultimate control over armaments exports remains with the State parties, who shall determine the conditions for granting, withdrawing and cancelling the Global Project Licences in accordance with Art. 12(4) FFA. In this regard, the FFA is more extensive than the NFGAAE, which only implicitly reaffirms national control over armaments exports in its preamble and resulting from the option to deny export licences in cases where a party's immediate interests or national security are concerned. This has been discussed at length in part *3.1.5. Mistakes were remade? – the New Franco-German Agreement on Armaments Exports.* What makes Art. 12 of the FFA particularly noteworthy is that its Global Project Licences regime closely resembles the intent and function of the General Transfer Licences regime under Art. 5 Transfer Directive, intended to further facilitate and harmonise intra-EU armaments transfers. However, as has been discussed, the possibility of using general licences for collaborative programmes is optional under the Directive (Art. 5(3)) and has not been transposed into the legislation of all Member States, including Germany and France (see part *3.2.1.3. The European Armaments Policy and its future*). A likely reason for this non-transposition is that under the FFA and the NFGAAE, procedures for simplified licencing issuance already exist, making the Transfer Directive's full transposition superfluous in the eyes of Germany and France. This however comes again at the cost of entrenching the fragmentation of European defence procurement.

Even more relevant for the discussions around lacking convergence of European armaments export policies is Art. 13 FFA, which deals with armaments exports to non-parties to the agreement in a detailed manner.

Under Art. 13(2) FFA, the parties participating in a cooperative armaments programme shall agree basic principles governing exports to non-parties from that programme and procedures for such export decisions. These decisions are made by consensus. This is especially relevant with regards to export destination decisions. Those decisions are made by consensus following consultations (Art. 13(3)(a) FFA). According to this provision, these consultations also take into account the parties' national export control policies, the fulfilment of their international commitments, including the EU CoC[869] criteria (see part *3.2.1.4. Towards a Comprehensive European Arms Export Regime?*), and the protection of the Parties' defence interests, including the preservation of a strong and competitive EDTIB.

Modifications of the whitelists are likewise consensus-based. According to Art. 13(3)(b) FFA, a permitted export destination may only be removed in the event of significant changes in the third country's internal situation, for example full-scale civil war or a serious deterioration of the human

---

869 Today (n 61), see part *2.1.1. Historical Evolution of European Defence and Armaments Integration.*

rights situation, or if that third country becomes a threat to regional or international peace, security and stability, for example as a result of aggression or the threat of aggression against other nations. If the participating parties in the cooperative programme are unable to reach consensus on the removal of a permitted export destination at the working level, the issue will be referred to the ministers for resolution. This however also does not ensure that consensus on the matter will be reached.

Once agreement on the export principles mentioned in Art. 13(2) FFA has been reached, the responsibility for issuing an export licence for the permitted export destination lies with the party within whose jurisdiction the export contract falls (Art. 13(4) FFA). This reflects EU-wide practice regarding exports of armaments stemming from collaborations and is applied in the same fashion in the NFGAAE (Annex 5 NFGAAE, see part 3.1.5. *Mistakes were remade? – the New Franco-German Agreement on Armaments Exports*).

The resulting whitelists of permitted export destinations determined through consensus-based consultations by the six parties marks the abandonment of the non-veto principle utilized in the SDA (see parts 2.1.2. *Historical Evolution of the Franco-German Armaments Collaboration* and 3.1.2. *Mistakes were made in Franco-German Armaments Collaboration – the Schmidt Debré Agreement*).

Perceiving the SDA's aforementioned unreliability vis-à-vis ensuring that Germany would not principally (or unpredictably) block France's exports of jointly produced armaments despite its non-veto principle, the six parties to the FFA consequently introduced a shift away from the non-veto principle by designing consensus-based rules for export procedures. The resulting whitelist of permitted export destinations was thus intended to avoid (formally impermissible) German export vetoes on a frequent basis. In this regard, it is noteworthy that the NFGAAE marks a return back to the non-veto principle afterwards, despite the unreliabilities of the SDA. This can only be explained by the FFA's deficits in terms of ensuring reliable export decisions.

By introducing consensus-based export destination lists, the parties to the FFA wanted to avoid unilateral decisions on armaments exports in their armaments cooperations based on political preferences, changes in administration or legal revisions.[870] Nevertheless, the fact that under Art. 13(3)(a)

---

870 Cops and Buytaert (n 146).

the FFA explicitly takes national armaments export policies into account allows for restrictive national armaments export policies (like Germany's), which can be (an subsequently were) applied unrestrictedly to collaborative armaments projects due to the consensus-based principle.[871] Germany's aforementioned (see part *2.1.2. Historical Evolution of the Franco-German Armaments Collaboration*) licence denials for British *Eurofighter Typhoon Meteor* missile exports to Saudi Arabia are a prominent example in this regard, which led to significant disgruntlement among the LoI partners and demonstrates why the consensus-based principle was likewise insufficient to ensure reliable armaments export decisions and consequently reliable trans-European armaments cooperation.

Like OCCAR, the LoI Group is linked to EDA. Apart from the UK, all parties to the FFA are EDA members. The aforementioned Art. 26(2) EDA Statute stipulates that besides with OCCAR, EDA 'shall pursue close working relations with [...] those established under the LoI Framework Agreement, with a view to incorporating those elements or assimilating their principles and practices in due course, as appropriate and by mutual agreement.' However, like in the case of OCCAR, this incorporation has not been realised to this day. Instead, the LoI Group has established working relationships with the Commission and EDA to influence their policies.[872] The LoI mission of ongoing defence-industrial restructuring in Europe is shared with EDA, duplicating EDA's efforts.

### 3.3.1.3. Integrating OCCAR and LoI into EDA?

The political, defence-industrial, and military landscape has changed significantly since the creation of OCCAR and the LoI in 1998. EDA was established in 2004 and the European Commission has taken an ever-closer interest in EDEM issues. The creation of OCCAR and LoI outside EU structures was originally meant to accommodate British scepticisms towards developing EU defence structures that would potentially compete with NATO.[873] However by now, the UK has left the EU and the EU is faced with an increasingly challenging geopolitical environment.

---

871  Brzoska and Küchle (n 354) 24.

872  Ministry of Defence, 'Letter of Intent: restructuring the European defence industry' (*gov.uk*, 12 December 2012) <https://www.gov.uk/guidance/letter-of-intent-restruct uring-the-european-defence-industry> accessed 7 October 2022.

873  Biermann and Weiss (n 211) 234.

The continuing non-incorporation of OCCAR and LoI into EDA till today is due to lack of political interest by OCCAR's and the LoI Group's Member States, which is in turn based on their protectionist concerns over losing control over defence-industrial matters and their defence-strategic concerns over potentially less efficiently realising collaborative armaments projects within more inclusive frameworks such as EDA or PESCO (see part *2.2.1. European Defence and Armaments Integration today*).

Furthermore, the UK's withdrawal from the EU has made it more difficult to incorporate OCCAR and LoI into EDA since the UK is now a third country to EDA, but an equal member to OCCAR and LoI. Incorporating OCCAR and LoI into EDA would thus require an EDA-UK administrative agreement, similar to agreements that EDA has signed with Norway, Switzerland, Serbia, and Ukraine, to enable EDA-UK cooperation. At the same time, notwithstanding OCCAR's and the LoI Group's relationships with EDA, OCCAR and LoI enable trans-European armaments cooperation between the largest armaments manufacturing States in Europe on a flexible basis, which ultimately serves European capability development.

Nevertheless, in the end, this multitude of frameworks and policies inside and outside EU structures leaves European armaments procurement legally and institutionally fragmented and inefficient due to costly duplications. Furthermore, the exclusive character of OCCAR and LoI undermines the coherence of a common European approach to armaments cooperation as part of broader defence integration.

The main advantage of multilateral armaments cooperation frameworks lies in their flexibility. Compared to initiatives within the EU framework, like PESCO for example (which also has its reliability and enforcement deficits, see part *3.2.1.2. The Future of European Armaments Cooperation and PESCO*), significant far-reaching legal commitments are avoided by the participating States, which is a central motive for them to participate in multilateral armaments cooperation frameworks. Consequently, certain large-scale armaments projects would likely not have been realised other than within such flexible, multilateral frameworks. Furthermore, since the number of participating States is lower than the number of EU Member States, multilateral armaments cooperation is easier to execute due to a lower number of diverging interests and country-specific defence requirements. This can make multilateral armaments cooperation more efficient.

On the other hand, this level of flexibility is accompanied by unreliability. States can unilaterally withdraw from OCCAR (Art. 56(1)) and the FFA (Art. 57(2)) within a six-month period. Furthermore, the dispute settlement mechanism through consultation for disputes over armaments exports has proven to be ineffective when it comes to national armaments export policy divergence. More effective decision-making and enforcement processes are theoretically conceivable (see part *3.3.4. A Future for Multilateral European Armaments Cooperation?*), however they are bound to fail because of the continuing political divergence and sovereignty concerns in Europe.

In this context, it is also noteworthy that notwithstanding the lacking political interest and continuing sovereignty concerns, which also apply to harmonising defence procurement on the European level, the EU already possesses a well-established, effective dispute settlement and enforcement body in the form of the CJEU, which's jurisdiction could be further extended in EDEM matters. This ultimately makes further European defence procurement integration more promising in terms of enhancing efficiency and reliability from a legal perspective.

### 3.3.2. The Bilateral Franco-German Armaments Collaboration in the context of European Union Law – exclusive cooperation within common integration

As discussed in several parts of this thesis (see for example parts *2.2.1. European Defence and Armaments Integration today* and *3.3.1. OCCAR and LoI – unreliable and ineffective?*), the myriad of European and trans-European armaments initiatives and frameworks has left European capability development fragmented and is contrary to a common European approach within the already fragmented CSDP or potentially within EDU. The lack of a common approach to capability development entails fiscal losses and weakens the effectiveness of Europe's and the Member States' defence capability development.

From a legal perspective, it is thus relevant to analyse the compatibility of intergovernmental defence cooperation formats outside EU structures with EU law if they undermine closer defence cooperation on a common European level. In this part, the compatibility of the current Franco-German armaments collaboration as a form of non-EU defence cooperation with EU law will therefore be analysed.

### 3.3.2.1. Franco-German Agreements and EU Law Links

The Aachen Treaty (see part *3.1.4. Let's try again – the Aachen Treaty*) and as well as the NFGAAE (see part *3.1.5. Mistakes were remade? – the New Franco-German Agreement on Armaments Exports*) are not isolated inter-governmental agreements located inherently outside the EU framework. Both international agreements feature distinct links to EU law, in particular the CFSP, and therefore need to be analysed also in this context.

In their respective preambles, the Aachen Treaty expressly mentions Germany's and France's commitment to the EU and European integration and the NFGAAE expressly refers to the shared European obligations for armaments exports, for example the EU's CP[874]. Para. 4 of the Aachen Treaty's preamble further states that the Franco-German cooperation is meant to further Europe's unity, capability, and cohesion and to leave their cooperation accessible to other EU Member States (*'in dem Bestreben, ihre Zusammenarbeit in der Europapolitik mit dem Ziel zu verstärken, die Einheit, die Leistungsfähigkeit und den Zusammenhalt Europas zu fördern und diese Zusammenarbeit zugleich allen Mitgliedstaaten der Europäischen Union offen zu halten'*). This provision highlights Germany's and France's sensitivity to the fears of other EU Member States that the Franco-German "couple" will become too dominant within the EU (especially after Brexit)[875] and it also reflects the legal and political tension between bilateral Franco-German defence integration in contrast to common European defence integration.

However, simply conceptionally aligning their new bilateral defence integration with the CSDP and broader European defence integration could potentially not suffice to make it legally compatible with EU law.

The current Franco-German cooperation is in practice already less accessible to other EU Member States than so inclusively formulated in the aforementioned Aachen Treaty's Preamble (Para. 4). This concerns the area of armaments cooperation in particular. By now, Spain has been allowed to join the FCAS project, however the "onboarding" process took four years after the project was initiated by Germany and France during the 2017 Franco-German Ministerial Council summit. Poland's request to join the MGCS project was rejected by France.[876] This was due to reasons

---

874 (n 61).
875 Ukrow (n 130) 23.
876 Müller (n 215).

that are typical for trans-European armaments cooperation (see part *2.2.2. Franco-German Armaments Cooperation today*). France has a strong interest to support its national defence industry and does not want to share sensitive knowledge and production shares if not necessary for financial reasons.[877] Also, past collaborative projects (for example the development of the *A400M* transport aircraft[878]) have been significantly more challenging to execute with higher numbers of participating States, which each had different defence requirements and disagreed over cost and productions shares, which in turn led to higher development costs.[879] These practical justifications aside, this exclusive Franco-German form of defence cooperation furthers legal and political fragmentation in the area of European defence and armaments cooperation, and is also potentially not compatible with EU law. This will now be discussed.

### 3.3.2.2. Enhanced Cooperation (Art. 20 TEU)

Generally, the enhanced Franco-German armaments integration on the basis of the Aachen Treaty is yet another building block within the European Treaty system, which is (not only in the field of security and defence policy) increasingly less characterized by a single unifying block of common rules which apply to all Member States, but rather by increasing, complex, and interdependent international and supranational integration mechanisms and approaches.[880] They are possible because EU law allows for so-called enhanced cooperation (under Art. 20 TEU), which is further integration between certain EU Member States seeking deeper integration in specific policy fields, without all Member States taking part.[881] Through enhanced cooperation, EU law takes the Member States' great variety in terms of interests, capabilities and historically evolved political reservations against further integration in certain policy fields into particular consideration

---

877  Hanke (n 216); Meta-Défense (n 216).

878  Mawdsley (n 213) 14–32; Hébert (n 45) 201–217.

879  Brink (n 276).

880  Hermann-Josef Blanke, 'Art. 20 EUV' in Eberhard Grabitz et al. (eds), *Das Recht der Europäischen Union Kommentar 1* (January 2016 EL 58, C.H.Beck 2022) 4–5; Matthias Pechstein, 'Art. 20', in Rudolf Streinz (ed), *EUV/AEUV* (3rd edn, C.H.Beck 2018) 230–233; Ukrow (n 130) 28; Isabelle Pingel, 'Titre VII Dispositions sur la coopération renforcée', in Isabelle Pingel (ed), *Commentaire Article par Article des Traités UE et CU* (2nd edn, Helbing Lichtenhahn 2010) 213–228; Priollaud and Siritzky (n 187) 103–108.

881  Kielmanssegg (n 174) 139; Kielmansegg (n 641) 556.

while also enabling further integration between willing Member States. While enhanced cooperation facilitates partial further integration, it also entails political and legal fragmentation. There are various examples today which showcase the field of tension between exclusive enhanced cooperation on the one hand and common European enhancement of European integration on the other. One of these examples is the increased Franco-German defence integration on the basis of the Aachen Treaty.

Art. 20 TEU authorizes enhanced cooperation in accordance with detailed conditions set out in the TFEU (Arts. 326–334[882]). It grants willing Member States the right to establish enhanced cooperation between themselves within the framework of the EU's non-exclusive competences and even the possibility to use the EU's institutions. Furthermore, enhanced cooperation shall aim to further the objectives of the EU, protect its interests, and reinforce the integration process. There must be a minimum of nine Member States wishing to participate for enhanced cooperation to be used (Art. 20(2) TEU). The cooperation must be open at any time to all Member States, in accordance with Art. 328 TFEU.[883] It is also emphasized in Art. 20(2) TEU that enhanced cooperation is a means of last resort, to be used where the Council has established that the objectives of such cooperation cannot be attained within a reasonable period by the EU as a whole.[884]

---

882 Matthias Ruffert, 'Art. 326' in Christian Calliess and Matthias Ruffert (eds), *EUV/AEUV* (6th edn, C.H.Beck 2022) 2557; Ulrich Becker, 'Artikel 326' in Hans von der Groeben et al. (eds), *Europäisches Unionsrecht* (7th edn, Nomos 2015) 1765–1770; Matthias Ruffert, 'Art. 327 in Christian Calliess and Matthias Ruffert (eds), *EUV/AEUV* (6th edn, C.H.Beck 2022) 2558; Ulrich Becker, 'Artikel 327' in Hans von der Groeben et al. (eds), *Europäisches Unionsrecht* (7th edn, Nomos 2015) 1770–1771; Matthias Ruffert, 'Art. 328' in Christian Calliess and Matthias Ruffert (eds), *EUV/AEUV* (6th edn, C.H.Beck 2022) 2558; Ulrich Becker, 'Artikel 328' in Hans von der Groeben et al. (eds), *Europäisches Unionsrecht* (7th edn, Nomos 2015) 1772–1774; Matthias Ruffert, 'Art. 329' in Christian Calliess and Matthias Ruffert (eds), *EUV/AEUV* (6th edn, C.H.Beck 2022) 2558–2559; Ulrich Becker, 'Artikel 326' in Hans von der Groeben et al. (eds), *Europäisches Unionsrecht* (7th edn, Nomos 2015) 1775–1779; Matthias Ruffert, 'Art. 334' in Christian Calliess and Matthias Ruffert (eds), *EUV/AEUV* (6th edn, C.H.Beck 2022) 2562; Priollaud and Siritzky (n 187) 394–396.
883 Matthias Ruffert, 'Art. 328' in Christian Calliess and Matthias Ruffert (eds), *EUV/AEUV* (6th edn, C.H.Beck 2022) 2558; Ulrich Becker, 'Artikel 328' in Hans von der Groeben et al. (eds), *Europäisches Unionsrecht* (7th edn, Nomos 2015) 1772–1774.
884 Paul Craig and Grainne de Búrca, *EU Law Text, Cases and Materials* (6th edn, OUP 2015) 145–146.

Enhanced cooperation is today the standard mechanism of flexibility in EU law.[885] It was originally introduced by the 1997 Amsterdam Treaty, although CFSP matters were excluded at the time.[886] Yet, Art. J.7(4) TEU-Amsterdam offered the possibility for closer defence cooperation between two or more Member States on a bilateral level (or within NATO or WEU frameworks) as long as it did not run counter to or impede the CFSP under the Amsterdam Treaty. Examples of such closer defence cooperation between two or more Member States on a bilateral level in the following years and based on Art. J.7(4) TEU-Amsterdam included multilateral defence cooperation frameworks such as the Dutch-German Corps, the Euro Corps or OCCAR.[887] This provision however does not exist anymore under the Lisbon Treaty, where PESCO instead offers a distinct framework for closer defence cooperation within the CSDP. This could mean that the Franco-German armaments cooperation must therefore be conducted within PESCO instead of the current contrasting bilateral approach (see below).

The 2001 Nice Treaty then extended the scope of enhanced cooperation to the CFSP, but defence matters remained excluded (Art. 27(b) TEU-Nice). This was due to the UK's traditional concerns that an overly strong continental and EU-focused defence integration by the Member States would weaken the transatlantic alliance (i.e. NATO).[888] These limitations were however then lifted in the 2009 Lisbon Treaty and enhanced cooperation made available to the CFSP, including the CSDP.

Enhanced cooperation is today a cross-sectional policy instrument to enable further EU integration efforts, which is in principle applicable to all EU policy fields of non-exclusive competence.[889] This includes the CSDP as part of the CFSP (Arts. 2(4), 3(1) TFEU, 24(1) subpara. 2 TEU). Enhanced cooperation even features specific provisions for the CFSP in Arts. 329(2), 331 TFEU, however they have never been seriously considered for the CSDP, also because PESCO (Arts. 42(6), 46, Protocol No. 10 TEU) by now presents a special form of enhanced cooperation for defence mat-

---

885  Kielmanssegg (n 174) 139.
886  Thym (n 641) 159; Isabelle Pingel, 'Article 43 UE' in Isabelle Pingel (ed), *Commentaire Article par Article des Traités UE et CU* (2nd edn, Helbing Lichtenhahn 2010) 214; Priollaud and Siritzky (n 187) 104–105.
887  Trybus (n 34) 85.
888  Kielmansegg (n 641) 553.
889  Kielmanssegg (n 174) 139.

ters (see part *3.2.1.2. The Future of European Armaments Cooperation and PESCO*).[890]

### 3.3.2.3. Unlawful Enhanced Franco-German Armaments Cooperation?

The recently reinitiated bilateral Franco-German armaments cooperation on the basis of the Aachen Treaty is situated in the field of tension between continuous efforts towards further and deeper European integration while taking into account the EU Member States' differences in terms of interests, capabilities and historically evolved policies, even if that leads to further legal and political fragmentation. This field of tension is principally governed by Art. 20 TEU provision on enhanced cooperation.

The current enhanced (in the sense of deepened) Franco-German armaments cooperation does however not fall into the category of enhanced cooperation under Art. 20 TEU. It is a bilateral enhanced cooperation outside the scope of this provision, because it does not fulfil the conditions set out in Arts. 20 TEU, 326–334 TFEU to qualify as such.

Firstly, since the Aachen Treaty is a bilateral agreement, it does not include the required nine participating Member States (Art. 20(2) TEU). Secondly, there has been no request to the Council to establish enhanced cooperation (Art. 329(2) TFEU) and thus also no corresponding Council decision (Art. 20(2) TEU). Thirdly, the Franco-German armaments cooperation has an exclusive character as discussed above and is therefore not accessible to all Member States as required by Arts. 20(1) TEU, 328(1) TFEU. This however raises the question whether such an exclusive defence integration project, situated outside the CSDP and enhanced cooperation under EU law, is compatible with EU law.

Every enhanced cooperation between selected EU Member States principally contrasts a common European approach and must deal with the fine balancing act of a Member State's own integration ability on the one hand and the fragility of the broader European integration framework on the other.[891] EU law is guided by the principles of unity and solidarity (expressed amongst other provisions in the preambles of the TEU and the TFEU), which are contrasted by such a bilateral approach outside the EU framework.

---

890  Kielmansegg (n 641) 556.
891  Blanke (n 880) 4.

However, it has been pointed out that the EU as a Union of law is not an objective as such, but rather a means for integration.[892] Considering that the Franco-German armaments cooperation is only a geographically limited cooperation which within the broader integration and enlargement context of an ever-closer Union promotes further integration, there is no basis to regard it as unlawful under EU law. As Ukrow[893] points out, this is due to semantic and teleologic considerations. According to Art. 20(1) TEU, there is a right to and not an obligation for enhanced cooperation, following from the wording of Art. 20(1) TEU (Member States "may make use").[894] This means that the Member States are entitled to make use of other means of integration, which are not provided for in the EU Treaties.[895] Art. 20 TEU offers the possibility for enhanced cooperation, but does not feature an obligation to conduct all integration and cooperation efforts within the EU framework. Also, for armaments cooperation, EU primary law now offers PESCO as a distinct framework, where Member State participation is also explicitly voluntary (Arts. 42(6), 46 and Protocol No. 10 TEU). On that basis, trans-European armaments cooperation frequently takes place outside EU structures (see parts *2.2.1. European Defence and Armaments Integration today* and *3.3.1. OCCAR and LoI – unreliable and ineffective?*). The CFSP (which includes the CSDP) is deliberately arranged in an intergovernmental manner[896] to take the Member States' – as "Masters of the Treaties" – sovereignty and competence over their respective foreign and security policy matters into account.[897] The CFSP is not an exclusive competence of the EU and the Member States therefore remain in control over their respective national foreign and security policies.[898]

---

892 Tobias Bender, 'Die Verstärkte Zusammenarbeit nach Nizza. Anwendungsfelder und Bewertung im Spiegel historischer Präzedenzfälle der differenzierten Integration' [2001] 61 ZaöRV 730, 730–769.

893 Ukrow (n 130) 29.

894 Bender (n 892) 738–741; Blanke (n 880) 14.

895 Claus-Dieter Ehlermann, 'Engere Zusammenarbeit nach dem Amsterdamer Vertrag: Ein neues Verfassungsprinzip?' [1997] EuR 362; Andreas von Arnauld, '„Unions(ergänzungs)völkerrecht". Zur unions- und verfassungsrechtlichen Einbindung völkerrechtlicher Instrumente differenzierter Integration' in Marten Breuer et al. (eds.), *Der Staat im Recht. Festschrift für Eckart Klein zum 70. Geburtstag* (Duncker&Humblot 2013) 514.

896 Pechstein (n 59) 425–432.

897 Ibid. 426.

898 Frenz (n 101) 492.

They are only bound by the EU's principles of loyalty and mutual solidarity (Art. 24(3) TEU).[899]

This means that the bilateral Franco-German armaments cooperation cannot violate supranational norms and the objectives of the EU (mentioned in Art. 3 TEU).[900] Since one of the Aachen Treaty's objectives is to promote European integration (not only in the area of defence) and no violation of any supranational norms or EU objectives is recognisable, the current Franco-German defence cooperation is consequently compatible with Art. 24(3) TEU. While the bilateral approach furthers political and legal fragmentation in the area of CSDP and thus undermines it effectiveness, this corresponds with the intergovernmental (intentionally not supranational) structure of the CSDP. This is also underlined by Art. 42(3) subpara. 2, which requires the Member States to progressively improve their military capabilities without specifying the manner.

Furthermore, EU primary law therefore does not prohibit other forms of "enhanced cooperation", meaning outside the scope of Art. 20 TEU, and correspondingly does not obligate the Member States to cooperate exclusively within the EU framework, even if the concerned policy areas are also within the scope of the EU Treaties, such as the current Franco-German armaments collaboration based on the Aachen Treaty due to its defence dimension. The only limits are posed by the principles of loyalty and mutual solidarity, which the Aachen Treaty respects.

Since the current Franco-German armaments collaboration does not fall in the category of enhanced cooperation under Art. 20 TEU and because there is no legal obligation to conduct said collaboration within this mechanism, there is consequently also no requirement to make Franco-German armaments collaboration accessible to other EU Member States,[901] even if that is politically contrary to the CSDP. The exclusion of Poland from the MGCS project for example is therefore compatible with EU law on enhanced cooperation. A potential violation of EU Internal Market rules through the exclusion of Poland from Franco-German armaments collaboration is precluded due to Art. 346(1)(b) TFEU, which excludes the application of the EU's Internal Market rules to the national defence industries

---

899   Rudolf Streinz, 'Art. 24' in Rudolf Streinz (ed), *EUV/AEUV* (3rd edn, C.H.Beck 2018) 29–43.

900   Blanke (n 880) 14; Martin Schauer, *Schengen – Maastricht – Amsterdam Auf dem Weg zu einer flexiblen Union* (Verlag Österreich 2000) 150–151.

901   Matthias Pechstein, 'Art. 20', in Rudolf Streinz (ed), *EUV/AEUV* (3rd edn, C.H.Beck 2018) 234–235; Ukrow (n 130) 31.

(see discussions in part *3.2.1.3. The European Armaments Policy and its future*).

Therefore, the Franco-German armaments collaboration as a bilateral defence integration initiative outside the EU framework is compatible with EU law. While offering the possibility for armaments cooperation within EU structures, EU law deliberately leaves the possibility open for such cooperation outside EU structures and thus intentionally allows for fragmentation.

### 3.3.3. A Future for Multilateral European Armaments Cooperation?

The lack of Member State willingness to take substantial steps towards increasing reliability of the European framework for armaments cooperation, in particular with regard to furthering EU-wide convergence of national armaments export policies to enable joint capability development, make it appropriate to rethink a refocus on multilateral agreements and convergence as a more practical way forward.

In this regard the NFGAAE is a prime example of national reorientation towards multilateral armaments export policy convergence. Furthermore, it could pioneer other multilateral ad hoc armaments export agreements in the future which European States will increasingly rely on to further defence-industrial consolidation and joint capability development on a flexible basis. In this regard, other European States will therefore also closely observe Germany's adherence to the NFGAAE and judge accordingly whether Germany is a reliable partner for armaments collaboration (again) and whether the NFGAAE serves as a reliable model for such collaboration.

It is submitted again that finding convergence of armaments export policies is a precondition to enable (more) trans-European armaments collaboration. Enhancing reliability of the collaboration frameworks will then ensure that trans-European armaments projects will be more consistently realised.

Multilateral agreements like the NFGAAE or the FFA serve several advantages. Firstly, they are relatively easy to conclude as State parties do not cede far-reaching sovereignty-related competences over defence and armaments matters by giving up ultimate control over export decisions (see parts *3.1.5. Mistakes were remade? – the New Franco-German Agreement on Armaments Exports* and *3.3.1. OCCAR and LoI – unreliable and ineffective?*). National legislation and decision-making mostly remain unaffected.

For certain Member States, Germany in particular, this also has a constitutionality dimension (see part *3.1.5. Mistakes were remade? - the New Franco-German Agreement on Armaments Exports*). Secondly, such agreements are usually concluded between small groups of States that work together on a joint project. This makes reaching a decision much easier than achieving EU-wide unanimity. Furthermore, the respective agreements can be tailored to the specific needs of the States parties involved in specific projects, including the level of armaments export policy convergence. This level of flexibility would not exist in supranational harmonisation. It however comes at the cost of legal and political fragmentation and unreliability, which has been discussed throughout this thesis.

This bottom-up convergence in Europe could be furthered in several regards. By finding common standards and criteria for armaments exports, similar to the FFA regime, and by introducing simplified licencing procedures, dispute settlement mechanisms and non-veto principles, similar to the NFGAAE, which could potentially go even further to achieve more reliability. The different possible configurations of how ad hoc agreements can be arranged underlines the level of flexibility that multilateral agreements inhibit, but also the potentially greatly varying levels of convergence they induce.

The issue of lacking enforcement with commitments made will however persist under multilateral armaments export convergence. This issue is of course not new in international law. There are possible solutions as to how to address lacking obligation observance, for example by establishing arbitration mechanisms or by adjusting national legislation to harmonise armaments export laws on a multilateral basis. These solutions however are also unfeasible for the foreseeable because of the continuing political divergence and sovereignty concerns of those States in the EU that would have to agree to those solutions. Furthermore, it is noteworthy to point out that supranational EU harmonisation would exactly solve these issues of lacking harmonisation and enforcement (via the CJEU), but cannot be introduced because of these known sovereignty concerns.

In the end, finding legal convergence to ensure more reliability is entirely dependent on political convergence and a corresponding political will. It comes at the cost of national sovereignty, although in multilateral convergence to a lesser degree than supranational harmonisation. The political will to enable armaments cooperation even if it entails a loss of sovereignty varies greatly in Europe and also explains the fragmented state of armaments cooperation in Europe. Europe's increasingly challenging geopolitical environment will however elevate the need for more efficient capability development, which in turn will most likely elevate the need to find convergence of armaments export policies and potentially realise far-reaching proposals. This process could take place both within and outside EU structures.

This thesis has previously argued that European capability development within EU structures offers the bigger efficiency gains and the European legal framework could be correspondingly developed to allow for more efficient and reliable capability development (see for example part *3.2.2. Making European Armaments Cooperation reliable?*). However, considering continuing Member State reservations against such proposals, multilateral capability development is still better than none and the most likely future of European (and Franco-German) armaments cooperation will therefore likely be a mixture of intra- and extra-EU cooperation resulting from varying defence integration-political and defence-industrial considerations. The functionality of dysfunctionality has always been part of broader European integration, including defence and armaments cooperation. Considering the extent of armaments cooperation outside EU structures, it is clear that there is a future for multilateral armaments cooperation in Europe, despite the known issues of fragmentation and unreliability, simply because States can protect their sovereignty interests that way. Fortunately for European capability development, also within multilateral armaments cooperation frameworks, reliability could be enhanced.

Lastly, while a variety of multilateral agreements have the potential to further legal fragmentation, they could also serve a valuable purpose by furthering convergence of European armaments export policies over time. Like pieces of a puzzle, a number of similar agreements like the NFGAAE could gradually harmonise the Member States armaments export regimes or at least enhance Member State acceptance for such harmonisation. In the long run, this could even make supranational harmonisation attainable and shows the continuing dialectic development of European defence integration.

# 4. Conclusion and Outlook – The Future of Franco-German Armaments Collaboration in the context of the European Defence Policy

Russia's 2022 invasion of Ukraine marks the preliminary low point in Europe's increasingly challenging and less rules-based geopolitical environment. Against this backdrop, Europe now realises that it has immense defence capability gaps and cannot defend itself without extremely relying on the US. To close Europe's capability gaps, efficient and reliable armaments cooperation in Europe is urgently required.

This can compensate the spiralling development costs of large-scale armaments projects, which are required to close Europe's capability gaps, but which even the larger European States cannot finance on their own anymore. Furthermore, European armaments cooperation significantly contributes to defence system interoperability between the European States' armed forces, which in turn facilitates defence cooperation within NATO and EU and thus credible deterrence against potential adversaries.

However, this objective need for efficient and reliable armaments cooperation is contrasted by opposing subjective national sovereignty concerns vis-à-vis losing control over defence(-industrial) policy. Defence integration touches upon core national sovereignty interests and States therefore remain reluctant to cede any sovereign powers in this area. Perpetual uncertainties regarding potential future geopolitical developments and how they could threaten national security thereby guide Nation State thinking. Defence capabilities and defence-industrial capacities often take decades to be built-up. Ultimately, any Nation State still wants to be able to rely on itself in security and defence matters, since security and mutual assistance guarantees never apply unconditionally. Therefore, defence capabilities and defence-industrial capacities are only reluctantly shared or surrendered.

Consequently, European defence and armaments integration are characterised by ambivalence and are dialectically event-driven. While to some degree there certainly is a European conviction for deeper integration as an objective in itself, in the end it has almost always been external geopolitical necessities which forced Member States to reluctantly give up defence-related sovereignty, and almost always only as little as possible.

Franco-German armaments collaboration is situated in this field of tension. This thesis has evaluated the legal frameworks for Franco-German armaments collaboration in the context of the European Defence Policy. It has analysed whether reliable rules are established which ensure that collaborative projects are consistently realised. The analysis has shown that neither the bilateral Franco-German legal framework for armaments collaboration nor EU law as an alternative, potentially more reliable framework are sufficiently reliable to ensure that large-scale collaborative armaments projects will be reliably realised. This lack of legal reliability is explained by these underlying national sovereignty concerns mentioned above, which have prevented the establishment of sufficiently reliable legal frameworks in the past and currently prevent the establishment of more reliable frameworks.

The main challenges of Franco-German armaments collaboration stem from their diverging national interests and strategic cultures. They manifest themselves especially in lacking convergence of armaments exports regimes. The lack of Franco-German convergence in this area is a prime example of the underlying national ambivalent stances with regard to armaments cooperation. On the one hand, there is a political will and interest for armaments cooperation, arising out of geopolitical and economic pressure, and thus for realising joint armaments projects to obtain defence capabilities. On the other hand, both States are not willing to give up (substantial) national sovereignty in defence-related matters. These ambivalent stances are then reflected in the underlying legal frameworks for armaments cooperation. Since States fear the loss of national sovereignty in armaments cooperation, they avoid those legal commitments that would be necessary to increase reliability of armaments cooperation in terms of efficient and consistent realisation of armaments projects, but nevertheless expect that these projects will be realised. The consequence of this contradiction is the dysfunctionality of the underlying legal frameworks.

Problematically, sufficient convergence of armaments exports policies is a prerequisite for reliable European armaments collaboration, meaning that joint armaments projects are realised. This is because export decisions by one partner affect the other(s). This applies to Franco-German armaments cooperation in particular because of Germany's restrictive armaments export policy, but it is also a significant point of contention in broader European armaments integration.

Without convergence of armaments export regimes, including the establishment of reliable rules on how to treat exports of armaments stemming from joint projects, armaments cooperation remains unreliable. France will simply not collaborate with Germany in armaments production if it cannot rely on Germany to not unpredictably impede French armaments exports. Reliable armaments cooperation therefore requires a legal framework that reconciles the tensions between diverging national interests in the interest of reliable capability development. Argumentum e contrario, the lack thereof endangers the success of Franco-German armaments cooperation as a whole. On the broader European level, lacking Member State convergence of national defence interests also undermines the necessary steps to further European defence integration. If finding convergence on the bilateral level is that difficult to achieve, finding convergence of the EU-27 becomes even more daring to imagine.

Alarmingly, this thesis has shown that the bilateral Franco-German legal framework for armaments collaboration is not sufficiently reliable to ensure that large-scale armaments projects will be consistently realised because sufficient convergence of the diverging armaments export policies is not found and sufficiently reliable rules to deal with armaments exports stemming from joint projects are not established. Many legal and political unreliability risks remain, ultimately endangering the bilateral armaments cooperation's success as a whole.

The central identified unreliability risk revolves around the lasting failure of the bilateral Franco-German legal framework to ensure (especially Germany's) consistent compliance with commitments made as preconditions to enable the bilateral armaments collaboration, i.e. to not impede France's exports of armaments stemming from collaborative projects in an unpredictable manner. The legal framework is by far not immune to national policy changes which could adversely affect the ultimate realisation of Franco-German defence capability projects. This risk is furthered since large-scale armaments projects, such as FCAS or MGCS, are usually realised over decades and thus require long-term legal and political certainty and predictability, which must be ensured by the underlying frameworks. However, as the bilateral framework currently presents itself, short-term political shifts are a constant risk that the bilateral projects are ultimately not realised.

The lasting lack of reliability in the bilateral framework puts Franco-German armaments collaboration at a continuous risk of failure. This in turn would have serious adverse consequences for European defence capability development.

Firstly, these large-scale armaments projects, which are urgently required for European strategic autonomy and Europe's ability to defend itself, would then not be realised.

Secondly, it is to be expected that France would refrain from another attempt to collaborate with Germany in armaments production for decades to come if the current bilateral legal framework ultimately proves unreliable. This would likewise significantly undermine any current and future efforts to make Europe more resilient against geopolitical threats.

The observations made on the bilateral level can likewise be generalised on the broader European level. Since the bilateral Franco-German legal framework for armaments cooperation is too unreliable to ensure the ultimate realisation of urgently necessary capability development, this thesis has discussed EU law as a potentially more reliable alternative framework for armaments cooperation.

European armaments cooperation now increasingly takes place within common EU structures, such as PESCO and EDA, and they are incentivised by programmes like the EDF. The Europeanisation of national and trans-European capability development would solve the contradiction between exclusive multilateral approaches to defence capability development and a genuine common European defence policy. Besides its unreliability risks, Franco-German armaments cooperation as an exclusive bilateral cooperation format also principally contrasts common European capability development in that regard. Furthermore, a common European approach to capability development offers significant defence-strategic (interoperability) and fiscal (economies of scale) efficiency gains. Problematically, this thesis has found similar unreliabilities in the ECAP, principally rooted in the same individual national sovereignty concerns and likewise preventing the reliable realisation of European defence capability development.

This is because of the ECAP's fragmented and primarily intergovernmental arrangements, which allows the Member States to avoid armaments-related commitments and prevents the EU from establishing a comprehensive regime for armaments procurement and armaments exports.

Despite the increasingly unstable geopolitical environment of the EU, which has significantly increased the relevance of European defence integration and enabled the EU to become increasingly active in facilitating European armaments cooperation, the ECAP's dysfunctional underlying conditions have never been fundamentally changed. The EU's competences in this area are severely restricted, especially on the basis of the CSDP's principle of voluntariness and the TFEU's infamous armaments exception.

Ultimately, armaments-related policies remain the Member States' domain réservé. Consequently, European armaments integration remains far being completed and significant fragmentations and unreliabilities therefore persist.

Consequently, the current European framework for armaments cooperation is likewise unreliable when it comes to ensuring the consistent realisation of large-scale armaments projects. In many respects, intra-EU and extra-EU forms of armaments cooperation are similar, due to their intergovernmental arrangement and the resulting reliability and enforcement deficits. Ultimately, Member States participating in EDA and PESCO remain free to withdraw from these frameworks relatively easily, just like they can in conventional multilateral armaments cooperation arrangements. The fulfilment of PESCO's binding, but still intergovernmental commitments will be difficult to enforce and will thus be largely subject to the volatile and diverging interests of the Member States. While the increasingly common approach within EU structures has the potential to lead to more coherence and reliability due to the at least rudimentary enforcement system of PESCO obligations, Member State peer pressure, and potentially normative effect of EU law, it does not suffice Europe's needs for efficient and reliable capability development in the face of current threats by far.

There have been several highly praised and arguably significant initiatives in European armaments integration since 2017. However, it remains overall incomplete and fails to establish an effective and comprehensive ECAP, including creating a Single Market for defence equipment and an integrated procurement system, and finding convergence on armaments exports. Consequently, the ECAP runs short of closing Europe's capability gap by far. Especially Art. 346(1)(b) TFEU continues to impede further integration attempts. The Commission has gone as far as the Treaties permit to consolidate the EDTIB and stimulate armaments cooperation. Despite supranational legislation, the EDF and the CJEU's case law, Art. 346(1)(b) TFEU continues to significantly impede the creation of an EDEM and a comprehensive and coherent ECAP.

Currently, the ECAP aims at facilitating more joint capability development between the Member States through various programmes and incentives. This is meant to convince Member States of the overall advantages of armaments cooperation and reduce perceived disadvantages because of sovereignty losses. However, these programmes and incentives do not ensure the ultimate realisation of joint armaments programmes. EDA does not have the mandate to manage capability development on its own, and the Commission even less so. Consequently, the EDEM continues to be fragmented. The unnecessary duplications and the uncoordinated development and procurement of defence capabilities by the Member States continue to entail cost inefficiencies and undermine the effectiveness of European defence. Furthermore, as a result of market and industrial fragmentation, defence systems lack interoperability, which in turn undermines effective cooperation between the Member States' armed forces, for example in multinational units or CSDP missions, because capabilities cannot be shared.

Harmonising the fragmented and diverging armaments exports regimes in the EU could only be achieved on a rudimentary level so far. Further harmonisation on the basis of current EU law is currently unfeasible and would ultimately be bound to fail against the CFSP's intergovernmental structure and the armaments exception. Consequently, addressing this central issue in European armaments cooperation remains out of sight for now. This is turn continues to undermine reliable European armaments cooperation, which requires sufficient convergence of armaments export matters. Seeing that European armaments cooperation increasingly takes place within EU structures (PESCO and EDF being the most noteworthy) and potentially within an EDU, a coherent and coordinated European armaments export control regime is needed and has the potential to strengthen European armaments cooperation and integration by overcoming the export issue. PESCO already demonstrates the challenges that arise from a multitude of project partners and complex interests which increase the risk of dysfunctionality (see part *3.2.1.2. The Future of European Armaments Cooperation and PESCO*). In this regard, it is concerning that the Member States insist on their national sovereignty in this policy area and remain primarily in control over their respective armaments export regimes.

In the end, the EU framework for armaments cooperation is – just like multilateral frameworks – characterised by national ambivalence and inconsistencies towards joint capability development. It is supposed to enable reliable and efficient capability development but at the same time safeguard national defence interests as much as possible, which then undermines consistent and efficient capability development. You can't have your cake and eat it too.

The different frameworks for armaments cooperation in Europe thus currently fail to reconcile the tensions between national sovereignty desires and the common European need for security. This thesis has discussed several legal options how the European framework(s) for armaments cooperation could be made more efficient and reliable. However, this thesis has also shown that due to continuing national sovereignty concerns vis-à-vis surrendering national security and defence competences, enhancing these framework remains unfeasible for the foreseeable future. On the EU level, fundamental change to enhance efficiency and reliability would require changes to EU primary law. Especially the armaments exception would need to be abolished. However, even short of treaty change and under the impression of current geopolitical threats, existing potentials of primary law are not even fully made use of, as the non-activation of the TEU's common defence provision shows. EU law as a potential means for defence integration and reliable capability development thus falls short of its potentials by far.

Now, what do the findings of this thesis as a whole mean for the future of Franco-German armaments cooperation and European defence integration?

The answer is concerning. Even when faced with an all-out war in Europe, efficient and reliable defence capability development in Europe is not ensured so far. This is rooted in lacking (national) political will to enhance European capability development because the European States are not willing to give up their sovereignty over defence-related matters. This in turn is reflected in the underlying legal frameworks and prevents their necessary enhancements.

Armaments cooperation in Europe will most likely remain intergovernmental for the foreseeable future, despite the significant deficits in terms of efficiency and reliability. Moreover, such cooperation will most likely continue to take place within a myriad of different frameworks, both within and outside the framework of the EU. This continuing double hybrid of intergovernmental intra- and extra-EU cooperation and intergovernmental and supranational intra-EU cooperation entrenches fragmentation and consequently inefficiencies (fiscal and defence-strategic) and unreliabilities (legal and political) in European defence capability development. European defence integration is thus also another example of "two-speed Europe".

Franco-German armaments cooperation is a prime example of these shortcomings. It remains unreliable due to diverging national interests and undermines coherency and consistency in common European approaches. While both States had an incremental role in launching PESCO, they still decided to develop their large-scale armaments projects FCAS and MGCS outside EU structures, contrasting current efforts to increase efficiency and reliability in European defence policy. The future success of EDA and

PESCO in terms of strengthening coherence and efficiencies in European capability development will thus also depend on whether such large-scale armaments projects will be primarily integrated (or integrable) in these frameworks.

Necessary, fundamental changes of the current frameworks for armaments cooperation in Europe require prior convergence of national defence interests and overcoming national sovereignty concerns in the interest of an autonomous and resilient Europe. This objective need of course continues to be contrasted by individual national interests and a strong resilience against sovereignty-restricting compromises. Fundamental changes are only to be expected if the political sense of urgency will further increase and then find its way into the legal frameworks. This dialectic has always driven European defence integration, beginning after the Yugoslav Wars and then accelerating again after Russia's annexation of Crimea. And further geopolitical pressure is already in sight, for example with regard to the US's questionable long-term security guarantee for Europe and its increasing focus on a likely military conflict in the Indo-Pacific. This underlines the urgent need for effective European defence capabilities and might provide a window of opportunity to address existing deficits.

On that basis, several reflections on the future development of Franco-German and European armaments cooperation in the medium to long term can be made. These depend entirely on future geopolitical pressure. This backdrop again underlines how this thesis cannot be read in a legal vacuum. It is situated in the ever-changing field of tension between diverging and converging political, social, economic, cultural and military considerations that have always influenced, enabled and often prevented European defence integration, reflected in the underlying legal frameworks. They continue to explain current regulatory complexities, the legal fragmentation, the contradictions between visions and realities, and existing dysfunctionalities of course. Immensely increasing geopolitical pressure thus could entail rapid adaptions of policy and law.

In this regard, the Commission's Reflection Paper on the Future of European Defence (discussed in part *3.2.1.1. Towards a European Defence Union and potential consequences for European Armaments Cooperation*) already outlines in a detailed fashion three potential future scenarios for European defence integration, of which armaments integration forms the central aspect.

There is of course the possibility that the status quo remains untouched. Since the reflection paper's publication, several European defence integration initiatives have been introduced, however they have remained within the narrow limits of EU primary law. Consequently, fragmentation, inefficiencies, and unreliabilities in the legal frameworks for armaments cooperation have persisted.

Seeing the positive impact of PESCO and the EDF, it is likely from a present-day perspective that European capability development will increasingly take place within EU structures in the future, gradually overcoming fragmentation. At some point, this might ultimately conclude in supranational capability development. Although, at the moment, it remains entirely unclear when that point comes and what the ultimate legal configuration will then look like. The current pace is certainly too slow in the face of the EU's increasingly challenging geopolitical environment. Furthermore, again, revolutionary armaments integration is not provided for in the current progression of the CSDP and would consequently only be possible within the narrow limits of current EU primary law.

Then again, conceivable are also regressions of European defence integration. Fundamental scepticism in parts of the French political spectrum regarding the EU and Franco-German armaments cooperation[902] or developments like Brexit demonstrate that there is also this negative integration dialectic based on refocuses on the Nation State. Against this scenario, the EU's defence integration achievements appear more remarkable by comparison. At least, there is currently some functionality in the ECAP's overall dysfunctionality. Better deficient armaments cooperation than none.

These possible scenarios will then also affect future Franco-German armaments collaboration. Will it become increasingly Europeanised? Even supranationalised? Will it remain intergovernmental? Will capability development take place exclusively nationally?

The Commission's outlined scenarios of course remain within the contested limits of current EU primary law. However, as this thesis has shown, it is doubtful whether EU law could ever provide for sufficiently efficient and reliable armaments cooperation in the face of the *Zeitenwende*, even if the common defence provision was activated, without fundamental change of EU primary law.

While the ultimate configuration of common defence also remains uncertain, its configuration and the process leading up to its eventual activation remain within the intergovernmental limits of the CSDP and do not address the armaments exception provision. This is also the reason

---

902   Die Zeit (n 337).

why the recent initiatives (PESCO, EDF, CARD, RDC) only build upon the established features of the CSDP. Consequently, European armaments cooperation thus runs short of Europe's security needs.

The establishment of a sufficiently efficient and reliable European framework for capability development would consequently require Treaty change. This issue however is not being discussed by the Commission. Also not discussed is the possibility of an entirely different scenario, only conceivable under immense, currently unconceivable geopolitical pressure. For example, if there was a military conflict between "the West" on the one side and China and Russia on the other. If Europe was then forced to show it colours and become a federal State, including the total supranationalisation of defence policy to survive.

There are current instances for defence integration in Europe that would have been inconceivable only a few years ago. The Netherlands is now integrating its land forces into Germany's – the armed forces of country that once brutally occupied it. The Scandinavian countries are building a joint air defence to counter Russian aggression.

So, the crucial questions are how much will geopolitical pressure increase the political sense of urgency regarding armaments integration and when will the European States act on it? The proposals for legal change and development made in this thesis might then serve as options for political action.

On top of its increasingly challenging geopolitical environment, Europe is also faced with its decreasing demographic, economic, and political influence on the global level. If Europe does not want to become marginalised, it needs to pool its resources to retain its ability to act. In the area of defence, this means efficient and reliable defence and armaments cooperation. This will likely also further increase the pressure to act and adapt the underlying legal frameworks. Unfortunately, European defence integration has always been shaped retroactively. This entails the risk that necessary adaptions to the legal frameworks come far too late. Moreover, far-reaching integration steps have often provoked strong national backlash.

Europe will have to decide whether it wants effective and reliable capability development and be strategically autonomous or not. Indeed, it comes at the loss of national sovereignty. But is clamping to national sovereignty really worth the risk of global insignificance and dependency on others? Under these circumstances, national sovereignty would be lost after all. Whether Europe succeeds in enhancing its defence capability development really is a fateful question.

# List of Cases

C-409/05, Commission v Greece, [2009] ECR I-11859

C-461/05, Commission v Denmark, [2009] ECR I-11887

C-38/06, Commission v Portugal, [2010] ECR I-1569

C-246/12 P, Commission v Ellinika Nafpigeia, [2013] ECLI:EU:C:2013:133

Case C-348/12 P, Council v Manufacturing Support & Procurement Kala Naft, [2013] ECLI:EU:C:2013:776

C-474/12, Schiebel Aircraft, [2014] ECLI:EU:C:2014:2139

Case C-455/14 P, H v Council and Others, [2016] ECLI:EU:C:2016:569

Case C-72/15, Rosneft, [2017] ECLI:EU:C:2017:236

# Bibliography

## Primary Sources

### International Treaties

Administrative Arrangement between the European Defence Agency and the Organisation for Joint Armaments Cooperation (OCCAR) (EDA-OCCAR) (27 July 2012)

Agreement between the Government of the Federal Republic of Germany and Government of the French Republic on Export Controls in the field of Armaments (NF-GAAE) (*Abkommen zwischen der Regierung der Bundesrepublik Deutschland und der Regierung der Französischen Republik über Ausfuhrkontrollen im Rüstungsbereich / Accord sous forme d'échange de lettres entre le Gouvernement de la République française et le Gouvernement de la République fédérale d'Allemagne relatif au contrôle des exportations en matière de défense*) (Germany-France) (14 November 2019)

Agreement on the Export of Jointly Developed and/or Produced Armaments (SDA) (*Vereinbarung über die Ausfuhr von gemeinsam entwickelten und/oder gefertigten Kriegswaffen und sonstigem Rüstungsmaterial / Accord sur les exportations vers les pays tiers des matériels d'armement développés et/ou produits en cooperation*) (Germany-France) (1972)

Arms Trade Treaty (ATT) (signed 2 April 2013, entered into force 24 December 2014) 3031 UNTS

Convention on the establishment of the Organisation for Joint Armaments Cooperation (United Kingdom, France, Germany, Italy) (9 September 1998)

Framework Agreement Between the French Republic, the Federal Republic of Germany, the Italian Republic, the Kingdom of Spain, the Kingdom of Sweden, and the United Kingdom of Great Britain and Northern Ireland Concerning Measures to Facilitate the Restructuring and Operation of the European Defence Industry (FFA) (France, Germany, Italy, Spain, Sweden, United Kingdom) (27 July 2000)

North Atlantic Treaty (signed 4 April 1949, entered into force 24 August 1949) 610 UNTS 205

Treaty between the Federal Republic of Germany and the French Republic on Franco-German cooperation and integration (Aachen Treaty) (*Vertrag zwischen der Bundesrepublik Deutschland und der Französischen Republik über die deutsch-französische Zusammenarbeit und Integration / Traité sur la coopération et l'intégration franco-allemandes*) (Germany-France) (22 January 2019)

Treaty between the Federal Republic of Germany and the French Republic on Franco-German cooperation (Elysée Treaty) (*Vertrag zwischen der Bundesrepublik Deutschland und der Französischen Republik über die deutsch-französische Zusammenarbeit / Traité d'amitié franco-allemand*) (Germany-France) (22 January 1963)

Vienna Convention on the Law of Treaties (VCLT) (signed 23 May 1969, entered into force 27 January 1980) 1155 UNTS 331

**European Union Documents**

Common Military List of the European Union adopted by the Council on 17 February 2020 (equipment covered by Council Common Position 2008/944/CFSP defining common rules governing the control of exports of military technology and equipment) [2020] OJ C85/1

Consolidated Version of the Treaty on European Union (TEU-Maastricht) [1992] OJ C325/5

Consolidated version of the Treaty on European Union (TEU) [2012] OJ C326/01

Consolidated version of the Treaty on the Functioning of the European Union (TFEU) [2016] OJ C202/1

Council Common Position 2003/468/CFSP of 23 June 2003 on the control of arms brokering [2003] OJ L156/79

Council Common Position 2008/944/CFSP of 8 December 2008 defining common rules governing control of exports of military technology and equipment [2008] OJ L335/99

Council Decision 2015/1835 of 12 October 2015 defining the statute, seat and operational rules of the European Defence Agency [2015] OJ L266/55

Council Decision (CFSP) 2017/2315 of 11 December 2017 establishing permanent structured cooperation (PESCO) and determining the list of participating Member States [2017] OJ L331/57

Council Decision (CFSP) 2019/1560 of 16 September 2019 amending Common Position 2008/944/CFSP defining common rules governing control of exports of military technology and equipment [2019] OJ L239/16

Council Decision (CFSP) 2022/1965 of 17 October 2022 in support of the United Nations Programme of Action to Prevent, Combat and Eradicate the Illicit Trade in Small Arms and Light Weapons in All Its Aspects [2022] OJ L270/67

Council Joint Action 2004/551/CFSP of 12 July 2004 on the establishment of the European Defence Agency [2004] OJ L245/17

Council of the European Union, Council conclusions on implementing the EU Global Strategy in the area of Security and Defence – Council conclusions (14 November 2016), CFSP/PESC 906 CSDP/PSDC 637 COPS 327 POLMIL 127 CIVCOM 219, 14 November 2016

Council of the European Union, Council conclusions on the Global Strategy on the European Union's Foreign and Security Policy – Council conclusions (17 October 2016), CFSP/PESC 814 CSDP/PSDC 572, 17 October 2016

Council of the European Union, Council conclusions on the review of Council Common Position 2008/944/CFSP of 8 December 2008 on the control of arms exports, COARM 154 CFSP/PESC 684, 16 September 2019

Council of the European Union, Council conclusions on the review of Council Common Position 2008/944/CFSP defining common rules governing control of exports of military technology and Equipment, COARM 245 PESC 1404, 19 November 2012

Council of the European Union, Council conclusions relating to the review of Common Position 2008/944/CFSP on arms exports and the implementation of the Arms Trade treaty (ATT), COARM 174 CFSP/PESC 401, July 2015

Council of the European Union, Extract of the Council Decision 255/58 of 15 April 1958, 14538/4/08 REV 4, 26 November 2008

Council of the European Union, User's Guide to Council Common Position 2008/944/CFSP defining common rules governing the control of exports of military technology and equipment, COARM 153 CFSP/PESC 683, 16 September 2019

Council Regulation (EC) No 428/2009 of 5 May 2009 setting up a Community regime for the control of exports, transfer, brokering and transit of dual-use items [2009] OJ L134/1

Directive 2009/43/EC of the European Parliament and of the Council of 6 May 2009 simplifying terms and conditions of transfers of defence-related products within the Community [2009] OJ L146/1

Directive 2009/81/EC of the European Parliament and of the Council of 13 July 2009 on the coordination of procedures for the award of certain works contracts, supply contracts and service contracts by contracting authorities or entities in the fields of defence and security, and amending Directives 2004/17/EC and 2004/18/EC [2009] OJ L216/76

EC Treaty (Treaty of Rome) [1957]

EDA, The Code of Best Practice in the Supply Chain [2014], available via <https://eda.europa.eu/docs/documents/EDA_Code_of_Best_Practice_in_the_Supply_Chain> accessed 17 December 2022

EDA, The Code of Conduct on Defence Procurement of the EU Member States participating in the European Defence Agency [2005], available via <https://eda.europa.eu/docs/documents/code-of-conduct-on-defence-procurement.pdf?sfvrs> accessed 7 October 2022

European Commission, Commission Recommendation of 30 November 2016 on the harmonisation of the scope of and conditions for general transfer licences for armed forces and contracting authorities as referred to in point (a) of Article 5(2) of Directive 2009/43/EC of the European Parliament and of the Council, C/2016/7711 final, 30 November 2016

European Commission, Commission Recommendation of 30 November 2016 on the harmonisation of the scope of and conditions for general transfer licences for certified recipients as referred to in Article 9 of Directive 2009/43/EC of the European Parliament and of the Council, C/2016/7728 final, 30 November 2016

European Commission, Communication from the Commission to the European Parliament, the Council, the European Economic and Social Committee and the Committee of the Regions – A strategy for a stronger and more competitive european defence industry, COM/2007/764 final, 5 December 2007

European Commission, Communication from the Commission to the European Parliament, the European Council, the Council, the European Economic and Social Committee and the Committee of the Regions, "European defence action plan", COM/2016/950 final, 30 November 2016

European Commission, European Defence–Industrial and Market Issues: Towards an EU Defence Equipment Policy, COM/2003/0113 final, 12 March 2003

European Commission, Evaluation of Directive 2009/43/EC of the European Parliament and of the Council of 6 May 2009 simplifying terms and conditions of transfers of defence-related products within the Community, COM/2016/760 final, 30 November 2016

European Commission, Evaluation of Directive 2009/81/EC on public procurement in the fields of defence and security, SWD/2016/407 final, 30 November 2016

European Commission, Evaluation of the Transfers Directive Accompanying the document Report from the Commission to the European Parliament and the Council on the evaluation of Directive 2009/43/EC of the European Parliament and of the Council of 6 May 2009 simplifying terms and conditions of transfers of defence-related products within the Community, SWD/2016/0398 final, 2 December 2016

European Commission, Green Paper Defence procurement, COM/2004/608 final, 23 September 2004

European Commission, Joint Communication to the European Parliament, the European Council and the Council: EU-China – A strategic outlook, JOIN/2019/5 final, 12 March 2019

European Commission, Joint Communication to the European Parliament, the European Council, the Council, the European Economic and Social Committee and the Committee of the Regions on the Defence Investment Gaps Analysis and Way Forward, JOIN/2022/24 final, 18 May 2022

European Commission, Launching the European Defence Fund, COM/2017/0295 final, 7 June 2017

European Commission, Proposal for a Council Implementing Regulation amending Implementing Regulation (EU) No 282/2011 as regards the update of the VAT and/or excise duty exemption certificate, COM/2022/8 final, 13 January 2022

European Commission, Proposal for a Regulation of the European Parliament and of the Council on establishing the European defence industry Reinforcement through common Procurement Act, COM/2022/349 final, 19 July 2022

European Commission, Reflection paper on the Future of European Defence, COM/2017/315, 7 June 2017

European Commission, Report from the Commission to the European Parliament and the Council Evaluation of Directive 2009/43/EC of the European Parliament and of the Council of 6 May 2009 simplifying terms and conditions of transfers of defence-related products within the Community, COM/2016/0760 final, 30 November 2016

European Commission, Report from the Commission to the European Parliament and the Council on the implementation of Directive 2009/81/EC on public procurement in the fields of defence and security, to comply with Article 73(2) of that Directive, COM/2016/762 final, 30 November 2016

European Commission, Report on the Transposition of directive 2009/81/EC on Defence and Security Procurement, COM/2012/565 final, 2 October 2012

European Council, European Council 19/20 December 2013 Conclusions, EUCO 217/13, 20 December 2013

European Council, European Council meeting (24 and 25 March 2022) – Conclusions, EUCO 1/22, 25 March 2022

European Council, European Council Presidency Conclusions 28 and 29 June 1991, SN 151/3/91, 29 June 1991

European Parliament Resolution 2016/2052(INI) of 22 November 2016 on the European Defence Union [2016] OJ C224/18

Joint Action of 17 December 1998 adopted by the Council on the basis of Article J.3 of the Treaty on European Union on the European Union's contribution to combating the destabilising accumulation and spread of small arms and light weapons [1999] OJ L9/1

Regulation (EU) 2015/479 of the European Parliament and of the Council of 11 March 2015 on common rules for exports (codification) [2015] OJ L83/34

Regulation (EU) 2018/1092 of the European Parliament and of the Council of 18 July 2018 establishing the European Defence Industrial Development Programme aiming at supporting the competitiveness and innovation capacity of the Union's defence industry [2018] OJ L200/30

Regulation (EU) 2019/125 of the European Parliament and of the Council of 16 January 2019 concerning trade in certain goods which could be used for capital punishment, torture or other cruel, inhuman or degrading treatment or punishment (codification) [2019] OJ L30/1

Regulation (EU) 2021/697 of the European Parliament and of the Council of 29 April 2021 establishing the European Defence Fund and repealing Regulation (EU) 2018/1092 [2021] OJ L170/149

Regulation (EU) 2021/821 of the European Parliament and of the Council of 20 May 2021 setting up a Union regime for the control of exports, brokering, technical assistance, transit and transfer of dual-use items (recast) [2021] OJ L206/1

Treaty of Amsterdam amending the Treaty on European Union, the Treaties establishing the European Communities and certain related acts (TEU-Amsterdam) [1997] OJ C340/1

Treaty of Lisbon amending the Treaty on European Union and the Treaty establishing the European Community (Lisbon Treaty) [2007] OJ C306/1

Treaty of Nice amending the Treaty on European Union, the Treaties establishing the European Communities and certain related acts (TEU-Nice) [2001] OJ C80/1

### German Legislation

1949 Basic Law (*Grundgesetz*) (GG) (current version 29 September 2020)

1961 War Weapons Control Act (*Gesetz über die Kontrolle von Kriegswaffen (Ausführungsgesetz zu Artikel 26 Abs. 2 des Grundgesetzes)*) (KrWaffKontrG) (current version 19 December 2022)

2013 Foreign Trade Law (*Außenwirtschaftsgesetz*) (AWG) (current version 17 July 2020)

2013 Foreign Trade Regulation (*Außenwirtschaftsverordnung*) (AWV) (current version 19 December 2022)

2019 Official Journal (*Bundesgesetzblatt Jahrgang 2019 Teil II Nr. 18*) (current version 14 November 2019)

**French Legislation**

1958 French Constitution (*Constitution française*) (current version 4 October 1958)

1953 International Commitments Implementation Law (*Décret n° 53–192 du 14 mars 1953 relatif à la ratification et à la publication des engagements internationaux souscrits par la France*) (current version 11 April 1986)

2019 Official Journal (*Décret n° 2019–1168 du 13 novembre 2019 portant publication de l'accord sous forme d'échange de lettres entre le Gouvernement de la République française et le Gouvernement de la République fédérale d'Allemagne relatif au contrôle des exportations en matière de défense (ensemble une annexe), signées à Paris le 23 octobre 2019 (1)*) (current version 13 November 2019)

**Government Documents**

Bundesregierung, 'Erklärung von Meseberg' (*Bundesregierung*, 19 June 2018) <https://www.bundesregierung.de/breg-de/suche/erklaerung-von-meseberg-1140536> accessed 26 October 2022

Bundesregierung, 'Politische Grundsätze der Bundesregierung für den Export von Kriegswaffen und sonstigen Rüstungsgütern' (*Bundesregierung*, 26 June 2019) <https://www.bmwi.de/Redaktion/DE/Pressemitteilungen/2019/20190626-bundesregierung-beschliesst-politische-grundsaetze-fuer-ruestungsexporte.html

Bundesregierung, 'Politische Grundsätze der Bundesregierung für den Export von Kriegswaffen und sonstigen Rüstungsgütern vom 28.4.1982' (*Rüstungsexport-info*, 28 April 1982) <http://ruestungsexport-info.de/fileadmin/media/Dokumente/R%C3%BCstungsexporte___Recht/Politische_Grunds%C3%A4tze/Politische-Grundsaetze-1982.pdf> accessed 26 October 2022

Deutsch-Französischer Ministerrat, 'Gemeinsame Erklärung' (*France-Allemagne*, 13 July 2017) <https://www.france-allemagne.fr/Deutsch-Franzosischer-Ministerrat-am-in-Paris.html> accessed 16 December 2021

Bundesregierung, 'Koalitionsvertrag zwischen SPD, Bündnis 90/Die Grünen und FDP' (*Bundesregierung*, 2021) <https://www.bundesregierung.de/breg-de/service/gesetzesvorhaben/koalitionsvertrag-2021-1990800> accessed 24 March 2022

Bundesregierung, 'Weissbuch 2016 Zur Sicherheitspolitik und der Zukunft der Bundeswehr' (*BMVG*, July 2016) <https://www.bmvg.de/resource/blob/13708/015be272f8c0098f1537a491676bfc31/weissbuch2016-barrierefrei-data.pdf> accessed 26 October 2020

Governments of France and the United Kingdom, 'Joint Declaration on European Defence' (*cvce*, 4 December 1998) <https://www.cvce.eu/obj/franco_british_st_malo_declaration_4_december_1998-en-f3cd16fb-fc37-4d52-936f-c8e9bc80f24f.html> accessed 1 March 2022

Federal Government of Germany, 'White Paper on German Security Policy and the Future of the Bundeswehr' (*Bundeswehr*, July 2016) <https://www.bundeswehr.de/re source/blob/4800140/fe103a80d8576b2cd7a135a5a8a86dde/download-white-paper-2 016-data.pdf> accessed 25 October 2022

## Secondary Sources

### Books

Bhat I, *Idea and Methods of Legal Research* (OUP 2020)

Boysen S, Rechtsfragen des deutsch-französischen Abkommens über Ausfuhrkontrollen im Rüstungsbereich vom 23. Oktober 2019 (Greenpeace 2020)

Butler L, *Transatlantic Defence Procurement* (CUP 2017)

Cops D et al., *Towards Europeanized arms export controls? Comparing control systems in EU Member States* (Flemish Peace Institute 2017)

Dyson T and Konstadinides T, *European Defence Cooperation in EU Law and IR Theory* (Palgrave Macmillan 2013)

Ernst&Young, *Rüstung und Beschaffung in Deutschland Stand und Herausforderungen, Dilemmata konstruktiv managen* (Ernst&Young 2017)

Heuninckx B, *The Law of Collaborative Defence Procurement in the European Union* (CUP 2017)

Kielmansegg S, *Die Verteidigungspolitik der Europäischen Union* (Boorberg 2005)

Knop D, *Völker- und Europarechtsfreundlichkeit als Verfassungsgrundsätze* (Mohr Siebeck 2013)

Kotthoff M, *Die Entwicklung der deutsch-französischen Sicherheitskooperation seit dem Ende des Ost-West-Konflikts* (Springer 2011)

Krotz U, *Flying Tiger International Relations Theory and the Politics of Advanced Weapons* (OUP 2011)

Mann T, *Australian Law Dictionary* (OUP 2010)

Mölling C, *Der europäische Rüstungssektor Zwischen nationaler Politik und industrieller Globalisierung* (SWP 2015)

Priollaud F and Siritzky D, *Le Traité de Lisbonne Texte et Commentaire Article par Article des nouveaux Traités Européens (TUE-TFUE)* (La Documentation française 2008)

Schauer M, *Schengen – Maastricht – Amsterdam Auf dem Weg zu einer flexiblen Union* (Verlag Österreich 2000)

Schorkopf F, *Staatsrecht der internationalen Beziehungen* (C.H.Beck 2017)

Seiler F, *Rüstungsintegration: Frankreich, die Bundesrepublik Deutschland und die Europäische Verteidigungsgemeinschaft 1950 bis 1954* (De Gruyter 2015)

Trybus M, *Buying Defence and Security in Europe* (CUP 2014)

Trybus M, *European Union Law and Defence Integration* (Hart Publishing 2005)

Thym D, *Ungleichzeitigkeit und europäisches Verfassungsrecht* (Nomos 2004)

Zippelius R, *Grundbegriffe der Rechts- und Staatssoziologie* (Mohr Siebeck 2012)

Zoller E, *Droit des relations extérieures* (PUF 1992)

**Edited Books**

Calliess C, *Staatsrecht III* (4th edn, C.H.Beck 2022)

Craig P and Búrca G, *EU Law Text, Cases and Materials* (6th edn, OUP 2015)

Jabko N, *Playing the Market: A Political Strategy for Uniting Europe, 1985 – 2005* (1st edn, Cornell University Press 2012)

Renoux T and Villiers M, *Code constitutional* (10th edn, LexisNexis 2019)

Schimmelfennig F, *Internationale Politik* (4th edn, utb 2015)

Schweitzer M and Dederer H, *Staatsrecht III* (12th edn, C.F. Müller 2020)

Shaw M, *International Law* (7th edn, CUP 2014)

Stein T et al., *Völkerrecht* (14th edn, Franz Vahlen 2017)

Verpeaux M, *Droit constitutionnel français* (2nd edn, PUF 2015)

**Book Chapters**

Arnauld A, „Unions(ergänzungs)völkerrecht". Zur unions- und verfassungsrechtlichen Einbindung völkerrechtlicher Instrumente differenzierter Integration' in Breuer M et al. (eds.), *Der Staat im Recht. Festschrift für Eckart Klein zum 70. Geburtstag* (Duncker&Humblot 2013)

Becker U, 'Artikel 326' in Groeben H et al. (eds), *Europäisches Unionsrecht* (7th edn, Nomos 2015)

Becker U, 'Artikel 327' in Groeben H et al. (eds), *Europäisches Unionsrecht* (7th edn, Nomos 2015)

Becker U, 'Artikel 328' in Groeben H et al. (eds), *Europäisches Unionsrecht* (7th edn, Nomos 2015)

Becker U, 'Artikel 329' in Groeben H et al. (eds), *Europäisches Unionsrecht* (7th edn, Nomos 2015)

Béraud-Sudreau L, 'Integrated markets? – Europe's defence industry after 20 years' in Fiott D (ed), *The CSDP in 2020 The EU's legacy and ambition in security and defence* (EUISS 2020)

Biervert B, 'Artikel 288' in Schwarze J et al. (eds), *EU-Kommentar* (4th edn, Nomos 2018)

Blanke H, 'Art. 20 EUV' in Grabitz E et al. (eds), *Das Recht der Europäischen Union Kommentar 1* (January 2016 EL 58, C.H.Beck 2022)

Bungenberg M, 'Artikel 215' in Groeben H et al. (eds), *Europäisches Unionsrecht* (7th edn, Nomos 2015)

Butzer H et al., 'Art. 59' in Hofmann H and Henneke H (eds), *Grundgesetz* (15th edn, Carl Heymanns Verlag 2022)

Calliess C, 'Art. 3' in Calliess C and Ruffert M (eds), *EUV/AEUV* (6th edn, C.H.Beck 2022)

Calliess C, 'Art. 348' in Calliess C and Ruffert M (eds), *EUV/AEUV* (6th edn, C.H.Beck 2022)

Cottier T and Trinberg L, 'Artikel 207' in Groeben H et al. (eds), *Europäisches Unionsrecht* (7th edn, Nomos 2015)

Cremer H, 'Art. 21' in Calliess C and Ruffert M (eds), *EUV/AEUV* (6th edn, C.H.Beck 2022)

Cremer H, 'Art. 25' in Calliess C and Ruffert M (eds), *EUV/AEUV* (6th edn, C.H.Beck 2022)

Cremer H, 'Art. 29' in Calliess C and Ruffert M (eds), *EUV/AEUV* (6th edn, C.H.Beck 2022)

Cremer H, 'Art. 42' in Calliess C and Ruffert M (eds), *EUV/AEUV* (6th edn, C.H.Beck 2022)

Czeguhn I, 'Rechtsgeschichte' in Hilgendorf E and Joerden J (eds), *Handbuch Rechtsphilosophie* (J.B. Metzler Verlag 2017)

dell'Aria E, 'L'UE dans sa relation avec l'OTAN et quelques autres acteurs: bilan et perspectives' in Raccah A (ed), *Le traité de Lisbonne De nouvelles compétences pour l'Union européenc?* (L'Harmattan 2012)

Denza E, 'Article 48 Treaty Revision Procedures' in Blanke H and Mangiameli S (eds), *The Treaty on European Union (TEU) A Commentary* (Springer 2013)

Dietrich F, 'Recht als Sonderfall einer Normordnung' in Hilgendorf E and Joerden J (eds), *Handbuch Rechtsphilosophie* (J.B. Metzler Verlag 2017)

Dittert D, 'Artikel 346' in Groeben H et al., *Europäisches Unionsrecht* (7th edn, Nomos 2015)

Dittert D, 'Artikel 348' in Groeben H et al. (eds), *Europäisches Unionsrecht* (7th edn, Nomos 2015)

Fischer M and Thym D, 'Article 42 CSDP: Goals and Objectives; Mutual Defence' in Blanke H and Mangiameli S (eds), *The Treaty on European Union (TEU) A Commentary* (Springer 2013)

Fortunato S, 'Article 40 The Relationship Between Powers and Competences Under the TEU and Under the TFEU' in Blanke H and Mangiameli S (eds), *The Treaty on European Union (TEU) A Commentary* (Springer 2013)

Frenz W, 'Artikel 346' in Pechstein M et al., *Frankfurter Kommentare Band IV AEUV Artikel 216–358* (Mohr Siebeck 2017)

Geiger R and Kirchmair L, 'Art. 21' in Geiger R et al. (eds), *EUV AEUV* (7th edn, C.H.Beck 2023)

Geiger R and Kirchmair L, 'Art. 334', in Geiger R et al. (eds), *EUV AEUV* (7th edn, C.H.Beck 2023)

Hatje A, 'Artikel 334' in Schwarze J et al. (eds), *EU-Kommentar* (4th edn, Nomos 2018)

Hébert J, 'D'une Production Commune à Une Production Unique? La Coopération Européenne En Matière d'armement Comme Moyen de Renforcement de l'autonomie Stratégique Européenne' in Hébert J and Hamiot J (eds), *Histoire de La Coopération Européenne dans l'armement* (CNRS Editions 2004)

Herrnfeld H, 'Artikel 48' in Schwarze J et al. (eds), *EU-Kommentar* (4th edn, Nomos 2018)

Herrnfeld H, 'Artikel 114' in Schwarze J et al. (eds), *EU-Kommentar* (4th edn, Nomos 2018)

Heinegg W and Frau R, 'Art. 26' in Epping V and Hillgruber C (eds), *Grundgesetz* (3rd edn, C.H.Beck 2020)

Hutchinson T, 'Doctrinal Research' in Watkins D and Burton M (eds), *Research Methods in Law* (2nd edn, Routledge 2018)

Kaufmann-Bühler W, 'Art. 29 EUV' in Grabitz E et al. (eds*), Das Recht der Europäischen Union Kommentar 1* (Juli 2010 EL 41, C.H.Beck 2022)

Kaufmann-Bühler W, 'Art. 46 EUV' in Grabitz E et al. (eds), *Das Recht der Europäischen Union Kommentar 1* (März 2011 EL 43, C.H.Beck 2022)

Kielmansegg S, 'Article 46. [Permanent Structured Cooperation]' in Hermann- Blanke J and Mangiameli S (eds), *The Treaty on European Union (TEU) A Commentary* (Springer 2013)

Kielmansegg S, 'Auf dem Weg zur Europäischen Armee? Ambitionen und Grenzen des Unionsrechts bei der Schaffung integrierter Streitkräfte' in Kielmansegg S et al. (eds), *Multinationalität und Integration im militärischen Bereich. Eine rechtliche Perspektive* (Nomos 2018)

Kielmansegg S, 'Gemeinsame Verteidigung und Verteidigungspolitik' in Kadelbach S (ed), *Die Welt und Wir. Die Außenbeziehungen der Europäischen Union* (Nomos 2017)

Kielmansegg S, 'Permanent Structured Cooperation: A New Mechanism of Flexibility' in Blanke H and Mangiameli S (eds), *The European Union after Lisbon* (Springer 2011)

Kielmanssegg S, 'The Common Foreign and Security Policy – A Pool of Flexibility Models' in Giegerich T et al. (eds), *Flexibility in the EU and Beyond. How Much Differentiation can European Integration Bear?* (Nomos 2017)

Kingreen T and Wegener B, 'Art. 346' in Calliess C and Ruffert M (eds), *EUV/AEUV* (6th edn, C.H.Beck 2022)

Klatt M, 'Juristische Hermeneutik' in Hilgendorf E and Joerden J (eds), *Handbuch Rechtsphilosophie* (J.B. Metzler Verlag 2017)

Klein E, 'Der Elysée-Vertrag vom 22. Januar 1963' in Bezzenberger T et al. (eds), Die deutsch-französischen Rechtsbeziehungen, Europa und die Welt. Les relations juridiques franco-allemandes, l'Europe et le monde (Nomos 2014)

Kokott J, 'Art. 215' in Streinz R (ed), EUV/AEUV (3rd edn, C.H.Beck 2018)

Kokott J, 'Art. 346' in Streinz R (ed), EUV/AEUV (3rd edn, C.H.Beck 2018)

Korte S, 'Art. 114' in Calliess C and Ruffert M (eds), EUV/AEUV (6th edn, C.H.Beck 2022)

Levêque J, 'L'Europe de la Défense après Lisbonne: enjeux, réalités et perspectives' in Raccah A (ed), *Le traité de Lisbonne De nouvelles compétences pour l'Union européene?* (L'Harmattan 2012)

Maulny J, 'No time like the present – Towards a genuine defence industrial base for the CSDP?' in Fiott D (ed), *The CSDP in 2020 The EU's legacy and ambition in security and defence* (EUISS 2020)

Mölling C and Schütz T, 'European Armament Collaboration: What We Can Learn from History and Concepts' in Karampekios N et al. (eds), *The Emergence of EU Defense Research Policy* (Springer 2018)

Nettesheim M, 'Art. 207' in Streinz R (ed), *EUV/AEUV* (3rd edn, C.H.Beck 2018)

Pasquale P, 'Article 25 The Instruments for the Conduct of the CFSP' in Hermann-Blanke J and Mangiameli S (eds), *The Treaty on European Union (TEU) A Commentary* (Springer 2013)

Pechstein M, 'Art. 20' in Streinz R (ed), *EUV/AEUV* (3rd edn, C.H.Beck 2018)

Pechstein M, 'Art. 334', in Streinz R (ed), *EUV/AEUV* (3rd edn, C.H.Beck 2018)

Pelka S, 'Artikel 4' in Schwarze J et al. (eds), *EU-Kommentar* (4th ed, Nomos 2018)

Pieper S, 'Art. 59' in Epping V and Hillgruber C (eds), *Grundgesetz* (3rd edn, C.H.Beck 2020)

Pingel I, 'Article 43 UE' in Pingel I (ed), *Commentaire Article par Article des Traités UE et CU* (2nd edn, Helbing Lichtenhahn 2010)

Pingel I, 'Titre VII Dispositions sur la coopération renforcée', in Pingel I (ed), *Commentaire Article par Article des Traités UE et CU* (2nd edn, Helbing Lichtenhahn 2010)

Poujol M, 'Article 48 UE' in Pingel I (ed), *Commentaire Article par Article des Traités UE et CU* (2nd edn, Helbing Lichtenhahn 2010)

Schmalenbach K and Cremer H, 'Art. 215' in Calliess C and Ruffert M (eds), *EUV/AEUV* (6th edn, C.H.Beck 2022)

Schneider H and Terhechte J, 'Art. 215' in Grabitz E et al. (eds), *Das Recht der Europäischen Union Kommentar 2* (May 2014 EL 53, C.H.Beck 2022)

Raccah A, 'Le traité de Lisbonne: de nouvelles compétences pour l'Union européene?', in Raccah A (ed), *Le traité de Lisbonne De nouvelles compétences pour l'Union européene?* (L'Harmattan 2012)

Regelsberger E and Kugelmann D, 'Art. 21' in Streinz R (ed), *EUV/AEUV* (3rd edn, C.H.Beck 2018)

Regelsberger E and Kugelmann D, 'Art. 24' in Streinz R (ed), *EUV/AEUV* (3rd edn, C.H.Beck 2018)

Ruffert M, 'Art. 288' in Calliess C and Ruffert M (eds), *EUV/AEUV* (6th edn, C.H.Beck 2022)

Ruffert M, 'Art. 326' in Calliess C and Ruffert M (eds), *EUV/AEUV* (6th edn, C.H.Beck 2022)

Ruffert M, 'Art. 327 in Calliess C and Ruffert M (eds), *EUV/AEUV* (6th edn, C.H.Beck 2022)

Ruffert M, 'Art. 328' in Calliess C and Ruffert M (eds), *EUV/AEUV* (6th edn, C.H.Beck 2022)

Ruffert M, 'Art. 329' in Calliess C and Ruffert M (eds), *EUV/AEUV* (6th edn, C.H.Beck 2022)

Ruffert M, 'Art. 334' in Calliess C and Ruffert M (eds), *EUV/AEUV* (6th edn, C.H.Beck 2022)

Schorkopf F, 'Völkerrechtsfreundlichkeit und Völkerrechtsskepsis in der Rechtsprechung des Bundesverfassungsgerichts' in Giegerich T (ed), *Der „offene Verfassungsstaat" des Grundgesetzes nach 60 Jahren* (Duncker&Humblot 2010)

Starski P, 'Art. 59' in Kämmerer J and Kotzur M (eds), *Grundgesetz Kommentar Band 1: Präambel bis Art. 69* (7th edn, C.H.Beck 2021)

Streinz R, 'Art. 24' in Streinz R (ed), *EUV/AEUV* (3rd edn, C.H.Beck 2018)

Streinz R, 'Art. 26' in Sachs M (ed), *Grundgesetz* (9th edn, C.H.Beck 2021)

Streinz R, 'Art. 59' in Sachs M (ed), *Grundgesetz* (9th edn, C.H.Beck 2021)

Terhechte J, 'Artikel 21' in Schwarze J et al. (eds), *EU-Kommentar* (4th edn, Nomos 2018)

Terhechte J, 'Artikel 25' in Schwarze J et al. (eds), *EU-Kommentar* (4th edn, Nomos 2018)

Terhechte J, 'Artikel 29' in Schwarze J et al. (eds), *EU-Kommentar* (4th edn, Nomos 2018)

Terhechte J, 'EUV Art. 42 [Aufgaben und Tätigkeiten; Europäische Verteidigungsagentur]' in Becker U et al. (eds), *EU-Kommentar* (4th edn, Nomos 2019)

Terhechte J, 'EUV Art. 45 [Aufgaben der Europäischen Verteidigungsagentur]' in Becker U et al. (eds), *EU-Kommentar* (4th edn, Nomos 2019)

Terhechte J, 'EUV Art. 46 [Ständige Strukturierte Zusammenarbeit]' in Becker U et al., *EU-Kommentar* (4th edn, Nomos 2019)

Terpan F, 'Article 45 Tasks and Powers of the European Defence Agency' in Blanke H and Mangiameli S (eds), *The Treaty on European Union (TEU) A Commentary* (Springer 2013)

Thym D, '§ 18 GASP und äußere Sicherheit' in Arnauld A and Bungenberg M (eds), *Enzyklopädie Europarecht Band 12* (2nd edn, Nomos 2022)

Weitzel L, 'Article 296 CE' in Pingel I (ed), *Commentaire Article par Article des Traités UE et CU* (2nd edn, Helbing Lichtenhahn 2010)

Welz C and Engel C, 'Traditionsbestände politikwissenschaftlicher Integrationstheorien: Die Europäische Gemeinschaft im Spannungsfeld von Integration und Kooperation' in Bogdandy A (ed), *Die europäische Option. Eine interdisziplinäre Analyse über Herkunft, Stand und Perspektiven der europäischen Integration* (Nomos 1993)

Zabel B, 'Europa denken. Das Recht der Moderne zwischen staatlicher und entstaatlichter Freiheitsverwirklichung' in Griesser W (ed), *Die Philosophie und Europa. Zur Kategoriengeschichte der "europäischen Einigung"* (Königshausen&Neumann 2015)

Zabel B, 'Europarecht' in Hilgendorf E and Joerden J (eds), *Handbuch Rechtsphilosophie* (J.B. Metzler Verlag 2017)

### *Journal Articles and Papers*

Anderson J, 'European defence collaboration. Back to the future' [2015] 19 European Union Institute for Security Studies 1

Becker F, 'Völkerrechtliche Verträge und parlamentarische Gesetzgebungskompetenz' [2005] 3 Neue Zeitschrift für Verwaltungsrecht 289

Bender T, 'Die Verstärkte Zusammenarbeit nach Nizza. Anwendungsfelder und Bewertung im Spiegel historischer Präzedenzfälle der differenzierten Integration' [2001] 61 ZaöRV 730

Béraud-Sudreau L, 'Building Franco-German Consensus on Arms Exports' [2019] 61(4) Survival 79

Béraud-Sudreau L et al. 'Réguler le commerce des armes par le Parlement et l'opinion publique: Comparaison du contrôle des exportations d'armement en Allemagne, France, Royaume-Uni et Suède' [2015] 48 Politique européenne 82

Béraud-Sudreau L, 'The policy model for French arms exports' [2016] 58(475–476) Adelphi Series 19

Biermann F and Weiss M, 'Power without a cause? Germany's conflict avoidance and the integration of European defence procurement' [2021] 43(2) Journal of European Integration 227

Biscop S, 'European Defence: Give PESCO a Chance' [2018] 60(3) Survival 161

Blockmans S and Crosson D, 'Differentiated integration within PESCO – clusters and convergence in EU defence' [2019] 4 CEPS Research Report 1

Blockmans S and Faleg G, 'More Union in European Defence' [2015] Centre for European Policy Studies 1

Blockmans S, 'The EU's modular approach to defence integration: an inclusive, ambitious and legally binding PESCO?' [2018] 55(6) Common Market Law Review 1785

Bromley M and Brzoska M, 'Towards a Common, Restrictive EU Arms Export Policy? The Impact of the EU Code of Conduct on Major Conventional Arms Exports' [2008] 13(3) European Foreign Affairs Review 333

Bromley M, 'The Review of the EU Common Position on Arms Exports: Prospects for Strenghtened Controls' [2012] 7 Non-Proliferation Papers 1

Brzoska M and Küchle H, 'Folgen, Auswirkungen und Gestaltungsmöglichkeiten internationaler Abkommen für eine restriktive deutsche Rüstungsexportpolitik', 19 [2002] BICC 1

Calcara A, 'Cooperation and non cooperation in European defence procurement' [2019] 42(6) Journal of European Integration 799

Cops D and Buytart A, 'Sustainable EU funding of European defence cooperation' [2019] Policy Brief Flemish Peace Institute 1

DeVore M and Weiss M, 'Who's in the cockpit? The political economy of collaborative aircraft decisions' [2014] 21(2) Review of International Political Economy 479

Dhommeaux J, 'Le rôle du parlement dans l'élaboration des engagements internationaux: continuité et changement' [1987] RDP 1448

Dietrich S, 'Die rechtlichen Grundlagen der Verteidigungspolitik der Europäischen Union' [2006] 66 Zeitschrift für ausländisches öffentliches Recht und Völkerrecht 663

Dinh N, 'La Constitution de 1958 et le droit international' [1959] RDP 515

Ehlermann C, 'Engere Zusammenarbeit nach dem Amsterdamer Vertrag: Ein neues Verfassungsprinzip?' [1997] EuR 362

Faure S, 'Varieties of international co-operation: France's "flexilateral" policy in the Context of Brexit' [2019] 17 French Politics 1

Fink-Hooijer F, 'The Common Foreign and Security Policy of the European Union' [1994] 5 European Journal of International Law 173

Fiott D et al., 'Permanent structured cooperation: What's in a name?' [2017] 142 Chaillot Paper 1

Fiott D, 'Strategic autonomy: towards 'European sovereignty' in defence?' [2018] 12 European Union Institute for Security Studies 1

Frenz W, 'Die neue GASP' [2010] 70 Zeitschrift für ausländisches öffentliches Recht und Völkerrecht 487

Hansen S, 'Taking ambiguity seriously: Explaining the indeterminacy of the European Union conventional arms export control regime' [2016] 22(1) European Journal of International Relations 192

Heuninckx B, 'A Primer to Collaborative Defence Procurement in Europe: Troubles, Achievements and Prospects' [2008] Public Procurement Law Review 17(3) 123

Hoeffler C, 'Differentiated Integration in CSDP Through Defence Market Integration' [2019] 6(2) European Review of International Studies 43

Hofmann T, 'Der Grundsatz der völkerrechtsfreundlichen Auslegung' [2013] 4 JURA 326

Howorth J, 'The European Draft Constitutional Treaty and the Future of the European Defence Initiative: A Question of Flexibility' [2004] 9 European Foreign Affairs Review 1

Hutchinson T and Duncan N, 'Defining and Describing What We Do: Doctrinal Legal Research' (2012) 17 Deakin Law Review 83

Kempin R, 'Die deutsch-französische Zusammenarbeit in der Sicherheits- und Vertei-digungspolitik – Vernunftehe vor dem Aus?' [2012] 5 Zeitschrift für Außen- und Sicherheitspolitik 203

Kempin R, 'Frankreichs Außen- und Sicherheitspolitik unter Präsident Macron' [2021] 4 SWP 1

Kielmansegg S, 'Die verteidigungspolitischen Kompetenzen der Europäischen Union' [2006] 2 Europarecht 182

Kunz B, 'Defending Europe? A Stocktaking of French and German Visions for European Defense' [2015] 41 Institut de Recherche Stratégique de l'Ecole Militaire

Lavallée C, 'The European Commission's Position in the Field of Security and Defence: An Unconventional Actor at a Meeting Point' [2011] 12(4) Perspectives on European Politics and Society 371

Lippert B et al. (eds), 'European Strategic Autonomy' [2019] 4 SWP Research Paper 1

Lonardo L, 'Integration in European Defence: Some Legal Considerations' [2017] 2 (3) European Papers 887

Luchaire F, 'The Participation of Parliament in the Elaboration and Application of Treaties' (1991) 67(2) Chicago-Kent Law Review 341

Mawdsley J, 'The A400M Project: From Flagship Project to Warning for European Defence Cooperation' [2013] Defence Studies 13(1) 14

Missiroli A (ed), 'From Copenhagen to Brussels' [2003] 67 Chaillot Papers 1

Mörth U, 'Competing Frames in the European Commission – the case of the defence industry and equipment issue' [2000] 7(2) Journal of European Public Policy 173

Neuwahl N, 'A Partner with a Troubled Personality: EU Treaty-Making in Matters of CFSP and JHA after Amsterdam' [1998] 3(2) European Foreign Affairs Review 177

Pechstein M, 'Die Intergouvernementalität der GASP nach Lissabon: Kompetenz-, Wirkungs-, Haftungs- und Grundrechtsfragen' [2010] 65(9) JZ 425

Potacs M, 'Effet utile als Auslegungsgrundsatz' [2009] 4 Zeitschrift Europarecht 465

Rogers J and Gilli A, 'Enabling the future European military capabilities 2013–2025: challenges and avenues' [2013] European Union Institute for Security 1

Rutten M, 'From St-Malo to Nice European Defence: core documents' [2001] 47 Chaillot Paper 1

Schmitt B, 'From Cooperation to Integration: Defence and Aerospace Industries in Europe' [2000] 40 Chaillot Papers 1

Schreer B, 'Trump, NATO and the future of Europe's defence' [2019] 164(1) The RUSI Journal 10

Talmon S, 'Die Grenzen der Anwendung des Völkerrechts im deutschen Recht' [2013] 68(1) JuristenZeitung 12

Trybus M and Butler L, 'The internal market and national security: Transposition, impact and reform of the EU directive on Intra-Community Transfers of Defence Products' [2017] 54(2) Common Market Law Review 403

Ukrow J, 'Élysée 2.0 im Lichte des Europarechts – Der Vertrag von Aachen und die „immer engere Union"' [2019] 22(1) Zeitschrift für Europarechtliche Studien 3

Warmke, R 'Verwaltungsabkommen in der Bundesrepublik Deutschland' [1991] 24 Die Verwaltung 455

Wisotzki S and Mutschler M, 'No common position! European arms export control in crisis' [2021] 10 Zeitschrift für Friedens- und Konfliktforschung 273

### Press Releases

Bundesministerium der Verteidigung, 'Future Combat Air System: Kampfjet-Entwicklung schreitet voran' (*BMWG*, 28 April 2023) <https://www.bmvg.de/de/aktuelles/future-combat-air-system-kampfjet-entwicklung-schreitet-voran-5614922> accessed 5 May 2023

Bundesministerium der Verteidigung, 'PESCO Permanent Structured Cooperation: Ein Meilenstein auf dem Weg zur Verteidigungsunion' (*BMVG*, 13 November 2017) <https://www.bmvg.de/de/aktuelles/pesco-ein-meilenstein-auf-dem-weg-zur-verteidigungsunion-19806> accessed 22 April 2022

Bundesministerium für Wirtschaft und Klimaschutz, 'A Restrictive, Responsible Policy on the Export of Military Equipment' (*BMWK*, 2019) <https://www.bmwk.de/Redaktion/EN/Dossier/export-controls-for-military-equipment.html> accessed 26 October 2022

Council of the EU, 'EU defence cooperation: Council welcomes Denmark into PESCO and launches the 5th wave of new PESCO projects' (*EU*, 23 May 2023) <https://www.consilium.europa.eu/en/press/press-releases/2023/05/23/eu-defence-cooperation-council-welcomes-denmark-into-pesco-and-launches-the-5th-wave-of-new-pesco-projects/> accessed 10 December 2023

EDA, 'Bringing Transparency into the European Defence Equipment Market: Code of Conduct on Offsets comes into force' (*EDA*, 1 July 2009) <https://eda.europa.eu/docs/news/EDA_-_Code_of_Conduct_on_Offsets_Comes_into_Force.pdf?Status=Master> accessed 18 December 2022

EDA, 'Capability Development Plan' (*EDA*, 2008) <https://eda.europa.eu/what-we-do/all-activities/activities-search/capability-development-plan> accessed 19 December 2022

EDA, 'Code of Conduct on Pooling & Sharing' (*EDA*, 2012) <https://eda.europa.eu/docs/news/code-of-conduct.pdf> accessed 17 December 2022

EDA, 'EDA finds record European defence spending in 2020 with slump in collaborative expenditure' (*EDA*, 6 December 2021) <https://eda.europa.eu/news-and-events/news/2021/12/06/eda-finds-record-european-defence-spending-in-2020-with-slump-in-collaborative-expenditure> accessed 16 April 2022

EDA, 'EDA study analyses defence industrial strategies' (*EDA*, 11 October 2022) <https://eda.europa.eu/news-and-events/news/2022/10/11/eda-study-analyses-defence-industrial-strategies> accessed 19 October 2022

EDA, 'EU Commission, EDA and OCCAR sign European Defence Fund agreements' (*EDA*, 14 December 2022) <https://eda.europa.eu/news-and-events/news/2022/12/14/european-commission-signs-european-defence-fund-agreement-with-eda-and-occar> accessed 14 March 2023

EDA, 'REACH' (*EDA*, 2015) <https://eda.europa.eu/what-we-do/all-activities/activities-search/reach> accessed 17 December 2022

European Commission, 'A European Defence Fund: €5.5 billion per year to boost Europe's defence capabilities' (*European Commission*, 7 June 2017) <https://ec.europa.eu/commission/presscorner/detail/en/IP_17_1508> accessed 22 April 2022

European Commission, 'Defence Procurement: Commission opens infringement procedures against 5 Member States' (*European Commission*, 25 January 2018) <https://ec.europa.eu/commission/presscorner/detail/en/IP_18_357> accessed 10 September 2022

Ministère de l'Europe et des Affaires Étrangères, 'Press release – Franco-German Agreement on Defence export controls (14 November 2019)' (*gouv.fr*, 14 November 2019) <https://www.diplomatie.gouv.fr/en/country-files/germany/events/article/franco-german-agreement-on-defence-export-controls-14-nov-19> accessed 27 October 2022

### Blog Posts

Atzpodien H, 'Deutscher Rüstungsexport. Restriktionen, Regelungsbedarfe und der europäische Kontext' (*Bundesakademie für Sicherheitspolitik*, 2019) <https://www.baks.bund.de/de/arbeitspapiere/2019/deutscher-ruestungsexport-restriktionen-regelungsbedarfe-und-der-europaeische> accessed 21 June 2020

Bachmann D et al. 'More European, More Connected and More Capable Building the European Armed Forces of the Future' (*Munich Security Conference*, 2017) <https://security conference.org/assets/02_Dokumente/01_Publikationen/MSCEuropeanDefe nceReport2017.pdf> accessed 26 October 2022

Béraud-Sudreau L, 'Towards convergence in European arms export policies: How to overcome the Franco-German stalemate?' (*Atlantic Community*, 29 August 2019) <https://atlantic-community.org/towards-convergence-in-european-arms-export-po licies-how-to-overcome-the-franco-german-stalemate/> accessed 22 June 2020

Besch S and Oppenheim B, 'The EU needs an effective common arms export policy' (*Centre for European Reform*, 4 June 2019) <https://www.cer.eu/publications/archiv e/bulletin-article/2019/eu-needs-effective-common-arms-export-policy> accessed 22 June 2020

Besch S and Oppenheim B, 'Up in arms: Warring over Europe's arms export regime' (*Center for European Reform*, 10 September 2019) <https://www.cer.eu/publicatio ns/archive/policy-brief/2019/arms-warring-over-europes-arms-export-regime> accessed 30 January 2022

Descôtes A, 'Vom „German-free" zum gegenseitigen Vertrauen' (*Bundesakademie für Sicherheitspolitik*, 2019) <https://www.google.com/url?sa=t&rct=j&q=&esrc=s&sou rce=web&cd=1&cad=rja&uact=8&ved=2ahUKEwjPi5SCrOLiAhWLUhUIHUIGAzs QFjAAegQIAhAB&url=https%3A%2F%2Fwww.baks.bund.de%2Fde%2Farbeitspapi ere%2F2019%2Fvom-german-free-zum-gegenseitigen-vertrauen&usg=AOvVaw3w30 k-lzufGnct9yxMHABx> accessed 11 June 2020

Grebe J, 'For a Europeanisation of Arms Export Controls. More power for Brussels will lead to a stronger Common Foreign and Security Policy of the EU' (*Bundesakademie für Sicherheitspolitik*, 2018) <https://www.baks.bund.de/en/working-papers/2018/f or-a-europeanisation-of-arms-export-controls-more-power-for-brussels-will-lead> accessed 23 June 2020

Keul K and Bütikofer R, 'Gegenseitiges Vertrauen durch gemeinsame Exportkontrolle. Eine Erwiderung auf Anne-Marie Descôtes' (*Bundesakademie für Sicherheitspolitik*, 2019) <https://www.baks.bund.de/en/node/2024> accessed 21 June 2020

Kielmansegg S, 'The Historical Development of EU Defence Policy: Lessons for the Future?' (*Verfassungsblog*, 25 March 2019) <https://verfassungsblog.de/historical-dev elopment-lessons-for-the-future%ef%bb%bf> accessed 8 October 2019

Peters J, 'Convenient, but controversial: Why the European Defence Fund should not be expanded as the Commission becomes 'geopolitical' (*European Law Blog*, 5 July 2022) <https://europeanlawblog.eu/2022/07/05/convenient-but-controversial-why-t he-european-defence-fund-should-not-be-expanded-as-the-commission-becomes-ge opolitical/> accessed 2 September 2022

### Reports

Bundesministerium für Wirtschaft und Klimaschutz, 'Bericht der Bundesregierung über ihre Exportpolitik für konventionelle Rüstungsgüter im Jahre 2020' (*BMWK*, 2020) <https://www.bmwk.de/Redaktion/DE/Downloads/B/bericht-der-bundesregi erung-ueber-ihre-exportpolitik-fuer-konventionelle-ruestungsgueter-im-jahre-2020. pdf?__blob=publicationFile&v=6> accessed 26 October 2022

Bundesregierung, 'Antwort der Bundesregierung auf die Kleine Anfrage der Abgeordneten Sevim Dağdelen, Heike Hänsel, Christine Buchholz, weiterer Abgeordneter und der Fraktion DIE LINKE – Drucksache 19/9317' (*Deutscher Bundestag*, 6 May 2019) <https://dserver.bundestag.de/btd/19/099/1909902.pdf> accessed 26 October 2022

Bundesregierung, 'Strategy Paper of the Federal Government on Strengthening the Security and Defence Industry' (*BMWK*, 14 February 2020) <https://www.bmwk.de/Redaktion/DE/Downloads/S-T/strategiepapier-staerkung-sicherits-und-verteidigungsindustrie-en.pdf?__blob=publicationFile&v=4> accessed 19 June 2022

Commission de la défense nationale et des forces armées, 'Audition de Mme Florence Parly, ministre des Armées, sur les opérations en cours et les exportations d'armement' (*Assemblée nationale*, 7 May 2019) <https://www.assemblee-nationale.fr/dyn/15/comptes-rendus/cion_def/l15cion_def1819032_compte-rendu#> accessed 26 October 2022

Commission de la défense nationale et des forces armées, 'Audition de Mme Florence Parly, ministre des Armées, sur le rapport au Parlement sur les exportations d'armement de la France' (*Assemblée nationale*, 4 July 2018) <https://www.assemblee-nationale.fr/dyn/15/comptes-rendus/cion_def/l15cion_def1718070_compte-rendu#> accessed 26 October 2022

Commission de la défense nationale et des forces armées, 'Audition de Monsieur Stéphane Mayer, président-directeur général de Nexter' (*Assemblé nationale*, 15 May 2019) <https://www.assemblee-nationale.fr/dyn/15/comptes-rendus/cion_def/l15cion_def1819034_compte-rendu#.> accessed 26 October 2022

European Commission, 'Evaluation of Directive 2009/43/EC on the Transfers of Defence-Related Products within the Community Final Report' (*europa*, 2016) <https://op.europa.eu/en/publication-detail/-/publication/538beabd-92af-11e7-b92d-01aa75ed71a1/language-en> accessed 6 May 2023

European Parliamentary Research Service, 'EU Defence Package: Defence Procurement and Intra-Community Transfers Directives European Implementation Assessment' (*europa*, 2020) <http://www.europarl.europa.eu/RegData/etudes/STUD/2020/654171/EPRS_STU(2020)654171_EN.pdf> accessed 25 December 2023.

European Parliamentary Research Service, 'The Cost of Non-Europe in Common Security and Defence Policy' (*europa*, 2013) <https://www.europarl.europa.eu/RegData/etudes/etudes/join/2013/494466/IPOL-JOIN_ET%282013%29494466_EN.pdf> accessed 17 April 2022

Ministère des Armées, 'Revue Stratégique de Défense et de Sécurité Nationale' (*gouv.fr*, 2017) <https://www.diplomatie.gouv.fr/IMG/pdf/2017-rs-def1018_cle0b6ef5-1.pdf> accessed 26 October 2020

Président du Groupe de travail VIII "Défense" à la Convention, 'Rapport final du Group de travail VIII "Défense CONV 461/02' (*cvce*, 16 December 2002) <https://www.cvce.eu/en/obj/rapport_final_du_groupe_de_travail_viii_defense_16_decembre_2002-fr-71dbaa92-ac9e-4556-a639-3c7665fd0812.html> accessed 22 October 2022

Sandrier J et al., 'Rapport d'information sur le contrôle des exportations d'armament' (*Assemblée nationale*, 25 April 2000 <http://www.assemblee-nationale.fr/rap-info/i2334.asp> accessed 26 October 2022

Bauer S et al., 'The further development of the Common Position 944/2008/CFSP on Arms Exports Control' (*European Parliament*, July 2018) <https://www.europarl.eu ropa.eu/RegData/etudes/STUD/2018/603876/EXPO_STU(2018)603876_EN.pdf> accessed 25 October 2022

Valero B, 'Arms export: implementation of Common Position 2008/944/CFSP' <https:/ /oeil.secure.europarl.europa.eu/oeil/popups/ficheprocedure.do?lang=en&reference= 2015/2114(INI)> (*European Parliament*, 2015) accessed 25 October 2022

Wissenschaftliche Dienste Deutscher Bundestag, 'Das Deutsch-Französische Abkommen vom 21. Oktober 2019 über Ausfuhrkontrollen im Rüstungsbereich im Lichte des Art. 59 Abs. 2 GG (WD 2 – 3000 – 122/19)' (*WD*, 2019) <https://www.bundestag. de/resource/blob/673972/3921230d2453e988b485aae981323a35/WD-2-122-19-pdf-da ta.pdf> accessed 20 October 2020

Wissenschaftliche Dienste Deutscher Bundestag, 'Die deutsch-französische Rüstungskooperation. Bilaterale deutsch-französische sowie multilaterale Entwicklungs- und Beschaffungsprojekte mit deutscher und französischer Beteiligung (WD 2 3000 – 070/18)' (*WD*, 2018) <https://www.bundestag.de/resource/blob/576770/c53 59790a0d6d943e4ccb2900cc6d3a1/wd-2-070-18-pdf-data.pdf> accessed 21 October 2021

### Websites

AFP, 'La gauche réclame la "transparence" sur la vente d'armes au Yémen' (*L'OBS*, 15 April 2019) <https://www.nouvelobs.com/politique/20190415.OBS11593/la-gauche-r eclame-la-transparence-sur-la-vente-d-armes-au-yemen.html> accessed 26 October 2022

Ayrault J and Steinmeier F, 'Ein starkes Europa in einer unsicheren Welt' (*Ministère de l'Europe et des Affaires Étrangères*, 28 June 2016) <https://www.diplomatie.gouv .fr/de/neuigkeiten/article/ein-starkes-europa-in-einer-unsicheren-welt-28-06-16> accessed 14 June 2022

Baume M and Herszenhorn D, 'Merkel Joins Macron in Calling for EU Army to Complement NATO' (*Politico*, 14 November 2018) <https://www.politico.eu/articl e/angela-merkel-emmanuel-macron-eu-army-to-complement-nato/> accessed 22 April 2022

Besch S, 'Can the European Commission develop Europe's defence industry?' (*Centre for European Reform*, 18 November 2019) <https://www.cer.eu/insights/can-europea n-commission-develop-europes-defence-industry> accessed 23 June 2020

Besch S, 'No escaping an arms export policy' (*Centre for European Reform*, 10 October 2019) <https://www.cer.eu/in-the-press/no-escaping-arms-export-policy> accessed 22 June 2020

Briani V, 'The Costs of non-Erope in the Defence Field' (*Istituto Affari Internazionali*, April 2013) <https://www.iai.it/sites/default/files/CSF-IAI_noneuropedefence_april 2013.pdf> accessed 26 October 2022

Brink N, 'Die Wunderwaffe' (*Internationale Politik*, 1 May 2021) <https://internationale politik.de/de/die-wunderwaffe> accessed 13 April 2022

Cabirol M, 'Eurofighter, A330 MRTT, Casa C295, H145 ... bloqués à l'export: Berlin fragilise Airbus' (*La Tribune*, 25 February 2019) <https://www.latribune.fr/entreprise s-finance/industrie/aeronautique-defense/eurofighter-a330-mrtt-casa-c295-h145-blo ques-a-l-export-berlin-fragilise-airbus-808239.html> accessed 30 October 2021

Collins Dictionary, 'sovereignty' < https://www.collinsdictionary.com/de/worterbuch/ englisch/sovereignty> (*Collins Dictionary*, 2023) accessed 11 April 2023

Cops D and Duquet N, 'Reviewing the EU Common Position on arms exports: Whither EU arms transfer controls?' (*Flemish Peace Institute*, 2019) <https://vlaamsvredesi nstituut.eu/wp-content/uploads/2019/12/VI_policy-brief_EU_arms_export_2019web .pdf> accessed 28 October 2022

Dean S, 'Main Ground Combat System (MGCS): A Status Report' (*European Security&Defence*, 23 January 2023) <https://euro-sd.com/2023/01/articles/29122/main-gr ound-combat-system-mgcs-a-status-report/> accessed 7 March 2023

Die Zeit, 'Marine Le Pen will Verteidigungsprojekte mit Deutschland stoppen' (*ZEIT*, 13 April 2022) <https://www.zeit.de/politik/ausland/2022-04/frankreich-marine-le-p en-verteidigung-deutschland-nato> accessed 13 April 2022

Duden, 'Souveränität' <https://www.duden.de/rechtschreibung/Souveraenitaet> (*Duden*, 2023) accessed 11 April 2023

EDA, 'Defence Data 2019–2020' (*EDA*, 2021) <https://eda.europa.eu/docs/default-sour ce/brochures/eda---defence-data-report-2019-2020.pdf> accessed 3 May 2023

EDA, 'Denmark joins the European Defence Agency' (*EDA*, 25 March 2023) <https:/ /defence-industry.eu/denmark-joins-the-european-defence-agency> accessed 27 March 2023

EDA, 'Germany – From PESCO to a European Defence Union' (*EDA*, 2017) <https://e da.europa.eu/webzine/issue15/cover-story/pesco-drivers-the-floor-is-yours#example Accordion2> accessed 22 April 2022

EEAS, 'A Strategic Compass for Security and Defence' (*EEAS*, 2022) <https://www.eeas .europa.eu/sites/default/files/documents/strategic_compass_en3_web.pdf> accessed 24 April 2022

EEAS, 'Denmark: Statement by the High Representative on the outcome of the referendum on the opt-out in defence matters' (*EEAS*, 1 June 2022) <https://www.eeas.euro pa.eu/eeas/denmark-statement-high-representative-outcome-referendum-opt-out-d efence-matters_en> accessed 17 December 2022

EEAS, 'EU Global Strategy' (*EEAS*, 28 June 2016) <https://www.eeas.europa.eu/eu-glo bal-strategy_en> accessed 13 June 2020

EU, 'Permanent Structured Cooperation (PESCO)' (*EU*, 2022) <https://www.pesco.eur opa.eu/> accessed 21 December 2022

European Commission, 'The European Defence Fund' (*European Commission*, 28 April 2021) <https://ec.europa.eu/defence-industry-space/document/download/69a a3194-4361-48a5-807b-1a2635b91fe8_en> accessed 25 November 2021

European Commission, 'The von der Leyen Commission: One year on' (*European Commission*, 2020) <https://ec.europa.eu/info/sites/default/files/von-der-leyen-com mission-one-year-on_en.pdf> accessed 11 September 2022

European Council, 'The Versailles declaration' (*European Council*, 10 and 11 March 2022) <https://www.consilium.europa.eu/media/54773/20220311-versailles-declarati on-en.pdf> accessed 2 September 2022

European Court of Auditors, 'The Preparatory action on defence research' (*ECA*, 26 April 2023) <https://www.eca.europa.eu/ECAPublications/SR-2023-10/SR-2023-10_ EN.pdf> accessed 27 April 2023

FAZ, 'Rüstungsindustrie warnt vor zu starken Exportbeschränkungen' (*FAZ*, 3 January 2022) <https://www.faz.net/aktuell/wirtschaft/mehr-wirtschaft/ruestungsindustrie -warnt-vor-starken-exportbeschraenkungen-17713099.html> accessed 4 January 2022

Guillermard V, 'Dassault appelle à une harmonisation des règles à l'export' (*Le Figaro*, 28 Feburary 2019) <https://www.lefigaro.fr/societes/2019/02/28/20005-20190228 ARTFIG00295-dassault-appelle-a-une-harmonisation-des-regles-a-l-export.php> accessed 3 December 2021

Handelsblatt, '"Wir Europäer müssen unser Schicksal in unsere eigene Hand nehmen"' (*Handelsblatt*, 28 May 2017) <https://www.handelsblatt.com/politik/deutschland/an gela-merkel-wir-europaeer-muessen-unser-schicksal-in-unsere-eigene-hand-nehme n/19861340.html?ticket=ST-14653270-UNvsjicXuGBjWHnqEVPT-ap6> accessed 16 June 2021

Hanke T, 'Europas grösstes Rüstungsprojekt steckt in der Krise' (*NZZ*, 3 March 2021) <https://www.nzz.ch/international/ruestung-deutsch-franzoesisches-projekt-steckt-i n-der-krise-ld.1604493> accessed 26 October 2022

Hanke T, 'Rüstungskonzerne Airbus und Dassault bemühen sich um Rettung von Mega-Projekt' (*Handelsblatt*, 8 March 2021) <https://www.handelsblatt.com/politik/ international/kampfflugzeugsystem-ruestungskonzerne-airbus-und-dassault-bemue hen-sich-um-rettung-von-mega-projekt/26984414.html> accessed 25 March 2022

Hegmann G, 'Der neue Superfighter ist der Schlüssel für Europas Verteidigungsstrate-gie' (*Welt*, 29 July 2020) <https://www.welt.de/wirtschaft/plus212412279/Der-Supe rfighter-ist-der-Schluessel-fuer-Europas-Verteidigungsstrategie.html> accessed 30 October 2021

Hegmann G, 'Europas Rüstungskonzerne wollen auf US-Technik verzichten' (*Welt*, 02 August 2020) <https://www.welt.de/wirtschaft/article212684375/Europas-Ruestungs konzerne-wollen-auf-US-Technik-verzichten.html> accessed 29 October 2021

Heimbach T, '„Future Combat Air System": Das steckt hinter dem Milliarden-Projekt der Bundeswehr, das den Luftkampf revolutionieren soll' (*Business Insider*, 27 March 2022) <https://www.businessinsider.de/politik/deutschland/future-combat-air-syste m-das-steckt-hinter-dem-milliarden-projekt-der-bundeswehr-das den luftkampf-rev olutionieren-sollltet/> accessed 28 March 2022

Hemicker L, 'Rechtliche Zweifel an deutsch-französischem Rüstungsabkommen' (*FAZ*, 26 February 2020) <https://www.faz.net/aktuell/politik/inland/bundeswehr-uni-krit isiert-deutsch-franzoesisches-ruestungsabkommen-16649444.html?premium=0x79c 76a4a56672c7a0fd0c63c954fe016&GEPC=Share_SMS> accessed 22 June 2020

Jungholt T, 'Geschäft mit dem Tod oder Beitrag für Deutschlands Sicherheit?' (*Welt*, 13 March 2019) <https://www.welt.de/politik/deutschland/article190276603/Ruestun gsexporte-Geschaeft-mit-dem-Tod-oder-Beitrag-zur-Sicherheit.html> accessed 15 November 2021

Kilcommins S, 'Doctrinal Legal Method (Black-Letterism): assumptions, commitments and shortcomings' (*University of Limerick*, 2015) <https://core.ac.uk/download/pdf/84112166.pdf> accessed 6 April 2023

Kunz B and Kempin R, 'The Treaty of Aachen. New Impetus for Franco-German Defense Cooperation?' (*IFRI*, 22 January 2019) <https://www.ifri.org/en/publicatio ns/editoriaux-de-lifri/treaty-aachen-new-impetus-franco-german-defense-cooperat ion> accessed 22 June 2020

Küstner K, 'Lücken in der EU-Verteidigungsunion' (*tagesschau*, 14 December 2019), <https://www.tagesschau.de/ausland/pesco-105.html> accessed 13 April 2022

Martin K, 'Observatoire des marchés publics de défense et de sécurité européens' (*Fondation pour la Recherche Stratégique*, October 2019) <https://www.frstrategie.or g/programmes/observatoire-des-marches-publics-de-defense-et-de-securite-europee ns/bulletins/2019/2> accessed 16 September 2022

McCarthy N, 'UK arms exports to Saudi Arabia fuel Yemen conflict' (*Statista*, 28 March 2017) <https://www.statista.com/chart/8708/uk-arms-exports-to-saudi-arabia-fuel-y emen-conflict/> accessed 2 December 2022

Leyen U, 'Strengthening the Soul of our Union' (*European Commission*, 15 September 2021) <https://ec.europa.eu/commission/presscorner/detail/en/SPEECH_21_4701> accessed 28 September 2021

Macron E, 'Initiative for Europe' (*ouest-france*, 26 September 2017) <http://internation al.blogs.ouest-france.fr/archive/2017/09/29/macron-sorbonne-verbatim-europe-1858 3.html> accessed 13 April 2022

Macron E, 'Speech by Emmanuel Macron at the closing ceremony of the Conference on the Future of Europe' (*europa*, 10 May 2022) <https://presidence-francaise.consil ium.europa.eu/en/news/speech-by-emmanuel-macron-at-the-closing-ceremony-of-t he-conference-on-the-future-of-europe/> accessed 13 June 2022

Mbengue M, 'Preamble' (*OPIL*, September 2006) <https://opil.ouplaw.com/view/10. 1093/law:epil/9780199231690/law-9780199231690-e1456?prd=EPIL> accessed 30 October 2022

Merkel A, 'Rede von Bundeskanzlerin Merkel zur 55. Münchner Sicherheitskonferenz am 16. Februar 2019 in München' (*bundeskanzlerin*, 16 February 2019) <https://ww w.bundeskanzlerin.de/bkin-de/aktuelles/rede-von-bundeskanzlerin-merkel-zur-5 5-muenchner-sicherheitskonferenz-am-16-februar-2019-in-muenchen-1580936> accessed 21 October 2021

Meta-Défense, 'SCAF, MGCS: Die Politik übernimmt wieder die Kontrolle über die deutsch-französische Rüstungsindustriekooperation' (*Meta-Défense*, 23 September 2022) <https://meta-defense.fr/de/2022/09/23/scaf-mgcs-Politiker-gewinnen-die-Ko ntrolle-%C3%BCber-die-deutsch-franz%C3%B6sische-Verteidigungsindustrie-Koo peration-zur%C3%BCck/> accessed 26 October 2022

Michel C, 'The chaotic withdrawal in Afghanistan forces us to accelerate honest think-ing about European defence' (*europa*, 2 September 2021) <https://www.consilium.eu ropa.eu/en/european-council/president/news/2021/09/02/20210902-pec-newsletter -afghanistan/> accessed 16 June 2022

Ministry of Defence, 'Letter of Intent: restructuring the European defence industry' (*gov.uk*, 12 December 2012) <https://www.gov.uk/guidance/letter-of-intent-restructu ring-the-european-defence-industry> accessed 7 October 2022

Müller B, 'Die Hürden für Europas gemeinsamen Kampfpanzer' (*FAZ*, 31 October 2019) <https://www.faz.net/aktuell/politik/ausland/ruesten-fuer-europa-huerden-fu er-den-gemeinsamen-kampfpanzer-16439321-p2.html> accessed 2 December 2021

Nguyen A, 'Macron's Call for a European Army: Still Echoing or Forgotten?' (*European Law Blog*, 22 June 2020) <https://europeanlawblog.eu/2020/06/22/macrons-call-for -a-european-army-still-echoing-or-forgotten/> accessed 3 December 2021

Parly F, 'Minister sets out defence priorities for French EU presidency in 2022' (*French Embassy in* London, 14 December 2021) <https://uk.ambafrance.org/Minister-sets-o ut-defence-priorities-for-French-EU-presidency-in-2022> accessed 10 January 2022

Rescan M, 'A l'Assemblée, des élus s'invitent dans le débat miné sur les ventes d'armes à l'Arabie saoudite' (*Le Monde*, 8 June 2019) <https://www.lemonde.fr/politique/articl e/2019/06/08/l-assemblee-s-invite-dans-le-debat-mine-sur-les-ventes-d-armes_5473 357_823448.html> accessed 26 October 2022

Scholz O, 'Regierungserklärung von Bundeskanzler Olaf Scholz am 27. Februar 2022' (*Bundesregierung*, 27 February 2022) <https://www.bundesregierung.de/breg-de/su che/regierungserklaerung-von-bundeskanzler-olaf-scholz-am-27-februar-2022-2008 356> accessed 30 March 2023

Schubert C, 'Zweifel an der Harmonie' (*FAZ*, 16 October 2019) <https://www.faz.net/a ktuell/wirtschaft/deutschland-und-frankreich-zweifel-an-der-harmonie-16436447.h tml> accessed 18 August 2020

Schuman R, 'The Schuman Declaration' (*EU*, 9 May 1950) <https://europa.eu/europ ean-union/about-eu/symbols/europe-day/schuman-declaration_en> accessed 16 February 2022

Seliger M, 'Die schwierige Geschichte der deutsch-französischen Rüstungskooperation' (*NZZ*, 2 April 2019) <https://www.nzz.ch/international/deutsch-franzoesische-ruest ungskooperation-ist-muehselig-ld.1470274> accessed 15 June 2020

Silva D et al., 'Trends in World Military Expenditure, 2021' (*SIPRI*, April 2022) <https:/ /www.sipri.org/sites/default/files/2022-04/fs_2204_milex_2021_0.pdf> accessed 1 September 2022

SPON, 'Deutsch-französisches Geheimpapier regelt Waffenexporte neu' (*SPON*, 15 February 2019) <https://www.spiegel.de/politik/deutschland/ruestungsexporte -deutsch-franzoesisches-geheimpapier-a-1253393.html> accessed 24 April 2023

SPON, 'Frankreich beklagt Blockade von Rüstungsdeal durch Berlin' (*SPON*, 24 De cember 2012) <https://www.spiegel.de/politik/ausland/bundesregierung-soll-ruestu ngsgeschaefte-mit-saudi-arabien-blockieren-a-874593.html> accessed 25 May 2022

The Economist, 'Emmanuel Macron in his own words (French)' (*Economist*, 7 Novem ber 2019) <https://www.economist.com/europe/2019/11/07/emmanuel-macron-in-hi s-own-words-french> accessed 16 June 2021

Vogel D, 'Future Combat Air System: Too Big to Fail' (*SWP*, 8 January 2021) <https://w ww.swp-berlin.org/publikation/armament-project-future-combat-air-system-too-big -to-fail> accessed 12 April 2022

Wassenaar Arrangement Secretariat, 'Wassenaar Arrangement on Export Controls for Conventional Arms and Dual-Use Goods and Technologies, Public Documents Volume II, List of Dual-Use Goods and Technologies and Munitions List' (*WAS*, December 2022) <https://www.wassenaar.org/app/uploads/2022/12/List-of-Dual-U se-Goods-and-Technologies-Munitions-List-Dec-2022.pdf> accessed 6 December 2022

Warrel H and Pfeifer S, 'Italy joins forces with UK in European fighter jet race' (*FT*, 11 September 2019) <https://www.ft.com/content/d8bcb02e-d49e-11e9-8367-807ebd53a b77> accessed 3 April 2022

Weisflog C, 'Der Krieg in der Ukraine offenbart: Ohne den Beistand der USA gibt es kein freies und sicheres Europa' (*NZZ*, 24 June 2022) <https://www.nzz.ch/meinung /ukraine-krieg-die-usa-sind-europas-geringgeschaetzter-schutzengel-ld.1686754?red uced=true> accessed 13 April 2023

Wezeman P et al., 'Trends in International Arms Transfers, 2020' (*SIPRI*, March 2021) <https://www.sipri.org/sites/default/files/2021-03/fs_2103_at_2020_v2.pdf> accessed 31 October 2021

Wezeman P et al., 'Trends in International Arms Transfers, 2021' (*SIPRI*, March 2022) <https://www.sipri.org/sites/default/files/2022-03/fs_2203_at_2021.pdf> accessed 1 September 2022

Wiegel M, 'Ärger in Paris über Deutschlands Tempo' (*FAZ*, 24 March 2021) <https://w ww.faz.net/aktuell/politik/ausland/deutsch-franzoesische-ruestungsprojekte-komme n-nicht-voran-17261344.html> accessed 25 March 2022

Wolfstädter L, „Europäische Verteidigungsunion": eine rechtliche Einordnung' (*Hertie School Jacques Delors Centre*, 1 August 2018) <https://www.delorscentre.eu/de/publik ationen/detail/publication/europaeische-verteidigungsunion-eine-rechtliche-einord nung> accessed 21 June 2020

Zhu M, 'Obstacles to Macron's "true European army"' (*Harvard Political Review*, 19 April 2020) <https://harvardpolitics.com/european-security/> accessed 27 October 2022